# Logos & Revelation

# Logos & Revelation

IBN 'ARABI, MEISTER ECKHART, AND
MYSTICAL HERMENEUTICS

Robert J. Dobie

The Catholic University of America Press

*Washington, D. C.*

The paper used in this publication meets the minimum requirements of
American National Standards for Information Science—Permanence
of Paper for Printed Library materials, ANSI Z39.48-1984.
∞

Library of Congress Cataloging-in-Publication Data
Dobie, Robert J.
Logos and revelation : Ibn 'Arabi, Meister Eckhart, and mystical
hermeneutics / Robert J. Dobie.
p. cm.
Includes bibliographical references and index.
ISBN 978-0-8132-1677-5 (pbk. : alk. paper)    1. Eckhart, Meister,
d. 1327.    2. Ibn al-'Arabi, 1165–1240.    3. Mysticism—Catholic
Church—Comparative studies.    4. Mysticism—Sufism—
Comparative studies.
I. Title.
BV5095.E3D63 2009
248.2´2—dc22                    2009022580

# Contents

## Acknowledgments

This book had its genesis some fifteen years ago as a dissertation for Fordham University on the doctrine of the transcendentals in Meister Eckhart and Thomas Aquinas. For his wisdom, insight, and patience in shepherding an often wandering graduate student, I thank my dissertation mentor, Fr. Joseph Koterski, S.J. I also have to thank Fr. W. Norris Clarke, S.J., now deceased, who read my dissertation with great interest and offered many corrections and clarifications, always with consummate gentleness!

For the continuation of my book project, especially when it morphed into a comparative study of Christian and Islamic mystical thought, I have many people at La Salle University to thank, including Marc Moreau, the chair of the Philosophy Department, whose moral support, good humor, and letters of recommendation did much to win me time and resources to do my research, and Michael J. Kerlin, who, as the senior member of the department, took me under his wing when I first started teaching at La Salle in 2002. Since he passed away in November 2007 he has been sorely missed, but I shall never forget his kindness to a new and inexperienced colleague.

I want to thank the Catholic University of America Press for seeing the potential for a book in a rough manuscript, in particular James Kruggel, Theresa Walker, and Elizabeth Benevides for bringing the manuscript to publication, and Ellen Coughlin for expert copyediting of an often unruly manuscript. I would like to thank the readers, Donald Duclow, David Burrell, and William Chittick, for so carefully reading the manuscript and offering many valuable suggestions. Don, in particular, has been a good friend and mentor to me and, since we are neighbors, I have had the pleasure hearing his insights on Western mysticism over many a refreshing beer! Needless to say, however, all errors of either fact or interpretation are mine alone.

Most important of all, I want to thank my family and especially my wife, Aurora. Not only have her skills as a librarian and an artist given me much needed help at crucial stages in the writing of this book, but her warmth, love, and companionship have been a real refuge from the often lonely work of a scholar. I must also thank my son, Aubin Anthony, who, although he may not be aware of it, has filled my life with indescribable joy. Finally, I want to thank my parents, Robert Aubin and Margaret Rose Puglisi Dobie. The selfless love, generous support, and quiet Catholic faith with which they nourished me as a child have made possible so much of what is good in my life as an adult.

# Abbreviations and Note on Translations

MEISTER ECKHART

The critical edition of Meister Eckhart's works is *Meister Eckhart: Die deutschen und lateinischen Werke herausgegeben im Auftrag der deutschen Forschungsgemeinschaft* (Stuttgart/Berlin:Kohlhammer, 1936–). The volumes that constitute the Latin works will be referred to simply as LW, and the Middle High German as DW. I have used the following standard abbreviations for the various works in the critical edition.

*Latin Works*

| | |
|---|---|
| In Eccl. | *Sermones et Lectiones super Ecclesiastici* (LW II: 229–300) |
| In Exod. | *Expositio Libri Exodi* (LW II: 1–227) |
| In Gen. I | *Expositio Libri Genesis* (LW I: 185–444) |
| In Gen. II | *Liber Parabolorum Genesis* (LW I: 447–702) |
| In Ioh. | *Expositio sancti Evangelii secundum Iohannem* (LW III) |
| In Sap. | *Expositio Libri Sapientiae* (LW II: 301–643) |
| Prol. op. trip. | *Prologus generalis in Opus tripartitum* (LW I: 148–65) |
| Prol. op. prop. | *Prologus in Opus propositionum* (LW I: 166–82) |
| Quaes. Par. | *Quaestiones Parisienses* (LW V: 27–83) |
| Sermo | Latin sermon (LW IV) |

*German Works*

| | |
|---|---|
| Pr. | *Predigt* or German language sermon (DW I–IV) |
| BgT | *Daz buoch der goetlichen troestunge* (DW V: 1–105) |
| Vom Abg. | *Vom abegescheidenheit* (DW V: 400–434) |

*Translations*

    EE     *Meister Eckhart: The Essential Sermons, Commentaries, Treatises and Defense*

    Maurer  *Master Eckhart: Parisian Questions and Prologues*

    TP     *Meister Eckhart: Teacher and Preacher*

IBN ʿARABI

The critical edition of Ibn ʿArabi's main masterpiece, *The Meccan Revelations*, is *Futūḥāt al-makkīyya*, ed. O. Yahia, 4 vols. (Cairo: al-Hay'at al-Misriyya al-ʿAmma li'Kitāb, 1972.) Extensive translations from the *Meccan Revelations* accompanied by commentary can be found in two works by William Chittick:

    SPK    *The Sufi Path of Knowledge*

    SDG    *The Self-Disclosure of God*

In my citations from either SPK or SDG that reproduce Chittick's translations from the *Futuhat*, Roman and Arabic numerals refer to the volume and page number of the critical edition edited by O. Yahia.

OTHER WORKS

    *Bezels*   *The Bezels of Wisdom*

OTHER ABBREVIATIONS

    *S.Th.*   Thomas Aquinas, *Summa Theologiae*

    *Sharḥ*  Dawoud Al-Qaysari, *Maṭlaʿ khuṣlūṣ al-ḥikam fi maʿāni fuṣūṣ al-ḥikam*

# Logos &
# Revelation

# Introduction

## What Is the "Mystical" in the Middle Ages?

If one looks closely at the works and thought of at least two very prominent and influential mystical writers in Islam and Christianity, Muhyaddin Ibn 'Arabi and Meister Eckhart, one does not find "mysticism" understood as a noun, i.e., a system of thought or practice separate from or parallel to the religious traditions to which it belongs, but instead one finds a "mystical" way or mode of appropriating these traditions. From its root meaning in the Greek, the "mystical" is the hidden or inner sense of Scripture. Thus, for both Ibn 'Arabi and Meister Eckhart, the inner or "mystical" sense is the sense that is universally applicable to the inner life of each and every soul. This is the way in which both Ibn 'Arabi and Meister Eckhart understood the mystical, to the degree that they were conscious of having a "mystical" approach at all. As far as we can tell, both were simply trying to develop a deeper and living appropriation of their faith as conveyed to them by their revealed scriptures.

For both the Sufi and the Christian mystic, the mystical is not something outside or alongside the revealed text and its exegetical tradition, but is a development and deepening of that tradition. The mystical is none other than the uncovering, indeed recovery, of the inner, original sense of Scripture such that the soul may come to subsist in and think and act out of that inner, original sense, which is nothing other than the divine Word or *Logos* itself. To uncover the inner sense of the revealed Word is

1

to allow God to unite with the soul and transform it in its very substance.

Mystical reflection is therefore always *embodied* in a specific religious tradition and that tradition is formed and maintained by the revealed text and its interpretation. "Mysticism" does not float disembodied in any "pure experience" of a purely personal, subjective nature. If there is a common core or universal referent to mystical thought and experience, it lies not in any natural realm, but in the transcendent. If one is to find a common core to mystical thought and experience, it can only be found *in and through* the religious traditions that give life to it, and not outside of them. Mystical reflection cannot dispense with revelation and religious tradition for the simple reason that it recognizes that God cannot be captured in a concept or set of concepts. This will be the assertion that I shall attempt to argue throughout this book.

In short, what Ibn ʿArabi and Meister Eckhart are doing, as mystical writers, is thinking back, not to being as such, but to the primal *revelation of being*. What they both assert is that prior to any concept we might have of "being" is the revelation of being, its "presencing" to us. As Eckhart puts it, the Gospel of John does not say, "In the beginning was being," but rather, "In the beginning was the Word (*Logos*)." "Being" or "existence" as such cannot be captured by our finite minds, but rather our finite minds must be captured by it, conformed to it. Hence, for both Ibn ʿArabi and Eckhart, revelation as such becomes the main datum of their thinking. This does not mean that they dispense with a science of being or a metaphysics; rather, it means that, in order for us to have a proper understanding of being or existence, in order to be *conformed* to pure being or existence, we must be open completely to its revealed character. This is not a retreat into irrationalism. To the contrary, it is a recognition that all creatures, insofar as they exist, are intelligible and, when the mind is conformed to them, all creatures are causes of truth. Norris Clarke expresses this insight of medieval thought well when he says:

Being itself is *for* intelligence. Its ultimate meaning and fulfillment require that it be brought into the light of consciousness, that it be *unveiled*, i.e., revealed ( = remove the veil: *revelation*) to mind. This unveiling of being to mind is *truth*, expressed beautifully by the Greek word for truth (*aletheia* = the unveiled). Thus, the fundamental intellectual vocation of every mind-endowed being, and hence of human beings as the only intellectual beings we know of in our material cosmos, is to *unveil* being, bring it into the light of consciousness and speak it out in a *logos,* or meaningful word.[1]

And, as Fr. Clarke and any scholar of the Middle Ages, Christian or Muslim, would add: being is for intelligence because being has within itself a primal *Logos* or Word that is expressed in every being. This primal Word or *Logos* makes possible every finite act of knowing or "unveiling" by created intelligence.

The whole goal of the mystical project, then, is to listen to this primal *Logos.* But, for Ibn 'Arabi and Meister Eckhart, working respectively in the Muslim and Christian religious traditions, this *Logos* has spoken to human beings directly: for Ibn 'Arabi, in the Qur'an, and for Meister Eckhart, in the Person of Christ. It has spoken to human beings directly because, as we shall see, it is the tendency of human beings, as both mystical writers note again and again, to become closed off to the revealed nature of being, to become, instead, "stuck" on the being itself or, even worse, on our *created concepts* about being or beings, and not on the act of revelation itself. Or to put it another way, it is the tendency of human beings to become enclosed in and attached to their own finite subjectivity. As William Chittick explains in discussing the Muslim intellectual tradition, human beings, even (or maybe especially) the most brilliant among them have the distinct tendency to fall into what the Muslim tradition calls *taqlīd,* or the "blind imitation" of what others have said, written, or thought without experiencing the truth of these things for themselves. This "blind imitation" is attractive to human beings because it gives them a sense of power over the world, a body of knowledge that allows them to manipulate the world for worldly ends. But what is necessary for true or authentic religion is not blind imitation but what the Muslim tradition calls *tahqīq* (from the causative form of *haqq,* "truth," "reality," therefore = "to make real," "to make true").[2] That is, instead of merely passing on handed-down truths, the mystic is the one who *realizes their truth by having their nature "unveiled" or "revealed" to him or her.* The mystic "sees" the divine truths and does not merely repeat them or even simply "understand" them in the sense of mere analytic understanding. And in order to do this, the mystic

1. W. Norris Clarke, S.J., *The One and the Many: A Contemporary Thomistic Metaphysics* (Notre Dame, Ind.: University of Notre Dame Press, 2001), 29.

2. William Chittick, *Science of the Cosmos, Science of the Soul: The Pertinence of Islamic Cosmology in the Modern World* (Oxford: One World Publications, 2007).

must let go of the finite self and allow him- or herself to be conformed to revealed, transcendent truth.

The mystical project of medieval writers like Ibn 'Arabi and Meister Eckhart, then, is to know God as self-revealed and self-revealing *Logos*. Hence, the primal Word that is spoken is always spoken by God, not human beings. We live in truth only to the degree that we fall silent and let God's Word, the *Logos* of all things, speak in and through us. For, in the end, it is not we who speak, but rather we who are spoken. For mystics like Ibn 'Arabi and Meister Eckhart, therefore, self-understanding begins not with any immediate reflection upon oneself. To make oneself an object of reflection is to lose oneself, for, as soon as one tries to grasp oneself in any concept or image, one's "I" has retreated "behind" the reflection. Rather, one comes to self-understanding only through reflection upon the Word of revelation, because only there can we find ourselves in our truth, i.e., as God knows, sees, and loves us. That is why, for the medieval mystic, all authentic self-knowledge must begin and end with a complete letting-go of the self, a radical *fana'* (extinction) or *abgeschiedenheit* or *gelassenheit* (a detachment or letting-be) from the finite, created self so that one may live and abide in and through the divine *Logos*. Medieval mystical writing, therefore, is through and through hermeneutical in that it assumes no fixed and abiding "self" that is the stable and absolute locus of truth. In fact, as we shall see, the whole effort of medieval mystical thought, in the writings of people like Ibn 'Arabi and Meister Eckhart, is to *destabilize* and *de-center* the self, for only then can the human being become open to truth as such. Their understanding is hermeneutical insofar, then, as it realizes that, for truth to occur, to be "unveiled," the very knower of truth with all of his or her limitations and prejudices must be put into question and ultimately transformed into the truth of the matter itself. Many modern theories of mysticism and mystical "experience" fail to understand this basic hermeneutical nature of mysticism, assuming, as we shall see, the Cartesian model of the self as the absolute and abiding "substratum" of "experiences." But first, let us turn to what is probably the best model so far of thinking through the essence of what we call the "mystical."

## Scholem on the Nature of Mystical Thought and Experience

The essentially hermeneutical nature of mystical writing and thinking has not gone unnoticed by contemporary scholars of Christian or Muslim mysticism. Scholars of Eckhart such as Bernard McGinn and Donald Duclow and scholars of Ibn 'Arabi such as William Chittick and Michel Chodkiewicz have done much to understand these writers on their own terms and within the context of their times and religious traditions.[3] In particular, these scholars have investigated how deeply rooted is the thought of Ibn 'Arabi and Meister Eckhart in the hermeneutics of sacred texts. Indeed, they have shown how the "mystical" itself is inseparable from this hermeneutic activity.

Already some sixty years ago, Gershom Scholem described with great perspicacity the nature of mystical thought and experience, and his observations form a corrective even today to many current popular views on the nature of mysticism. Scholem, in the first essay of his important book *Major Trends in Jewish Mysticism*, gives us the salutary reminder that "there is no mysticism as such, there is only the mysticism of a particular religious system, Christian, Islamic, Jewish mysticism and so on."[4] Even if the mystical is the universal meaning of a particular revelation, applicable to the inner journey toward God of any soul, there still cannot be a mysti-

---

3. For Meister Eckhart and Christian mysticism in general, see Bernard McGinn's monumental history of Christian mysticism, *The Presence of God: A History of Western Christian Mysticism*. In particular, see the first and fourth volumes: *The Foundations of Mysticism: Origins to Fifth Century* (New York: Crossroad, 1991) and *The Harvest of Mysticism in Medieval Germany* (New York: Crossroad, 2005). McGinn also has a monograph on Eckhart, *The Mystical Thought of Meister Eckhart: The Man from Whom God Hid Nothing* (New York: Crossroad, 2001). For some very insightful articles on Eckhart and his mystical hermeneutics, see the collected articles of Donald F. Duclow in *Masters of Learned Ignorance: Eriugena, Eckhart, Cusanus* (Aldershot, England: Ashgate Publishing, 2006). For Ibn 'Arabi, see Claude Addas, *Quest for the Red Sulphur*, trans. Peter Kingsley (Cambridge: Islamic Texts Society, 1993); William Chittick, *The Sufi Path of Knowledge: Ibn 'Arabi's Metaphysics of Imagination* (Albany: State University of New York Press, 1989); Chittick, *The Self-Disclosure of God: Principles of Ibn al-'Arabi's Cosmology* (Albany: State University of New York Press, 1998); Chittick, *Imaginal Worlds: Ibn 'Arabi and the Problem of Religious Diversity* (Albany: State University of New York Press, 1994); Michel Chodkiewicz, "Ibn 'Arabi et la lettre de la loi," in *Actes du colloque: Mystique, culture et societé*, ed. M. Meslin (Paris: 1983); Chodkiewicz, *An Ocean without a Shore: Ibn 'Arabi, The Book, and the Law*, trans. David Streight (Albany: State University of New York Press, 1993).

4. Gershom Scholem, *Major Trends in Jewish Mysticism* (New York: Schocken Books, 1974), 6.

cal tradition outside the revealed text and the religious community that interprets the text. Mystical thought is always embedded in a religious tradition and, more specifically, in an interpretive tradition that has legal or liturgical aspects. A personal experience is, indeed, central to the mystical path in the Middle Ages, but it is an experience of, in, and through the revealed text and the way that text is read and experienced, be it in the liturgy, in the scholar's study, or in the application of legal judgments. For Ibn ʿArabi and Eckhart, it is the revealed Word of God, not the individual, that must be allowed to shape human experience.

Scholem posits three stages of religious development. They are helpful as a way of understanding the place of mystical thought in a religious tradition (even if his schema is not without its own problems and owes much to that archmodernist, Hegel). The first stage Scholem names the "mythical" epoch: "In this first stage, Nature is the scene of man's relation to God."[5] Gods are seen to walk the earth and to represent the forces of nature. This epoch sets the stage for the second epoch of what Scholem calls "classical" or "revealed" religion: "For in its classical form, religion signifies the creation of a vast abyss, conceived as absolute, between God, the infinite and transcendental Being, and Man, the finite creature."[6] In this stage, God reveals himself in historical events and gives laws or commands to the community of faith. God is seen as transcendent, apart from nature both ontologically and ethically. Here we have a much more sublime and exalted notion of God, but one that comes at a price—the sundering of the primal unity between God and man of the first epoch. The third, or "romantic" period strives "to bring back the old unity which religion has destroyed, but on a new plane, where the world of mythology and that of revelation meet in the soul of man."[7] It is here that the mystical element in religion properly speaking arrives. Thus the mystical is not a primary but a secondary phenomenon for Scholem: it is an attempt to recover the primal unity between God and man that had been sundered by revealed or "classical" religion. But it does this not by trying to return to the first, or mythical stage, of religion. It attempts to preserve both the transcendent and sublime spirit and content of the second stage while trying to restore the unity of the first. It does this by interpreting the revealed scriptures of

5. Ibid., 7.                                                6. Ibid.
7. Ibid., 8.

the second epoch in a new way, a way that tries to understand the revelation of God as a dual movement, from without into human history, but also and correspondingly from within the heart or ground of the believer back to God:

Revelation, for instance, is to the mystic not only a definite historical occurrence which, at a given moment in history, puts an end to any further direct relation between mankind and God. With no thought of denying Revelation as a fact of history, the mystic still conceives the source of religious knowledge and experience which bursts forth from his own heart as being of equal importance for the conception of religious truth. In other words, instead of the one act of Revelation, there is a constant repetition of this act.[8]

In other words, the mystical thinker conceives of revelation as both a transcendent and an immanent act. Both aspects necessarily belong together. Revelation is a transcendent act because it breaks through the finite, created mental categories of human thought. But precisely because it transcends these finite limits, revelation also transcends all attempts by the human mind to make it into a mere object of thought; instead, it is also the immanent *ground* of the soul's self-understanding. As such, the goal of the mystical project is to see the Word of God in its dialectical unity, as both the ultimate subject and object of the soul's blessedness. God is within the soul, but only in an analogical way: He is fully present by his creative power, but he is and remains always transcendent, "beyond" the innermost depths of the soul. Ibn 'Arabi and Meister Eckhart thus see the "inner revelation" of the mystical life not as a revelation separate from or parallel to the revealed text but as the living completion and fulfillment of the Word of God. In fact, the "inner" revelation is nothing but the "outer" or "textual" revelation become the lived ground of the soul's being, thinking, and acting.

A key distinction, therefore, that both Ibn 'Arabi and Meister Eckhart constantly posit is a distinction between "God the Creator" and "God as He is in Himself." Eckhart talks about the distinction between God, as the highest being and cause of creation, and the "Godhead" (*gottheit, deitas*), who is "beyond God," beyond all distinctions and relations, even those of the Trinity. Ibn 'Arabi makes a distinction between God in himself, as the

---

8. Ibid., 9.

"Real," *al-ḥaqq*, and God as "Lord" or *rabb* of creation and, thus, as conditioned by his relation with creation.[9] These sorts of distinctions have led many to confuse the thought of Ibn ʿArabi and Meister Eckhart with gnostic speculation. The gnostic posits an opposition between the evil "Creator God" of revelation (Yahweh) and the "good God" "beyond" the created world and its "archons, principalities, thrones and powers." But, as Scholem asserts, this is not the case for the "orthodox" mystics of the Jewish, Christian, and Islamic traditions, no matter what the superficial similarities their thought may bear to gnostic theories. Scholem remarks, referring to the Jewish mystical tradition:

Kabbalism in other words is not dualistic, although historically there exists a close connection between this way of thinking and that of the Gnostics, to whom the hidden God and the Creator are opposing principles. On the contrary, all the energy of "orthodox" Kabbalistic speculation is bent to the task of escaping from dualistic consequences; otherwise they would not have been able to maintain themselves within the Jewish community.[10]

In other words, the whole thrust behind the thought of "orthodox" mystical thinkers, whether Jewish, Christian, or Muslim, is to show the *identity* between the God of revelation, the Creator God, and the God "beyond God," the Essence or "God in Himself." Indeed, for these mystical thinkers, it is the purpose of revelation to overcome this division, even as it posits it; in the words of Jacques Maritain, revelation distinguishes in order to unite.[11] The same movement by which God reveals himself in creation and, in particular, in the Holy Book, is the same movement by which he takes the believer who enters into its deepest meaning back up into himself. Meister Eckhart and Ibn ʿArabi belong squarely in this group of "orthodox" mystical thinkers. This is a second major thesis of this book, and one, as we shall show, supported by much evidence.

And we should not forget the importance of the faith community to

9. Scholem mentions a parallel or analogous concept in Jewish mysticism: "The mystic strives to assure himself of the living presence of God, the God of the Bible, the God who is good, wise, just and merciful and the embodiment of all other positive attributes. But at the same time he is unwilling to renounce the idea of the hidden God who remains eternally unknowable in the depths of His own Self, or, to use the bold expression of the Kabbalists 'in the depths of His nothingness.'" Scholem, 12–13.

10. Ibid., 13.

11. See his book *Distinguish in Order to Unite or The Degrees of Knowledge*, trans. Gerald Phelan (Notre Dame, Ind.: University of Notre Dame Press, 1995).

both Eckhart and Ibn 'Arabi. What ultimately gives their thought and practice grounding and validity is this community. Eckhart's mystical reading of Scripture occurred almost always in a liturgical context. Ibn 'Arabi's mystical hermeneutics of the Qur'an is firmly situated within the study of Islamic law, its interpretation, and its application. What he looks for is simply the inner meaning of that Law. To separate the mystical writings of either from their respective communal contexts would be to misunderstand their intention and effect.

## Twentieth-Century Scholarship and the "Antinomies of Mysticism"

In advancing this approach to comparative mystical studies, I hope to reverse at least somewhat a trend, common in scholarship on mysticism and religion until quite recently, wherein scholars attempted to identify a core set of characteristics common to all mystical experience.

Involved in this quest was the elaboration of complex categories and taxonomies of various kinds of mysticism.[12] Many of these categories and taxonomies of types of mystical experience and thought have, no doubt, been very helpful in enabling scholars to get a better grasp of the mystical phenomenon. But too often these categorizations and taxonomies operate on the basis of modern assumptions that are foreign to the mystical texts themselves and certainly extraneous to whatever the writers wished to illuminate through them. Such characterizations of a "mystical core" end up either leaving in too much of the plethora of evidence, or leaving too much out. Even more fundamentally, such modern scholarship on mystical thought and experience runs into difficulties of a purely logical nature, which I call "antinomies of mysticism."

For example, it is disputed whether mystical "experience" is purely

---

12. Two influential books on mysticism that perpetuate the notion that there is a universal "core" to mysticism that is some sort of "pure" experience "transcending" religious norms and conventions are W. T. Stace, *Mysticism and Philosophy* (London: Macmillan, 1961), and F. Staal, *Exploring Mysticism* (Harmondsworth, England: Penguin, 1975). For various taxonomies of mysticism such as that between "monist" and "theist" mysticism or that between the "numinous" or "prophetic" mysticism of the Semitic religions as opposed to the more "introverted" mysticism of East Asia, there are the books by Robert Zaehner, *Mysticism: Sacred and Profane* (Oxford: Oxford University Press, 1961), and Ninian Smart, *Reasons and Faith: An Investigation of Religious Discourse, Christian and Non-Christian* (London: Routledge and Kegan Paul, 1958).

contextual—i.e., determined decisively by the structure of the human mind and the religious, political, cultural, and social structures "created" by it—or whether mystical experience is a "pure experience" or "pure consciousness event" that escapes or goes beyond these a priori structures of human understanding.[13] But if mystical experience is essentially hermeneutical, then such a debate is moot. Of course, mystical experience is contextual precisely because it arises in and out of a religious tradition and in intimate contact with its revealed text. There can be, therefore, no authentic mystical "pure experience" that is empty of specific content precisely because the living Word of God is the content as well as the subject of that experience. This, however, is also why mystical experience is not purely contextual either: an Ibn 'Arabi or a Meister Eckhart experiences the revealed text as that which "breaks through," "dissolves," or "shatters" conventional and pre-established notions, concepts, and imagery. Revelation is revelation because it breaks through the "hard shell" of accepted human cultural, intellectual, and, most of all, linguistic conventions and expectations. As I shall show, in both Ibn 'Arabi and Meister Eckhart, it is not philosophical or metaphysical thought that tries to cut revelation down to size but rather the reverse: it is revelation that fundamentally alters the meaning and significance of all traditional philosophical or metaphysical categories. Being hermeneutical, mystical writing recognizes that all spiritual meaning for human beings is embodied in creatures, texts, and traditions. But for all that, it also recognizes that they have a deep and inner meaning that point beyond their embodied natures.

If it were not out of place here, I could point to many other such examples of modern approaches to medieval mystical writing that have been, to say the least, inadequate. It is my contention that this inadequacy stems, for the most part, from an uncritical acceptance of the modernist assumption, going back to Descartes, that all human knowledge must be founded on the experience of a discrete, self-contained, and self-transpar-

---

13. For a defense of the "contextualist" approach to mysticism, see the articles by S. T. Katz in S.T. Katz, ed., *Mysticism and Philosophical Analysis* (London: Sheldon Press, 1978); Katz, ed., *Mysticism and Religious Traditions* (Oxford: Oxford University Press, 1983); and Katz, ed., *Mysticism and Language* (Oxford: Oxford University Press, 1992). For a defense of the essence of mysticism as a "pure consciousness event," see R. K. C. Forman, ed., *The Problem of Pure Consciousness* (Oxford: Oxford University Press, 1990), and *Meister Eckhart: Mystic as Theologian* (Rockport, Mass.: Element Books, 1991).

ent human subject.[14] As Descartes argued, the only indubitable truth is "I think, therefore I am"; everything "outside" the thinking subject is doubtful. Although he criticized Descartes's philosophy in some of its details, Immanuel Kant did not challenge but only deepened the force of this assumption and argued that the human subject cannot know "things in themselves" but only as they "appear" to and are structured by the *a priori* concepts of the, albeit universal and therefore "transcendental," human subject. "Revelation" from outside the structure of the human mind could come only in the form of the moral law, which is known by pure reason anyway, special divine revelation being unnecessary to know it. Curiously, however, this leads to a contradiction—curious, because Kant's position is the logical conclusion of Cartesian premises: if one follows Descartes, it is only the "pure experience" or "pure consciousness event" of the subject that would count as authentic "mystical knowledge" because only such experience would be immediately accessible to the "pure subject." But at the same time, this leads to the opposite Kantian contention: that all mystical experience must be contextual, because we would not be able to know reality outside the structure of the human mind and its scientific, cultural, and political products.

In other words, most modern commentators on mysticism have missed the hermeneutical nature of the writings of Ibn 'Arabi and Meister Eckhart and of medieval mystical writing in general. Human beings do not experience the world as either pure concepts or mere material things. Just as human beings are not pure minds or pure bodies, but embodied spirits, so human beings experience the world as a realm of meaningful things, things with their own *logoi* or essences that point beyond themselves to a spiritual reality.

Thus, "experience," to be sure, is essential to the mystical projects of Ibn 'Arabi and Meister Eckhart. But as such, the "experience" does not "belong" to the human subject, but transcends it. The thirst for individual and extraordinary experiences of divine things, already prevalent in the high Middle Ages but even more so in the modern era, misses the essential nature of the mystical as understood by Meister Eckhart and Ibn

14. For this change in outlook, which infected even many of the greatest mystics after the sixteenth century, see Michel de Certeau, *La Fable mystique: XVI et XVII siècle* (Paris: Gallimard, 1982).

'Arabi. They both combated these tendencies in their writings. The goal of Ibn 'Arabi and Meister Eckhart's thinking is not to lead the soul to new, discrete experiences, but to lead it to a new *way* of experiencing the world and the self in and through God.

That is why there are always two poles to the mystical: the subjective inner experience but also the objective outer content of revelation. Authentic mystical experience, at least as it was conceived in the Middle Ages, demands both poles. Vladimir Lossky, in his book on the mystical theology of the Eastern Church, puts this necessary tension very nicely when he says:

> Outside the truth kept by the whole Church personal experience would be deprived of all certainty, of all objectivity. It would be a mingling of truth and of falsehood, of reality and of illusion: "mysticism" in the bad sense of the word. On the other hand, the teaching of the Church would have no hold on souls if it did not in some degree express an inner experience of truth, granted in different measure to each one of the faithful. There is, therefore, no Christian mysticism without theology; but, above all, there is no theology without mysticism.[15]

One can say the same thing, mutatis mutandis, for the relationship of personal experience to Islamic theology and law in the writings of someone like Ibn 'Arabi. The point that Lossky makes here is very important: mystical experience is always an experience in and out of an objective content which, by definition for the mystic, is always a *revealed* content. The revealed content, to be objective, valid, *true,* cannot be private, but rather common to all. There is, therefore, nothing, technically speaking, *esoteric* about mystical experience. But, as Lossky also reminds us, if revelation is to have a hold on us, if it is to be *lived* and to have transformative power, it must also have an inner correlate, it must come as much from deep within the soul as from without it.

The goal, then, of the mystical project, whether that of Ibn 'Arabi or that of Meister Eckhart, is to come personally and inwardly to participate in the realities revealed or unveiled by revelation. Thus, mystical thinking and experiencing are always exegetical thinking and experiencing and mystical exegesis is itself always a participatory exegesis.[16] That is, it is al-

---

15. Vladimir Lossky, *The Mystical Theology of the Eastern Church* (Crestwood, N.Y.: St. Valdimir's Seminary Press, 1957), 9.

16. See the book by Matthew Levering, *Participatory Biblical Exegesis: A Theology of Biblical Interpretation* (Notre Dame, Ind.: University of Notre Dame Press, 2008).

ways an exegesis of revealed texts whose goal and purpose is for the reader, hearer, or exegete to participate in the divine realities revealed in the text. But, in this sense, all medieval exegesis, whether Christian or Muslim, is a participatory exegesis, because, as the theologian Matthew Levering argues, all medieval exegesis, at least until the advent in the Christian world of nominalism in the fourteenth century, was a participatory exegesis.[17] In other words, what Ibn ʿArabi and Meister Eckhart are doing in their mystical writing is not radically different from the main streams of thinking and interpretation in their respective faith traditions and times.

## Comparative Mysticism and Analogy

I have chosen to focus on Ibn ʿArabi and Meister Eckhart in this study for several reasons. The clearest and simplest reason is that both were thinkers of great power whose influence extended widely, deeply, and often covertly in their respective traditions. Ibn ʿArabi earned for himself the appellation *al-Shaykh al-ākbar*, or "the greatest master," and his works spawned many schools of Sufism—along with much controversy—in the Muslim world for centuries after his death. Meister Eckhart profoundly influenced such prominent and influential Christian mystics as Johannes Tauler, Henry Suso, Jan van Ruysbroeck, Nicholas of Cusa, and, through them, the great Spanish mystics of the sixteenth century, John of the Cross and Theresa of Avila.

But there is a deeper reason for the choice of Ibn ʿArabi and Meister Eckhart. They are excellent examples of mystical writers who appear to defend the very proposition that I wish to refute in this work: i.e., the modernist assumption that the mystical is somehow independent of or even opposed to religious tradition. This misunderstanding is primarily due to a neglect of the hermeneutical nature of medieval mystical writing in general. To a certain extent, it is understandable why many have interpreted their writings in this way. Meister Eckhart, after a distinguished career as a professor, administrator, and preacher within the Dominican order, ran afoul of Church authorities. Several propositions taken from his

17. Levering does note a slight weakening of what he calls participatory exegesis in Eckhart, remarking that the Dominican indulges too much in abstract allegory. Nevertheless, Eckhart remains true to the tradition of participatory exegesis as handed down to him by Aquinas. Besides, as we shall show, Eckhart's method of exegesis is, strictly speaking, not allegorical.

works were condemned as heretical in a papal bull published a year after his death (although, it should be made clear, Eckhart himself was never condemned as a heretic, since he was prepared, as his vows of obedience required, to abjure any propositions that were found heretical or even "smacking" of heresy). For this reason, it is often assumed that Eckhart was something of a "revolutionary," even "heretical," thinker. Ibn 'Arabi had no such entanglements with the Islamic authorities, but that was probably due only to the fact that he was much more discreet in his teaching activities. As Alexander Knysh shows,[18] the posthumous reputation of Ibn 'Arabi in the Islamic world came into bitter dispute, with many of the *'ulema* denouncing his writings as thoroughly heretical. So he, too, has acquired in recent times the reputation of being an "outsider" to the tradition, a maverick, and a rebel.

Yet in each case, their reputation is undeserved, because, as I wish to show here, for both of them, the revealed text as handed down and interpreted by their respective religious traditions is essential to their mystical thought and, in general, their interpretations of these texts are decidedly orthodox and conservative in character. Thus, for example, Meister Eckhart's writing and reflection are in no way opposed to Thomistic teaching, but rather an extension and application of it. Neither Meister Eckhart nor Ibn 'Arabi pursues his mystical reflection outside the main currents of medieval Christian and Islamic thought, but within them.

What's more, Ibn 'Arabi and Meister Eckhart belong to obviously different religious traditions, Muslim and Christian respectively, but have much in common in their writings. These commonalities may very easily tempt many to conclude that both somehow "rose above" their respective traditions and taught a sort of universal religion. I want to show that neither one in any way rose above his respective religious tradition but, to the contrary, entered very deeply into it. It is precisely in entering into the depths of their traditions that we find points of convergence. Here again, the convergence between Ibn 'Arabi and Meister Eckhart lies in their attempt to realize through rational reflection upon their respective scriptures the inner, lived meaning or truth of divine revelation.

There can be no univocal meaning to "mysticism" or "the mystical"

18. See Alexander Knysh, *Ibn 'Arabi in the Later Islamic Tradition: The Making of a Polemical Image in Medieval Islam* (Albany: State University of New York Press, 1999).

precisely because mysticism or the mystical cannot subsist apart from the mystical interpretation of revealed texts within the context of a religious tradition, with its own liturgical and hermeneutical practices. Indeed, the mystical *is* this interpretation with a view toward inward appropriation of an outward meaning leading to self-transformation. There is no "pure" or "natural" mysticism, no "common core" that we can access independent of any religious matrix. There is, to repeat the words of Gershom Scholem, no mysticism as such, only "Islamic mysticism" or "Christian mysticism." Does this mean, then, that these mystical manifestations have nothing in common, that they do not point to a common origin? Not at all. Rather, we must understand them as *analogous* manifestations that refer to a singular and absolute divine origin.[19] Mystical or analogical readings exist precisely because the divine cannot be grasped by the human mind empirically or conceptually, but only analogically.

Islamic mysticism and Christian mysticism are each unique, with their own revealed texts and thus their own inner potentialities and capacities. And yet, Ibn 'Arabi and Meister Eckhart develop these potentialities and capacities in strikingly and proportionately analogous ways. They both use philosophical concepts to unlock the inner meaning of Scripture and, by doing so, give, in turn, a new meaning not only to philosophical concepts and to one's own inner experiences as well. We can see now, from the perspective of seven centuries, that Ibn 'Arabi and Meister Eckhart were pursuing analogous paths within their traditions. Their writings are fully

19. This account of the proper understanding of the universality of mystical thought and experience across traditions bears, some readers may note, a strong resemblance to the Perennial or Traditionalist school of comparative religion represented most forcefully in the many books by Frithjof Schuon, particularly *The Transcendent Unity of Religions* (Wheaton, Ill.: Quest Books, 2nd ed., 1993). In this book Schuon argues, as we do, that the "unity" of religions, properly speaking, lies only in the transcendent deity and not in any universal "experience" or, even less, in any philosophical system. Our account of this universality, however, differs from Schuon's in two important respects. (1) Schuon's account relies on the problematic distinction between an "esoteric" and an "exoteric" religion: the former gives us access to this transcendent unity while the latter makes available this access to the wider masses. There is some basis for this distinction, especially in Muslim sources; but the distinction is not always clear, especially when applied to a Christian context. Our account relies on no such distinction. (2) Relying as it does on Thomistic principles, our account is rooted even more firmly in "tradition" than Schuon's. Schuon's accounts of religion, as insightful as they often are, are still redolent of a nineteenth-century romanticism that seeks "authentic" religion in esoteric teachings and initiations. Our Thomistic account of the analogous nature of mystical thought and experience is itself rooted in the medieval thought-world and is, besides, a more straightforward account of the proper understanding of religious "universality."

embodied in their respective traditions, and yet they point beyond their traditions, not to some universal religion, but to the divine truth. That is, the hermeneutical reason that is embodied in their mystical writings also forms the ground for a new understanding between religious traditions. It is unfortunate that the full potential of their writings for interreligious dialogue could not be realized in any full way during the Middle Ages.

Does this mean, then, that all religious or mystical paths are equal? Neither Ibn 'Arabi nor Meister Eckhart thought so. To be sure, Ibn 'Arabi, in his *Interpreter of Desires (Tarjumān al-ashwāq)*, talks about his religion as the "religion of love," and that all religions are valid manifestations of the divine Reality, as well as vehicles that carry us toward that Reality. I shall have an opportunity to look at Ibn 'Arabi's religious "universalism" in due course. But, at the same time, it should never be forgotten that Ibn 'Arabi sees Islam and the Law of the prophet Muhammad as the fulfillment of all previous religious manifestations. His adherence to the norms of Islamic law was scrupulous and single-minded and, despite (or, maybe, because of) his universalism, he thought the strictures of this law should be applied with utmost rigor to the *dhimmi* communities of Christians and Jews living in realms under Muslim rule. We have, for example, a letter of Ibn 'Arabi to Kayka'us, the sultan of Konya (Rum), advising him in his treatment of his Christian subjects:

The worst thing that Islam and Muslims suffer in your realm is the sound of bells, the manifestation of infidelity, the affirmation of an associate of God, and the disappearance of the rules instituted by the Prince of Believers, 'Umar b. al-Khattab, regarding *dhimmis:* namely that neither in the city itself nor in the surrounding regions are they to build new churches, monasteries or hermitages, that they are not to repair any of these buildings if they become dilapidated, that they are not to prevent any Muslim from being given food and shelter in their churches for a period of up to three days, that they are not to hide spies, that they are not to conspire in secret against Muslims, that they are not to teach the Qur'an to their children, and that they are not to make public show of their polytheism.[20]

We should note that these provisions were not out of the ordinary or harsh relative to the time. Ibn 'Arabi is probably also thinking of his Spanish experience, at a time when the Christian kingdoms were on the cusp

20. Cited in Addas, 235.

of driving the Muslims out of Spain. But it should also put us on guard against too quickly attributing to Ibn 'Arabi a facile religious universalism.

While Eckhart, unlike Ibn 'Arabi, does not have anything explicit to say about the relation of Christianity to other religions nor anything specific to say about Islam, it is safe to suppose that Eckhart had no doubts about Christ as the perfection and fulfillment of all revelation and that his adherence to the letter of the Gospel was absolute as well. We can agree with Fernand Brunner when he remarks that Eckhart is no radical; otherwise he would not have such a strong influence on mystics of impeccable orthodoxy, many of whom I named above.[21] For Eckhart, Christ is the inner mystical meaning of all authentic revelation, whether Jewish or Christian. If Eckhart had at any time reflected upon Islam, like all of his colleagues he would most likely have thought it a Christian heresy.[22]

If, then, all mystical experience and reflection are embodied in religious tradition, taking their very essence and substance from the hermeneutics of the sacred text that is the ground and center of that tradition, where does that leave comparative mysticism and, a fortiori, comparative religion? Such a strictly contextualized approach might at first glance leave no basis for dialogue among religious traditions, even—or especially—on the level of mystical reflection and practice. I shall show, however, that this is not the case; to reject the notion of a universal core to religious reflection and experience is by no means a rejection of a universalism per se. If mystical reflection and experience point to any universal core, it is to the transcendent Deity given in revelation rather than to any human mode of thought or experience.

21. Fernand Brunner, *Maître Eckhart: Approche de l'oeuvre* (Geneva: Editions Ad Solem, 1999), 6.
22. After all, Eckhart consistently refers to Muslim philosophers as "heathens," even if he does so without any trace of animosity and with not a little respect!

.

# PART I

# ✦ Revelation

For medieval mystical writers, Christian or Muslim, the authority of the sacred text was unquestioned. Meister Eckhart and Ibn 'Arabi were no exception. But if we read the writings of these two with care, we find that their obedience to the authority of a revealed text did not at all stifle free inquiry. Both Ibn 'Arabi and Meister Eckhart held that finite human reason could not be its own ultimate authority. Human reason is indeed powerful and *capax veritatis (sive Dei)*, but, left to its own devices, it is liable to error and, most important, to confusing its own limited, finite and provisional formulations of the Truth with the infinite Truth itself. Human reason cannot grasp the infinite without the help of the infinite. Reason is in need of illumination or an *unveiling* that frees it from its own finitude.[1]

Hence, both men argue that we need *revelation*. "Revelation" in its original sense means an "uncovering"—a pulling away of a "veiling" (*velatio*). What is the "veil"? It is all the limits and finite boundaries that cover over or veil the nature of Being or Reality, of

---

1. See the two articles by Nicholas Largier that develop this argument in relation to the work of Meister Eckhart: "Intellekttheorie, Hermeneutik und Allegorie: Subjekt und Subjektivität bei Meister Eckhart," in *Geschichte und Vorgeschichte der modernen Subjektivität*, ed. Reto Fetz, Roland Hagenbüche, and Peter Schulz, 460–86 (Berlin: de Gruyter, 1998), and "*Figuratio Locutio*: Hermeneutik und Philosophie bei Eckhart von Hochheim und Heinrich Seuse," in *Meister Eckhart: Lebensstationen—Redesituatationen*, ed. Klaus Jacobi, 303–32 (Berlin: Akademie Verlag, 1997).

God, in its (or his) nakedness. These limits are twofold. On the one hand, there are the limits entailed by the materiality or finitude of creatures: creatures, by their very nature as creatures, cannot reveal adequately the infinity of God. On the other hand, there is the finitude of the human mind: the human mind, in abstracting concepts from creatures, cannot think beyond what it can clearly conceive, and these concepts are necessarily limited and limiting. For both of our mystical writers, the second limit is by far the greater obstacle to knowing God and the one that they are most concerned to overcome, since, by his or her intellectual nature, the human being is open, at least potentially, to all being as such.

Now Ibn ʿArabi and Meister Eckhart, like most medieval theologians, understood revelation in two senses. In a wide and very fundamental sense, all that exists is revelation, because it reveals or uncovers in some way what God is. If a doctrine as fundamental to both Christianity and Islam as that of creation teaches that all things have their existence and nature from God, then quite literally everything reveals in a limited and finite way who and what God is. So in this sense, every human mind, even that of the atheist or agnostic, is illuminated by what the theologians call "general" revelation, which is creation itself. Reason, therefore, is in harmony with revelation and depends upon it to the degree that reason grasps truth only to the degree that its judgments conform to reality. But this general revelation is so general that it is of limited usefulness to the soul who wants to know whether God exists or, if he does, what sort of being he is. If *everything* is a divine revelation, then it is very easy for the human mind to conclude that *nothing* is such a revelation or fail to recognize anything as revelation in the first place. The fish does not know as water the water in which it swims. It becomes too easy to take material reality as all there is and the concepts of the human mind as all we can know. In other words, without revelation, the human mind does not recognize creatures or concepts as what they truly are: limited.

But there is a narrower meaning of revelation called "specific" revelation that especially concerns mystical writers like Ibn ʿArabi and Meister Eckhart. This is the revelation contained in the books of the Bible or the Qur'an, written historical documents that address human beings directly about the nature and commands of God and, in some cases, claim to be the very words of God himself. This sense of revelation is of prime importance because it is through this revelation that the soul comes to know God as God, revelation as revelation, and both creatures and concepts as what they truly are, finite limits on the infinity of being or existence. Here there is a direct address to the human mind and heart. What is important for mystical writers like Ibn 'Arabi and Meister Eckhart is that, in attending to this address made by revelation, the inner truth of general revelation is revealed as well, because, by understanding more specifically who God is and what he demands, the human mind is in a better position to understand the ends and purposes of creation and, most particularly, of creatures like ourselves. The human mind is better able to understand the nature of both creatures and concepts as *analogical,* i.e., as embodying truths that refer beyond themselves to a transcendent existence and unity. In short, special revelation is the key to the meaning of general revelation.

Nevertheless, revelation needs reason to interpret the full import and explicit meaning of the revealed text. Thus, both Ibn 'Arabi and Meister Eckhart (the first implicitly, the second explicitly) use the categories of philosophy and even physics, to unlock the inner meaning of revelation. But they do this not, as many other such writers have done, simply to say that the truths of reason and those of revelation accord and amount to the same principles (one thinks here of Ibn 'Arabi's older Andalusian contemporary Averroes); rather, they use these principles and categories to unlock *the inner meaning of the text that is also the inner meaning of the philosophical or scientific concept.* In other words, by using philosophical reason to unlock the inner meaning of the revealed text, both Ibn 'Arabi and Meister Eckhart wish to disclose the *inner meaning for the life of the soul and its ascent to God.* They want to disclose the meaning not just of the sacred text, but of all creatures and all sciences. They wish to show how all creatures and all the sciences by which human beings know creatures refer back to God and to the Word of God as found in the sacred text. Thus, for Eckhart, the principles of Aristotelian physics, for example, are analogies for the union of the soul with God, as we shall see below.

But this is not all. This understanding of Scripture, which also transforms our understanding of all creatures and also of all the products of human reason such as philosophy and the sciences, should also transform the understanding of ourselves. Indeed, it should lead to a transformation of the self, in which the soul is conformed completely to God's Word. According to the great French scholar of Sufism and Islamic thought Henry Corbin, the mystical thinker discloses out of revelation itself the hidden, inner meaning of that revelation so that, in turn, that meaning can be appropriated and lived from the inside out, so to speak, by the believer.[2] This openness of interpretation, as Corbin notes, paradoxically presupposes a closed or fixed text, for it is only when the prophetic revelation is closed can the interior vivifying work of interpretation begin: "Thus, prophetic Revelation is closed, but precisely because it is closed, it implies openness of prophetic hermeneutics, of the *ta'wīl, or intelligentia spiritualis*."[3]

Ibn 'Arabi, to be sure, makes use of philosophical concepts inherited from both the Peripatetic and Neoplatonic traditions in order to draw out, make clear and render universal and hence available for inner appropriation the inner meaning of Scripture. Revelation for him is not simply philosophy or science decked out in symbolic guise to make these truths all the more accessible to the masses. The "real truth" of revelation is not some collection of scientific or historical facts and theories. Rather it is the inverse: by making use of philosophy to explicate Scripture, the "real truth" of philosophy (or science or history) is revealed and disclosed *out of Scripture*. For it is in Scripture that the lived, inner sense of *anything whatsoever* is disclosed and that lived, inner sense is how the thing, idea or self relates back to God, its source and end.

In this process, Ibn 'Arabi places much importance on the *imagination* of the human soul to "guide, anticipate and mold sense perception" so that it may transmute "sensory data into symbols."[4] As we shall explain extensively below, for Ibn 'Arabi, the imagination, in this very specific sense, is that crucial faculty by which the seeker of God actually sees the spiritual

---

2. "To create a phenomenology of Sufism is not to derive it causally from something else or to reduce it to something else, but to look for what reveals itself to itself in this phenomenon, to distinguish the intentions implicit in the act which causes it to reveal itself.... What is made manifest in this phenomenon is the act of mystic consciousness disclosing to itself the inner, hidden *meaning* of a prophetic revelation, for the characteristic situation of the mystic is a confrontation with a prophetic message and revelation." Henry Corbin, *Alone with the Alone: Creative Imagination in the Sufism of Ibn 'Arabi* (Princeton, N.J.: Princeton University Press, 1969), 78.

3. Ibid., 79.

4. "Unlike common knowledge, which is effected by a penetration of the sense impressions of the outside world into the interior of the soul, the work of prophetic inspiration is a projection of the inner soul upon the outside world. The active Imagination guides, anticipates, molds sense perception; that is why it transmutes sensory data into symbols." Ibid., 80.

in the material and is thus able to refer all things back to their one Source, God. The human faculty of imagination, when used in this sense, I call the *analogical imagination*, because such use of the human power of forming images is employed to disclose meanings that are related to the material images, but transcend those images and forms at the same time.[5] The Qur'an provides the imagination of the human soul with its guide and content; but it is the analogical imagination, by virtue of its resemblance to God's creative power as revealed in Scripture, that is in turn able sympathetically to disclose the inner, lived meaning of the prophetic revelation.

In the same way, Eckhart uses (more explicitly than Ibn 'Arabi) the categories of Aristotelian physics and Neoplatonic metaphysics not to "reduce" the truths of Scripture to the "truths" of science and philosophy, but to reveal the true inner meaning of the Gospel, who is Christ. The goal of interpretation is not mastery or control over the world, over the text, or even over oneself, but to allow the Son of God to be born in the ground of the soul, because only then is God not an object of "scientific" research and control but, to the contrary, the lived basis of all truth that is "born" in the soul, precisely because God cannot become the object of any inquiry. That is why, as described by Robert Lewis Wilken, Eckhart follows the procedure of the early Church Fathers such as Justin:

For the Greeks, God was the conclusion of an argument, the end of a search for an ultimate explanation, an inference from the structure of the universe to a first cause. For Christian thinkers, God was the starting point, and Christ the icon that displays the face of God. "Reason became man and was called Jesus Christ," wrote Justin. Now one reasoned from Christ to other things, not from other things to Christ. In him was to be found the reason, the *logos*, the logic, if you will, that inheres in all things.[6]

---

5. Ibn 'Arabi himself simply uses the word "imagination" (*khayāl*) to describe this faculty. Henry Corbin terms Ibn 'Arabi's particular understanding of *khayāl* the "creative imagination," since it is a faculty that shares in the creative power of God and discloses intentionally the inner meanings of things. I prefer to use the term "analogical imagination," because it describes more clearly and accurately what Ibn 'Arabi means by this special human faculty that perceives "higher" spiritual things. But the reader must keep in mind that the word "imagination," in Ibn 'Arabi's texts, has no descriptive adjective.

6. Robert Lewis Wilken, *The Spirit of Early Christian Thought: Seeking the Face of God* (New Haven, Conn.: Yale University Press, 2003), 15.

Thus, for Eckhart, as for the early Christian thinkers, "understanding was achieved not by stepping back and viewing things from a distance but by entering into the revealed object itself."[7] Or, another way of putting it: "All 'true' *knowing* depends on a *being* in the truth."[8] That is, for Eckhart, we cannot know God as an object over and against us, simply because God is not and cannot be solely an object. As the purity of being, God is source and sustainer of all that is; one cannot, so to speak, step outside of God to know God and experience God. One must *enter into* God in order to know God. And to enter into God is nothing other than to enter into his Word, or *Logos*. The essence of mystical exegesis is to discover, in and through the sacred text, the analogical meaning or nature of all creatures and all sciences so that the soul itself may be led back to God in all that it thinks, knows, and perceives.

Self-understanding is drawn out—evoked (from the Latin *e-vocare*, "to call out")—by something that is higher than itself or transcendent, i.e., by the revealed Word. And, as I will demonstrate, it is in this self-understanding that is also a self-transformation that Eckhart, like Ibn 'Arabi, finds the analogical meaning of the revealed text. For what Wilken says of early Christian thought can equally apply to Eckhart and even Ibn 'Arabi: "The distinctive feature of early Christian thinking was the interplay between biblical text, the spiritual reality discerned in the text, and theological reasoning. The *res* was understood by means of the text, and *res* in turn interpreted the text."[9] Without the revealed text, there is no mystical consciousness and only in their application to the text of revelation do the concepts and categories of natural philosophy and metaphysics reveal their lived and inner sense and origin in the soul's quest for God.

7. Ibid., 45.

8. Louis Dupré, *Religious Mystery and Rational Reflection: Excursions in the Phenomenology and Philosophy of Religion* (Grand Rapids, Mich.: Eerdmans, 1998), 20.

9. Wilken, *The Spirit of Early Christian Thought*, 320.

1

# "His Character Was the Qur'an"

*Ibn 'Arabi, Analogical Imagination, and Revelation*

The thought of Ibn 'Arabi is inseparable from the Qur'an. Indeed, we can view his thought, no matter how speculative it might appear, as nothing but an extended commentary on the letter and spirit of that holy book (as well as on the *aḥādīth* [sing., *ḥadīth*] of the Prophet—sayings of Muhammad gathered in the first two or so centuries after his death into several large authoritative collections and having an importance second only to the Qur'an among the founding texts of the Muslim tradition). Thus, many of the subsequent opponents of Ibn 'Arabi were, according to one of his defenders, 'Abd al-Ghani al-Nabulusi, faced with an intractable problem: if they were to destroy Ibn 'Arabi's works, they would also have to destroy the Qur'an itself, so intimately linked were the words of the Shaykh with those of the Qur'an. As Michel Chodkiewicz relates:

'Abd al-Ghani al-Nabulusi underscores, referring to the *auto-da-fe* of Ibn 'Arabi's works barred by certain jurists who sought out heresy with indefatigable zeal, that those who desire to execute such sentences find themselves in a paradoxical situation: if they leave the countless Qur'anic quotations in Ibn 'Arabi's books that they are tossing into the flames, they end up burning the word of God. On the other hand, if they erase the passages before burning, then the works to be burned are no longer those of Ibn 'Arabi, for the Qur'an is such an integral part of them.[1]

1. Michel Chodkiewicz, *An Ocean Without a Shore*, trans. David Streight (Albany: State University of New York Press, 1993), 20.

Thus, the thinking of Ibn ʿArabi is not a philosophical system separable from the text of revelation nor is it a search for some kind of extraordinary "experience." The Shaykh's thinking is always a thinking in, with, and through the sacred text. For Ibn ʿArabi, any thinking that is to transcend discursive reasoning and attain to reality has no other choice than to rely on revelation. As we shall see in later chapters, discursive reasoning does not, for the Shaykh, attain to reality as such or existence as such in its irreducible unity but only to regions of reality that can be classified into genera and species. Reality as such, then, can only be hinted at through imagery and symbol that have a surplus of meaning, a surplus that carries reason beyond its categories to a sort of "opening" (*futūḥ*) onto the Real in which reason does not grasp the Real but rather it is the Real that reveals itself to reason.

Like the Platonists before him, Ibn ʿArabi sees the realm of sensible, temporal being as a realm between absolute being or existence—eternal existence as such that is necessary and cannot not be—and sheer nothingness. All creatures are between these extremes; they both are and are not. They are insofar as they manifest to us existence; but they are bounded neither by time or essence nor by non-being insofar as that manifested existence is fleeting and borrowed. They exist only for a limited time and to a degree limited by their essential features. Understanding this principle is essential for understanding Ibn ʿArabi's great *summa* of Sufi wisdom, his *Futūḥāt al-makkīyya* or "Meccan Revelation." This is an immense encyclopedia of the Islamic sciences that, if translated into a Western language, would probably run to some thirty quarto volumes. Fortunately, many of the principles expounded in the *Futūḥāt* are summed up in his *Fuṣūṣ al-ḥikam* or *Bezels of Wisdom,* a much shorter but also much denser version of the *Futūḥāt.* Since the latter is more compact and also has the advantage of having been written toward the end of his life, therefore reflecting most fully Ibn ʿArabi's mature thought, this work has by far been the most popular subject matter of commentary by scores of Sufi masters. My account of Ibn ʿArabi's thought and practice will also base itself primarily on this work, supplemented, of course, by passages from the *Futūḥāt* and other works. (Catalogs list some seven hundred works! Even if, as is likely, only half or a third of the titles are genuine, it is still a vast corpus of work. Most of it lies hidden away in unedited and unpublished manuscripts.)

To put it in a more provocative way, the existence of this world is for the Shaykh analogous to a dream. Like a dream, it has a certain existence in the mind of the dreamer but, at the same time, compared to the state of being awake and the things experienced while awake, the dream has only an ephemeral reality.[2] The dream, for Ibn 'Arabi, is therefore analogous to the ontological status of the created world, the world in which we live. It is important from the beginning to emphasize the word *analogous*, for Ibn 'Arabi does not argue that the world *is* unequivocally a dream. Rather, we have here, as the scholastics would say, an analogy of proportionality: as a reflection in the water is to its object, or as a dream is to the dreamer, so is the relation of the creature to its Creator. The relationships are analogous but not identical. This is important for understanding Ibn 'Arabi's doctrine of the imagination: the realm of symbolism we find in dreams, and its intermediate state—a sort of Platonic *metaxu* between the material and the spiritual—give us a clue and entry into the ontological status of creation and its true relationship to its Creator, but not directly. It does so only through analogy.

Insofar, therefore, as this world is analogous to a dream, it is not made up of inert objects or things but rather is made up of *symbols* of true, eternal, and unlimited existence, which is the Real, the Truth (*al-ḥaqq*), God. Thus, as Chittick notes,

the Shaykh stresses the fact that calling this world "dreamlike" can only mean that, like a dream, the world and everything within it need interpretation. It is utter folly to think that what we perceive, whether outside or inside ourselves, is anything but an image that reflects something else.[3]

That is why the great commentator on Ibn 'Arabi's *Bezels*, Dawud al-Qaysari, says that, in effect, the meaning of revelation is found in the faculty of imagination, the ability to strike similitudes for what transcends reason.[4] While the revelation of the Qur'an was given in time and has an outward historical sense, this outward sense points to a transcendent, uni-

---

2. It should be mentioned here, however, that this exploration of the "world of imagination" is not unique to Ibn 'Arabi; it plays a considerable role in Ismaili Shiite thought. See Claude Addas, *Ibn 'Arabi et le voyage sans retour* (Paris: Edition de Seuil, 1996), 58.

3. William Chittick, *Imaginal Worlds: Ibn 'Arabi and the Problem of Religious Diversity* (Albany: State University of New York Press, 1994), 27.

4. *Sharḥ*, I 460.

versal, and eternal sense.[5] But this transcendent, universal, and eternal sense is accessible only by a mode of interpretation that is analogous to interpreting dreams, and is thus also a matter of inward vision and creative imagination. For this reason many of the early Sufis, starting with Hakim al-Tirmidhi, made a distinction between "gnosis" (*ma'rifa*) and "wisdom" (*ḥikma*): wisdom connotes knowledge of the outer law, while gnosis is a deeper knowledge of the inner meaning of the law.[6] It is the realization of this inner meaning that is the core of Ibn 'Arabi's mystical project, a meaning that exists pre-eminently, eternally, and essentially in God. Thus, in a proper hermeneutics of the Qur'an, understanding is becoming what one ultimately *is* in the Real. The goal of hermeneutics is also pure bliss or happiness,[7] for it is the uncovering of what the divine Word means *for me and my life,* which is to say what it means for me insofar as I exist only in and through God and am what I am in God. It follows that, for Ibn 'Arabi, the imagery of the Qur'an is not a drawback for the rational seeker but an advantage, for through the "imaginal world" (i.e., the interlocking symbolic logic) of the Qur'an and the Prophet (in the *ḥadīth* traditions), the inner meaning of creation manifests itself in and through a creative appropriation of that imaginal world by the believer.[8]

## The Wisdom of Light in the Word of Joseph

In the chapter of the *Bezels* on the prophet Joseph, Ibn 'Arabi teaches that the ontological status of creation is akin to that of the imagination.

5. "Formé à l'école du Coran, la conscience musulmane est spontanément anhistorique, c'est-à-dire mythique." Paul Nwyia, *Exégèse coranique et langage mystique: Nouvel essai sur le lexique technique des mystiques musulmans* (Beirut: Dar el-Machreq Sarl, 1991), 74.

6. Ibid., 144–45.

7. "'Perfect happiness belongs to those who join the external meaning with the internal meaning.' In his eyes, a little knowledge of the *batin* leads away from the *zahir*, whereas a lot of knowledge of *batin* leads back to it." Chodkiewicz, *An Ocean Without a Shore,* 24.

8. This, as Corbin recognizes, points to a dissimilarity between the mystical thought of Ibn 'Arabi and that of Meister Eckhart, since the latter emphasizes quite rigorously and consistently the eradication of images with a view to making way in the ground of the soul for the event of the divine birth: "Here perhaps we should anticipate a question: Does not spirituality, does not mystical experience cast off images, to forgo all representation of forms and figures? Yes, indeed, some masters have sternly and implacably rejected all imaginative representation, all use of images. Here, however, we shall be dealing with an effort to utilize the image and the Imagination for spiritual experience." Corbin, *Alone with the Alone.* 6. Nevertheless, we shall see in what ways this opposition is more apparent than real.

This is not surprising, since Joseph is famous in both the Bible and the Qur'an as the great interpreter of dreams. But for Ibn 'Arabi, Joseph is also the interpreter par excellence: he represents the hermeneutical principle at the basis of all reasoning about the created world. For creation is illuminated for human knowledge in and through the symbols of the imagination, which is the first principle of revelation: "The light of this luminous Wisdom extends over the plane of the Imagination, which is the first principle of revelation according to the people of Providence."[9] In reporting what 'A'ishah said about the conditions under which the Qur'an was revealed to Muhammad, Ibn 'Arabi cites a *ḥadīth* in which the Prophet compares this sensible world to a dream and realization of the Real to a state of wakefulness from that dream:

"Men sleep and when they die they shall awake," all that is seen in sleep being of a similar nature, although the conditions are different. She ['A'ishah] stated a period of six months, whereas [in truth] his whole earthly life was after this fashion, [earthly existence] being a dream within a dream.[10]

The realm of the imagination is not a merely private affair—a subjective fantasy. The Shaykh continues, "What he [Muhammad] perceived [in this state] he perceived only in the plane of Imagination, except that he was not considered to be sleeping."[11] There is an analogical relationship between Joseph and Muhammad: both tap into the imaginal world, but while Joseph interprets dreams *qua* dreams, Muhammad, as the seal of the prophets, interprets creation *as a dream*. The functions of Joseph and Muhammad parallel two of the ways in which Ibn 'Arabi understands the realm of imagination: it can be understood in its more proper but relative sense as the realm of the private fantasy, or it can be understood in its more ontological and absolute sense as that of the created world itself, which, as the realm of becoming, is midway between the absolute and eternal Being of God and sheer nothingness.[12] Joseph deals with the imagination in the relative sense, though even here it should be emphasized that, for the Shaykh, imagination is not pure subjective fantasy: the im-

9. *Bezels*, 120/99 (the second number refers to the Arabic text of 'Affifi).
10. *Bezels*, 121/99.
11. *Bezels*, 121/99.
12. See Caner K. Dagli's translation and commentary in *The Ringstones of Wisdom (Fuṣūṣ al-ḥikam)* (Chicago: Great Books of the Islamic World, 2004), 95 n.6.

ages have some independence from the dreamer and follow a logic of their own.[13] The difference between Joseph and Muhammad is that the latter and all who follow him had (and have), in the Qur'an, the hermeneutic key for the proper interpretation not just of dreams but of all of reality as we encounter it in our awakened state. For creation may be a dream, but it is not a private fantasy; it is an imaginal projection or emanation from God and thus a sort of "objective imagination." Thus creatures are "real" in the sense that they are independent from our control and private fantasy.[14] And the greatness of a prophet lies in his ability to express eternal truths in symbolic form in such a way that they not only are accessible to the great majority of human beings but also may awaken by their suggestive or interpretive power in the elect few a unitative self-awareness that necessarily transcends discursive reason.[15]

That Joseph represents the "wisdom of light" in the Real is in this context significant. The "light" referred to in the title of this chapter is the Platonic intelligible light that illumines the mind and thus makes all thought possible, a concept developed in Islam by, among others, al-Ghazali in his *Mishkāt al-ānwār*. Al-Ghazali makes no specific reference to Plato; rather, his treatise is a commentary on a Qur'anic verse in which God is referred to as "light" (one of the "exalted names" of God is *al-nūr*, or "light"). For, like the light of the sun, the divine Reality illuminates all creatures insofar as it renders them intelligible to the eye of the mind, and enables that eye to see the intelligible forms of the creatures. Al-Ghazali therefore argues that it is the divine or intelligible light that is "real," while physical or visible light is but a "metaphor" *(mijāz)* for the divine light. But the light of the divine Reality is usually not directly perceived because the forms of things, while revealing the light that manifests them, also hide that light. Lacking pure existence, they do not have light of their own, but only a reflected light. They themselves, lacking any inherent existence, are "dark."

13. As al-Qaysari notes, Joseph received and interpreted images not of his own choosing but rather as symbolic forms that have a degree of independence as to both their existence and their meaning. The function of the Prophet, then, is, in a sense, to interpret the meaning of creation in such a way as to allow us to read, as it were, the dream of creation. *Sharh,* I 464–65.

14. See Toshihiko Izutsu, *Sufism and Taoism: A Comparative Study of Key Philosophical Concepts* (Berkeley: University of California Press, 1983), 11.

15. Ibn 'Arabi, *La Sagesse des prophètes (Fuçuç al-hikam)* translation and introduction by Titus Burckhardt (Paris: Albin Michel, 1974) , 109 n.1. See also al-Ghazali's *Mishkat al-anwar* or *The Niche of Lights,* trans. David Buchman (Provo, Utah: Brigham Young University Press, 1998).

Or, to put it another way, creatures in themselves are but shadows cast by the divine Light. As Ibn 'Arabi describes it:

Know that what is "other than the Reality," which is called the Cosmos, is, in relation to the Reality, as a shadow is to that which casts the shadow, for it is the shadow of God, this being the same as the relation between Being and the Cosmos, since the shadow is, without doubt, something sensible. What is provided there is that on which the shadow may appear, since if it were possible that that whereon it appears should cease to be, the shadow would be an intelligible and not something sensible, and would exist potentially in the very thing that casts the shadow.[16]

As represented in Plato's story of the cave, the sensible world is really a world of shadows compared to the Real or Absolute Being, which is pure light. That upon which the shadow of this light is cast is the immutable essence of the creature. The light is "shadowy" because, relative to the divine light, visible light and even the created light of human reason are as dim shadows. Without this essence upon which the shadow may be cast, the creature would not be a sensible, created thing, but rather an intelligible idea in the mind of God. In other words, for the world to arise, what is necessary is the union of two things: the essence (shadowy because not yet given existence) and the existentiating light of God's Being. Ibn 'Arabi continues:

The thing on which this divine shadow, called the Cosmos, appears is the [eternally latent] essences of contingent beings. The shadow is spread out over them, and the [identity] of the shadow is known to the extent that the Being of the [original] Essence is extended upon it. It is by His Name, the Light, that it is perceived. This shadow extends over the essences of contingent beings in the form of the unknown Unseen. Have you not observed that shadows tend to be black, which indicates their imperceptibility [as regards content] by reason of the remote relationship between them and their origins? If the source of the shadow is white, the shadow itself is still so [i.e., black].[17]

The action of the light (read: existence) makes the arising of the shadow possible and the shadow is thus a reflection, in some sense, of its source; but, in another sense, the shadow is other than, indeed has qualities opposite to, its source (such as the black shadow of a white thing). Shadows

16. *Bezels*, 123/100.          17. *Bezels*, 123/101–2.

have, in comparison with light, a relative "blackness" or nonexistence; at best, creatures have a latent or virtual existence in God, since they depend on the Real for giving them existence, just as shadow depends on the light for its existence. "In the same way the essences of contingent beings are not luminous, being nonexistent, albeit latent. They may not be described as existing because existence is light."[18] And while the emanation of light or existence from the Real is constant, universal, and one, its reception by creatures is varied because their essential features are varied, each receiving a varied combination of light and shadow depending on the receptivity of its "surface." As Izutsu explains, following one of Ibn 'Arabi's most important interpreters, al-Qashani, what receives the shadow are not the things of the world directly but rather their individual archetypes or eternal fixed essences (al-'ayān al-thābita):

Al-Qashani makes it clear that the "shadow" is cast not on what we call the "world" directly, but on the archetypes of the things. In other words, the "world" begins to exist on a higher level than the one on which our common sense usually thinks it exists. The moment the shadow of the Absolute is cast on the archetypes, the world is born, although, strictly speaking, the archetypes themselves are not the "world" but rather the "locus of the appearance of the world."[19]

Bringing this discussion to bear on our focus here, the nature of revelation, the immutable or fixed entities of creatures are not so much "things in themselves" as the loci or places in which God may become manifest, for it is God alone who gives existence; the fixed entity of the creature simply limits God's existential manifestation to a particular "locus" or "place" in the manifestation of his existence. As such, the "symbolical" or "fixed" essence of any creature is both logically and existentially prior to the creature itself. The difficulty here, of course, is that it is unclear in this Platonic metaphor who or what casts the shadow, for if God casts the light while the fixed entities of creatures receive the shadow, what is it that casts the shadow?[20] God is both source of the "light" as well as the "object" from which the shad-

---

18. *Bezels*, 123/102.

19. Izutsu, *Sufism and Taoism*, 90

20. Dagli mentions this problem in a note to his translation of this passage: "The immutable identities are the surfaces, as it were, where the shadow of God appears. Here Ibn al-'Arabi takes the forms within God's knowledge (immutable identities), His Essence, and His emanating Light, all of which are none other than God Himself, and conceives of them in terms of an object, its shadow, and the light which allows the shadow to be cast. The identities of existent

ows are cast, for God is existence itself. Nevertheless, the relation between these two modes in God's essence Ibn 'Arabi does not explain.

From the standpoint of creatures, however, God is not just light but also darkness: not in himself, but due to the limited preparedness of the creaturely essences to receive and perceive the superabundant purity of the divine light. This is why the Shaykh is fond of the *hadith* in which the Prophet says, "God has seventy veils of light and darkness; were He to lift them, the august glories of His face would burn up everyone whose eyesight perceived Him."[21] Thus, the overflowing, dynamic reality of the divine light can be as much a "veil" as any created thing since, relative to the limited powers of perception of the creature, it is a sort of darkness. In this sense, Ibn 'Arabi says that God is known in one way in every act of knowing but unknown in another:

> No more is known of the Cosmos than is known from a shadow, and no more is known of the Reality than one knows of the origin of a shadow. Insofar as He has a shadow, He is known, but insofar as the form of the one casting the shadow is not perceived in the shadow, the Reality is not known. For this reason we say that the Reality is known to us in one sense and unknown in another.[22]

Just as when we look at the source of a shadow we can see, through the light shining behind it, the outline of its source but, because of the very brightness of the light, we cannot see the source itself, so is it the same with our perception of God and the fixed entities in God. In this way, the Real is known qua shadow but unknown qua Real itself.[23] But all creatures *are* the Real insofar as they are its shadows. Thus, the world and God are one and their duality is only relative to the creature:

---

things are receptacles for the emanation of existence from God, because they represent the possible manifestations of God's Names and Qualities. The shadow of an object is a manifestation of that object which is made possible by a receptive locus and a shining light. The way in which one object will cast a shadow will depend upon the nature of the surface where the shadow will appear. For example, the same object will cast a different shadow on rocky ground than it will on rippling water or a flat plane. The light of existence is universal in its emanation, but the shadows (the world) are differentiated as a function of the differentiation of the surfaces (the immutable entities) upon which the shadow is cast. Every shadow is God's shadow, because each immutable identity is none other than a surface for the one Object's shadow to appear. The analogy becomes a bit difficult because God is both the object and the source of light." Dagli, *The Ringstones of Wisdom*, 98 n.17.

21. This *hadīth* is discussed by al-Ghazali in the third chapter of his *Mishkāt al-ānwār*, in which he performs a hermeneutics of the light verse of the Qur'an (24:35).

22. *Bezels*, 123/102.              23. *Sharh*, I 470.

*Then We take it back to Ourselves easily* [25:46], only because it is His shadow, since from Him it is manifest and to Him the whole manifestation returns, for the shadow is none other than He. All we perceive is nothing other than the being of the Reality in the essences of contingent beings. With reference to the Identity of the Reality, it is Its Being, whereas, with reference to the variety of its forms, it is the essences of contingent beings. Just as it is always called a shadow by reason of the variety of forms, so it is always called the Cosmos and "other than the Reality." In respect of its unity as the shadow [of God], it is the Reality, being the One, the Unique, but in respect of the multiplicity of its forms it is the Cosmos; therefore understand and realize what I have elucidated for you.[24]

In a sense, then, creatures are nothing but what arises from the relative privation of light or existence in the Real, who is God. As such, creatures are ambiguous: they both manifest God's creative power and share in God's nature and existence, but as finite things they also cover over and obscure that nature and power. It is almost as if their finitude negates any positive revelation they may make of the divine Reality. This is why for Ibn 'Arabi, the general revelation of creation, as magnificent as it is and as much truth as it gives human beings about God, is inadequate for coming to a full knowledge of God and, in particular, of God's commands as to how human beings are to live rightly.

To recognize creation as an act of divine imagination, then, is to recognize, to be sure, the ambiguity of creation. But it is also to see all creation as rooted in the divine Reality. The meaning of the divine creative imagination is that there is in reality nothing but one Existence:

If what we say is true, the Cosmos is but a fantasy (*mutawahm*) without any real existence, which is another meaning of the Imagination. That is to say, you imagine that it [the Cosmos] is something separate and self-sufficient, outside the Reality, while in truth it is not so. Have you not observed [in the case of the shadow] that it is connected to the one who casts it, and would not its becoming disconnected be absurd, since nothing can be disconnected from itself? Therefore know [truly] your own self [essence], who you are, what is your identity and what your relationship with the Reality. Consider well in what way you are real and in what way [part of] the Cosmos, as being separate, other, and so on. It is in this respect that the sages are better than one another; so heed and learn![25]

24. *Bezels*, 124/103.
25. *Bezels*, 124/103.

Here Ibn 'Arabi does say that the cosmos "is but a fantasy (*mutawahm*)," in the sense that the cosmos is not separate and self-sufficient in itself, only God is. But more fundamentally, this basic ontological point is also an epistemological one: in themselves, creatures are meaningless; they are "brute facts" without any Truth. Ontologically dependent, creatures are also dependent on the Truth (*al-ḥaqq*) for their truth or meaning with respect to the intellect. This means that all creatures are but reflections or, better, symbols of higher, eternal Truths because, limited and finite as they are, they cannot reflect these Truths fully but only suggestively.

In other words, creatures have to be interpreted as if they were images in a dream,[26] so it is therefore logical that Ibn 'Arabi compares the cosmos and, most particularly, the created human self to colored glass that reflects, in various colors, the one and simple Light of the divine Being:

The Reality is, in relation to a particular shadow, small or large, pure or purer, as light in relation to the glass that separates it from the beholder to whom the light has the color of the glass, while the light itself has no [particular] color. This is the relationship between your reality and your Lord; for, if you were to say the light is green because of the green glass, you would be right as viewing the situation through your senses, and if you were to say that it is not green, indeed it is colorless, by deduction, you would also be right as viewing the situation through sound intellectual reasoning. That which is seen may be said to be a light projected from a shadow, which is the glass, or a luminous shadow, according to its purity. Thus, he of us who has realized in himself the Reality manifests the form of the Reality to a greater extent than he who has not. There are those of us in whom the Reality has become their hearing, sight, and all their faculties and limbs, according to signs taught us by revealed Law that tells us of God.[27]

Each creature is a locus (made possible by its latently eternal fixed entity) in which the divine Light of Being shines as colored by that locus. "Hence the locus is identical with the light, and the locus is other than it."[28] The

---

26. "Quand les maîtres soufis affirment que «le monde est imagination» (*al-kawnu khayal*), ils entendent par là qu'il est illusoire, qu'il n'a pas de réalité propre, mais aussi, qu'il est constitué d'«images» ou de reflets des réalités éternelles; car l'imagination (*khayal*) considerée comme une fonction cosmique correspond au milieu formel; le «monde des analogies» ('*alam al-mithal*), qui comprend la manifestation subtile et la manifestation corporelle, est aussi appelé «le monde de l'imagination» ('*alam al-khayālī*)." Burckhardt, *La Sagesse*, 108 n.2.

27. *Bezels*, 124–25/103–4.

28. "In the same way, sunlight strikes diverse colors in glass and gives lights that are diverse in

creature reflects or symbolizes the divine Truth, but at the same time, as creature, it "colors" or distorts it. By analogy, the saint is the one who has become a locus where the divine Light shines, but where it shines most clearly with the least color or refraction, because, in the saint, the Light by which we perceive the sensible world, its intelligible forms and the imaginal symbolic forms that mediate between the sensible world and its intelligible forms, becomes the very subject-matter of the saint's vision. As al-Qaysari explains, we can say that God is more manifest in the power of perception itself than in what that power of perception perceives. God is most purely present in the light by which we perceive than in that which is perceived by this light.[29] And we come to know the degree to which the saint has passed away from created things and identified himself with his eternal pre-existence in the Real through the signs taught to humanity by the Qur'an. The ultimate criterion for whether we or any saint has realized this "transparency" to the divine Light is through the Qur'an and the Law. As James Morris puts it: "Ibn 'Arabi's entire understanding of the metaphysical teaching of the Qur'an could be simply described as a 'theology of trans-parition' (transparaître)."[30] That is to say, the Qur'an, by imaging the world in terms of symbols and parables, points to the inner reality of the world as symbolic imagination of a higher reality. The more the saint penetrates that higher reality through the symbols and parables of the Qur'an, the more he or she realizes that higher Reality in him or herself.

Ibn 'Arabi puts this matter directly: we are all an imagination. That is to say, we human beings, qua creatures, are but an image of a higher reality or archetype in God. Only God is beyond being imagined, even if he is known partially by his revealed Names which, on the one hand, reveal who God is but, on the other hand, conceal his true essence:

If things are as we have decided, know that you are an imagination, as is all that you regard as other than yourself an imagination. All [relative] existence is an imagination within an imagination, the only Reality being God, as Self and the

---

color, whether red, yellow, blue, or something else, in keeping with the color of the glass in the view of the eye. The diversity that arrives newly in the light derives only from the locus. No part of the light becomes designated in itself as different from other parts save through the locus. Hence the locus is identical with the light, and the locus is other than it." SDG, 325; III 554.6.

29. *Sharḥ*, I 476.

30. James Morris, *The Reflective Heart: Discovering Spiritual Intelligence in Ibn 'Arabi's Meccan Illuminations* (Louisville, Ky.: Fons Vitae, 2005), 115.

Essence, not in respect of His Names. This is because the Names have two con-notations: The first connotation is God Himself Who is what is named, the sec-ond that by which one Name is distinguished from another. Thus the Forgiving is not [in this sense] the Manifest or the Unmanifest, nor is the First the Last. You are already aware in what sense each Name is essentially every other Name and in what sense it is not any other Name. As being essentially the other, the Name is the Reality, while as being not the other, it is the imagined Reality with which we are here concerned.[31]

Compared to the one and immutable Essence of God which is indepen-dent of all relations, even the "Ninety-nine Most Beautiful Names" of God, as codified and hallowed in Islamic tradition,[32] are inadequate in expressing God's essential nature, since the division of the name from the one named is a duality that cannot subsist in God's utter unity. Even the greatest and first of the names, Allah, is ultimately inadequate in denoting who God is, because it also denotes a relation of Creator and Lord to cre-ation and thus a duality.[33] Ibn ʿArabi puts it this way in his *Futūḥāt*:

We have already explained that God as an essence cannot be understood in the same way as God as a god. Therefore there are two different levels (*martaba*) though there is nothing in entified existence (*al-wujūd al-ʿaynī*) save the One Entity. In respect of Himself, He is "independent of the worlds," but, in respect of the Most Beautiful Names which demand the cosmos because of its possibil-ity (*imkān*) in order for their effects to become manifest within it, He demands the existence of the cosmos. If the cosmos already existed, He would not have sought its existence.[34]

As Izutsu points out, "God is a 'phenomenal,' i.e., self-manifesting, form assumed by Something still more primordial, the Absolute Being. Indeed,

31. *Bezels*, 125/104.

32. The names of God, however, are theoretically unlimited, as was recognized by Islam-ic tradition. See Abu Hamid al-Ghazali, *al-Maqṣad al-asnā fī sharḥ asmā' Allah al-ḥusnā* (*The Ninety-nine Most Beautiful Names of God*), part 3, chap. 1.

33. "The 'effects' or 'properties' of the divine names are the phenomena of the cosmos. In other words, they are the creatures—the things, the entities, the forms—considered inasmuch as they make the divine names manifest. In the Shaykh al-Akbar's vocabulary the word 'creature' immediately calls to mind 'Creator,' 'existent entity' conjures up 'immutable entity,' and 'form' implies 'meaning.' In the same way, 'properties' and 'effects' bring to mind the names, realities, and roots. Or rather, to see the properties and effects is to see the names and realities exercising their influence and determining the nature of the cosmos. And to see the names and realities is to see the manifestation of the Essence Itself." SPK, 39.

34. III 316.27 in SPK, 41.

the concept of Being is the very foundation of this world-view."[35] As such, the name Allah, while the highest and most potent of the Names, cannot denote the divine Reality in itself apart from its relation to creatures.[36] More precisely, the divine Names "denote the actual reality of *wujūd*, and hence they delineate the modes in which *wujūd* comes to manifest itself through its 'signs,' the things of the cosmos."[37] That is, the Names indicate the modes in which the immutable entities of things may manifest themselves as creatures in the world. [38] As such, the divine Names, as revealed in the Qur'an, mediate between creation and God.

Using a term that the Shaykh is very fond of (because found in the Qur'an), the Names are a *barzakh* or isthmus linking God and the cosmos even if, should the cosmos disappear, the Names (though not the Named) would disappear.[39] As Claude Addas puts it, the Names are "the shadow of God, the rays of His Essence." Just as the rays of the sun are not the sun itself but not other than the sun, so are the Names not God himself but also not other than God since they manifest God in some way.[40] As

35. "The concept of Being in the double meaning of *ens* and *esse* is the highest key-concept that dominates his entire thought. His philosophy is theological, but is more ontological than theological. That is why even the concept of God *(Allah)* itself which in Islam generally maintains its uncontested position is given here only a secondary place. As we shall see presently, God is a 'phenomenal,' i.e., self-manifesting, form assumed by Something still more primordial, the Absolute Being. Indeed, the concept of Being is the very foundation of this world-view." Izutsu, *Sufism and Taoism*, 19.

36. "There are two fundamental levels: God and the cosmos, independence and poverty, or Lordship *(rubūbīyya)* and servanthood *(al-'ubudīyya)*. All the other levels have to do with the various modalities that tie these two basic levels together." SPK, 50. "All the divine names belong to the Level, not to Me, except only the name One *(al-wāḥid)*. It is a name that pertains exclusively to Me. No one shares with Me in its reality in any respect, none of the names, none of the levels, and none of the possible things." I 322.33 in SPK, 54.

37. Chittick, *Imaginal Worlds*, 21.

38. Ibid.

39. "If the names, realities, roots, and supports denote the Essence in terms of relationships, they also point to things and phenomena within the cosmos, relating them back to God. The names are an intermediate stage between God and the universe. Though they have no existence separate from God and cannot be understood correctly except as relationships, they provide our only means of grasping the connection between man and God. In Ibn al-'Arabi's terms, they are a *barzakh* or isthmus between God and the cosmos." SPK, 39.

40. "Les Noms sont l'ombre de Dieu, les rayons de Son Essence. . . . Les créatures sont les réceptacles qui les réfléchissent à plus ou moins grande échelle selon leur configuration propre, c'est-à-dire selon leur prédisposition essentielle. De même que les rayons ne sont ni le soleil niautre chose que le soleil, les Noms ne sont pas Dieu, mais ils ne sont pas autre chose que le Nommé." Addas, *Ibn 'Arabi et le voyage sans retour*, 97–98.

for the creatures, they receive these "shadows" or "rays" to the extent that their essential nature permits their receiving them.

That is why, for Ibn 'Arabi, Existence or Being is one, while creation is characterized by multiplicity and is, therefore, the realm of the imagination: "There is naught in Being but is implicit in the divine Unity, and there is naught in the Imagination but is implicit in [Cosmic] multiplicity."[41] All multiplicity arises from a relationship to the one divine essence and is, as such, not ultimately or absolutely real, but only real relative to this or that aspect of the divine essence. Therefore, the boundless multiplicity of creatures cannot of itself give us knowledge of God. In citing the short *sura* from near the end of the Qur'an, *al-Ikhlas,* in which God's absolute unity is affirmed, he neither "begetting" nor being "begotten," Ibn 'Arabi asserts:

We, for our part, beget and are begotten, we depend on him and we compete one with another. However, the Unique One transcends all these attributes, having no need of them or of us. Indeed, the Reality has no [true] description better than this chapter, *al-Ikhlas,* which was revealed precisely for this reason.[42]

The divine Reality is beyond any relationship, any duality and this truth, for Ibn 'Arabi, also reveals our true relationship with God:

God created shadows lying prostrate to right and left only as clues for you in knowing yourself and Him, that you might know who you are, your relationship with Him, and His with you, and so that you might understand how or according to which divine truth all that is other than God is described as being completely dependent on Him, as being [also] mutually interdependent. Also that you might know how and by what truth God is described as utterly independent of men and all worlds, and how the Cosmos is described as both mutually dependent.[43]

As creatures, we are dependent on each other and, ultimately, upon God for our existence. But God is, as the Shaykh says above, "utterly independent of men and all worlds." God exists and cannot not exist; creatures can exist and not exist. But only the human being can share in the true and necessary existence of God or the ephemeral and contingent existence of the creature. It all depends on how he relates himself to God.

41. *Bezels,* 125/104.   42. *Bezels,* 126/105.
43. *Bezels,* 126/105.

Ibn 'Arabi on the Nature of Existence

As we have seen, created existence both reveals and conceals the Reality, God. But as such, it also reveals the hermeneutical principle by which human reason can interpret the world. It must interpret the world as it would interpret a dream. All creatures have a significance and meaning that should lead the soul to self-understanding, and this self-understanding is nothing other than understanding its significance in the realm of divine affairs. For this understanding, as we shall see, the Qur'an shall provide the key. Thus, for Ibn 'Arabi, creation as an act of imagination is crucial to understanding the relation between the "book of nature" and the "divine book of revelation."

So what is the meaning of "existence" in Ibn 'Arabi? The meaning of existence, wujūd, in Arabic, connotes fundamentally the notion of "finding" or "coming upon" since this is the basic meaning of the Arabic root, w-j-d. As Chittick points out:

The expression wājib al-wujūd has been consistently translated in Western sources as "Necessary Being" or "necessary existence," but it can also be rendered as "necessary finding" or "necessary awareness." God finds Himself and cannot not find Himself. The possible thing may or may not find itself and God, depending upon whether or not God gives preponderance to its finding over its not-finding ('adam). The Verifiers [those who practice taḥqīq or the realization of al-ḥaqq, the Truth or the Reality] are the People of Unveiling and Finding (ahl al-kashf wa'l-wujūd), since the reality of things has been disclosed to them and they have found God in both the cosmos and themselves.[44]

The human being may "lose" him or herself by straying from awareness of his or her (relative) identity with God, who is existence in itself. But the human being may also find him or herself in finding (or being found by) God, who is absolute "finding" or absolute awareness itself that makes possible any finite act of "self-finding" or self-awareness. And, as Chittick points out in the quote above, this self-finding is also the root meaning of "existence." Thus, "to exist" is "to be self-aware." But this self-awareness in which one truly exists cannot come from oneself, since that self is finite, "losing itself" in the world by being conditioned by the world, ultimately lacking any being and awareness in itself. Only by listening to the Divine

44. SPK, 212.

Speech and by interpreting it properly can one come to true existence and self-awareness. Chittick continues:

In short, we come to find our own existence through listening to the Divine Speech, which is "Be!" By the same token, we come to find God through listening to His Speech in the form of revelation. Finding and existence are two aspects of the same reality, which at root is God's own Finding of Himself, His Necessary Being. All goes back to Him and His names.[45]

To find God is to be found by God, for God's word "Be!" is prior to all finite existence. Thus, God's Word is prior to existence and prior to any understanding of God. To interpret God's Word, then, is to have our own existence interpreted for us. We find that, instead of ascribing meaning to existence, the meaning of existence finds us and in-scribes itself in us in and through the revelation of the Qur'an.

To summarize, therefore, knowing essentially involves interpretation: we read the meaning of creation through the Names revealed to us in the Qur'an. The divine Names have causal powers, manifesting creation as God's "speech." Thus, our "true names are God's names":

Without any doubt, the Cosmos is fundamentally dependent on causes, the greatest of which enjoys the causality of the Reality. The divine causality on which the Cosmos depends is the Divine Names, which are every Name on which the Cosmos depends, whether on [a Name manifested in] a cosmos or the divine Essence. Whichever it be, it is [essentially] God, no other. Thus, He says, *O Men, your need of God is total, while He is the Self-sufficient, the Praised.* Besides this it is well known that we are also mutually dependent. Therefore, our [true] names are God's Names, since all depends on Him. At the same time our essential selves are His shadow. He is at once our identity and not our identity. We have paved the way for you, so consider![46]

God reveals himself to us in symbols and images because, at bottom, we also are symbols and images of God. By interpreting the Qur'an through the data of creation (and vice versa), Ibn 'Arabi maintains that we come to a deeper understanding of our own essential nature and its relation to its temporal manifestation. The meaning of the Qur'an is not at all alien to our innermost selves, but rather it reveals that innermost self to us as

---

45. SPK, 213.

46. *Bezels*, 126–27/105–6. Al-Qaysari notes that this name is our essential nature as it exists eternally in God, its finite manifestation but a shadow of this nature. See *Sharh*, I 480.

a "theophany" of God, realized most fully in the Universal Man.[47] Clearly, he is not saying that our material manifestation—or for that matter, secondary causes—are unimportant. Secondary causes are important because it is through them that God reveals himself to us.[48] But, at the same time, secondary causes, i.e., the Names, are veils hiding God, which is why, as was mentioned above, in certain respects the Names are not identical with God.[49] Thus, God is, to borrow the Latin scholastic terminology of Eckhart, both *innominabile* and *omninominabile*—unnamable and all-namable. This is because all things—and no-thing—can name God, who is utterly one and unique, but at the same time the true cause of the existence of all. For God is beyond relationships and therefore beyond levels, even of perfection and existence.[50] That is why God cannot be known as an object or even as the subject of knowing, but only in the interpretive interplay of the human being realizing internally the meaning of revelation.

As Ibn 'Arabi says in his *Futūḥāt*:

47. This insight is, of course, not new to Ibn 'Arabi: al-Ghazali, in his treatise *The Ninety-nine Most Beautiful Names of God,* points out how meditation on the meaning of each divine Name should work a transformation in our character such as to make us like the quality signified by that name.

48. "Many Sufis held that it was blameworthy to take the *āsbāb* or 'secondary causes' seriously, since this would mean turning one's gaze away from the Causer of Secondary Causes. But Ibn al-'Arabi reinstates the secondary causes as fundamental constituent elements of the cosmos. The secondary causes are important because they are names of God through which we come to know Him. Without them we would have no access to Him. Here one has to understand that 'secondary causes' is merely another name for existent things, creatures, or divine acts." SPK, 44. See also Ibn 'Arabi's criticism of al-Ghazali in the chapter of the *Bezels* on Abraham, where he takes al-Ghazali to task for denying the efficacy of secondary causes and for asserting that we can know God without any reference to the created cosmos.

49. "All secondary causes brought into existence by God are forms and veils, or effects and properties of His names. In the last analysis the secondary causes denote only the Causer. They must be considered His names. . . . Therefore, in fact, when we have need of the secondary causes, we have need of God. The forms and phenomena are merely veils hiding God's Reality, or rather, various names that He assumes in disclosing Himself to His creatures. Poverty toward secondary causes is in truth poverty toward the First Cause." SPK, 45.

50. "The terms Essence and Divinity are applied to the same Reality, but from different points of view. In respect of the Essence, nothing positive can be said about God; attributes must be negated from Him. But in respect of the Divinity, all names can be ascribed to Him. In other words, God cannot be understood in a positive, affirmative way in respect of His Essence, but He can be understood so in respect of His names. In the same way, levels—which, like the names, are relationships—can only be discerned in respect of the Divinity, not in respect of the Essence. So the Essence itself is not a level, and the first level that can be discerned in all that exists is God as Divinity." SPK, 49.

The Real is not known in the things without the manifestation of the things and the lifting of their properties. The eyes of the common people fall only upon the properties of the things, but the eyes of those who have the opening of unveiling fall only upon the Real in the things.[51]

The "eyes of those who have the opening of unveiling" see all things as manifestations of God's speech in the Holy Qur'an. They are able to see the world through the lens of what Corbin called the *mundus imaginalis* or "imaginal world" or, in Sufi terminology, the *barzakh*, "isthmus," "boundary," or "limit," made manifest in the Qur'an, in and through which, like in a dream, material objects acquire spiritual meanings and spiritual meanings acquire material forms. But we shall discuss this peculiar feature of Ibn 'Arabi's Sufism in the following section, where we discuss his interpretation of the prophetic wisdom of Isaac.

### The Wisdom of the Real/True in the Word of Isaac

In the chapter on the prophet Isaac, Ibn 'Arabi begins by discussing the biblical story, as reported in the Qur'an, of Abraham's abortive sacrifice of his son Isaac and how a ram was substituted in Isaac's place.[52] But, the Shaykh asks, how can a ram symbolize a human being, a prophet who is the "vice-regent" of God on earth? Or, to put it in other words, how can the lower (in perfection of being, that is) signify the higher? But this is precisely what creation does and what the revealed Word of God in the Qur'an does. The reason is that, in many respects, animals and even plants and minerals signify divine qualities with more purity and directness than does the human being:

> Do you not perceive a certain logic in the matter,
> The realization of gains and the diminution of loss?
> No creation is higher than the stone, and after it the plant,
> In a certain sense and according to certain measures.
> After the plant comes sentient being, all know their Creator
> By a direct knowledge and on clear evidence.

51. II 507.30 in SPK, 225.
52. Affifi notes the deep thematic affinity between this chapter and the one on Joseph. See his *Remarks*, 70, in his Arabic edition of the *Bezels*.

As for the one called Adam, he is bound by intelligence,
Thought, and the garland of faith.[53]

Well before Pico della Mirandola's *Oration on Man*, the Sufi Shaykh recognized that the position of the human being vis-à-vis God is ambiguous: the human being is a microcosm, potentially reflecting by virtue of his intellect all of creation, and thus the most perfect creaturely reflection of God but by virtue of his vice and ingratitude toward God, the human being usually reflects God *the least* of all creatures. This paradoxical situation arises because, as Ibn 'Arabi mentions, the human being is also "bound by intelligence," which is to say, he or she is bound by the limitations of reason, with its finite concepts and categories. The very faculty that makes the human being rise above other creatures, the intellect, is also what can bring human beings below other creatures. As such, the human being often takes what he can grasp and understand with his reason as "god" and not the Real in itself. He or she, therefore, can—and usually does—fall from submitting to God completely and thus reflecting the Real perfectly. Animals, plants, and even inanimate objects, on the other hand, are not bound by intelligence and thus cannot fall from imitating God with the perfection that their essential natures permit.

But even more important, animals, plants, and minerals often are clearer, more direct, and richer symbols of aspects of the divine than the human being. Thus, "the flight of an eagle expresses the meanings of freedom and elevation in a more direct, simple, obvious, and unambiguous manner than does a person we know who has these as qualities of soul."[54] The crystalline and geometric perfection of a mineral (such as a diamond) can signify the orderly and unified complexity of the divine Intellect better than the usually disordered and dispersed human intellect. But the point here is that the appropriateness of a symbol has nothing to do with its *similitude* to the divine Reality because that similitude does not exist. As Ibn 'Arabi constantly emphasizes, there is nothing comparable in any

53. *Bezels*, 98/184–5. Here there is a reference to al-Tustari's notion that, unlike in other creatures, the human being's knowledge of God is not *fiṭriyya*, i.e., primordial. That is, by his or her rational nature, the human being tends to cut him- or herself off from God and is therefore in need of constant reminders back to his or her potential status of vice-regent of God on earth. See Affifi, *Remarks*, 73.

54. Dagli, *The Ringstones of Wisdom*, 69.

way to God. Rather, there is a hierarchy of symbols in religious imagery due to the fact that the human mind is open to the meaning-valence of some creatures over others. In other words, the symbolic power of a creature comes from its meaning-resonance with the human mind.

Regarding religious symbols, Louis Dupré has this to say: "Their [symbols'] hierarchy constitutes an anthropological order. Not because their signifying power is purely subjective; that power is real and objective, but it resides in a particular ability to *disclose* a transcendent presence, not in a presumed similarity with that reality."[55] This applies even to the human being him or herself; he or she is a microcosm not out of similarity to the divine Reality but solely because of his or her (potential) awareness of the divine presence in him or herself and in all things (qua symbols): "Even humans owe their unique status as religious symbol not so much to their elevated rank in being as to their singular *awareness* of the divine presence both in themselves and in other beings."[56] Thus, in sleep, when we dream and the "bounds of intelligence" are loosened, our intellect often reflects more clearly and directly the symbolic nature of sensible things, not limiting them to what it can grasp through genera and species but sensing in them a presence that transcends the sense-data. It is therefore a mistake to understand dreams literally, as simply the sensible world perceived while awake transposed into the dream world.

This error of literalism was the mistake of Abraham, according to Ibn ʿArabi (and, as we shall see, this will not be the last time that Ibn ʿArabi will chide a prophet, despite all his wisdom, for an elementary mistake in metaphysics!): "The state of sleep is the plane of the Imagination and Abraham did not interpret [what he saw], for it was a ram that appeared in the form of Abraham's son in the dream, while Abraham believed what he saw [at face value]."[57] Notice here how the situation is the inverse of what we expect when thinking about the dream of Abraham in which he is asked to sacrifice his son: it is not, as we would expect, the ram that represents the son but rather the son that represents the ram. In other words, the symbolic form belongs not to the dream but to the sensible world that we perceive *while awake*.[58] It is the world we perceive while awake, as we

---

55. Dupré, *Religious Mystery*, 100.    56. Ibid.
57. *Bezels*, 99/85.
58. Thus, Chittick notes: "This is not unrelated to the idea that the cosmos, as Unbounded

saw in his chapter on Joseph, that is the true dream and that constitutes the realm of symbol and thus needs interpretation and not the dream properly speaking. Or, more accurately, the prophet and saint view the world as a *mundus imaginalis,* neither completely sensible nor completely intelligible and neither completely objective nor completely subjective but as the intersection between these two worlds. In fact, for the prophet and saint both, the imaginal world *is* the created world viewed in its unity, i.e., in its relation to God. Thus, we need a science of the world as symbolic forms hiding a deeper, inner meaning for us.[59]

We should not, therefore, confuse the symbolic forms and the realm of imagination with the Ideas and Intelligible World of Plato. Rather, Ibn 'Arabi's concern is in what mediates between the sensible world and the intelligible world, the boundary or *barzakh* that at once separates and unites the spiritual and material into symbolic forms that are not unlike what we witness in dreams. It is the realm of, as Plato calls it in the *Symposium,* the *metaxu* or "in-between," in which intelligible forms become materialized in concrete symbol and material things become spiritualized in erotic reminiscence. As we saw in the previous section, the material or sensible world itself is imaginal in its very ontological status. But this realization comes most acutely to consciousness in the specific realm of the *mundus imaginalis,* accessible usually, though not exclusively, in dreams, but manifested most powerfully and concretely in prophetic revelation. Thus each of the prophets, in the *Bezels,* manifests an aspect of this *mundus imaginalis,* which, however, is not a separate ontological "layer" of created existence, but what relates and unites creation to uncreated Existence.

As such, the world cannot be known by sense perception alone nor

---

Imagination, is the dream of God." SDG, 336. Also: "While explaining the inadequacy of the philosophical approach to knowledge, Ibn al-'Arabi points to the cosmic root of imagination by identifying it, on the angelic level, with possibility (or contingency), the fact that everything other than God stands halfway between *wujūd* and nonexistence. It is well to remember here that the Shaykh identifies the philosophical term *possibility* with the Koranic term *poverty.* God alone is Independent and Self-Sufficient. Everything else, including even the First Intellect, is poor and needy toward God. The essential poverty of all things puts them in the station of intermediacy between the nothingness of themselves and the *wujūd* of the Real, and intermediacy is precisely the defining characteristic of both imagination and possibility. Thus, in a broad cosmological perspective, every possible thing is precisely an imaginal thing, an image of both *wujūd* and nonexistence." SDG, 345.

59. "The formal Self-revelation [of the Reality] on the plane of the Imagination requires an additional knowledge by which to apprehend what God intends by a particular form." *Bezels,* 99/85.

even by reason, for reason only grasps the intelligible form and not the *meaning* of the form—what inner reality it signifies. Hence, any understanding of the world is a hermeneutical understanding; it is an act of interpretation or, more specifically, as the Arabic word *ta'bīr* indicates, "dream interpretation": "Interpretation *(ta'bīr)* means to pass from the form of what one sees to something beyond it."[60] The root for the word for "interpretation" used here, *ta'bīr,* literally means "to cross" or "pass over." The act of interpretation allows the human self to cross over the *barzakh* or "isthmus" of the *mundus imaginalis,* i.e., from the visible to the hidden, from the sensible form to the invisible meaning, from the less real to the more real. *Ta'bīr* is related to another term that Ibn 'Arabi uses for interpretation, *ta'wīl,* whose literal meaning is "to return, to take back, and to take back to the origin."[61] But *ta'bīr* has the added connotation of returning to the origin of things as presented in the "dream world" of the imaginal world. That is, the act of interpretation is one of taking something back to its most concrete root meaning, which is in the invisible realm of spirit.[62] In this sense, then, Ibn 'Arabi, despite his criticisms of the power and scope of human reason, does not reject human reason: human reason and its use at a very high, sophisticated level is necessary in order to discern the concrete root meanings of the images and symbols.[63]

At the same time, however, the Shaykh's method is not allegorical: allegory is simply a "rationalization" of the imagery of the sacred text, a fit-

---

60. *Bezels,* 99/186.          61. SPK, 199.

62. This process is facilitated by the Arabic root system in which one cluster of (usually) three consonants, through a series of pattern permutations by the insertion of different vowels or vowel lengths or by consonantal infixes, can build many (again, usually) related meanings. In principle, at least, every Arabic word can be reduced to one root meaning. Thus, as Paul Nwyia shows, we can consider the development of Qur'anic exegesis in Islam as a movement away from the literal verification of the historical circumstances of the various revelations in the holy book (the *asbāb al-nuzūl* or "the occasions of the revelations") to a both more philological and more philosophical investigation of the root meanings of the words of the Qur'an. Finally, Sufi interpreters read the meanings of these roots in light of their own experiences, in turn, giving new meanings to these roots. See Paul Nwyia, *Exegèse coranique,* passim.

63. "For the most part, Ibn 'Arabi considers *ta'wīl* as interpretation of the Koran and the sayings of the Prophet in a way that will not compromise the principles of rational thought. Instead of having faith in the literal accuracy of the revelation and trying to understand it on God's terms (e.g., through the practice of the religion and 'godfearing'), the interpreter accepts the supremacy of reason and its ability to judge all things. In effect, reason becomes the scale in which everything else must be weighed, including the Word of God. Practically all modern hermeneutics and scriptural exegesis fit neatly into the category of *ta'wīl* as Ibn al-'Arabi understands it." SPK, 199.

ting of it into limited preconceived rational categories. Rather, his method is one of the *actualization* of the meaning of symbols, the nature of which Corbin explains very well:

The symbol announces a plane of consciousness distinct from that of rational evidence; it is the "cipher" of a mystery, the only means of saying something that cannot be apprehended in any other way; a symbol is never "explained" once and for all, but must be deciphered over and over again, just as a musical score is never deciphered once and for all, but calls for ever new execution.[64]

The act of interpretation demands a constant enactment or "performance" in the inner life of the one who unlocks its meaning. If all images conformed to our reason, then there would be no need for *ta'wīl* or interpretation. Interpretation, Ibn 'Arabi says, is what unites the external form to the internal meaning and, by doing so, unites the revealed Word to the innermost ground (or "heart") of the saint, just as the *mundus imaginalis* separates only in order to unite the material and the spiritual.

If the meaning of a verse in revelation is not contrary to reason, then we must accept the image as it is, as a manifestation of the Real:

Since, then, the vision has these two aspects and since God has taught us by what he did with Abraham and what He said to him, which teaching is connected to the station of Prophecy, we know, in respect of any vision we may have of the Reality in a form unacceptable to the reason, that we must interpret that form in accordance with a doctrinal [*mashrū'*] concept of the Reality, either from the standpoint of the recipient of the vision or the context or both. If, however, reason does not reject it, we accept it as we see it, even as we shall see the Reality in the Hereafter.[65]

But if the apparent sense of Scripture is repugnant to reason, it must be interpreted as revealing a hidden, inward dimension of the Law as applied either to the inner standpoint or state (*ḥāl*) of the interpreter or to its place in the overall scheme of images and symbols. Reason wants to reduce these images of Scripture to allegorical abstractions; but since God is manifest in them, this is impossible, for God cannot be reduced to our conceptual categories:

---

64. Corbin, *Alone with the Alone*, 14.
65. *Bezels*, 101/87.

In every abode [of being, becoming] the Unique, the Merciful has forms,
whether hidden or manifest.
If you say, "This is the Reality," you have spoken the truth,
If "something other," you are interpreting (*'abir*).
His determination applies in every abode equally,
Indeed, he is [ever] unfolding His Reality to creation.
When He manifests Himself to the sight, reason rushes to
bring proof against it [Him]
He is accepted as manifested on the intellectual plane as also
in the imagination, but direct vision sees true.[66]

Every creature is a form in which God discloses himself, and thus to say
"This is the Reality" is to recognize this truth. But to recognize every creature as creature is to interpret, because one is interpreting God *as* this or
that creature; one is "passing over" from God into creation just as interpreting images and symbols in creation is to pass over from creation to
God. But, as Ibn 'Arabi here notes, God is the original interpreter. Why?
Because God is ever "unfolding His Reality to creation," i.e., passing over
from his unique, nonmanifest and undivided Unity and Being into the
multiplicity and manifestation of creation. This is the primal revelation
or the original Qur'an and so the imagination is a necessary supplement to
the intellect, because only the imagination can understand, in its way, how
God can manifest himself in the finite creatures of the world.

Chodkiewicz explains that "given the extremely rich polysemy of Arabic vocabulary, rigorous fidelity to the letter of Revelation does not exclude but, on the contrary, it implies a multiplicity of interpretations."[67]
The meaning of creatures is ever unfolding, just as one root in Arabic
unfolds a multiplicity of words and related meanings. But, Ibn 'Arabi asserts, rational thinkers are blind to the necessity for interpretation when
it comes to ultimate Reality: "reason rushes to bring proof against it" by

66. *Bezels*, 101.
67. "Ibn 'Arabi insists on this point on a number of occasions, emphasizing that there is a
general rule applicable to all the revealed Books: 'Any meaning of whatever verse of the Word
of God—be it the Qur'an, the Torah, the Psalms or the "Pages"—judged acceptable by one who
knows the language in which this Word is expressed represents what God wanted to say to those
who interpret it so.' As a corollary, none of these meanings is to be rejected, regardless how surprising or even scandalous it might appear, for God, in uttering this verse, had to be aware of the
diversity of possible interpretations for each word or group of words. To deny the validity of this
rule is to limit divine knowledge." Chodkiewicz, *An Ocean Without a Shore*, 30.

asserting the utterly transcendent incomparability of the Real as over and against creation. This viewpoint is valid but incomplete. As he mentions in the *Futūḥāt*, a one-sided adherence to this position is the biggest mistake of the rationalist philosophers:

> Despite their knowledge of imagination's ruling authority, the philosophers give it no notice in the acquisition of the divine sciences. This is because, in their ignorance, they wish for that which cannot be wished for, which is disengagement from every sort of matter. This will never happen, whether in this world or the next world. This—I mean disengagement from matter—is an affair that is rationally conceivable, but not witnessed. The considerative thinkers have no greater mistake than this, but they are not aware of their mistake.[68]

Purely abstract thought is, for us embodied beings, an impossibility even in the next life, where we will still be embodied, albeit in glorified, "spiritual" bodies. Hence, there is the need of revelation for knowledge of what is truly and ultimately Real: without the symbols and images of the Qur'an, human reason would not know the Real but rather would only know the products of our own limited understanding and thus would fall into a radical solipsism.[69] Only through interpretation of the symbols of a sacred text in a deep and transformative way does human reason transcend itself and become united to the Real qua Real. Chittick puts well this mutual need of rational and imaginal understanding in coming to a knowledge of the Real:

> In sum, revelation has to do with the imaginal embodiment of meanings in language, but these embodiments are not haphazard. They take form on the basis of God's own knowledge of Himself. This helps explain both the necessity of revelation to establish human knowledge of God and the necessity of imaginalization for this knowledge to be complete. Rational operations have an indispensable function, because without them, God's incomparability cannot be understood; and indeed, the Koran frequently appeals to reason, as does the Shaykh. Tomes on philosophy and theology, which are rooted in the rational sciences, play useful and even necessary roles, so long as they do not become the exclusive source of

---

68. III 508.10 in SDG, 346–47.

69. "Note that the imaginalization of meanings through revelation demands that the prophet's message have more to do with God's similarity than His incomparability. This is because the prophet receives the images of God's attributes and qualities in sensory form, typically linguistic form. Imagination and images function by bringing together two sides—in contrast to reason and abstraction, which separate and establish difference. Precisely because of the predominance of images in revelation, rational thinkers insist upon interpreting *(ta'wīl)* the sacred text to bring it into line with their own abstract understanding of things." Chittick, *Imaginal Worlds*, 75.

knowledge. But imaginal understanding is also necessary, and revealed texts are full of images. Without images, God's similarity could never be grasped.[70]

Reason forgets that the rational knower is a finite and contingent possibility brought out of absolute nonexistence by God. Therefore, its thinking cannot grasp the utterly irreducible fact of existence in all its particularity: it can know only universal essence or universal and impersonal laws of nature, but not the lived and particular choices of existence.[71] In a very telling example, al-Qaysari, commenting upon this part of the *Bezels*, notes that reason, in declaring the exclusive incomparability of God, cannot recognize him in the form of the poor, the hungry, and the weak—referring to a *hadīth*, modeled evidently on Matthew 25:31–46, that insofar as you feed, clothe, and minister to the least of one's brethren, one serves God himself.[72] Reason cannot recognize God in those things because reason "abstracts" God "out of" creation. The "God of the philosophers" is a mere idea and not a concrete reality that one encounters. That is why the encounter of the imagination with the rich, polyvalent symbols of the Qur'an is necessary for any knowledge of the Absolute, for it brings about the embodiment of the truths of universal reason in lived existence.

In a sense, as Chodkiewicz reminds us, the Law or the revealed text is not just a cloak for the Real, but is, in a deeper sense, the Real itself: "In summary, then, we have a fundamental principle: the Law is not the cloak or the symbol of *haqīqa*, of a hidden truth that might be reached by transgression. It *is* the *haqīqa*. It thus imposes itself absolutely and up to the last iota on the *'ārif bi-Llāh* (the knower of God)—in the etymological sense of the word—as well as on the *umma*, the common believers."[73]

For Ibn 'Arabi, the reading and appropriation of revelation is not a

---

70. Ibid., 77.

71. "No rational faculty is safe from the ruling property of fantasy and imagination, which, in the world of angels and spirits, is possibility. No spirit and no knower of God is safe from the possibility that falls to him in everything that he witnesses. After all, the reality of everything other than God, in its essence, is possibility. A thing never leaves the property of its own self, so it never sees what it sees—whether the object be eternal or newly arrived—except through itself. So possibility accompanies it constantly, and no one is aware of this save those who know the affair as it is." III 508.10 in SDG, 347.

72. *Sharh*, I 399. Al-Qaysari adds (p. 400) that the problem with reason is that it is based too much on abstractions, while God, as the living basis of all existence, is beyond all abstraction or particularization.

73. Chodkiewicz, *An Ocean Without a Shore*, 57.

merely passive event but is fundamentally *creative*. By this he means that the realized saint, having access to all levels of the meaning of a symbol, from its physical manifestation all the way up to its ideal archetype in God, is able to realize some or even all these levels of meaning, at least temporarily.[74] Ibn ʿArabi, both in this chapter of the *Bezels* as well as throughout his other works,[75] practically ascribes a magical quality to this imaginative power. The realized sage is able to actualize on the plane of dreams or even physical existence various objects and even persons, such as long deceased Sufis or masters living far away.[76]

But in a more prosaic, but perhaps deeper, sense, what Ibn ʿArabi means by the creative power of imagination is its ability to perceive the transcendent, eternal meaning in the things of manifest temporality. Corbin describes this creative power well:

The active Imagination guides, anticipates, molds sense perception; that is why it transmutes sensory data into symbols. The Burning Bush is only a brushwood fire if it is merely perceived by the sensory organs. In order that Moses may perceive the Burning Bush and hear the Voice calling him "from the right side of the valley"—in short, in order that there may be a theophany—an organ of trans-sensory perception is needed.[77]

74. "Thus, I have expounded here a mystery that the Folk have always guarded from exposition, because it would seem to contradict their claim to be one with the Reality. The Reality is never unattentive, while the servant is always inattentive to something or other. With respect to the maintenance of something he has created, the gnostic may say, 'I am the Reality,' but his maintenance of that thing cannot be compared to the maintenance exercised by the Reality." *Bezels*, 102/89.

75. See *Bezels*, 102/89.

76. Although, as both the medieval commentator al-Qaysari and the modern commentator Affifi point out, this power is creative only relatively: only God can create something from nothing while the realized sage can only transpose a form from one level of existence to another. Affifi offers two explanations for Ibn ʿArabi's doctrine of the creative imagination: (1) that, as mentioned above, the realized sage is able through his spiritual power of concentration to manifest on one level of existence (and Ibn ʿArabi presupposes five: the Divine Essence, the First Intellect, the Realm of Spiritual Beings, the Imaginal Realm, and the Sensible Realm) what is unmanifest on another. An interesting and close connection with the description and explanation of the special powers of the yogi in such works as the *Yogasutras* of Patanjali is striking. Or (2) there occurs a sort of "occasionalism" (Affifi uses the English term in his Arabic text) in which, due to God's grace, God manifests an image of reality that the realized gnostic is concentrating on, for once, devoid of all attachment to created things, the realized gnostic has aligned all the activities of his heart and intellect with God's creative power. See his *Remarks*, 79–81, and also his book in English, *The Mystical Philosophy of Ibnul ʿArabi* (Lahore: Muhammad Ashraf, 1979), 133ff. Al-Qaysari also gives a similar account of the creative power of imagination; see his *Sharḥ*, I 404–6.

77. Corbin, *Alone with the Alone*, 80.

He continues: "The symbolic exegesis that establishes typifications is thus creative in the sense that it transmutes things into symbols, into typical Images, and causes them to exist on another plane of being."[78] The ability of the prophet is then "re-created" or "re-enacted" by the realized saint in his own creative imagination. Yet, the ability of the prophet itself presupposes the revealed text of the Holy Qur'an considered in its eternal aspect (i.e., as predating its revelation to Muhammad, accessible to previous prophets as well), for ultimately God is the first to "strike similitudes," since we cannot do so under our own power. Only God can symbolize himself. Nevertheless, the symbols of revelation have (by divine design?) a resonance with the human mind such that they disclose the divine in a special and striking way. Thus, as Dupré asserts, "Symbols do not signify because they are thought to be revealed, but they are selected to reveal because they are endowed with a natural significance."[79] In other words, the "evidentness" of the truth disclosed in these symbols does not derive from an external authority, i.e., the traditional authority that states that the Qur'an (or the Bible) is the "Word of God," but from the symbol's *own inherent* power to disclose the Real. The revealed text owes its authority primarily to what Dupré calls its "inherent religious expressiveness." From the standpoint of someone like Ibn 'Arabi, then, God chooses his symbols carefully, so that they may awaken a consciousness of himself independent of the authority of his Revelation.

The way, then, to such a creative realization of truth in creation is the assimilation into one's mind and heart of the text of the Qur'an. Ibn 'Arabi claims that only "one who has the Qur'an in his soul" knows of what he speaks:

This whole question, as I have been told, has never previously been committed to writing, either by me or any other, until now. It is indeed unique and without precedent. Take care lest you forget this, for that plane in which you remain present with the form may be compared to the Book of which God said, *We have missed nothing in the Book,* for it comprises all that has come to pass [into being] and all that has not come to pass. Only he will truly know what we have said whose essential self is a united totality *[qur'an]*. [Only one who has the Qur'an in his soul knows what we speak of—Dagli, 77.] For one who fears God, *He will make a discrimination for him,* and he is as we have mentioned in discuss-

78. Ibid., 243.
79. Dupré, *Religious Mystery,* 100.

ing the distinction between servant and Lord. This discrimination is the loftiest discrimination.[80]

This is also why, despite having, as we shall see, a very broad vision of the (relative) validity of other revelations, Ibn 'Arabi was a stickler in the observance of Islamic law for Muslims and its rigorous application even to *dhimmi* subjects.[81] As Chodkiewicz says, "Ibn 'Arabi's doctrine is not simply a meditation on the Qur'an. It is so organically linked to him that the two are really inseparable. For Ibn 'Arabi, the Word of God is 'the Way, the Truth, and the Life.' It is in the Qur'an that the voyage is made that leads man back to his original status, to his divine similitude."[82] And, as Chodkiewicz further points out, for the Shaykh, it is not so much the person who assimilates the Qur'an as it is the other way around:

There is no appropriation of Revelation on the part of the man. It is not the man who inhabits the Qur'an; it is the Qur'an that dwells within the man: Divine Word takes possession of the *'arif bi-Llāh* in such a way that the Qur'an becomes his "nature." The initiatory voyage (*sulūk*), its abodes, its trials, its length can be described in a number of ways: certainly, for Ibn 'Arabi they are nothing more than this possession by the Verb.[83]

The fully realized saint is, then, simply an incarnation of the word of the Qur'an just as the Prophet's character was not like that of the Qur'an but

80. *Bezels*, 103/89–90. Or, as al-Qaysari interprets the last phrase of this passage: "the distinction that removes all distinction." *Sharḥ*, I 408–9.

81. For this rigorous attitude by Ibn 'Arabi toward the law even to non-Muslims see: Claude Addas, *Quest for the Red Sulphur*, 270–71. In the *Bezels* itself, in the chapter on Aaron, the Shaykh has this to say about the importance for spiritual realization of the strict observance of *sharī'a* law: "As for the gnostics, who know things as they really are, they display an attitude of rejection toward the worship of forms, because their degree of knowledge makes them aware that they are, by the authority of the apostle in whom they believe and through whom they are called, believers, subject to the rule of time. Thus, despite their awareness that the polytheists do not worship the forms themselves, but only God in them, by the dominance of the divine Self-manifestation they discern in them, they are nevertheless servants of [their] time. The rejector, who has no knowledge of how He manifests Himself, is completely unaware of this, since the true gnostic hides all this from the prophet, the apostle, and their heirs. Instead, he orders the polytheists to shun such forms whenever the apostle of the time does so. This they do, adhering to the apostle and seeking the love of God, as He says, *Say: If you love God, then follow me and God will love you* [3:31]." *Bezels*, 248/196. That is, while the realized Sufi may himself recognize the only relative nature of the law, he will be scrupulous in observing it, if only not to lead the mass of Muslims astray but also, even more deeply, to realize the inward dimension of the law.

82. Chodkiewicz, *An Ocean Without a Shore*, 95.

83. Ibid., 96.

was and is the Qur'an. Ibn 'Arabi discusses this point in his *Futūḥāt* in relation to a *ḥadīth*:

When 'A'isha was asked about the character of the Messenger of God, she answered, "His character was the Koran".... So the Koran is his character. If a person in the community of the Messenger of God desires to see him, let him look upon the Koran. When he looks upon it, there is no difference between looking upon it and looking upon God's Messenger. It is as if the Koran takes the configuration of a corporeal form which is named Muhammad ibn 'Abdallah ibn 'Abd al-Muttalib. The Koran is God's Speech and His attribute, so Muhammad in his entirety is the attribute of God. "So he who obeys the Messenger has obeyed God" (Koran 4:80), since "He does not speak out of caprice" (53:3), for he is the tongue of God.[84]

In conclusion, then, the goal of the mystical project is not some extraordinary "experience" of God apart from revelation, nor, even less, is it an abstract metaphysics of reality. The goal is the complete assimilation of the self to the Word of God as revealed in the Qur'an. This assimilation happens, to be sure, through a thoroughly rigorous rational analysis of the text supplemented by a creative imagination that is able to go beyond rational categories to perceive the higher meanings intimated by the symbolic nature of the "two books" of creation and the Qur'an. But, most of all, what is required is an utter humility that thirsts not for "experiences" but for the realization that we as creatures are nothing but shadows of the divine Light. Ibn 'Arabi concludes his chapter on Isaac with this poem:

> At the time the servant is a Lord, without a doubt,
> At the time the servant is a servant, most certainly.
> If servant, he encompasses the Reality,
> If Lord, he is in a lowly state.
> As servant he perceives the essential self
> And hopes range widely from him.
> As Lord he sees all creation, both lower and higher,
> Making demands on him.
> In himself he is quite unable to answer their demands,
> And for this reason you may see the gnostic weeping.
> So be the servant of a Lord, not Lord of a servant,
> Lest you fall into Hell Fire.[85]

84. IV 60.33 in SPK, 241.
85. *Bezels*, 103/90.

As rational beings, we humans are lords of creation but, at the same time, as the opening verses of the chapter remind us, this reason that we possess is the source of our downfall because it is the limited categories of reason that cut us off from Reality as such. Only insofar as we are servants—indeed, *slaves*—of the Most High with nothing of our own does the Real then disclose itself to us in and through the speech of the Qur'an.

2

# "Revelatio proprie est apud intellectum"

*Meister Eckhart and the Birth of the Word in the Soul*

All of Meister Eckhart's works, including his famous vernacular sermons, are commentaries of some type on the text of Scripture. For Eckhart, genuine thought cannot be otherwise, seeing
that all real human thought is nothing but a response to the primal
Word or Logos that speaks to us, to be sure, in all creation, but
most directly in the revealed text of Scripture. According to Eckhart, therefore, in Scripture we find the ultimate truths not only
of God but of all the sciences, which are all clearly subordinate
to theology in that their ultimate truth comes to light only in the
interpretation of Scripture. "Eckhart believed that mystical consciousness was fundamentally hermeneutical; that is, it is achieved
in the act of hearing, interpreting, and preaching the Bible."[1] For
him "mystical" meant primarily the inner, hidden meaning of the

1. McGinn, *The Mystical Thought of Meister Eckhart*, 24–25. The centrality of
hermeneutical understanding, particularly the hermeneutics of Scripture, to Eckhart's
metaphysical-mystical thought is discussed by Donald Duclow in his article "Hermeneutics and Meister Eckhart," *Philosophy Today* 28 (1984): 36–43. Professor Duclow
draws some interesting comparisons between Eckhart's hermeneutics and contemporary philosophical hermeneutics as represented by Hans Georg Gadamer. For Reiner
Schürmann, preaching on the event of the Word is the model of Eckhart's metaphysics,
a model that "emphasizes event over substance and coming-forth over fixed objectivity."
See his *Meister Eckhart: Mystic and Philosopher* (Bloomington: Indiana University Press,
1978), 89 (republished as *Wandering Joy: Meister Eckhart's Mystical Philosophy* [Great
Barrington, Mass.: Lindisfarne Books, 2001]), as cited in Duclow, 37.

sacred text,[2] and precisely because this meaning is hidden, it is transformative, requiring the soul to enter at first with its intellect and then with its entire existence into the meaning of Scripture.

McGinn notes that we cannot separate Eckhart's biblical exegesis from his activity as a preacher: not only are all of his sermons mini-commentaries of sorts on sacred Scripture, but the activity of preaching and of putting into action the words of Scripture is an essential completing of the hermeneutic act—of giving birth to the inner sense of Scripture and hence of all the human sciences as well in both the preacher and the hearer.[3] Nevertheless, Eckhart's project is also a genuinely philosophical one as well and not only because he argues, as we shall see below, that it is necessary to apply philosophical categories to the "images and parables" of Scripture in order to uncover their inner and hence universal sense.[4] Eck-

2. See the introduction to Bernard McGinn, *The Presence of God*, vol. 1: *The Foundations of Mysticism*. The reading of Eckhart's mystical project as presented here attempts to stay close to the medieval (and hence Eckhart's) understanding of the term.

3. McGinn, *Mystical Thought of Meister Eckhart*, 29.

4. McGinn, in his *Mystical Thought of Meister Eckhart*, gives a good overview of the current scholarship on Eckhart and in what sense we can or cannot term him a "mystic." Heribert Fischer, for example, has argued that Eckhart lacked the "charismatic gifts" of the mystic and has preferred to label him a theologian; for C. F. Kelly, Eckhart's thought represents a "pure metaphysics" that is rooted in the experience of the individual self and therefore we would better call Eckhart a philosopher of the purest type rather than a mystic. Kurt Flasch and Burkhardt Mojsisch have taken up and furthered this position, arguing that Eckhart is a philosopher and not a mystic. See: Heribert Fischer, "Grundgedanken der deutschen Predigten," in *Meister Eckhart der Prediger: Festschrift zum Eckhart-Gedenkjahr,* ed. Udo Nix and Rapheal Öchslin, 55–59 (Freiburg: Herder, 1960); Fischer, "Zur Frage nach der Mystik in den Werken Meister Eckharts," in *La mystique rhénane,* 109–32 (Paris: Presses Universitaires de France, 1963); C. F. Kelly, *Meister Eckhart on Divine Knowledge* (New Haven, Conn.: Yale University Press, 1977); Kurt Flasch, "Die Intention Meister Eckharts," in *Sprache und Begriff: Festschrift für Bruno Lierbrucks,* ed. Heinz Röttges, 292–318 (Meisenheim am Glan: Hain, 1974); Flasch, "Meister Eckhart: Versuch, ihn aus dem mystischen Strom zu retten," in *Gnosis und Mystik in der Geschichte der Philosophie,* ed. Peter Koslowski, 94–110 (Darmstadt: Wissenschaftliche Buchgesellschaft, 1988); Burkhardt Mojsisch, *Meister Eckhart: Analogie, Univozität und Einheit* (Hamburg: Felix Meiner, 1983), 11–12, 111, and 146.

On the other hand, Kurt Ruh and Alois Haas, along with Bernard McGinn, argue that, if we are guided by a proper understanding of the term "mystical," we can with full justification label Eckhart's thought "mystical." See: Ruh, *Geschichte der abendländische Mystik,* vol. 2, *Frauenmystik und Franziskanische Mystik der Frühzeit* (Munich: C. H. Beck, 1993); and Haas, "Aktualität und Normativität Meister Eckharts," in *Eckardus Teutonicus, Homo doctus et sanctus: Nachweise und Berichte zum Prozeß gegen Meister Eckhart,* ed. Heinrich Stirnimann and Rüdi Imbach (Freiburg, Switzerland: Universitätsverlag, 1992). McGinn, for example, argues that a mystic is not so much someone who has transitory "experiences" of God or the Absolute as someone who lives in awareness of the presence of God.

hart also wants to show how, in being applied to Scripture, the lived inner sense or truth of these otherwise static objective categories of philosophical thought is revealed.

In other words, Eckhart attempts to show that philosophical categories of secular thought as found in the writings of, say, Aristotle attain the fullness of their truth-content only when understood in relation to the soul's ascent to and union with God, because only in this ascent and union is the soul able to come to know these categories in their ideal origin, who is, of course, God. Eckhart's thought, therefore, presents us with a sophisticated critique of philosophical reason by trying to show that the categories of philosophical reason are as much in need of interpretation as the text of Scripture. The Word of God as revealed in Scripture and not any human ratiocination, even that of the great Aristotle, provides the interpretive key necessary for understanding the inner truth of philosophical categories, because Scripture, under the cover of its images and parables, presents to us in the fullest way possible the story of the soul's ascent to and union with God, which is the final goal of all human knowing and action. The categories of secular philosophy, just as much as the images and parables of Scripture, have a lived, inner (dare one say "mystical"?) sense that must be disclosed by exegesis. And it is in their application to scriptural exegesis that the inner sense of any static, objective philosophical categories discloses itself.

Central to Eckhart's interpretation of Scripture is the birth of the Son in the soul. For Eckhart, all interpretive activity aims at cracking the "outer shell" of the text to reveal its "hidden marrow," which is precisely the process of this inner birth. Eckhart thus argues that the Christian life is not one of mere rational assent to the divine Word of Scripture but an actual giving birth to this Word in the innermost ground of the soul, which then bears fruit in a life of detached freedom and love. The Christian life is a life of *living the Word*, of proclaiming and manifesting the Word in all of one's actions. Without this existential transformation, the Word of God becomes a mere objective category of rational thought like any other category found in Aristotle and, just as importantly, without this birth, philosophy and science remain mere abstractions, cut off from vivifying Truth.

For Eckhart, then, the primal truth in which all other truths can be known is known only in this birth in which the soul does not merely have the divine Word or Truth as an object but in which its very mode of existing and knowing is transformed by this Word. This birth, then, is not a mere experience among other experiences[5] but is something much more fundamental—a new way of *structuring experience,* one in which the soul lets God be in himself and in all things and thus comes to exist in absolute freedom. In this way, Eckhart carries forward the Augustinian tradition of illumination: the birth of the Son in the soul describes a process of illumination in which is revealed the inner truth not only of Scripture but of all the sciences.

### Reason and Revelation in Eckhart

Meister Eckhart interprets Scripture using as his basic premise that truth is one: God is the True and, since God is one, the ultimate truth of things is one. All particular truths derive whatever truth they have from God, who is the *prima veritas* or "First Truth," and in whose light they are known.[6] Eckhart, of course, takes this basic premise not only from his fellow Dominican Thomas Aquinas; both take it from a broader Neoplatonic tradition. According to this tradition, all particular perfections in things, truth, for example, must derive from a level of reality in which they are perfectly united, for multiplicity follows upon change and decay and

5. This is, in effect, the argument of Denys Turner in his book *The Darkness of God: Negativity in Christian Mysticism* (Cambridge: Cambridge University Press, 1995). There, he argues that the habit in the current literature on mysticism has been to project back anachronistically on the medieval mystics the primacy in the modern mind of "experience" and to see all of mysticism as about special "experiences." Rather, Turner says, we must see the best medieval mystics, like Eckhart, providing a *critique* of such "experiences" and arguing that the properly Christian life is one that is grounded in what is beyond specific experiences. Louis Dupré, in his contribution, "*Unio Mystica: The State and the Experience,*" in *Mystical Union and Monotheistic Faith: An Ecumenical Dialogue,* ed. Moshe Idel and Bernard McGinn,3–23 (New York: Macmillan, 1989), makes a similar argument. There Dupré states: "It seems that consciousness in the unitative state remains on a different level that transforms *all* experience" (10).

6. See B. Welte, *Meister Eckhart: Gedanken zu seinen Gedanken* (Freiburg: Herder, 1992), 19–20, where he remarks: "Wir haben also noch einmal das klassische 'Fidens quaerens intellectum' in eigentümlicher Ausformung vor uns. Es muß *gedacht* werden, wenn das Wort Gottes klarwerden soll"; and: Goris, "Ontologie oder Henologie? Zur Einheitsmetaphysik Meister Eckharts," in *Was ist Philosophie in Mittelalter?* Miscellanea Mediaevalia, 26, ed. Jan Aertsen and Andreas Speer (Berlin: de Gruyter, 1998), 695: "Das Grundschema des Eckhartischen Denkens ist die Einheit von Natur und Offenbarung, von Glauben und Wissen."

no general perfections can change or decay. They must, then, be united in what the Neoplatonists call the "One" and which Eckhart identifies with God. Thus Eckhart will say in his general prologue to the *Opus triparti-tum* as a basic axiom of his thought, "What is divided in the inferior is always one and undivided in the superior. It clearly follows that the superior is in no way divided in the inferior; but, while remaining undivided, it gathers together and unites what is divided in the inferior."[7] To the degree that anything is perfect and a principle of the less perfect, to that degree it is one. This principle holds in particular for the perfection of truth: the cause of intelligibility in all created things, and thus the cause of the many truths that can arise from the created intellect's adequation with them, cannot itself be multiple, but must be one. Eckhart can therefore also say that "Moses, Christ, and the philosopher teach the same thing."[8] Eckhart is quick to add that the truth of all three is not of the same value, since what the philosopher teaches is only probable, while what Moses teaches is worthy of belief and what Christ teaches is truth in all its certainty.[9] Nevertheless, all truth, be it found in revelation or in creation as understood through philosophy, has the same source, God, who is Truth itself.

The difference between theology and philosophy, therefore, is not one of content;[10] the difference lies in the way in which the truth of that

7. *Prol. op. trip.*, n.10; LW I, 155/Maurer, 84. All translations from Eckhart's works are taken from the following editions: *Master Eckhart: Parisian Questions and Prologues*, trans. Armand Maurer (Toronto: Pontifical Institute for Medieval Studies, 1974); *Meister Eckhart: The Essential Sermons, Commentaries, Treatises, and Defense*, trans. Edmund Colledge and Bernard McGinn (New York: Paulist, 1981); and *Meister Eckhart: Teacher and Preacher*, ed. and trans. Bernard McGinn (New York: Paulist, 1986). If no reference to the above translations is given, then the translation is mine. All citations from the original Latin and Middle High German are from the standard critical editions of Eckhart's works: *Meister Eckhart: Die lateinischen Werke*, ed. Josef Koch and Georg Steer (Stuttgart: Kohlhammer, 1936–); and *Meister Eckhart: Die deutschen Werke*, ed. Josef Quint and Loris Sturlese (Stuttgart: Kohlhammer, 1936–).

8. *In Ioh.*, n.185; LW III, 155: "Idem ergo est quod docet Moyses, Christus et philosophus." Also, *In Ioh.*, n.185; LW III, 154: "Convenienter valde scriptura sacra sic exponitur, ut in ipsa sint consona, quae philosophi de rerum naturis et ipsarum proprietatibus scripserunt, praesertim cum ex uno fonte et una radice procedat veritatis omne quod verum est, sive essendo sive cognoscendo, in scriptura et in natura." Eckhart goes on to add that the Old Testament contains truths concerning what is movable and corruptible while the New Testament treats of what is eternal and incorruptible (*In Ioh.*, n.185; LW III, 155–56).

9. *In Ioh.*, n.185; LW III, 155. See also E. Winkler, "Wort Gottes und Hermeneutik bei Meister Eckhart," in *Freiheit und Gelassenheit: Meister Eckhart Heute*, ed. Udo Kern (Grünwald: Kaiser, 1980), 176.

10. "All scholastic theologians believed that there could be no *conflict* between faith and

content is appropriated. The one truth can be appropriated as an abstract objective truth, a revealed Law that is scrupulously to be fulfilled, or as a truth lived in the concrete particularity of the subject. It is this third mode of appropriation, the *truth as lived*, that interests Eckhart without, however, losing sight of its abstract, objective implications nor, most of all, its basis in the exegesis of the revealed Law.

As Eckhart implies, while truth is one, we human beings apprehend it in different ways, some more adequate than others. All human modes of knowing, even that mode of knowing that takes revelation as its primary source, are imperfect and inadequate when it comes to knowing God. God is one but the human intellect knows the truth, as Thomas Aquinas showed, only by forming judgments through composition and division.[11] This means that the human intellect, by virtue of the very mode of its operation, cannot of itself know truth in its utter simplicity. It can know it only in a roundabout fashion by forming judgments based on the separation and union of subjects and predicates. In other words, the human intellect, in trying to grasp God by means of the finite categories of its thought, breaks up the divine unity into a multiplicity of attributes that, in itself, already falsifies what it is trying to know.

Eckhart addresses this problem in his *Commentary on Exodus,* where the influence of Moses Maimonides is particularly strong, since the Jewish philosopher took as one of his central problems the relation of the multiple divine attributes to the divine unity and how it is possible for us humans to predicate accurately and adequately these attributes of God. In discussing a passage from Philippians 2, in which the Apostle says, "I have given him a name which is above every name," Eckhart notes:

reason because each has its source in the one divine Truth. Eckhart, as we have seen, went further, claiming that Moses, Aristotle, and Christ 'teach the same thing, differing only the way they teach' (*in Ioh.,* n.185). This suggests that there is no difference in the *content* of philosophy and theology, though there is certainly a difference in the way in which philosophers and theologians grasp the truth of their respective disciplines. Thus, philosophy as a discipline is not limited to what thinkers like Thomas Aquinas called natural truths about God (e.g., God's existence), but it includes teachings like the Trinity and the Incarnation, which Eckhart saw as fully rational because the philosopher could find evidence for them in the natural world. For Eckhart, creation itself reveals that God is Trinity and that the Second Person of the Trinity became flesh for our salvation." Bernard McGinn, *The Harvest of Mysticism,* 108.

11. See *S.Th.* I, 16, 2, and I, 85, 5.

From this the true answer of that knotty and famous question whether there is a distinction of attributes in God or only in our intellect's way of grasping is clear and evident. It is certain that the distinction of divine attributes, for example, power, wisdom, goodness, and the like, is totally on the side of the intellect that receives and draws knowledge of such things from and through creatures. Creatures, by the fact that they are from the One but below the One, necessarily fall into number, plurality, distinction, guilt, and fault, a condition by which they are numbered among all the things that are. That which commits an offense in the One and against the One incurs the guilt of distinction and happens to all things. This is one explanation of what is said in James 2: "He who offends in one point has been made guilty in all" (Jas 2:10). The distinction which the term "all" implies is indeed, guilt, fault, and defect in existence and unity. Everything that exists is either above all and above number, or is numbered among all things. But above all and outside number there is only the One. No difference at all is or can be in the One, but "All difference is below the One," as it says in the *Fountain of Life*, Book 5.[12]

When it comes to the problem of how we are to predicate any attributes of God, Eckhart clearly sides against Aquinas and with Maimonides (and another Andalusian Jewish philosopher, Avicebron, whose *Fountain of Life* is referred to here). Whereas Aquinas argued that some knowledge of God is open to us through the analogical predication of perfections from creatures to God, Eckhart argues that to conceive of any multiplicity even of perfections in God is already to misconceive God.[13] Maimonides, on the other hand, argued that any predication that we make from creatures to God will already be equivocal by the mere fact that what exists in a multiple fashion in creatures can only exist in perfect unity in God. But unity is such an integral aspect of divine perfection that any perfection in God will be totally unlike what that perfection is in the created thing, because in God it will exist in unity with all other perfections while in creatures it will not.

The upshot of this for Eckhart is that human reason is helpless to know God apart from revelation. Eckhartian thought, however, is not a species of irrational enthusiasm: to the contrary, Eckhart leaves human reason an essential role in coming to any knowledge of God. But for Eck-

---

12. *In Exod.*, n.58; LW II, 63–64/TP, 63.

13. Konrad Weiß notes the great influence that the works of Maimonides exercised over Meister Eckhart in his interpretation of Scripture. See Weiß, "Meister Eckharts biblische Hermeneutik," in *La mystique rhénane* (Strasbourg: Presses universitaires de France, 1963), 103.

hart, reason can operate effectively and according to its inner nature only under the tutelage of Scripture. The goal of any talk about God is not to describe God or to give us speculative knowledge about God, for all such talk is ultimately futile. It is rather to lead the believer to a *new mode of existing in* God, one that is possible, paradoxically, only when the human intellect has been stripped of any and all preconceptions about the nature of God, so that there is a new basis for knowing God not as this or that object of reason but as the very basis of all of one's knowledge of both God and creatures.[14]

From this we can understand why, in the prologue to his *Book of the Parables of Genesis*,[15] Eckhart states that the diversity of sciences was created together with the human soul and has no correlate in God, appealing, interestingly enough, to Plato for support: "This is the reason why the philosophers of the Academy used to hold that all the intellectual sciences, the theological and the natural, and even the virtues in relation to the ethical sciences, were created together with the soul."[16] The plurality of sciences, then, is something of a "falling away" from the divine unity and belongs to the multiplicity of the external and objective created world. The "objects" or "proper subject matters" of all the human sciences are therefore, in a sense, a creation of human reason because they multiply the oneness of God, the ultimate reality, into many different attributes or objects, a problem with which Maimonides and many Islamic thinkers, such as,

14. Indeed, recent scholarship on Maimonides and his relation to negative theology sees in Maimonides's philosophical-theological project something strongly akin to what I describe here as Eckhart's mystical project. See Kenneth Seeskin, "Sanctity and Silence: The Religious Significance of Maimonides' Negative Theology," and Diana Lobel, "'Silence Is Praise to You': Maimonides on Negative Theology, Looseness of Expression, and Religious Experience," both in the *American Catholic Philosophical Quarterly* 79 (2002), 7–24, 25–49.

15. Perhaps the most systematic account that Eckhart gives us of the understanding of his own "mystical" project is in the prologue to his *Book of the Parables of Genesis*. We have already had many occasions to refer to Eckhart's *Book of the Parables of Genesis*, in which he puts his particular understanding of the relation of reason and revelation to work. Indeed, Heribert Fischer remarks of this work that it is not a mere rehashing of the *Commentary on Genesis* but is rather a conscious methodological reflection on that first work: "Die *Expositio libri Genesis* ist das erste Werk, das sich im ersten Band der lateinischen Werke findet; ihm folgt ein zweites über das gleiche Thema: *Liber parabolarum Genesis*, und man kann bereits vermuten, daß hier nicht eine Wiederholung, sondern eine echte methodische Neubearbeitung zu erwarten ist." See Heribert Fischer, "Die theologische Arbeitsweise Meister Eckharts in den lateinischen Werke," in *Methoden der Wissenschaft und Kunst Mittelalters*, ed. Albert Zimmermann (Berlin: de Gruyter, 1970), 52.

16. *In Gen. II*, n.2; LW I, 450–51/EE, 93.

of course, Ibn 'Arabi, concerned themselves. Or, in an analogous way, the "objects" of science posit a plurality of sources of creation when there is really only one. Human reason is structurally unable to grasp God's oneness or the oneness of creation's source. Indeed, reason does not produce unity but division and diversity: it divides reality into "regions" of being and, even more fundamentally, it makes what is known into an object, separate and alien from the knower, when ultimately knower and known are one in the divine unity. As Aristotle demonstrated, all knowing is a unity of knower and known qua intelligible form and, if God is pure Intelligence, then knowledge in God would be absolute unity of knower and known. But this identity at the basis of human knowledge is only implicitly recognized by human reason and has been completely forgotten in modern times.

The only way to overcome this alienating effect of reason is to present reason's truths under the cover of parables or myths, so that it will stimulate the hearer to the activity of interpretation and thus to an inward penetration of the divine mystery and the indwelling of the transcendent Truth. As we had opportunity to note earlier, according to Louis Dupré and also Gershom Scholem, the myth is something that still retains the lived sense of the "primeval wholeness" of humanity with God that has been "lost through reflection." Thus, according to Eckhart even a philosopher and metaphysician like Plato spoke about divine, natural, and ethical problems in the form of myths or parables, because he recognized the inadequacy of static and objective categories of metaphysics for capturing the reality of God's dynamic unity.[17] But for Eckhart, the ultimate goal of interpreting Scripture is to find Christ, both within the text and within the soul, for ultimately Christ is born in the soul when that soul encounters Christ in the deepest meaning of Scripture. For it is in Christ that the eternal, transcendent divine Reality, expressed in these parables and myths, enters or, better, "intersects" with historical time and temporality and thus with the inner life of the believer.

From the oneness of God and the oneness of divine Truth, Eckhart draws the following conclusions: "God is the author of Sacred Scripture (*deus autem auctor sacrae scripturae*)" and "every truth comes from the

17. *In Gen. II*, n.2; LW I, 451/EE, 94.

Truth itself; it is contained in it, derived from it, and is intended by it."[18] As such, the literal meaning is what that author intends, not necessarily what is written on the page:

Since the literal sense is that which the author of a writing intends, and God is the author of holy scripture, . . . then every true sense is a literal sense. It is well known that every truth comes from the Truth itself; it is contained in it, derived from it, and is intended by it.[19]

The implications of this view are interesting, for Eckhart does not conceive himself as going beyond the literal intent of Scripture by submitting to a philosophical interpretation and its *rationes naturales*. To the contrary, he sees this interpretation as uncovering the more literal sense of Scripture— that of the mind of God, especially as it is known in and through Christ and his birth in our soul. Far from arbitrary whimsy, the blurring of the line between text and interpretation is precisely what makes the divine Truth "break through" the created rational categories of the believer and makes the divine Truth dwell within him or her. As McGinn explains:

By means of this procedure we might say that the exegete has become the text in the sense that it is he who provides the meaning adjudged as truly divine. Even more radically, the mystical interpreter has become one with, that is, indistinct from God, the author of the Bible. If the main concern of Eckhart's exegesis, as we have seen, is to "break through the shell" of literalism to reach the infinite inner understandings that become a new letter, exegesis of necessity implodes upon itself. It is the very nature of the Dominican's exegesis and his biblical preaching to encourage such a breaking-through that fuses both the text and the self into divine indistinction.[20]

When text and interpretation thus fuse, multiple meanings may arise that actually reflect more fully the divine intent of Scripture, for the divine intent cannot be contained by any finite text but must be enacted, as often as possible, in the lives of every hearer of the divine Word. Only in this enactment does the divine Word become living and its multiple meanings— every bit as literal as the meaning of the revealed text—become realized.

Thus, by contemporary standards at least, Eckhart at first glance seems cavalier in his interpretation of Scripture. He offers many different, even conflicting, interpretations of any single passage, all of which he as-

18. *In Gen. II*, n.2; LW I, 449/EE, 93.      19. *In Gen. II*, n.2; LW I, 449/EE, 93.
20. McGinn, *The Harvest of Mysticism*, 113.

serts may be equally valid and, indeed, implies in his commentaries that the more interpretations a passage has, the better. Moreover, he also states as a fundamental hermeneutical principle that one passage can be explained, regardless of context, by another passage elsewhere in the Bible: "In explaining a passage under discussion many other texts of the canon of Scripture are often brought forward, and all these passages can be explained in their proper places from this one, just as it is now explained through them."[21] Such a principle, of course, violates much of what we think of as good modern historical-critical scholarship, which is careful to establish layers of redaction, historical context, and a multiplicity of authorship and theological points of view.

But objective, depersonalized knowledge of the text was not what Eckhart or medieval exegesis was after: he was after the timeless meaning of the text precisely because this timeless meaning is the only meaning available for appropriation by the believer into his or her inner ground.[22] Only in such a reading of the text can the transcendent meaning become fully immanent in the life of the knower. To Eckhart, a purely objective historical-critical scholarship, while valuable as a propaedeutic study, would strip Scripture of its transcendence by reducing its meaning to purely historical human factors, leading to a grave difficulty: in stripping the text of its transcendent meaning and making that meaning purely historical, it makes that meaning unavailable for any living *present* appropriation *in historical temporality* precisely because that meaning has become, at least in the mind of the interpreter, wholly conditioned by uniquely historical "facts."[23] A more absurd situation could not be imagined for a mystical writer like Eckhart.

21. *Prologus opus expositum*, n.1; LW I, 183–84: "Primo quod in expositione auctoritatis, de qua tunc agitur, plurimae et plerumque adducuntur aliae auctoritates canonis, et illae omnes auctoritates possunt in locis suis exponi ex ista, sicut nunc ista per illas." See also *Prol. op. trip.*, n.14; LW I, 159.

22. McGinn, *The Harvest of Mysticism*, 112.

23. Describing the new sense of historical criticism that arose at the end of the eighteenth and beginning of the nineteenth centuries, Louis Dupré remarks: "Beyond the uniqueness of historical events, educated Europeans for the first time began to consider events as segments of a continuous line from which they could never be detached. Not only could the same event never occur twice in its existential singularity: it was not even seriously comparable to any more recent event, since its very *essence* restricted it to an irreversible past. Integrated with a unique and all-comprehensive cultural totality, it remained unrepeatable and excluded any repetition in another epoch." *Religious Mystery and Rational Reflection*, 84. This, as Dupré also points out, explains the

As pure unity or oneness, God is both the objective, transcendent existence on whom our own existence absolutely depends, and also the inner or immanent principle of our own existence.[24] God as the transcendent cause of creation also corresponds to the immanent ground of the soul; or, to put it another way, God as the eternal, transcendent principle of reality is also present in the lived temporality of the soul because of and through the Incarnation of the Word. As Eckhart argues in his *Commentary on Wisdom*, God's transcendence is defined by his very immanence in all things, most of all in the soul.[25] In the soul God comes to understanding and hence is received in his essential nature, transcendent to all created being. As Eckhart puts it in a sermon that we shall analyze more fully later: "God is in all things. The more he is in things, the more he is outside things; the more within, the more outside; the more outside, the more within."[26] In other words, God is the inner principle of our existence precisely because God is the absolute Existence on which our own existence and knowledge of God depends. And the more we turn our attention inward, the more we come to know God in both God's immanence and his transcendence.

In short, Eckhart maintains we cannot know God except by revelation, precisely because our existence depends absolutely on God and we cannot therefore know God as an object but as the ground of our existence. But at the same time, God is the inner principle of this knowledge and we can know this knowledge as an inner principle only through subjecting revelation in its outward form (i.e., as "sacred text") to a rigorous rational analysis that unlocks this inner, universal sense that is active and salvific in its effects.[27]

---

loss among many of the power of ritual—presumably also including the act of preaching or the sermon—since it is the purpose of ritual to take us out of the flow of homogenous, segmented time, to the eternal present by re-enacting the founding religious event.

24. B. McGinn, "Meister Eckhart on God as Absolute Unity," in *Neoplatonism and Christian Thought*, ed. D. O'Meara (Albany: State University of New York Press, 1982), 137.

25. *In Sap.*, nn.144-57; LW II, 481–94.

26. *Pr.*, 30; DW II, 94/TP, 292.

27. Thus Weiß notes that Eckhart rarely refers to the *allegorical* sense of Scripture but almost always to its *parabolic* sense. Eckhart uses the term *allegorice* only when referring to the exegeses of others. The difference between the two lies in their function: an allegory consists in a mere one-to-one correspondence between symbol and reality while a parable is a story that is designed to lead the reader or hearer into an inner experience of that reality. In other words, the allegory still remains on the plain of objective knowledge while the parable leads to an "inner" knowledge and represents such a knowledge. Weiß also notes that Eckhart makes very little use of the

This dialectic of immanence and transcendence is reflected in the sacred texts. The outer or literal sense of the text corresponds to an inner or parabolic meaning. "In his exegesis, as everywhere in his thought, Eckhart is concerned with the basic opposition between inner and outer"[28]— and one could also add, with their essential harmony. At the beginning of his *Commentary on John*, Eckhart asserts that he will explain, "as in all his works," the meaning of holy Scripture "through the help of the natural arguments of the philosophers."[29] But at the same time, Eckhart notes, this use of the "natural arguments" *(rationes naturales)* of the philosophers will also yield the truth of philosophy because the *inner sense* of these categories is intimated in a parabolic fashion in Scripture: "The truths of natural principles, conclusions and properties are well intimated for him 'who has ears to hear' (Mt 13:43) in the very words of sacred scripture, which are interpreted through the natural truths."[30]

It follows for Eckhart that the task of the metaphysician is no different from that of the theologian: to make the divine *ratio* in and through which all beings are created transparent to reason insofar as it is possible.[31] Both, therefore, must turn to an interpretation of Scripture for a proper investi-

---

traditional "four senses" of Scripture, more or less limiting himself to the literal and "parabolic" senses. See: Weiß, "Meister Eckharts biblische Hermeneutik," 95ff; also Fischer, "Die theologische Arbeitsweise Meister Eckharts in den lateinischen Werke," 64–65: "Christus selbst lehrt in Parabeln für die, welche Ohren zu hören haben, und er lehrt darin tiefe, abgründige, verborgene Wahrheiten. Alles in der Schrift läßt sich 'mystice' auslegen. Überall in der Schrift ist Christus verborgen, und Eckharts Theologie ist christologische, Heilstheologie. In den Parabeln ist verborgen, was Gott, dem ersten Prinzip, dem Grund eigen ist."

28. "Intertextuality of this sort was not new, but Eckhart's de-historicizing form of it fits his 'principial' way of knowing: that is, seeing all things from the divine perspective, the 'now' (*nû/ nunc*) of eternity in which all words and expressions are one in the eternal Word. For Eckhart such multiplicity does not introduce confusion, because all meanings come from one and the same source." McGinn, *The Mystical Thought of Meister Eckhart*, 27.

29. *In Ioh.*, n.2; LW III, 4/EE, 123.

30. *In Ioh.*, n.3; LW III, 4/EE, 123.

31. Henri de Lubac places Eckhart in the "rationalist school" (*l'école rationaliste*) insofar as he has little or no concern for the historical sense of Scripture but, instead, sees it as a mine for "hidden" or "mystical" truths which are trans-temporal. Eckhart's method, according to de Lubac, is nothing less than a "demythologization" of Scripture so as to make religious truth transparent to reason. This view of Eckhart is, of course, very reminiscent of Jonas's definition of the mystical project as developed in his article, "Myth and Mysticism: A Study of Objectification and Interiorization in Religious Thought," *Journal of Religion* 49 (1969): 315–29. See Henri de Lubac, *Exégèse médiévale: Les quatre sens de l'écriture*, vol. 4 (Lyon: Auber, 1959), 164–65. For a more recent discussion of Eckhart's "rationalism," see Jan Aertsen, "Is There a Medieval Philosophy?" *International Philosophical Quarterly* 39 (1999), 403–5.

gation of the truth because it is in Scripture that the metaphysician finds most clearly and directly expressed the primal idea or *ratio* by which all things were created. In holy Scripture all mysteries of the various human sciences, both speculative and practical, are hidden: "Sacred Scripture frequently tells a story in such a way that it also contains and suggests mysteries, teaches about the natures of things, and directs and orders moral actions."[32] The task of the interpreter is to disclose these mysteries to consciousness in their divine Truth, prescinding, for the sake of interpretation, from the effects of these truths in creation.

In his first *Commentary on Genesis*, Eckhart therefore says that what the metaphysician investigates is not the efficient or final causes of things. These causes belong to things insofar as they are distinct and particular and thus belong to the science of physics. The metaphysician, however, seeks to uncover formal causes, which is also to say ideal or exemplary causes. By asserting this position, Eckhart shows a strongly Platonic orientation derived from his—and Aquinas's—teacher, Albertus Magnus:

The reason of things is a principle in such a way that it does not have or look to an exterior cause, but looks within to the essence alone. Therefore, the metaphysician who considers the entity of things proves nothing through exterior causes, that is, efficient and final causes. This is the principle, namely, the ideal reason, in which God created all things without looking to anything outside himself.[33]

32. *In Exod.*, n.211; LW II, 178/TP, 110. Eckhart's conception of the scientific nature of Scripture, derived at least in part from Moses Maimonides, as well as other matters related to his biblical hermeneutics is discussed in Weiß, "Meister Eckharts biblische Hermeneutik," 104–5.

33. *In Gen. I*, n. 4; LW I, 187–88/EE, 83–84. This passage, of course, presumes a certain conception of metaphysics that was by no means shared by all or even most theologians during the Middle Ages. See A. Zimmerman, *Ontologie oder Metaphysik? Die Diskussion über den Gegenstand der Metaphysik im 13. und 14. Jahrhundert* (Leiden: E. J. Brill, 1965), and L. Honnenfelder, "Der zweite Anfang der Metaphysik. Voraussetzungen, Ansätze und Folgen der Wiederbegründung der Metaphysik im 13./14. Jahrhundert," in *Philosophie im Mittelalter: Entwicklungslinien und Paradigmen*, 165–86 (Hamburg: Felix Meiner, 1987), for a detailed discussion of the debates concerning the proper subject matter of metaphysics in the Middle Ages. To summarize this discussion briefly: for someone like Aquinas, following in the footsteps of Avicenna, the proper subject matter of metaphysics is not God but being qua being. God is studied by the metaphysician only insofar as God is the cause of being in general. But Eckhart, following the Averroist tradition, argues, in his prologues to the *Opus tripartitum*, that the proper subject matter of metaphysics is God, because being in its purity is none other than God. Thus Eckhart posits in his general prologue to the *Opus tripartitum* his chief thesis, "*Esse est Deus.*"

Eckhart repeats this conception of metaphysics again in the opening pages of his *Commentary on John*: metaphysics consists of an investigation of the *rationes* prior to all things, their causes, and that which the intellect accepts when it knows the thing in its intrinsic principles *(in ipsis principiis intrinsecis)*.[34] In this passage, Eckhart is operating with a classic scholastic distinction between concepts or *rationes* abstracted by the human intellect from sensible particulars and the transcendent "ideas" or *rationes divinae* in and through which God creates and which are identical with the divine substance. The concept or *ratio* abstracted from sensible particulars approximates the primal idea of the thing from which it has been abstracted, but it can never be identical with it because the created copy of the idea falls infinitely short of its ideal exemplar.

Thus Aquinas argues that we cannot, in this life *(in via)*, know created things in the divine ideas but know them only indirectly by abstracting the form from the sensible particular, which is in turn created in accordance with a divine idea.[35] Eckhart, however, argues that Scripture, insofar as it reveals the primal *ratio* or idea in which all things have been created, contains within itself the key to knowing created beings in their divine ideas.[36] Insofar as we apply the categories of reason to the interpretation of the parables of Scripture, what in effect happens is that human intellect is raised, by grace, to an intellection of all things in their divine ideas, and the limits of human discursive reasoning become palpable.

The truths of metaphysics and even physics, therefore, lie hidden under the "husk" of the images and parables of Scripture. In one of his vernacular sermons, Eckhart compares the "shell" of the outward form of Scripture to the "kernel" of its hidden, inner meaning:

I have said before the shell must be broken through and what is inside must come out, for if you want to get at the kernel you must break the shell. And also, if you want to find nature unveiled, all likenesses must be broken through, and

---

34. *In Ioh.*, n. 29; LW III, 22–23.

35. *S.Th.*, I, 84, 5.

36. See also Eckhart's sermon for the feast day of Saint Augustine, given by him in Latin at the University of Paris, in which he argues that the theologian properly speaking treats of things in a deeper fashion than the philosopher, mathematician, or physicist, since he treats of the ideas of things before they were instantiated in bodily or sensible substances, whereas the philosopher, mathematician, and physicist treat of things only insofar as they subsist in bodily substance. See LW V, 90ff.

the further you penetrate, the nearer you will get to the essence. When the soul finds the One, where all is one, there she will remain in the Single One.[37]

The interpreter who wishes to know the true sense of all human concepts and all categories of human reason must use them to penetrate into the hidden depths of Scripture, where all concepts and categories of reason are illuminated by the divine *ratio*, who is Christ himself. Christ is the *ratio rationum* or the Logos of the ideas of all things in and through whom all things derive their spiritual meaning or truth:

> No one can be thought to understand the scriptures who does not know how to find its hidden marrow—Christ, the Truth. Hidden under the parables we are speaking of are very many of the properties that belong to God alone, the First Principle, and that point to his nature. Enclosed there are to be found the virtues and the principles of the sciences, the keys to metaphysics, physics and ethics, as well as universal rules. Also there we find the most sacred emanation of the divine Persons.[38]

Scripture reveals the "properties that belong to God alone," which are, as the prologues to the *Opus tripartitum* tell us, "existence, unity, truth, and goodness" or the *transcendentalia*. These are the first or most basic concepts of the intellect corresponding to the most basic properties of things. Nevertheless, these properties, by their very infinitude and perfection, Eckhart argues, belong properly to God alone. They cannot be derived from creatures, since creatures are always limited to a genus and species while the *transcendentalia* are not, precisely because they "cut across" all categories; they can therefore only come from God and be revealed by God.[39] Revelation, then, can be the only source of a proper knowledge of

---

37. *Pr.* 51; DW II, 473. Translation from McGinn, *The Harvest of Mysticism*, 114.

38. *In Gen. II*, n.3; LW I, 453/EE, 94.

39. *Prol. op. trip.*, n.4; LW I, 132, and n.8; LW I, 152–53. Eckhart planned this work to be divided, as its name suggests, in three parts: a *Book of Propositions*, in which he would lay out in axiomatic fashion the metaphysical principles by which he would interpret revelation; a *Book of Questions* in which he would deal, as in Thomas's *Summa*, with specific theological questions; and a *Book of Commentaries*, in which he would apply the metaphysical principles of the first part to the interpretation of Scripture. As Eckhart himself says, the second and third parts would be of "little use" without the first part (n.11; 156). That is, we cannot understand revelation without also understanding the ultimate structure of reality. But the *transcendentalia* themselves and all first principles refer directly to God, since they do not belong to creatures as such. It follows that they cannot be fully understood except when applied to the interpretation of revelation where they find their full embodiment in Christ (see *In Ioh.*, n.97; LW III, 83). For an in-depth discussion of the importance of the prologues to the *Opus tripartitum* and his doctrine of the transcendentals

these most basic properties and, by extension, of the first principles of all the sciences. Eckhart asserts in his *Commentary on John* that "knowledge of God and cognition of divine things is not received from things outside of us but in accordance with revelation."[40] For Eckhart, this revelation finds its fulfillment in Christ, who is the embodiment of the divine *ratio* or rational principle of all things and in whom the *transcendentalia* and the first principles of all the sciences find their concrete expression.

It is significant that Eckhart includes the Trinity in his discussion of the transcendentals and other first principles, because the doctrine of the Trinity describes for Eckhart the formal emanation of the divine *ratio* within the Godhead and, as such, the process by which the soul also comes to understand the first principles of all things. For the emanation of persons within the Trinity is the formal cause or basis for the birth of God's Son in the innermost ground of the soul. By this birth the soul comes to a true understanding of the metaphysical principles of creation. Here, the basic principle of Plotinus is at work: "The demonstrations that we make concerning the Principle are, at the same time, the means by which we elevate ourselves to It."[41] That is, the act of interpretation is at the same time an enactment of the inner sense of revelation in the inner ground of the soul. To strip away the husk to get to the kernel is, in a sense, not to consume the kernel but to be consumed by it.

For these reasons, Eckhart is essentially what McGinn calls "an apophatic exegete."[42] To interpret is, for him, fundamentally, to strip away all that is created from the sense of Scripture, so that the uncreated may be born in the interpreter. And in this birth comes a true and effective understanding of the Trinity, distinct from all abstractions and hair-splitting. The analogy with Ibn 'Arabi's attitude to the Qur'an is here obvious. Just as one must use one's creative imagination to see within the Qur'an the inner truths of the soul's journey toward union with God, making his own the inner meaning of the sacred text's imagery, so must the hearer of the Gospel come to understand how the words of Christ speak to his own inner journey toward union with him.

---

for Eckhart's mystical project see my article, "Meister Eckhart's 'Ontological Philosophy of Religion,'" *Journal of Religion* 82 (2002): 563–85.

40. *In Ioh.*, n.347; LW III, 295: "scientia dei et divinorum cognitio non est ab extra a rebus accepta, sed secundum revelationem."

41. *Enneads*, I, 3, 3, 1–5.                      42. McGinn, *The Harvest of Mysticism*, 114.

Eckhart thus sees the opening verse of John, "In the beginning was the Word," as the metaphysical fulfillment of the "physics" of the Old Testament. According to Eckhart, "the gospel contemplates being qua being,"[43] or God as the formal cause of all things, whereas the Old Testament only gives us a knowledge of God as creator, i.e., God as the efficient and final cause of all things. When we know God as the efficient and final cause of creation, we know God as somehow divided off from creation and, therefore, we do not know God as God is in himself, i.e., in his absolute unity, which embraces all that exists.[44] Only when we strip God of such causality do we know him as the simultaneously transcendent and immanent *ratio* or *formal cause* of creation. Thus the Gospels give us a properly *metaphysical or philosophical* knowledge of God in his pure formal *ratio*, because Christ is the formal *logos* or *ratio* of creation. Christian Scripture, then, gives us direct access to the proper subject matter of metaphysics.

If, as Aristotle defined it, metaphysics is the study of "being qua being," then Eckhart is deeply engaged in a metaphysical project as well as a mystical one: Christ is the "being qua being" as lived by the fully detached soul. As Vladimir Lossky points out, Eckhart seeks to find, in the *abditum mentis* of Saint Augustine, the *ipsum esse* of Saint Thomas.[45] The science of being qua being is not a purely "objective" science, but one that demands

43. *In Ioh.*, n.444; LW III, 380: "evangelium contemplatur ens in quantum ens." In this passage of his commentary on John, Eckhart transfers Averroes's distinction between the proper subject matters of physics and metaphysics to that of the Old and New Testaments, where the New Testament, like metaphysics, treats of God, or being as such, and where the Old Testament, like physics, demonstrates the existence of the subject matter of metaphysics and, as such, is a necessary propaedeutic to the study of the New Testament or metaphysics: "Hinc est quod metaphysica, cuius subiectum est ens in quantum ens, duas tantum causas intrinsecas considerat; physica autem, cuius subiectum est ens mobile in quantum mobile, non tantum intrinsecas, sed etiam extrinsecas causas speculatur. Testes autem uniuscuiusque rei propriae sunt causae ipsius. De praemissis patet quod evangelium et lex vetus se habent ad invicem sicut demonstrator et topicus, sicut metaphysicus et physicus: evangelium contemplatur ens in quantum ens. Esse autem dicimus illa quae ipsa quidem natura incorporea sunt et immutabilis substantiae ratione vigentia ut ait Boethius I Arithmeticae et II Musicae." Here, as noted above, Eckhart presupposes Averroes's conception of the proper subject matter of metaphysics.

44. Thus, the first proposition of the *Book of Propositions* will be *"Esse est Deus"* or "Existence is God." Eckhart argues that God cannot be anything other than existence itself, since that would imply that God receives God's existence from another, which is impossible. It also follows that nothing can have existence outside of God, since if it did, it would have existence by something other than existence itself, which is also impossible. See: *Prol. op. trip.*, n.12; LW I, 156–58.

45. Vladimir Lossky, *Théologie négative et connaissance de Dieu chez Maître Eckhart* (Paris: Vrin, 1998), 31–32.

the inner appropriation of absolute Being. But for this appropriation revelation is necessary, because only revelation calls the soul inward. The truth of revelation is thus under the veil *(velamen)* of parables. As for Ibn 'Arabi so for Eckhart, the sensible imagery of the sacred text makes possible knowledge of God for the human intellect, immersed as it is in a corporeal form; but, at the same time, this imagery "veils" the "naked truth" of absolute Existence, God. All in all, however, the "veil" of Scripture is essential because it is what draws the soul into the inner sense of divine truths and thereby draws the soul into itself, where it can encounter and live these truths unhindered by the limitations put on the soul's life by the forms of finite rational thought.

To sum up what we have said so far: Eckhart's thought is a thoroughly hermeneutical endeavor almost wholly concerned with the interpretation of the sacred text and the reactivation in the soul of the believer of the inner unity of the soul with God at the core of that text's meaning, because, for Eckhart, the revealed Word is in a fundamental way prior not only in the order of knowing (with respect to God) but also in the order of being. In his first *Parisian Question*, disputations that date from his first professorship at Paris and therefore relatively early in his career, Eckhart notes: "The Evangelist did not say: 'In the beginning was being, and God was being' but rather he said, 'In the beginning was the Word, and the Word was with God.'"[46] That is, prior to "being" or, more accurately, our understanding of "being" is the *revelation of being* in the primal Word or *logos/ratio* of all things. Prior to our knowing beings or even being as such is the openness or clearing, to use Heidegger's term, in which beings and even being as such can appear. For Eckhart, what opens up beings and being itself to our understanding is the divine Word, which is contained in Scripture but understood fully only when we give birth to that Word in the innermost ground of our souls. Given this understanding of the relation of reason to revelation in the *Parisian Questions*, Eckhart will be forced subsequently to rethink quite radically the relationship of reason to revelation since, ultimately, the truths of human reason, which can be resolved into the most fundamental concept, "being," can in turn find their truth and fulfillment only in revelation.[47]

46. *Quaes. Par. I*, n.4; LW V, 40/Maurer, 45.
47. McGinn puts this very well when he says: "[The highest form of philosophy] also teaches natural reason's insufficiency to attain the ground unless it surrenders itself to the action of the

## From Outer Text to Inner Birth

Eckhart's entire intention, then, is to reinsert the objective categories of speculative thought, whether in theology or in metaphysics, into their origin and basis in the soul's living union with God in and through the divine Word or *ratio* and, by doing so, transform this union from one of potentiality to one of actuality. Eckhart's mystical thought is, then, just as much practical as it is speculative. The goal of his dialectical critique of reason and revelation is to *reactivate* in the believer an awareness of this union of the soul in its innermost ground with God, which for Eckhart is the inner core and source of revelation *and* of reason (as embodied in the philosophical sciences). In this section, I shall show how, in Eckhart's writings, speculative thought as well as the parables of Scripture are to be "deconstructed" so as to reveal what both presuppose: the absolute unity of all truth and the soul's inner experience of that unity in detached freedom. Speculative thought deconstructs revelation and revelation deconstructs speculative thought so as to reveal this inner union at the basis of both; thus this inner union may be available for appropriation in the soul of each and every believer. Or as Eckhart might say, only in "proclaiming the Word"—in bringing forth the Word and giving birth to it, in the act of preaching it or in the infinitely little actions of our lives—does the Word as primal *ratio* become understood.

The relation of the inner to the outer Word comes most to the fore in Eckhart's sermon *Praedica Verbum*. Here Eckhart starts by commenting on a verse of Scripture that refers to Saint Dominic, the founder of his order, the Dominicans or *Ordo Praedicatorum* (Order of Preachers). The verse is 2 Timothy 4:2, which Eckhart paraphrases as "Speak the word, speak it externally, speak it forth, bring it forth, give birth to the Word!" Following this paraphrase, Eckhart then launches into the following remark:

It is a marvelous thing that something flows out yet remains within. That a word flows out yet remains within is certainly marvelous. That all creatures flow out and yet remain within is a wonder. What God has given and what he has promised to give is simply marvelous, incomprehensible, unbelievable. And this is as

divine light. Some might call this 'mystical irrationality.' Eckhart thought of it as the higher form of suprarational knowing needed to bring reason to its goal." McGinn, *Mystical Thought of Meister Eckhart*, 24.

it should be; for if it were intelligible and believable, it would not be right. God is in all things. The more he is in things, the more he is outside the things; the more within, the more outside: the more outside, the more within.[48]

Eckhart understands God's presence in creation as one of simultaneous transcendence and immanence: to the degree that God is in all things, to that degree God is beyond all things, confined to none of them. And to the degree that God is beyond or outside of all things, to that degree is God their inner principle and source. These are the logical implications of God's absolute unity. Thus Eckhart compares God to a word: just as a word communicates its meaning to all that hear it and yet remains what it is independent of those who hear it, so does God communicate being to all those who receive or "hear" God while God remains who God is apart from creatures. In God as in a word, the inner and the outer coincide.

But which creature can be said to receive or "hear" God most fully? Which creature is potentially capable of having its being conform wholly to the divine being in listening to this divine communication? For Eckhart, both the human being and the angel are such creatures. For the human being and angel are present to themselves in a way that no other creatures are and, by being present to themselves, they are able to discover God within themselves as the "within" that is also wholly "without." Nevertheless, Eckhart focuses on the implications of this divine communication for human beings, for it was, after all, human nature that God assumed and in which God gave birth to his Son:

God is in all things; but God as divine and God as intelligent is nowhere so intensely present as he is in the soul and in the angels; if you will, in the innermost and in the highest [part] of the soul. . . . There, where time never entered nor image shined in, in this innermost and highest [part] of the soul, God creates this whole world. Everything that God created six thousand years ago when he made the world and everything he will yet create in a thousand years (if the world lasts that long), all this he creates in the innermost and in the highest of the soul. Everything that is past, everything that is present, and everything that is future God creates in the innermost of the soul. . . . The Father gives birth to his Son in the innermost of the soul and gives birth to you with his only-begotten Son, not less.[49]

---

48. *Pr.* 30; DW II, 94/TP, 292.
49. *Pr.* 30; DW II, 95–96/TP, 292–93.

All that God accomplishes, including the creation and the birth of the Son, occurs in the eternal "Now," which, being not subject to time, is known only in the innermost part of the soul, because only the intellectual soul is able to abstract from every *hic et nunc* or every here and now.[50] Since God creates all things in this inner and eternal Now, the inner meaning not only of Scripture but also of all of creation and of all the human sciences—physical, metaphysical, and moral—that study creation and ultimately God resides solely in this inner, eternal Now.

Only in bringing forth the inner Word in loving detachment does the soul come to understand the divine Truth, as it manifests itself in both the sciences of reason and in revelation. Eckhart continues:

"Speak the word, speak it externally, speak it forth, bring it forth, give birth to the Word!" "Speak it externally." That something is spoken from the outside is a common thing. This, however, is spoken within. "Speak it externally!" This means: Be aware that this is within you. The prophet says, "God spoke one thing, and I heard two" (cf. Ps 61:12). This is true. God has only ever spoken one thing. His speech is only one. In this one speaking he speaks his Son and, together with him, the Holy Spirit and all creatures; and there is only one speaking in God. But the prophet says, "I heard two," that is, I understood God and creatures. Where God speaks it, it is God; but here it is creature. People imagine that God only became man there [in Palestine]. This is not true. God has just as much become man here [in the soul] as there, and he has become man so that he might give birth to you, his only-begotten Son, and nothing less.[51]

Here Eckhart repeats a theme we have seen earlier: that human reason can only overlay God's utter oneness with a multiplicity of conceptual categories or figurative and parabolic images and therefore remains ignorant of God as God. When the soul, however, penetrates beyond the particularity of the historical events narrated in Scripture to their inner meaning, then it is able to allow God to give birth to his Son within it. The soul then resides in the eternal *hic et nunc* of the purified intellect, tapping into the eternal, formal (i.e., intellectual) emanation of the Divine Persons in love. When this happens, the soul is then able to understand God in his abso-

---

50. *In Ioh.*, n.318; LW III, 265–66: "Intellectus autem abstrahit ab hic et nunc, et secundum genus suum nulli nihil habet commune: impermixtus est, separatus est, ex III De anima. . . . Esto talis: humilis, scilicet subiectus deo, separatus a tempore et continuo, impermixtus, nulli nihil habens commune: venis ad deum, et deus ad te." See also, *In Ioh.*, n.38: LW III, 32.

51. *Pr.* 30; DW II, 97–98/TP, 293.

lute oneness. It understands not God along with creatures but creatures in God, because, giving birth to God's Son within itself, the soul comes to subsist in his eternal and absolutely free activity. Such an understanding can occur only in a soul that is completely detached from all creatures, for only in such a soul can God find the emptiness and receptivity into which God can give birth.[52]

Eckhart thus finishes his sermon with this remark: "Direct all your works to God. There are many people who do not understand this, and this seems to me hardly surprising. For the person who is to understand this must be totally detached and elevated above all things." For Eckhart, we know and live in the divine Truth only when we are free and we are free only insofar as we act with detachment. But what makes possible this detachment is not anything created or human, but the eternally detached freedom of God who, by giving birth to his Son in the soul, allows the soul to participate in that freedom. In other words, this birth can happen only by divine grace. But there is something in the soul, its ground, that allows the soul to seize and be seized by God in its freedom from all time and place. This ground of the soul makes possible the faculty of what Eckhart, following scholastic tradition, calls the "superior intellect":

It concerns the superior intellect and its relation to not only the sensible powers but also the discursive reason: a noble power of the soul, so high and so noble that it seizes God in the simplicity of his essence. This power has nothing in common with anything; from nothing it makes something and all things. It seizes nothing of yesterday and before yesterday, of tomorrow and the day after tomorrow, because in eternity, there is neither yesterday nor tomorrow, only an instantaneous present; what was a thousand years and what will be a thousand years is present, as is what is from the other shore of the sea. This power seizes God in his nudity. . . . For this power, nothing is hidden. A text says that the head of men should be uncovered while that of women should be covered (1 Cor 11:7). The "women" are the lower powers that should be covered, but the man is this power that should be naked and uncovered.[53]

By participating in God's freedom, the soul as intellect also comes to know the inner truth of Scripture, which is to say, of God, and the true inner

52. For a detailed discussion of the noetic dimension of detachment in Eckhart's thought, see my article, "Meister Eckhart's Metaphysics of Detachment," *The Modern Schoolman* 80 (2002): 35–54.

53. *Pr.* 11; DW I, 182.

sense of revelation and therefore of all truth. The superior intellect is not constrained by place or time and is therefore able to discern the eternal truth *for me and my life* of any passage or even word of Scripture. Yet, the soul paradoxically does not create this most intimate and personal of senses of Scripture, but is rather given this sense by God in his naked self-presence. Thus, divine grace is always at work in any proper understanding of Scripture and of its Author, God: for the very movement toward detachment and understanding can only come ultimately from God. It is simply up to us to accept or reject this movement.

As the passage cited above makes clear, the events and parables of Scripture signify not merely contingent historical events or ahistorical mythical archetypes. They signify eternal and universal processes bound up necessarily in the divine life *and* the personal inner life of the detached soul. The most notable of these processes is, of course, the birth of the Son in the soul, by which the historical-temporal soul is united to God in his eternal working and being.

In light of such a view of the biblical text, Eckhart sees these parables as signifying as well the inner truth and meaning of universal, objective philosophical categories (most notably for Eckhart, those of Aristotle). As we mentioned previously, Eckhart's hermeneutical method, no more than that of Ibn ʿArabi, is not one of allegory: Eckhart's intention is not to "translate" the tropes of Scripture into the language and categories of philosophy and contemporary science. To the contrary, Eckhart's hermeneutics shows how these categories are in need of interpretation themselves. As objective and abstract, these categories may be correct, in the sense of corresponding to "the nature of things"; but they cannot be true, unless we can show how they arise in the soul's inner, existential encounter with God, because knowing the truth, for a mystical thinker like Eckhart, as for Ibn ʿArabi, requires *being* in the truth, "entering into the revealed object." True knowing abolishes all distance between the knower and the known. Thus, for Eckhart (and, mutatis mutandis, for Ibn ʿArabi), the *lived, inner truth* of philosophy and science discloses itself only in the application of their language and categories to Scripture, for it is their use in the interpretation of Scripture that this ultimate inner sense, the union of the soul with God in the birth of his Son in the soul, comes to light. For Eckhart, only Scripture can show both the universal and the inner, lived (or, if you will, personal) significance of this truth.

As Vladimir Lossky points out, Eckhart takes the definition of meta-physics by Aristotle as the study of "being qua being" in a new direction: he sees this study of *ens inquantum ens* as explicated most directly and clearly in Exodus, where God says that he is *sum qui sum*: in other words, God proclaims that it is he that is being qua being. God is the self-reflexive act of being that returns upon itself as being. As such, being qua being is God; but it comes to dwell in the soul through Christ.[54] Insofar as we appropriate the eternal birth of Christ in the Father in the ground of our souls, we come to know being qua being by dwelling in and being dwelt in by being qua being.

Thus we find the use of Aristotle's notion of "natural place" in Eckhart's little vernacular treatise "On Detachment," to describe the necessity of the union between God and the detached soul:

I prove that detachment compels God to come to me in this way; it is because everything longs to achieve its own natural place (cf. Aristotle's *Physica* Δ, 212b17–22). Now God's natural place is unity and purity, and that comes from detachment. Therefore God must of necessity give himself to a heart that has detachment.[55]

And also:

The Father gives birth to his Son in the eternal knowledge, and the Father gives birth to the Son in the soul just as [he does] in his own nature. He gives birth in the soul as its own, and his being depends on his giving birth to the Son in the soul whether he likes it or not.[56]

Further on in the treatise, Eckhart makes reference to Aristotle's argument that the human intellect is a sort of empty tablet.[57] When God and the detached soul are united, then, it is in the same way that knower and known or perceived and perceiver are united in one activity.

Thus it is not the case for Eckhart that we can merely *illustrate* the principles of the spiritual life by, say, Aristotelian physics. Rather, the principles of the spiritual life *are*, fundamentally, the principles of physics and of all sciences, because they are the principles by which the soul lives its unity with the divine Truth, the cause of the truth in all things. As Aristotle argued, just as the motion by which the mover moves and the

54. Lossky, *Théologie négative chez Maître Eckhart*, 120.
55. *Vom Abg.*, DW V, 403/EE, 286.        56. *Pr.*, 4; DW I, 72/TP, 251.
57. See *Vom Abg.*, DW V, 425–26/EE, 292.

moved is moved is one motion and one act, so when we know something the act by which something is known is the exact same act by which the knower knows it. In other words, it is not the case that the detached soul's dynamic union with God is a species of union of mover and the moved (or of the knower and the thing known) but rather these later are merely species and imitations of the soul's union with God or, more fundamentally, of God's union with his only-begotten Son:

Matter and form are the two principles of things in such a way that they are still one in existence and have one act of existence and one activity. Operation follows existence. This is what the figure of chapter two declares, "They were two in one flesh" (Gn 2:24). And so the sense faculty and the sense object, the intellect and the intelligible object, though two in potency, are one in act. The one act belongs to both. The faculty of sight is actually seeing and the visible object is actually seen in the same utterly simple act.[58]

What Scripture reveals is the wider (and one can also say "deeper" or "personal") significance of Aristotelian philosophy (and of all philosophy in general) as having its primal root in the inner union of the detached soul with God, which then the soul, in its falling away into multiplicity of the created world and the various sciences, reformulates in the objective terms of philosophical or mythical-historical discourse, in the process forgetting and covering over that original concrete lived inner union with the divine unity. This union becomes covered over with stale speculative abstractions. In other words, philosophical/scientific activity is a sort of alienated knowing because it is an abstract, objective depersonalized knowing. As such, it is inherently a-theistic in the root sense of "without God." By contrast, for Eckhart, any knowing that is a true self-knowing, i.e., one that aims at the inner freedom of detachment and is rooted in the transformation and transcendence of the self, is inherently theistic, because it is God, as the transcendent cause of all existence, who makes this self-transcendence possible.

It follows that the inner sense or meaning of both revelation and of the truths of human reason or philosophy is primarily for Eckhart a practical sense. That is to say, its truth is only understood in free and detached activity that is in union with God's free and detached activity. Thus, in his Latin sermon given at Paris on the occasion of the feast day of Saint Au-

58. *In Gen. II*, n.33; LW I, 501/EE, 105.

gustine, Eckhart, in discussing Boethius's ordering of the sciences, mentions the practitioners of the three main speculative sciences, the *"physicus,"* the *"mathematicus,"* and the *"ethicus sive theologus"* (the ethical philosopher or theologian).[59] What this list implies is that all talk about God, whether in philosophy or theology, can only find its truth in a certain way of life, for the term *ethicus* is interchangeable for Eckhart with the term *theologus*. And that way of life is one that is embedded in an ethical activity that is utterly free and detached from created things, concepts, or volitions.

For this reason, Eckhart in several places, most notably in the beginning of his *Commentary on John*,[60] compares the relation of God and the free, detached soul to that of justice itself to the just man. The just man is the man who "seeks nothing in his works,"[61] who works out of complete detachment from created things, treating all creatures with perfect equality. Indeed, the just man, Eckhart says, is equal to nothing.[62] As a result, the just man does not work for anything outside of himself or for any goal external to justice itself. Or, as Eckhart puts it in one of his striking expressions, the just man works "without a why": he works simply for the sake of the work itself, because when a man is perfectly just, he seeks nothing in his own nature but everything in justice. And since God is, for Eckhart, justice itself, the just man lives, moves, and works in God: "The just man lives in God and God in him because God is born in the just man and the just man in God" and "God is justice. Therefore, whoever is in justice is in God and *is* God."[63] Thus insofar as the just man is just and lives in justice, he is of one nature with God; but because justice gives birth to the just man, they are also distinct. In other words, for the just man, who lives "without a why," detached from everything that is created, whether material or immaterial, justice is not a mere abstract concept—an intelligible form abstracted from sensible particulars—but a fully concrete and living idea that is the ground of the just man's very existence and, more particularly, of his living and acting and loving. This is perhaps why Eckhart chose to concentrate on the "notion" of justice in describing the kind of effective or "verbal" unity[64] that occurs between the detached soul and

59. LW V, 90.
61. *Pr.* 39; DW II, 253.
63. *Pr.* 39; DW II, 252/TP, 296–97.

60. *In Ioh.*, nn. 13–26; LW III, 13ff.
62. *Pr.* 6; DW I, 107.

64. Thus Reiner Schürmann talks about a notion of "operative identity" in Eckhart, which he contrasts with a notion of "substantial identity" that one would find in, say, the works of panthe-

justice. Justice cannot be understood by means of intellectual abstraction from sensible things; it can only be understood in perfectly detached, free, and loving action. Since justice looks entirely to the good of another and not one's own, it can be known and realized only in a radical *kenosis* or "self-emptying" in which one is completely at the disposal of the other. For Eckhart, this self-emptying is both manifested and given to the soul in, by, and through Christ. The idea of justice, therefore, becomes only a personal, living idea in and through Christ, who gives birth to himself in the soul by means of the Word of Scripture.

So, as Eckhart also puts it, the just man stands to justice as the word stands to its idea.[65] The just man, living without a why in detached freedom, "breaks through" to the primal Word or divine *ratio*, which is the inner truth of both revelation and philosophy. Thus Eckhart notes, in his sermon *iusti vivent in aeternum*:

> One should not accept or esteem God as being outside of oneself, but as one's own and as what is within one; nor should one serve or labor for any recompense, not for God or for his honor or for anything that is outside oneself, but only for that which one's own being and one's own life is within one. Some simple people think that they will see God as if he were standing there and they here. It is not so. God and I, we are one. I accept God into me in knowing; I go into God in loving. . . . Working and becoming are one. If a carpenter does not work, nothing becomes of the house. If the axe is not doing anything, nothing is becoming anything. In this working God and I are one; he is working and I am becoming. The fire changes anything into itself that is put into it and this takes on fire's own nature. The wood does not change the fire into itself, but the fire changes the wood into itself. So are we changed into God, that we shall know him as he is.[66]

In the practical life of detachment and justice the soul is united to God, indeed, is changed into God not by virtue of anything of its own but pure-

---

istic monists. Whereas the latter conceive of the union between the soul and God in terms of the "merging" into "one substance," Eckhart conceives of this unity as a "verbal" unity: that is, a unity of action or actuality (Aristotle's ἐνέργεια). Thus, Eckhart can maintain an utter oneness between God and the soul without claiming that they are one "substance" and avoid the pitfalls of monism or pantheism. See Schürmann, *Wandering Joy,* 22–23. Bernard Welte points out, in his seminal article "Eckhart as Aristotelian," how Eckhart uses in particular the categories from Aristotle's physics of motion, in which the mover and the moved are understood as having *one shared actuality* (ενέργεια) while still remaining distinct as mover and moved, to describe the union of God and the soul in the inner birth of the Son in the soul. See Bernard Welte, "Meister Eckhart als Aristoteliker," *Philosophisches Jahrbuch* 69 (1961): 64–74.

65. *In Ioh.,* n.15; LW III, 13.          66. *Pr.* 6; DW I, 113–15/EE, 188–89.

ly by its detached action. Only then the soul knows God not as some object "over there" but as the very ground of its existence and, as Eckhart here emphasizes, the soul and God are one in working, in giving birth to good works and to justice through the birth of the Son in the soul. Notice here how Eckhart mentions that, in this working, "working and becoming are one." In this free and detached working in its ground, the becoming of the soul becomes one with the unchanging Being of God. But, according to Eckhart, we only appropriate this truth in and through Christ because Christ, in his Incarnation, is the identity of Being and becoming, of the eternal and the temporal, that makes all such unity possible.[67]

The primal *ratio* or Word, then, speaks and is known by the soul as the *ratio* of all things only insofar as it is received *inwardly* in the intellect. For it is only in and by the intellect that God is stripped of all objective being *(esse)*—that is, of being understood as efficient or final cause (or in the vernacular sermons as the "why" and "wherefore")—and is known in himself. Thus according to Eckhart in one of his Latin sermons, in the intellect and in the intellect alone does revelation find "its fulfillment":

Note: revelation finds its fulfillment properly speaking in intellect or, even more, in the essence of the soul, which, properly speaking seeks existence *(esse)*. To be God, however, is to be naked without any veil *(Esse autem deus esse nudum sine velamine est)*. Or take both together: in the essence of the soul, insofar as it is intellectual, it is, according to Maimonides, bound to the supreme God himself and is thus of the "genus of God." It follows that the essence does not generate in the Godhead *(in divinis)* nor does it bring forth the Word. Nor does it give birth to the Word unless it has the character of intellect. The Son does not proceed unless under the property of intellect.[68]

Thus the very existence of God is his "nakedness" or his revelation of existence: *Esse autem deus esse nudum sine velamine est.* His very existence is to reveal himself, to be Word and this self-revelation can come about only in and through the intellect, which is why Eckhart, in the *Parisian Ques-*

67. For an interesting discussion of the "physics" of the Incarnation and its relevance to the inner life of the soul for Eckhart, see Emilie Zum Brunn and Alain de Libera, *Maître Eckhart: Métaphysique du Verbe et théologie négative* (Paris: Beauchesne, 1984), chap. 2 and passim.

68. *Sermo XI*, n.1; LW IV, 108: "Nota: revelatio proprie est apud intellectum vel potius in essentia animae quae proprie esse respicit. Esse autem deus esse nudum sine velamine est. Vel dic utrumque: in essentia, ut intellectiva, sic copulatur sui supremo deo, secundum Rabbi Moysen, sic est 'genus dei.' Unde essentia non generat in divinis nec verbum profert. Nec enim verbum gignit nisi sub ratione intellectus. Filius non procedit nisi per proprietatem intellectus."

*tions,* says that God is essentially intellect. And so the soul, "which properly speaking, seeks existence" finds existence only insofar as it is purely intellectual, i.e., detached from every finite existent and turned purely inward. Notice here how Eckhart refers again to Maimonides. While, for the Jewish sage, any predication we make of God is utterly inadequate, nevertheless our intellect, as intellect, is of the "genus of God" insofar as it detaches itself from creatures and becomes open to the revelations of God's being as such.

In Eckhart's assertion that "revelation finds its fulfillment properly speaking in the intellect," we find a statement of Eckhart's mystical project in its purity: revelation, properly understood, is a purely inner event immanent in and perfective of the intellect. Revelation is not something that comes from "without" but is an emanation from within, described by Eckhart as a "birth" that comes to the soul not by virtue of its finite existence but by virtue of its potentially infinite intellectual nature. Yet, at the same time, this emanation is not subjective precisely because, in this emanation, God reveals himself not simply "by means of" his Word but as the *Word Itself.* In other words, it is we who are addressed by revelation; our "being" is in question, not that of the Word. Thus, "Word" or communicability is as constitutive of the divine nature as is transcendence. "And I say that the Godhead depends on what he is able to communicate to anyone who is receptive to him and, if he is does not communicate himself, he would not be God."[69] This, for Eckhart, is what is revealed in the Incarnation: using the ancient Patristic formula, that God became man so that man might become God:

> Now it puzzles me that certain priests, who are certainly very learned and want to be important, are so easily satisfied and certainly let themselves be fooled in how they take these words our Lord spoke: "Everything that I have heard from my Father I have made known to you." They want to interpret them thus saying that he has revealed to us "on the way" as much as is necessary for attaining eternal happiness. I do not agree that it is to be thus understood; it just is not the truth. Why did God become man? So that I might be born the same.[70]

In other words, the purpose of revelation is not so much *epistemological* (i.e., to give us "information" about God, though it does do this) but *ontological:* to make us over by grace into God himself.

69. *Pr.* 73; DW III, 265. See also *Pr.* 63; DW III, 81.
70. *Pr.* 29; DW II, 83/TP, 289.

## Reason and Revelation in the Christian and Islamic Mystical Traditions

With regard to the topic of revelation and its place in mystical thought and experience, there can be no doubt that the mystical thought of Ibn ʿArabi and Meister Eckhart is thoroughly exegetical. For both, the mystical act is the recovery of the inner, hidden sense of Scripture, which is itself identical with an appropriation of that sense in the inner ground of the believer. This appropriation or enactment in the soul's ground of the inner sense of Scripture is not, therefore, a new "experience" or "understanding" alongside others but a new *mode* of experiencing and understanding the world and oneself, i.e., in and through God.

Which brings me to the important question that I have bracketed until now: What difference does it make that Ibn ʿArabi and Meister Eckhart appeal to different scriptures for their mystical projects? Is it simply irrelevant that Ibn ʿArabi affirms the Qurʾan as truly authentic revelation while Meister Eckhart affirms the Gospel of Christ as the fullness and perfection of God's revelation? The first and most direct answer is, of course, that it is indeed relevant: the different contents of the Qurʾan and the Bible (though also similar in many striking ways) make the appropriations of their meanings different as well. The most obvious of these differences is that, for Meister Eckhart, the center and root of the mystical meaning of Scripture is Christ, the divine Logos, and the goal of his exegesis is Christ's birth in the ground of the human soul through a detachment and stripping away of all images. Such a person, free from all creaturely being, is the true "nobleman." For Ibn ʿArabi, the center and root of the mystical meaning of the Qurʾan lies in the "wisdoms" (*hikam*, plural in the Arabic) of the prophets. The goal of his exegesis is the assimilation and recovery through the analogical imagination of the inner sense in which these prophets, summed up and completed by Muhammad, understood and enacted in their own lives their successive revelations. Such a person, who has assimilated this meaning, shares in the "word" or "spirit" of Muhammad, as the "seal of the prophets." Such a person is what Sufi terminology calls the "universal man." These goals reflect the differing emphases of the two revelations: for the Christian, the goal of the religious life is regeneration from a fallen and sinful nature in and through Christ; for the

Muslim, it is the return of the human being to his or her primal, Adamic nature.

The historian of Islam Marshall Hodgson sums up the difference between the two revelations in this way:

Christians have seen the world as first corrupted with Adam, thenceforth to be patiently redeemed by a loving God, tirelessly forgiving his people so soon as they respond to His grace, and finally revealing Himself most fully among them as a perfect Life of suffering love, to which they need only respond with love, to be saved from the corruption and made whole. Muslims have seen the world as the proper sphere of Adam's vice-regency; when Adam strayed into error, he turned to God for guidance and was guided; rather than a source of taint in his descendents, he is a model to them. Thenceforth, God continued the guidance through a series of prophetic summonses to a total pattern of living; finally He revealed His transcendent unity most clearly through a perfect Book; if people allow it to remind them of what they are if left to themselves, they will turn to Him and His guidance will enable them to live right and to rule the world in justice. The central event of history for Christians was Christ's crucifixion and resurrection, which most decisively evoke a sense of God's love in him who opens himself to their impact, and lead him to respond to others in the same spirit. The central event of history for Muslims was the descent and preaching of the Qur'an, which most decisively evokes a sense of God's majesty and his own condition in him who opens himself to its impact, and leads him to reflect and submit himself to its norms.[71]

We can see here, in a nutshell, the difference in the ways in which Ibn 'Arabi and Eckhart interpret their respective scriptures, which follows that of their respective religious traditions. For Eckhart, it is to have the Word of Scripture reborn in the very ground of a fallen and corrupted soul so that the soul may become a true Nobleman (*edele Mensch*); for Ibn 'Arabi, it is to understand the inner meaning of the Law or *sharī'ia* that restores the Muslim to the state of perfect vice-regency as the Universal Man (*al-insān al-kāmil*), which is itself a return to the pure, primal nature of humanity (or *fiṭra*) in which the human being was a perfect mirror of God's essential attributes.

This difference becomes most clearly defined in the role of the ana-

---

71. Marshall G. S. Hodgson, *The Venture of Islam: Conscience and History in a World Civilization*, vol. 2, *The Expansion of Islam in the Middle Periods* (Chicago: University of Chicago Press, 1974), 337–38.

logical imagination in the two thinkers. For Ibn 'Arabi, it is the use of the analogical imagination and its perception of the imaginal world that marks the true Sufi. As we have seen, the imaginal world is that ontologically distinct level of reality of symbolic forms that mediates between the world of sense perception and the realm of abstract ideas; it is the realm of prophecy and revelation precisely because it, unlike the other two realms, guides human beings to conformity with God's will through their suggestive power. By spiritualizing the material and materializing the spiritual, the imaginal world and the analogical imagination that perceives it is able to connect the nitty-gritty of daily sensual life and its religious duties as prescribed by the Law to the abstract concepts and commands of philosophy and science by revealing the inner harmony of the two. This is what, for example, al-Ghazali set out to do in his *Revivification of the Religious Sciences:* he set out to show how the requirements of the law can be given an inner, philosophically and even scientifically cogent sense. And the source of this harmony is contained in the symbolic, imaginal world of the Qur'an as perceived and experienced by the Sufi.

In Eckhart, however, we do not find, at least explicitly, the analogical imagination or the imaginal world playing any role. Corbin laments this disappearance of the *mundus imaginalis* in Christianity. For him, this possibility passed with the suppression of the Montanist "heresy" in the third century, making any "prophetic" development of the religion impossible and thereby imprisoning it in a static, bureaucratic ecclesiastical structure. The Incarnation becomes a "purely historical event," incapable of being understood as an eternal event that can be appropriated by esoteric interpretation.[72] Orthodox Christianity has emphasized the historical character of the person and mission of Christ at the expense of their eternal and transcendent character.

But here, despite his great perspicacity, Corbin misses the mark. One cannot read the Nicene Creed, for example, and come away with the impression that orthodox Christianity leaves the eternal nature of the Son unrecognized or ignored. One can also admit that Eckhart, more than perhaps was comfortable for some of the Church authorities of his time, tends to neglect the historical activity and character of the life of Jesus of

72. Corbin, *Alone with the Alone,* 82–83.

Nazareth and to focus most of his attention on Christ's eternal nature. But leaving aside the problem of Corbin's peculiarly Shi'ite understanding of Sufism and, in particular, of a Sunni thinker like Ibn 'Arabi, he fails to see that Eckhart, at least, sees the Incarnation as precisely both a temporal, historical and an eternal event. It is precisely because the Incarnation is both temporal and eternal that the Son can be reborn within the ground of any soul at any time and place, so long as that soul is receptive to this birth. True, Eckhart emphasizes the stripping away of images rather than their creative cultivation; but that is because in his view, Christ performs the function analogous to that of the *mundus imaginalis:* it is Christ who, in his person, materializes the spiritual and spiritualizes the material. To receive Christ is to receive the *mundus imaginalis,* which is to say, to receive the interpretive key not only to all Scripture but to all creation, for in Christ the material becomes spiritual and the spiritual becomes material and the eternal intersects with the temporal.

Thus, the stripping away of all images in order to give birth to the Son in the ground of the soul is itself a form of analogical imagination in reverse—a sort of de-imagination—for this is demanded by the regenerative task of Christianity. By contrast, Ibn 'Arabi enjoins upon the Sufi the assimilation of the Holy Book of the Qur'an, in and through which the imaginal world is received. Though the Qur'an is only a partial concretization of that world, it is, nevertheless, the Qur'an that guides the prophet's and saint's transmutation of creation into a kaleidoscopic theophany. The result should be that he or she in turn becomes a particularly clear and potent divine theophany him or herself. In this way, the prophet or saint returns not only himself but also all of humanity in his person to their primal Adamic nature, which is to be a microcosmic vice-regent of God on earth. For the Christian, however, this has already been achieved by Christ; one simply has to allow Christ to be reborn in the empty, transcendent freedom of one's ground. While Eckhart, therefore, does not have explicitly the concept of the *barzakh* or imaginal world and the "analogical imagination" that has access to that imaginal world, he does have it in deed. As I have shown, much of Eckhart's writing is concerned to show how, when reason is applied to the interpretation of Scripture, the inner meaning and significance of both human reason and divine revelation is disclosed. This disclosure of the inner meaning of reason and revelation opens the soul up for the birth of the Son in the ground of the soul. The concepts of reason and the parables of Scripture point beyond themselves toward the divine and, in particular, toward Christ and his immanent action in the soul when they operate in conjunction. Thus, Eckhart's hermeneutical approach to reason and revelation is a very close, if not exact, analogue of Ibn 'Arabi's use of analogical imagination.

If I may sum up, then: the holy text, in both mystical writers, is both *absolutely necessary* and *absolutely irrelevant* for the inward mystical realization of union with God. It is absolutely necessary because, as we have spent much time showing, the mystical realization is nothing but the realization (or enactment or appropriation) of the hidden, inner meaning of Scripture in the lived inwardness of the believer. It is absolutely irrelevant insofar as this enactment or appropriation of the inner sense of Scripture is inward and is not in the exterior, objectively accessible text itself. I would like to be clear here: it is not as if these are two separate moments in which the text of revelation can be dispensed with as a purely instrumental means to the inner realization. To the contrary, the revealed text is part of the very essence and content of the mystical enactment. In Eckhart, it is the divine Word, no more and no less than the Word of the Gospel, that is born in the ground of the soul. Similarly for Ibn 'Arabi, the Qur'an becomes the very substance of the saint, because the created self has, as such, passed away in the very act of interpretative appropriation and become the transcendent Word. Thus, in the mystical consciousness, there is a great tension between the inward subjective act of appropriation and the transcendent Word or Reality that makes that act possible. Indeed, the more inward the enactment of the hidden sense of revelation, the more transcendent does that sense become. Nevertheless, it is never the case that Ibn 'Arabi, Meister Eckhart, or any other mystical writer of their two traditions ever reaches a state of "pure experience" completely uncolored by their respective revealed texts and traditions—as we shall see, Ibn 'Arabi denies this explicitly and Eckhart implicitly. But what the two revelations do for these two mystical thinkers is that they, to the degree that their inner sense is recovered in mystical exegesis, make the transcendent Divinity ever more and more *present* and *immanent* to the individual soul.

# PART II

❖ Existence

We have all had experience of what the Hungarian chemist and philosopher of science Michael Polanyi called "tacit knowledge": a practical knowledge of "how to go about things" that we, however, cannot describe or explain in words. Saint Augustine gives an example of this sort of knowledge when he talks, in book 11 of his *Confessions*, about time. He notices the great paradox that as long as we do not talk about time, we know what it is, but as soon as we start trying to talk about it, we do not know what it is at all. This is also the great problem or paradox of talking about Being or Existence: as long as we do not talk about it, it seems to be something clear and obvious, but as soon as we start talking about Being or Existence, all of a sudden it becomes a topic fraught with obscurity. We can get at the meaning of existence, or of time or any other such thing, only by way of *analogy*. We say "existence" or "time" is *like* such and such, but in a limited or imperfect way.

Mystical writers such as Ibn 'Arabi and Meister Eckhart have a greatly heightened sense of the analogical nature of all things. All things reflect analogically their divine source insofar as they are all limited manifestations of God's absolute Existence and the infinite knowledge and power that flow from that unbounded Existence. But any idea or concept of God himself will remain elusive. Even creatures are of no help here, because, though they are analogues of the divine Being, that to which they refer remains hidden or obscure to human reason. For both Ibn 'Arabi and Meister Eckhart, reason needs revelation in order not only to know what creatures may tell us about God but also, even more basically, to know creatures as analogues of a divine Being or absolute Existence. For them, therefore, any thinking upon the nature of existence as existence, i.e., any metaphysics worth its salt, must begin with reflection upon the text revealed by God himself. Only God himself can give us an adequate idea of who God is. To our limited intellects, this text is obscure, but it is, at least, something. Sacred Scripture gives the analogical key (or keys) to the inner meaning of all creatures, making them understandable in light of God's own revelation of himself. Mystical thought and experience are, as I noted in the introduction, concerned first and foremost with making inwardly concrete and immanent in the soul the transcendent and absolute Existence of God. The soul cannot do this through thought or even through virtue alone, but only through a meditation upon the inner meanings of things given in the sacred text of his or her tradition.

For the contemporary reader, what is perhaps most remarkable about the writing of mystical thinkers like Ibn 'Arabi and Meister Eckhart is the lack of arguments or "proofs" of what the contemporary reader probably feels is most in need of demonstration: the existence of God. Such arguments are indeed lacking: in the general prologues to Eckhart's *Opus tripartitum,* there are what appear to be "proofs" of God's existence, which, upon closer inspection, are not quite what they seem. The initial temptation is to attribute this oversight simply to the fact that a pious Muslim or Christian of the thirteenth or fourteenth centuries could not have thought otherwise. They simply take the existence of God for granted, unlike us more sophisticated moderns. This response seems, prima facie, plausible; but I want to argue that it would be wrong.

In the first place, proofs or demonstrations of God's existence were not unknown to either thinker: there was already in both the Muslim and Christian traditions a long history of giving proofs or demonstrations of God's existence. Nor do Ibn 'Arabi or Eckhart take the existence of God for granted, merely assuming it and then moving on to their "mystical speculations." Their work lacks formal proofs of God's existence because what they are reflecting upon and writing about is deeper. For Ibn 'Arabi and Meister Eckhart, the notion of what is meant by "God" is thoroughly *dialectical.* In their way of thinking, "God" cannot be the "object" of any proof—indeed, God cannot be an object of any sort. In Ibn 'Arabi's understanding, the "Real" or "Truth" (al-ḥaqq) is God, and in Eckhart's, "existence" or *esse* is God, so God cannot be merely an object among other objects. The meaning of "God," these two medievals contend, must be grasped therefore as dialectical, as both the subject and the object of all thought and all being. Or to put it in other terms, God is both what is most transcendent to all things and also what is most immanent in all things.

What is very important to appreciate in Ibn 'Arabi and Eckhart is the logical rigor or necessity of this understanding of God's nature as dialectical. The absolute transcendence of God necessarily demands his immanence in all things, for what makes God transcendent is God's existence and sustenance of all that is. Likewise, God's true and utter immanence necessarily implies transcendence because what is inmost in all things is precisely that which escapes limitation and objectification into a "this" or a "that." Again, the logic here is clear: as Ibn 'Arabi puts it, to assert only the transcendence of God without his immanence is, in effect, to limit him, because you are marking him off from creatures. And to assert his immanence without asserting his transcendence is to limit him to the sum of finite creatures. Similarly for Eckhart, God's distinction from creatures, his transcendence, lies precisely in his indistinction from all things, i.e., in his immanence in all things as their existence, oneness, truth, and goodness—in short, as the transcendental properties that "run through" all the categories of existence and that all creatures have insofar as they exist.

As it stands so far, however, the two writers' understanding of God as dialectical is speculative and abstract, which, indeed, would be the case if such understanding were to be separated from the reading and interpretation of sacred texts. For both Ibn 'Arabi and Meister Eckhart, however, this dialectical theology arises out of and in turn informs an engagement of the whole person with the interpretation of the sacred text. As we saw in the last section, it is in applying the truths of reason as given by metaphysics and science to the interpretation of a transcendent revelation that the believer finds the inner meaning, which is to say the immanent presence of God in creation and, most of all, in oneself.[1] What is, then, innermost

---

1. See Largier's essay "*Figuratio Locutio*" in relation to Eckhart's work.

to the human being is also outermost to all beings. Thus revelation breaks the solipsism of human reason precisely by turning, paradoxically, the human soul away from its abstract speculations to its lived, inner experience of God's transcendent presence within itself and within all things. It follows from this that, while proofs of God's existence are important and in certain contexts useful, true, and necessary, they are, in the context of what Ibn 'Arabi and Meister Eckhart are doing, superfluous. They become superfluous because both Ibn 'Arabi and Eckhart ground their teachings of God not on abstract philosophical speculations but on a living contact with God as necessarily mediated by their respective scriptures.

3

# "You Are He and You Are Not He"

*The Dialectic of Transcendence and Immanence in Ibn 'Arabi*

In his *Futūḥāt al-makkiyya*, Ibn 'Arabi asserts the following about the power of human reasoning and its relation to prophetic revelation:

Know that, before his prophecy, no prophet ever knew God through rational consideration, and it is not proper for any prophet to do so. In the same way, the chosen friend of God has no prior knowledge of God through rational consideration. Any friend of God who has prior knowledge of God in respect of reflective consideration is not "chosen," even though he is a friend of God, nor is he one of those to whom God has given the inheritance of the Divine Book.[1]

For Ibn 'Arabi, true wisdom does not result from human reasoning, since human reasoning only limits reality to its measure: rather true wisdom is the intellect's "opening" (*futūḥ*), in which the divine Reality or Truth (*ḥaqq*) is revealed to it, what Ibn 'Arabi calls "unveiling" or *kashf*. In Ibn 'Arabi's thought, then, knowledge of God, whether by the prophet (*nabī*) or "friend of God" (*walī*)[2] can

---

1. III 402.13 in SDG, 14.

2. This is an important distinction that cannot be treated adequately here. See Michel Chodkiewicz, *The Seal of the Saints: Prophethood and Sainthood in the Doctrine of Ibn 'Arabi* trans. Liadain Sherrard (Cambridge: Islamic Texts Society, 1993). Basically, in Islam, there can be no prophet after Muhammad; the door to prophecy has been closed till the Last Judgment. But the door of "friendship with God" (*walāyya*) has not been

come not by rational consideration but by an "unveiling" that reveals the divine Reality, all the while showing the limits of human reason or what Ibn 'Arabi calls "rational consideration."[3] Thus the highest wisdom results in a sort of perplexity or *ḥayra* whereby the "knower by *kashf*" or unveiling (the *'ārif*, commonly translated "gnostic" or "knower") in the true Socratic fashion knows what he does not know.

God is both "incomparable" or transcendent to all things as well as "comparable" to or immanent in all things—or, to put it in Ibn 'Arabi's Sufi terminology, all creatures are "both He and not He." Thus, any rigorous way of speaking about God must employ paradoxes and contradictions, since to say one thing about God logically implies, by the very idea of God, its opposite. Thus we have the paradox that, for us to speak rationally and logically of God, we must do something that, on the face of it, is irrational and illogical or, as Ibn 'Arabi would put it, goes beyond rational consideration. Thus, in the works of Ibn 'Arabi, it becomes clear that when he talks about God, he does so in a dialectical manner, saying something of God and then immediately negating what he has said. Indeed, his dialectic is so thoroughgoing that it seems designed to lead to perplexity, to a "holy confusion" or "learned ignorance." This essentially dialectical theology, in both understanding and presentation, is probably what so bewildered his contemporaries and many of the more *sharī'a*-based scholars and theologians for centuries after his death.

### The Wisdom of Exaltation in the Word of Noah

In Islam, as in all the Semitic monotheisms, God is, in a sense, wholly other: as the Qur'an states, "There is none like unto Him" (42:11). "Islam"

---

closed and can be acquired by any gnostic who has insight into the inner meaning of revelation. Thus, while in the *Fuṣūṣ* Ibn 'Arabi is talking about prophets and the nature of prophecy, in general he means much of what he says to apply to the "friends of God" (*Āwliā'*) as well.

3. This is why Ibn 'Arabi is wary of and even hostile to rational proofs of God's existence: to try to prove rationally God's existence is to try to make God fit within the bounds of human reason, which is both blasphemous and idolatrous. We can know the Real only insofar as the Real reveals itself to us because otherwise we would have the absurdity of forcing the Real to conform to the categories of the less real. For the fact is that it is not God's nature and existence that are obscure but rather it is we who are obscure, in the sense that it is we who cover over Reality with our self-certain unexamined assumptions and categories: "No proof of Him can ever be safe from obfuscation, because He is the Greatest Proof, and we are His obfuscation." IV 442.31 in SDG, 15.

itself means "submission": i.e., submission to what is wholly other than oneself or any other creature. This otherness or transcendence of God was the message of the prophet Noah, one that Ibn ʿArabi interprets in the chapter of the *Fuṣūṣ* dedicated to the "wisdom" of Noah and, in particular, the *sura* of the Qurʾan (no. 71) named after Noah. The full title of the chapter, as for all the chapters of the *Fuṣūṣ*, is significant: "The Wisdom of Exaltation [*sabbūḥiyya*] in the Word of Noah." Every prophet in the *Fuṣūṣ* expresses a particular wisdom which is itself a manifestation of a divine name or "word." Thus, every prophet represents in the matrix of space and time an eternal facet of the divine.[4]

The particular wisdom that is manifested by the word of Noah is that of *exaltation*, that is, *tanzīh* or the "incomparability" or utter transcendence of the Reality or Truth *(al-ḥaqq)*. As the *sura* of Noah in the Qurʾan clearly states, Noah was sent by God to announce the "incomparability" of God and his utter distinction from the created idols that his people worshipped. In this sense, then, Noah is, like many of the other prophets, a messenger of pure monotheism to an idolatrous, polytheistic people.

Yet, as with many things in the thought of Ibn ʿArabi, the matter is not quite so simple. For the doctrine of *tanzīh*, taken alone and without its dialectical opposite, *tashbīh* (similarity or immanence), can itself become a form of idolatry. Ibn ʿArabi explains at the beginning of the chapter:

For those who [truly] know the divine Realities, the doctrine of transcendence imposes a restriction and a limitation [on the Reality], for he who asserts that God is [purely] transcendent is either a fool or a rogue, even if he is a professed believer. For, if he maintains that God is [purely] transcendent and excludes all other considerations, he acts mischievously and misrepresents the Reality and all the apostles, albeit unwittingly. He imagines that he has hit on the truth,

4. S. H. Nasr makes this same point very well when he says: "The human and individual nature of each prophet is in turn contained in the logos, or word *(kalimah)*, which is his essential reality and which is a determination of the Supreme Word, or the 'primordial enunciation of God.' That is why the chapters are entitled 'The Bezel of Divine Wisdom in the Adamic Word,' 'The Bezel of the Wisdom of Inspiration in the Word of Seth,' and so on, until it ends with the 'Bezel of the Wisdom of Singularity in the Word of Muhammad.' Whereas, humanly speaking, the human and individual aspects of the prophets seem to 'contain' their essential and universal aspects as the bezel 'englobes' the precious jewel, in reality the relation is reversed. It is the inner reality, the supra-individual aspect of the prophet that contains and determines the bezel. The divine revelation is 'colored' by its recipient while from a universal point of view the recipient itself is a divine possibility determined from above and contained by its celestial prototype." S. H. Nasr, *Three Muslim Sages* (Delmar, N.Y.: Caravan Books, 1964), 99.

while he has [completely] missed the mark, being like those who believe in part and deny in part.[5]

According to Ibn 'Arabi, *tanzīh*, or God's transcendence or "incomparability," must be negated by *tashbīh*, God's utter immanence or "comparability," if we are truly to grasp the truth about God's nature:

The truth is that the Reality is manifest in every created being and in every concept, while He is [at the same time] hidden from all understanding, except for one who holds that the Cosmos is His form and His identity. This is the Name, the Manifest, while He is also unmanifested Spirit, the Unmanifest. In this sense He is, in relation to the manifested forms of the Cosmos, the Spirit that determines those forms.[6]

Any doctrine of pure transcendence would make God a "thing" or "entity" distinct from creation; but that is the same as saying that God is limited and that there is distinction in his unity, which is impossible. Thus God is manifest (*zāhir*) in all things, but he is also nonmanifest or hidden (*bāṭin*) in all things for the very same reason that he is manifest in all things. Since human reason knows only by categorizing (i.e., limiting) what it perceives, God remains hidden behind his unlimited manifestation of himself in creation.[7] Or, as Ibn 'Arabi succinctly puts it in his *Futūḥāt*:

The manifest of the Real is creation,
    and the nonmanifest of creation is the Real.[8]

There is thus a sense in which God's incomparability, his *tanzīh*, is logically prior to his similarity or *tashbīh* with creation.[9] This incomparability,

5. *Bezels*, 73/68.

6. *Bezels*, 73/68.

7. Chittick puts it well when he says: "To Himself He is manifest, but to others He is non-manifest. Hence nonmanifestation is a quality that can only be understood in terms of creation." Also: "Inasmuch as *wujud* is hidden from us, God is the Nonmanifest, but inasmuch as the whole cosmos is *wujud*'s self-disclosure, God is the Manifest." SDG, 206.

8. IV 246.1 in SDG, 206.

9. "When Ibn al-'Arabi speaks about the Essence as such, he has in view God's incomparability. In this respect there is little one can say about God, except to negate (*salb*) the attributes of created things from Him. Nevertheless, the Essence is God as He is in Himself, and God must exist in Himself before He reveals Himself to others. Both logically and ontologically, incomparability precedes similarity. It is the ultimate reference point for everything we say about God. A great deal can indeed be said about Him—that, after all, is what religion and revelation are all about—but once said, it must also be negated. Our doctrines, theologies, and philosophies exist like other things, which is to say that they also are He/not He. Discerning the modalities and

since it is incomparable, is unknowable to the human intellect, which is why all those who, like Noah, speak correctly about God negate all that is limited and finite of God.[10] Likewise, Islam is right to emphasize, for the mass of believers, the transcendent side of the divine dialectic, but of course, though God's *tanzīh* is logically prior to his *tashbīh*, to assert the first without eventually asserting the second paradoxically ends up limiting God to the categories of human thought.

For Ibn 'Arabi the essential incomparability of God means, dialectically speaking, that God can be compared to everything, which leads to the assertion that any definition of the Reality or *ḥaqq* is ultimately impossible:

> Thus a [true] definition of the Reality is impossible, for such a definition would depend on the ability to define [fully] every form in the Cosmos, which is impossible. Therefore a [complete] definition of the Reality is impossible.[11]

Any knowledge of God is one that transcends definitions by uniting dialectically two opposites, that of comparability or immanence and that of incomparability or transcendence, in such a way that we know God not in detail or by definition but in a "general way":

> It is similar in the case of one who professes the comparability of God without taking into consideration His incomparability, so that he also restricts and limits Him and therefore does not know Him. He, however, who unites in his knowledge of God both transcendence and immanence in a comprehensive way, it not being possible to know such a thing in detail, owing to the infinitude of Cosmic forms, knows Him in a general way, but not in a detailed way, as he may know himself generally but not in detail.[12]

The point is that the true knower of God does not put *any* limit on the Real to the extent that even nonlimitation would be a limitation on the Real: God's *tanzīh* itself must be transcended. Al-Qashani, the well-known commentator on Ibn 'Arabi, explains:

---

relationships, distinguishing the true from the false and the more true from the less true, is the essence of wisdom." SPK, 9.

10. "Only Being—the Necessary Being—is absolutely unquestionable and unambiguous. But since It is utterly free of every limitation that can be applied to anything else, we can only know It by negating from it all the ambiguities of 'that which is other than Being.'... From this point of view, true knowledge of God can only come through negation." SPK, 12.

11. *Bezels*, 74/68.

12. *Bezels*, 74/69.

The gist of what is asserted here is the following. He who "purifies" God puri-fies Him from all bodily attributes, but by that very act he is (unconsciously) "assimilating" *(tashbīh)* Him with non-material, spiritual beings. What about, then, if one "purifies" Him from "limiting" *(taqyīd)* itself? Even in that case he will be "limiting" Him with "non-limitation" *(iṭlāq)*, while in truth God is "puri-fied" from (i.e., transcends) the fetters of both "limitation" and "non-limitation." He is absolutely absolute; He is not delimited by either of them, nor does He even exclude either of them.[13]

The Real, according to Ibn 'Arabi, cannot be bound or limited by anything other than itself, even to the point where it cannot be limited by non-limitation. As such, God is "rich" in himself, in need of nothing, including the limitation of being unlimited, in order to exist, nor of anything else in order to be such and such. By contrast, the creature is "poor" in existence because it is in need of another both for its existence and for the limits that make it essentially what it is.[14] The creature manifests the Real by its existence but covers it over by its essential limitedness and finitude. For this reason, Ibn 'Arabi states that we, as creatures, are both "He and not He": we are he insofar as we manifest his qualities in the realm of created manifestation; but we are not he insofar as we manifest these qualities in a limited way.[15]

It follows then that, as Ibn 'Arabi says above, we can know the Real, much like ourselves, only in a general way as manifesting an immeasurable and invisible depth. Concerning a *ḥadīth* that he was particularly fond of citing, he writes:

In this connection the Prophet said, "Who [truly] knows himself knows his Lord," linking together knowledge of God and knowledge of the self. God says, *We will show them our signs on the horizons,* meaning the world outside you, *and in yourselves,* self, here, meaning your inner essence, *till it becomes clear to them*

13. Al-Qashani, as cited in Toshihiko Izutsu, *Sufism and Taoism,* 50.

14. "As Ibn al-'Arabi constantly quotes from the Koran, God is 'Independent of the worlds' in respect of the Essence. The term *ghinā* signifies independence, wealth, and having need of noth-ing. God has all wealth—Being and all Its attributes—in Himself, so He is independent of the cosmos and needs nothing whatsoever from it. The opposite of *ghinā* is *faqr,* 'poverty' or 'need,' which . . . is the essential and inherent attribute of all created or 'temporally originated' *(ḥadīth)* things. Everything other than God is constantly in need of God, not only for its existence, but also for every positive attribute it displays, since these attributes are nothing but the properties and effects of the divine names." SPK, 64.

15. *Sharḥ,* I, 291.

*that He is the Reality,* in that you are His form and He is your Spirit. You are in relation to Him as your physical body is to you. He is in relation to you as the spirit governing your physical form.[16]

In other words, God stands in the same relation to the world as our inner self stands to our body. Our inner self is the "hidden" or *bāṭin* behind the "manifestation" or *ẓāhir* of the body. Nevertheless, the two are essentially and by definition one: the human body is only a human body insofar as it is a manifestation of the spirit hidden within, otherwise the body would be a mere statue called "human" only by equivocation.[17] The Aristotelian definition of the human being, that we are "rational animals," for example, takes account, in our two parts, of the outer and inner aspects of the human being: we are "animals" with respect to our outer aspect, but "rational" with respect to our inner aspect. Both aspects are essential; otherwise, our outer or formal aspect would be indistinct by definition from a statue in wood or stone of a human being.

Ibn 'Arabi extends this analogy to creation as a whole and its relation to God. The Real necessarily manifests itself in creation, but creation would be a dead, logical abstraction, i.e., mere *extension*, without the divinity animating it:

On the other hand, the Reality never withdraws from the forms of the Cosmos in any fundamental sense, since the Cosmos, in its reality, is [necessarily] implicit in the definition of the Divinity, not merely figuratively as with a man when living in the body.[18]

Moreover, as Ibn 'Arabi states above, this analogy also applies to the inner self of the human being: this inner self is, in turn, but an outer manifestation of the Real. Thus, in no way is the inner human being identical with the divine: rather its own nature is only analogous to the inner, hidden dimension of God's self-manifestation in the cosmos. As a created thing, human reason, with its categories and concepts, lays over the Real only so many limitations—and manifestations—of the Real and its essential possibilities, which Ibn 'Arabi calls the divine names. As such, the Real is the observer hidden in every act of consciousness, which is in turn but an out-

16. *Bezels,* 74/69.
17. *Bezels,* 74/69.
18. *Bezels,* 74/69.

er manifestation of the Real who is most intimately hidden in the soul.[19]

Thus every creature gives praise to God just as the tongue of the "outer man" gives praise to the "inner man" that governs it. Here, of course, we return to the theme of the chapter, which is the "wisdom of exaltation" or "praise" (*ḥikma sabbuḥiyya*) in the "word of Noah." As outer manifestations of the inner Real, all creatures exalt him who gives them life and breath. This praise Ibn 'Arabi sums up in several lines of poetry:

> If you insist only on His transcendence, you restrict Him.
>> And if you insist only on His immanence you limit Him.
> If you maintain both aspects you are right,
>> An Imam and a master in the spiritual sciences.
> Whoso would say He is two things is a polytheist,
>> While the one who isolates Him tries to regulate Him.
> Beware of comparing Him if you profess duality,
>> And, if unity, beware of making Him transcendent.
> You are not He and you are He and
>> You see Him in the essences of things both boundless and limited.[20]

A better and more concise statement of the dialectical nature of Ibn 'Arabi's idea of God can perhaps not be found. For Ibn 'Arabi, the most forceful teacher of the dialectical nature of God is the Holy Qur'an, which in subtle but powerful ways, calls us to experience God as simultaneously immanent and transcendent. In this light, the message (*risala*) of Noah was imperfect: he called his people to a worship of God only as utterly transcendent, neglecting God's immanence in all things—an imperfection that the Qur'an corrects. In this connection, Ibn 'Arabi distinguishes the Qur'an from what the Qur'an itself calls the *Furqān* (which is normally simply understood as a synonym for the Qur'an). The root of *furqān* is *faraqa*, which means to divide or discriminate. Thus, the message of Noah is one of *furqān* because Noah calls on his people to discriminate between the one God of creation and all created idols. The Qur'an, however, calls

19. There is thus, as al-Qaysari points out, a direct parallel between the relation of God to the world and the traditional Aristotelian definition of the human being as a "rational animal": as al-Qaysari explains, "animal" refers to the manifest nature of human beings, while "rational" refers to their nonmanifest or *batin* nature. As a microcosm, human beings are defined by the interplay of the manifest and nonmanifest and, as such, already have a hermeneutical "pre-understanding" of the existential interplay between God, nonmanifest Existence-in-itself, and the world, or manifested, created existence. *Sharḥ*, I, 285.

20. *Bezels*, 75/70.

humanity to experience God as immanent in all things, precisely because God is so utterly transcendent: "The whole truth is a conjunction [al-qur'ān (qarana) as the whole revelation] and not a discrimination [al-furqān (faraqa) a chapter of the Qur'an, i.e., a part]."[21] The difference between the "Qur'ān" and the "Furqān" is that the latter calls humanity to a pure transcendence, while the former corrects this one-sided message with one that calls humanity to embrace simultaneously God's transcendence *and* immanence.

There is thus a bit of a game that arises between Noah and his people, according to Ibn 'Arabi. On the one hand you have Noah, who "summoned his people *by night,* in that he appealed to their intellects and spirits, which are unseen, and *by day,* in that he appealed to the [evidence of] their external senses. But he did not unite the two as in the verse *There is none like unto Him.*"[22] On the other hand, you have the people of Noah, who recoiled—in a sense, justifiably, according to Ibn 'Arabi—from this doctrine of pure transcendence or discrimination. They were therefore, again, in a sense, right to turn away from Noah. Izutsu puts this dynamic well:

Thus we see that the relation of Noah with his people, as Ibn 'Arabi understands it, has a complex inner structure. On the one hand, Noah, as we have just observed, outwardly reproaches his people for their faithlessness, but inwardly he praises them because of the right attitude they have taken on this crucial question. On the other hand, the people, on their part, know, if not consciously, that pure monotheism in its true and deep sense is not to reduce God to one of his aspects such as implied by the kind of *tanzīh* advocated by Noah, but to worship the One God in all the concrete forms of the world as so many manifestations of God. Outwardly, however, they give the impression of committing an outrageous mistake by refusing to accept Noah's admonition and exhorting each other to stick to the traditional form of idol-worship.[23]

What Ibn 'Arabi is arguing is that the transcendence that the Qur'an teaches is not a purely abstract transcendence, but rather a concrete and dynamic transcendence that manifests itself in all things in a variety of apparently contradictory attributes (i.e., the manifest and the hidden, the merciful and the wrathful, etc.) that only it can unite in itself. Again, Izutsu is helpful here:

21. *Bezels,* 76/70.          22. *Bezels,* 76/70–71.
23. Izutsu, *Sufism and Taoism,* 59.

Real *tanzīh* is something quite different from this kind of logical *tanzīh*. And according to Ibn 'Arabi, the right kind of *tanzīh* was first advocated consciously by Islam. It does not consist in recognizing the absolute Unknowable alone with a total rejection and denial of the phenomenal world of things. The real *tanzīh* is established on the basis of the experience by which man becomes conscious of the unification of the Divine Attributes, each Attribute being actualized in a concrete thing or event in the world. In more plain terms, the real *tanzīh* consists in man's peeping through the things and events of this world into the grand figure of the One God beyond them. It is "purifying" *(tanzīh)*, no doubt, because it stands on the consciousness of the essential "oneness" of God, but it is not a purely logical or intellectual "purifying." It is a *tanzīh* which comprises in itself *tashbīh*.[24]

That is why, for Ibn 'Arabi, intellection of the Real can find a proper support only in the concrete imagery of the Qur'an and its interpretation and not in pure rational consideration.

A pure knowledge of God, then, in which we contemplate God as an object free from all similarity to creatures is impossible. "Whoever imagines that he sees the Reality Himself has no gnosis; he has gnosis who knows that it is his own essential self he sees. Thus are the Folk *(ahl)* divided into those who know and those who do not know."[25] Henry Corbin explains the Shaykh's meaning in this way: "The authentic mystic wisdom *(ma'rifa)* is that of the soul which knows *itself* as a theophany, an individual form in which are epiphanized the divine Attributes which it would be unable to know if it did not discover and apprehend them in itself."[26] The one who knows in the deepest sense of unveiling or *kashf* is one who knows himself and his knowledge as only a manifestation of one of the names or possibilities of the hidden divine unity. As Ibn 'Arabi puts it:

The heir of Muhammad knows that the summons to God is not a summons to His Ipseity [Essence or *huwiyya*], but to Him in respect of His Names [modes]. He says, *On the day when we will gather together the guarding ones in a band,* indicating that they will come before God in the [all-embracing] Name the Merciful [not before God in His Essence]. We know that the Cosmos is under the rule of a divine Name that makes all in it guarding [guarded—*mutaqayīn*].[27]

The true knower of God knows God not as an object over and against himself but rather he knows himself as a manifestation or theophany of a

---

24. Ibid., 62–63.  
26. Corbin, *Alone with the Alone,* 133.

25. *Bezels,* 77/71.  
27. *Bezels,* 78/72.

divine name. It is the Real (*al-ḥaqq*) that is the true subject of knowledge: the gnostic simply knows himself as a manifestation of the Essence that has no being of his own but, from the divine standpoint, is a pure dependent relation to the divine Existence.

The *tanzīh* of God indicates that God is beyond all that we can define and limit by our reason; but the *tashbīh* of God indicates that God is the true knower immanent in every act of knowledge. God is both what is most distant from our knowledge and what is closest and most intimate to every act of knowing. This is because God, as the Real, is the all-encompassing. God is both absolute object and absolute subject of all knowing. As Ibn 'Arabi says in the *Futūḥāt*:

He encompasses us, and in every direction the "behind" of us belongs to Him. In respect of this verse, we will never see Him, because our faces are turned toward the center point of the encompassing circumference. We have emerged from that point, so we are not able to turn our faces toward any but it. It is our *kiblah*, and it is our Imam and that of all who have this description.[28]

To use Ibn 'Arabi's spatial metaphor, God cannot be known in the usual way because God is both "behind" and "before" us. In other words, knowledge of God or existence in itself is not "linear": it does not consist in a line between the human subject and the divine object, each of them existing independently of the other. Rather, the knowledge of God is circular: the subject of the act of knowing is, in a very fundamental sense, the object known and the object known is the subject. Ibn 'Arabi prefers to think of the Real, insofar as it can be thought of all, as an encompassing sphere or circle that enfolds in itself subject and object, knower and known. Again, he says in the *Futūḥāt*:

The cosmos is between the center point and the encompassing circumference. The center point is the First, and the circumference is the Last. So the divine preservation accompanies us wherever we may be. It directs us away from Him toward Him. The affair is a circle. It has no extremity which can be witnessed or at which one can halt.[29]

It follows then that the thought of the realized knower (or "gnostic") moves in a circle: he or she does not try to grasp the Real as an object to

28. IV 13.32 in SDG, 226.
29. IV 13.32 in SDG, 226.

be fit into a category, but rather he or she is seized by the "object" in holy "perplexity" or *ḥayra*.

The movement of *ḥayra* is similar to that of a circle. The Sufi moves around God in a circle with God as the "pole" or *quṭb*. This is not, of course, to be thought of as opposed to the *ṣurāṭ al-mustaqīm* of the Qur'an, but rather as its fulfillment. The opposite of the Sufi movement of knowledge is movement that is *mustatil* ("drawn-out, linear, stretched, presumptuous, arrogant"). This is why the Prophet said, "Lord, increase me in my perplexity of You." Rational certainty abides in a cramped world cut down to the size of human reason; *ḥayra*, however, is open to the infinite play of the Real in creation and, in a deep sense, allows the realized knower to *become* the Real. As Ibn 'Arabi explains:

He who experiences this perplexity is ceaselessly centered on the Pole [God], while he who follows the "long" path [to a distant God] is always turning aside from the [Supreme] Goal to search after that which is [eternally] within him, running after imagination as his goal. He has an [imaginary] starting point and [what he supposes to be] a goal and what lies between them, while for the God-centered man there is no restriction of beginning or end, possessing [as he does] the most comprehensive existence and being the recipient of [divine] truths and realities.[30]

The gnostic is one who knows that God is not distant as an object "out there" but as the One who is immanent in his very being and the ground of his very knowing.[31] The knowledge of the Sufi is one that is able to grasp in its two distinct aspects the immanence and transcendence of being. The gnostic is God from one aspect and not God from another. Thus the Qur'anic verse, "There is none like unto Him."[32] The realized knower is able to intuit the ultimate unity of opposites in the divine Essence. As Izutsu explains:

What we must emphasize before everything else is that, in Ibn 'Arabi's worldview, the whole world is the locus of theophany or the self-manifestation of

30. *Bezels*, 79/73.

31. As al-Qaysari explains, the one who is possessed of *ḥayra* moves in a circle because, toward whatever creature he or she turns, there he or she beholds the divine Existence, realizing that the pole of existence, the eternal Essence that is Existence itself, is centered in no other than him- or herself. (*Sharḥ*, I, 309) Thus, in the state of *ḥayra*, the gnostic sees God *in all* manifestations. (I, 310)

32. Affifi, *Remarks*, 36.

the Absolute, and that, consequently, all the things and events of the world are self-determinations of the Absolute. Therefore, the world of Being cannot be grasped in its true form except as a synthesis of contradictions. Only by a simultaneous affirmation of contradictories can we understand the real nature of the world. And the "perplexity" is nothing other than the impression produced on our minds by the observation of the simultaneous existence of contradictories.[33]

What of course is difficult to understand is that we normally think of perplexity as the *starting point* of inquiry, which subsequent rational inquiry is supposed to remove. But, as is typical for Ibn 'Arabi in particular and Sufism in general, we must think in the reverse sense: when it comes to knowledge of God or the Reality, it is rather rational certainty that is the starting point that must be removed by a perplexity that puts the entire knower into question. We shall have an opportunity to return to this point at the end of this chapter. But first, let us turn to a chapter from the *Bezels* whose themes are intimately connected with that on Noah, namely the chapter on the Qur'anic prophet Hūd.[34] In this chapter of the *Bezels*, Ibn 'Arabi describes how the realized knower of God must look at creation with "two eyes," the "eye of transcendence" or "incomparability" and the "eye of immanence" or "comparability." The eyes of the realized knower do not see two separate things or aspects of reality, but see these aspects as one phenomenon, as one sees pure light through colored glass.

### The Dialectic of Divine Unity in the Word of Hūd

Ibn 'Arabi begins his discourse on divine unity in the chapter on Hūd with this poem:

The Straight Path of God is not hidden,
    But manifest universally.
He is essentially in all things great or small,
    Ignorant of truth or aware.
Thus does His Mercy embrace all things,
    Be they mean or mighty.[35]

---

33. Izutsu, *Sufism and Taoism*, 74.
34. For the close thematic connection between these chapters, see Affifi, *Remarks*, 127.
35. *Bezels*, 129–30/106.

As Ibn 'Arabi's medieval commentator al-Qaysari explains, it is the Truth (al-ḥaqq) that is primarily apprehended by the gnostic, while the creature is only surmised (ma'qul), whereas for most people it is only the creature that is apprehended and God who is surmised. But even ordinary people apprehend, if not explicitly like the gnostic, at least implicitly, the relative nature of creatures through a prior apprehension of the Truth.[36] For this reason, Ibn 'Arabi says that divine Mercy precedes divine Wrath. If the divine Mercy is that which embraces all things by giving them existence, according to Ibn 'Arabi, divine Mercy is logically and ontologically prior to divine Wrath. Just as error, which, as misapprehension of truth, presupposes truth, so does wrath ultimately stem from mercy and presuppose mercy, since it is through divine Mercy that all things have their existence. Thus, the realized knower is one who exists and knows in and through God, and not in and through himself, because the gnostic apprehends God but only "surmises" himself.[37] The gnostic intuits directly the priority of the Real to the point where the reality of finite creatures, including himself, becomes only a conjecture; whereas those who are lacking in this inner awareness perceive only finite, limited things first and then, if they are more thoughtful than average, conjecture the Oneness of the Real.[38] In this way, the gnostic calls upon God not from the habit of mere tradition, but from insight and self-knowledge: "The gnostic calls on God with spiritual perception, while he who is not a gnostic calls on Him in ignorance and bound by a tradition."[39]

The realized knower or gnostic therefore does not limit the Real in thought or will, but allows it to be to such a degree that subject and object become inverted in the act of knowing: the known becomes the knower. Therefore, "in the Shaykh's view, existence and knowledge are two names for the same reality; it is impossible to discuss one without the other."[40] As the Shaykh says in the Futūḥāt:

> My entity is nothing but He,
>     So I do not refuse Him.

36. *Sharḥ*, II, 14.
37. *Bezels*, 130/106.
38. *Bezels*, 132/108. *Sharḥ*, II, 16.
39. *Bezels*, 132/108.
40. SPK, 91.

Whoever witnesses with the eye
      Of *wujud* witnesses Him.
In Him we are equal—
      As He sees me, I see Him.[41]

Indeed, what the gnostic knows is that there is no knower save God, the Real: "Further, there is no Knower save He; so who are you? Therefore, know your true reality and your way, for the truth has been made clear to you on the tongue of the Interpreter [Muhammad], if you will only understand."[42] When the knower does not realize this insight, then his or her "knowledge" of God is not knowledge but a concealment of the true situation.[43] For Ibn 'Arabi, therefore, reason can be "meddlesome" (*fuḍūl*) because it covers over with its preconceptions and categories the direct apprehension of the Real that is within and is the ground of our existence.[44] Ibn 'Arabi does not, however, recommend that we cast reason aside; far from it. But what the true gnostic knows is that reason conceals as much as it reveals and that a higher intellection is necessary if we are to know God in truth.

So what is this higher intellection? For Ibn 'Arabi, it is self-knowledge and it is this that he pursues in his chapter on Hūd, a quest that he sees as essentially bound up in the quest for the divine unity. Without knowledge of the self, its preconceptions, assumptions, and self-made "gods" and "lords," the soul cannot have any true knowledge of the Real itself. As William Chittick puts it: "Self-knowledge is an absolutely necessary precondition for any real knowledge, that is, any knowledge of the Real. But the

41. III 549.20 in SDG, 83.

42. *Bezels*, 132/109.

43. "Then it is said to him, 'Be cautious of the folk of the curtains lest they lead you on step by step to the curtains. They are the folk of deceit and deception. Is there a curtain over Him who, in relation to you, is *nearer than the jugular vein* [50:16]? He is curtained from you only through you, so you are identical with His curtain over you. Were you to see your own nonmanifest side, you would see Him." III 229.8 in SDG, 121.

44. "Some rational faculties are meddlesome (*fuḍūl*) because of the faculties which are their tools [e.g., reflection and consideration]. . . . This meddlesome nature leads to rational consideration of the Essence of God, though the Law has prohibited reflection upon God's Essence. Such a rational faculty slips into considering the Essence, thereby transgressing and wronging itself. It sets up what it supposes are proofs . . . that the Essence of God cannot be such and such, nor can It be in such a manner. Reason negates from the Essence everything that is attributed to temporally originated things so that It will be distinct from them. Thereby it constricts the Essence and considers It delimited." II 389.1 in SPK, 71.

cosmos is full of veils, and the greatest of veils, even greater than the quest for objectivity, is the self that knows."[45] In innumerable ways that escape the rational mind, we cover over and "color" Reality with our concepts and categories, our desires and fears. For Ibn ʿArabi, the essential Self of all things is God, while the finite, created self of the human being is simply a veil or covering of this essential Self or Unity:

God, Most High, has described Himself as Jealous [that aught should exist but Himself], and it is because of this that He "forbade excesses," which means that which is manifest and apparent. As for that which is unmanifest, it is [excessive] for him to whom it is apparent [in himself]. Thus, He forbade excesses [relative existence], that is, He prevented the real secret from being known, namely that He is the essential Self of things. He conceals it by otherness, which is you [as being not He]. Otherness asserts that the hearing [referred to in the Tradition] is Zaid's hearing, while the gnostic [who sees beyond that to the Oneness of Being] asserts that it is the Reality Himself, and similarly with the other organs and faculties. Not every one knows the Reality, some men excelling others according to [known] spiritual ranks, so that it is plain who is superior [in this respect] and who is not.[46]

Thus it is not really "I" who acts but the Real in me.[47] And insofar as we know this, then we are transparent "windows," so to speak, for divine action. Insofar as we do not know this, then the divine actions in us are "colored" by our selfish desires and preconceptions. Hence, it is impossible to know the Real of our selves by reason, for our reason automatically colors what it knows and thus limits it. As Ibn ʿArabi himself says, it was the prophet Hūd himself, who, in Cordoba, in the Hegira year 586, disclosed to him this truth, and this truth is completed by Muhammad to whom is attributed the ḥadīth that God is the hearing by which his servant hears, the seeing by which he sees, the foot by which he walks, etc.[48] We can therefore think of the chapter on Hūd as applying the dialectic of transcendence and immanence that Ibn ʿArabi describes in his chapter on Noah to the human subject and its self-knowledge. God, Ibn ʿArabi argues, becomes the seeing by which the gnostic sees, the foot by which he walks,

---

45. SDG, 120.　　　　　　　　　46. *Bezels*, 133/109–10.

47. Or, as al-Qaysari puts it, God is the subject of all things, while we are the predicate. *Sharḥ*, II, 28.

48. Muhammad Ibn Ismaʿil al-Buhkari, *Sahih Abi ʿAbd Allah al-Bukhari*, 25 vols. (Cairo: al-Matbaʿa al-Bahiya al-Misriya, 1933–62), LXXXI:38.

etc., only insofar as his servant, the gnostic, assimilates into his being the language, metaphors, and thought of the Qur'an.

Ibn 'Arabi asserts that we cannot know the Real save through limitation: "For our part, whenever God has revealed or informed us [through Holy Traditions] concerning Himself, whether it assert His transcendence or comparability, we always see it in terms of limitation."[49] By the very structure of our finite minds, we limit God, the Real. But the Real itself is unlimited, even, paradoxically, as we saw above in our discussion of the chapter on Noah, by the fact of being unlimited. Ibn 'Arabi explains:

The first limitation [to which He subjects Himself] is "The Dark Cloud having no air above or beneath it." The Reality was in it before He created His creation. Then He says, *He established Himself on the Throne*, which also represents a Self-limitation. He then says that He descended to the lower heaven, also a limitation. He says further that he is in the Heaven and on the Earth, that He is with us wherever we are, and finally that He is, in essence, us. We are limited beings, and thus He describes Himself always by ways that represent a limitation on Himself. Even the verse *There is none like unto Him*, constitutes a limitation if we regard the *kaf* as simply emphatic, since one who is distinguished from what is limited is himself limited because he is not that thing; to deny all [possibility of] limitation is itself a limitation, the Absolute being [in a sense] limited by His Own Absoluteness.[50]

This is a point that we have already seen in Ibn 'Arabi's exegesis of the sura of Noah: essential to the absoluteness or transcendence of the Reality is its ability to limit itself and become immanent in the essences of all things. But even more importantly, as the chapter on Hūd makes clear, it is through self-limitation that the Real or Absolute is able to manifest itself in all things, while, at the same time, transcending them.[51] In other words, the very transcendence of God makes possible his immanence and hence the very unknowability of God makes possible his knowability. When God escapes the clutches of reason, seeking the certainty of first principles, God reveals himself immanently in the figures, images, and symbols of revelation, the Qur'an. Revelation supplies logically and necessarily, in this sense, what our reason fails to provide.

49. *Bezels*, 134/110.
50. *Bezels*, 134–35/111.
51. That is why al-Qaysari notes that the Absolute limits itself by virtue of its very absoluteness, for otherwise it would be limited by its very absoluteness, which is absurd. *Sharḥ*, II, 32–33.

Through the self-limitation of his absoluteness, God is both the outer and the inner, the existence of all things and the consciousness or awareness of all things:

> He is Being Itself, the Essence of Being, *He is the Preserver of all* by His Essence, nor do His preservations *weary Him*. In preserving all things, He is preserving His Form, lest aught assume a form other than His Form, which is not possible. He is the observer in the observer and the observed in the observed; the Cosmos is His Form and He is the governing Spirit of the Cosmos, which is the Great Man [Macrocosm].[52]

God is the essence of all existence and the essence of existence is God. Thus, God preserves all things in existence just as the spirit preserves the body in life. Here Ibn ʿArabi refers to the concept of the "Great Man" (*al-insān al-kabīr*) or the Macrocosm. Just as the human being is a synthesis of an outer (the body) and an inner (consciousness), so is the Cosmos a Great Man in that it is a synthesis of an outer (the observable essences) and an inner (its existence). Thus, to know the "small man" or microcosm is to know the "Great Man" or Macrocosm:

> He is all Becoming and He is the One by Whose
> Becoming I become, therefore I say He feeds
> On my being, so we are modeled in His Image.
> As also, from a certain respect, I seek refuge in Him from Him.[53]

To seek refuge in him from him is to seek our eternal being in God as opposed to the fleeting becoming of God's own self-manifestation in the world. This is possible only because God is in one respect other than the world and, in another respect, identical to the world.

Ibn ʿArabi, therefore, prefers not to think of God as the "first cause" of the universe, because such a notion does not permit the interplay of immanence and transcendence that is essential to any adequate notion of God. Rather, Ibn ʿArabi prefers to think of God as the necessary condition for the existence of the world rather than its cause.[54] In other words,

---

52. *Bezels*, 135/111.    53. *Bezels*, 135/111.

54. SDG, 19. Also, Rom Landau clarifies this rather subtle point of Akhbarian metaphysics: "For Ibn ʿArabi, the One is not the cause but the essence of everything. This difference in the two doctrines is fundamental. To be the maker of the thing I produce is one matter; it is quite another matter to be the thing itself or, rather, to share with it my essence. To paint the picture of a child is not identical with giving birth to a child." Rom Landau, *The Philosophy of Ibn ʿArabi* (New York: Macmillan, 1959), 32.

there is a nonreciprocal dependent relation between the world and its inner Reality.[55] A reciprocal relation is one in which two independently existing entities enter into a relation, while remaining independent of that relation; but it is nonreciprocal and dependent when one depends on the other for its very being and existence. Thus, the relation of the creature to God is a real one, because the creature depends upon God entirely for its existence. But the relation of God to the creature is not a real relation, because the relation of the creature to God adds nothing to God's existence. Therefore, their relation is nonreciprocal. Rather the relation of the creature to God, from the divine standpoint, is more adequately described as *imaginal*: i.e., the ontological status of the creature to God in God is that of the image, a reflection of an aspect of the divine being, having no being independent of God, and since creation has an entirely imaginal status in relation to God, God is both totally immanent to it as its existence, but totally transcends it insofar as he is utterly independent of it, being existence itself.

55. "Though multiplicity *is* real for Ibn 'Arabi in its seeming opposition to unity, the reality of this opposition is conceptual, while unity is the overriding ontological truth in its ultimate subsuming and absorbing of all diversity. But again, it is the presumed and felt tension between these two 'sides' which provides the rich intellectual core of Ibn 'Arabi's Sufi metaphysics in its integration with traditional religion and in its fullest expression." Ronald Nettler, *Sufi Metaphysics and Qur'anic Prophets: Ibn 'Arabi's Thought and Method in the Fusus al-Hikam* (Cambridge: Islamic Texts Society, 2003), 11. In her book, *Toward an Alternative Theology: Confessions of a Non-Dualist Christian* (Notre Dame, Ind.: University of Notre Dame Press, 2002), Sara Grant notes that this nonreciprocal dependent relation is also key to understanding such diverse traditional thinkers as Shankaracarya and Thomas Aquinas. Indeed, Thomas gives a good account of this nonreciprocal dependent relationship in *STh.* I, 13, 7: "Quandoque vero relatio in uno extremorum est res naturae, et in altero est rationis tantum. Et hoc contingit quandocumque duo extrema non sunt unius ordinis. Sicut sensus et scientia referuntur ad sensibile et scibile, quae quidem, inquantum sunt res quaedam in esse naturali existentes, sunt extra ordinem esse sensibilis et intelligibilis: et ideo in scientia quidem et sensu est relatio realis, secundum quod ordinantur ad sciendum vel sentiendum res; sed res ipsae in se condideratae, sunt extra ordinem huiusmodi. Unde in eis non est aliqua relatio realiter ad scientiam et sensum; sed secundum rationem tantum, inquantum intellectus apprehendit ea ut terminos relationum scientiae et sensus. Unde Philosophus dicit, in V *Metaph.*, quod non dicuntur relative eo quod ipsa referuntur ad ipsa. Et similiter *dextrum* non dicitur de columna, nisi inquantum ponitur animali ad dextram: unde huiusmodi relatio non est realiter in columna, sed in animali. Cum igitur Deus sit extra totum ordinem creaturae, et omnes creaturae ordinentur ad ipsum, et non e converso, manifestum est quod creaturae realiter referuntur ad ipsum Deum; sed in Deo non est aliqua realis relatio eius ad creaturas, sed secundum rationem tantum, inquantum creaturae referuntur ad ipsum. Et sic nihil prohibet huiusmodi nomina importantia relationem ad creaturam, praedicari de Deo ex tempore: non propter aliquam mutationem ipsius, sed propter creaturae mutationem; sicut columna fit dextera animali, nulla mutatione circa ipsam existente, sed animali translatio."

Another way in which Ibn 'Arabi expresses the relationship of God to creation is through the image of the divine breath: creation is the breath of the All-Merciful. Because, like human breath, the "breath" of creation is nonsubstantial, yet, again like human breath, its source is living and, in a certain sense, life itself (for, in Arabic, the word for "breath" and for "soul"— nafs—is the same). Creatures are as insubstantial as breath compared to the Real, and yet they are expressions of and, in a certain way, extensions of the divine Life, being "words" articulated by the divine speech and thus having a specific reality or fixed entity to which comes existence when God says for it to "Be." For it is in the divine Breath that God expresses his Names.[56] These Names denote the various ways in which the divine Essence may be imitated finitely by creatures. The Qur'an talks about God's "most beautiful names," but there are, in principle, as many names of God as there are creatures, and for every human being, there is a divine Name that governs his or her relation to the Real, a Name that is identical with what Ibn 'Arabi calls the "Lord" of each human being. Thus, the realized knower sees that his own relationship to himself as an independent creature is not a real relation but an imaginal one. Thus Ibn 'Arabi remarks:

> The eye perceives naught but Him
>     Only He is determined [by Himself].
> We are His, by Him we exist and by Him we are governed.
>     And we are in His Presence at all times, in all states.

Ibn 'Arabi continues:

Because of this [inevitable limitation by definition] He is both denied and known, called incomparable and compared. He who sees the Reality from His standpoint, in Him by Him is a gnostic. He who sees the Reality from His standpoint, in Him, but with himself as the seer, is not a gnostic. He who does not see the Reality in this way, but expects to see Him by himself, is ignorant.[57]

In short, the gnostic is one for whom there is no seer but God, and so the realized knower of God is to be distinguished from two other types of

---

56. *Bezels*, 136/112: "Since He created the forms in the Breath, and there became manifest the dominion of the relations, called the Names, the divine connection with the Cosmos is established, all beings deriving from Him. He says, 'This day have I reduced your relationship and raised My connection,' that is, I have taken away your relationship to yourselves and have returned you to your [proper] relationship with me."

57. *Bezels*, 137/113.

knower. The first says, "God is the Truth," the second, more ignorant, says, "God is a creature." The first is more knowledgeable than the second, but still not perfect, not a realized knower of God, because the third and most perfect knower says, "God, as pure existence, is *both* the Truth *and* the creature."[58] That is, God is both the transcendent truth and the immanent existence of any creature. The realized knower is careful not to assert the transcendence of God at the expense of God's immanence in the knower.

For Ibn 'Arabi, then, the realized knower has an acute sense of how human knowledge of the Real is deformed by the limited notions and concepts that humans create and lay over the Real. As Ibn 'Arabi puts it:

In general, most men have, perforce, an individual concept [belief] of their Lord, which they ascribe to Him and in which they seek Him. So long as the Reality is presented to them according to it they recognize Him and affirm Him, whereas if presented in any other form, they deny Him, flee from Him and treat Him improperly, while at the same time imagining that they are acting toward Him fittingly. One who believes [in the ordinary way] believes only in a deity he has created himself, since a deity in "beliefs" is a [mental] construction. They see [in what they believe] only themselves [as relative beings] and their own constructions within themselves.[59]

Most only "worship" gods of their own making—even those who profess some sort of adherence to a monotheistic religion. The human tendency is to make the divine conform to human ideas of what the divine should be. According to Ibn 'Arabi, God discloses himself only to the degree to which a particular person or people is prepared to receive him.[60] But the preparation of most people and nations is incomplete. This incomplete preparation therefore limits our idea of God in some respect. Only the realized knower is prepared to receive God as such, being freed from the desire to limit him. Thus, Ibn 'Arabi exhorts his reader to "be completely and utterly receptive to all doctrinal forms, for God, Most High, is too All-embracing and Great to be confined within one creed rather than another, for He has said, *Wheresoever you turn, there is the face of God,* without mentioning any

58. See *Sharḥ,* II, 40.
59. *Bezels,* 137/113.
60. "When God discloses Himself, the extent to which a thing 'receives' the self-disclosure is determined by its 'preparedness' to receive it, and this in turn is determined by the thing's own reality. . . . In Ibn al-'Arabi's view receptivity must be taken into account not only on the cognitive level, but also on the existential level." SPK, 91.

particular direction."[61] The realized knower is one who is able to see the oneness of being at the root of all religions and varieties of belief.

Therefore, for such a realized knower, the plurality of religions is not a difficulty. This is not to say that such a knower, for Ibn 'Arabi, ceases to be a Muslim: on the contrary, the "straight path" of the *shari'a* leads ultimately and *necessarily* to this oneness.[62] Nevertheless, the realized knower is the one who knows to what degree the structure of the human mind distorts its perception of the oneness of being. As Ibn 'Arabi states in the *Futūḥāt*, using one of his favorite metaphors taken from one of the seminal masters of Sufism, Junayd:

> Junayd was asked about knowledge (*ma'rifa*) and the knower (*'ārif*). He replied, "The water takes on the color of its cup." In other words, the container displays its effects in what it contains. Junayd said this to let you know that you will never judge your object of knowledge except by yourself, since you will never know anything but yourself. Whatever may be the color of the cup, water becomes manifest in that color. The person without knowledge judges that the water is like that, since sight gives that to him. Water discloses itself in the forms of all the cups in respect to their colors, but it does not become delimited in its essence. You only see it that way. In the same manner, the shapes of the containers in which water appears display their effects in it, but in all of them it is still water. If the container is square, the water becomes manifest as square.[63]

The true knower of the Real knows to what extent his knowledge of the Real is limited by the limitedness of his own created self; it is not that he experiences the water apart from all colors and forms, as he knows that there is a difference between the form or color of the water and the water itself. The believer does not know this as long as he is not detached from

---

61. *Bezels*, 137/113.

62. Ibn 'Arabi would not be one to advocate the slightest departure from orthodox Muslim belief and practice: "To think that all beliefs are limited and therefore should be scrapped becomes in turn another belief and dogma, equally limiting and limited, if not more so. To be free of the limiting condition is to be free of the dominion of intellectual thought. This requires the most penetrating insight into the very structure and root of belief, which by its nature simultaneously accepts and rejects. This insight is the seeing of the heart. Only then is it possible not to be tied to any one form of belief. It implies accepting things as they really are without the bias of a particular viewpoint or 'room.' In this light all 'things' are equal, as they are His revelations, and all hierarchy is subsumed in the Divine order. The viewpoint adopted is thus His viewpoint, and it is this which Ibn 'Arabi stresses throughout his writings." Stephen Hirtenstein, *The Unlimited Mercifier: The Spiritual Life and Thought of Ibn 'Arabi* (Oxford: Anqa Publishing, 1999), 134.

63. III 161.24 in SPK, 341.

all created things and has surrendered himself completely in *'ubudīyya* or servanthood to God. When this does happen, the knower not so much sees the Real as tastes it: he no longer contemplates the glass of water but drinks from it.

This true knowledge is forcefully described by al-Ghazali in his *Deliverance from Error*: not to reason about the Real with the mind but to taste the Real to the point where one's entire being is in turn drunk or consumed by the Real.[64] The goal of the Sufi, therefore, is to see the created as rational, i.e., mediate and abstract, and the Truth as "sensible," i.e., immediate and concrete and not the other way around, which can only happen in "extinction" or *fanā,'* whereby human qualities are extinguished and only divine qualities remain, a manifestation of the only true state of affairs, since only God truly exists, while the existence of the creature is borrowed and fleeting. As Ibn 'Arabi explains in the *Futūḥāt:*

When the Real delimits Himself within a form to the recipient of self-disclosure, without doubt the form delimits the viewer. He is with each viewer in a form that is not seen by any other viewer. Hence, no one sees Him nondelimited by existences except him who is destitute, him from whose witnessing all forms have disappeared.[65]

Only when the knower is no longer limited in thought or will by finite, created things does he know the Real as it is. To *abide in* the Truth (*baqā' bi*) one must first be *extinguished from* all created things (*fanā' an*), which represents the practical realization of the theoretical dialectic of *tanzīh* and *tashbīh*. The realized knower must separate himself in incomparability from all creatures (*tanzīh—fanā' an*) in order to abide in comparability in God (*tashbīh—baqā' bi*).

In the normal state of affairs, human beings cannot worship anything but themselves and their own created images of themselves:

64. In connection with the wisdom of unity as exemplified by the word of Hūd, Izutsu points out the centrality of knowledge by "taste" or *dhawq* in Ibn 'Arabi. By "taste," Ibn 'Arabi wishes to distinguish Sufi knowledge from the proofs of reason on the one hand, and from blind faith and obedience to tradition on the other. In this, he has much in common with the great Muslim theologian and Sufi al-Ghazali. "No philosophical explanation can do justice to his thought unless it is backed by a personal experience of the Unity of Being (*wāhdat al-wujūd*). The proposition: 'Adam married himself,' for example, will never cease to be perplexing and perturbing to our Reason until it is transformed into a matter of experience." Izutsu, *Sufism and Taoism,* 81.

65. III 105.8 in SPK, 378.

Hence you will see no one who worships an unmade god, since man creates in himself that which he worships and judges. But God is the Judge; He is not restricted by reason, nor does it rule over Him. On the contrary, to Him "belongs the command" in His creation, "before and after" (30:4). There is no god but He, the God and Master of everything.[66]

So the goal of true knowledge is not a certainty that derives from a dominance over its object but a perplexity, which is an openness to the Real as such. What is necessary is that the bounds of human reason be transcended, for in themselves they are ignorant of the real; what must abide is the knowledge of God, who is in truth the only genuine knower: "So ignorance is an essential attribute of the servant, and the whole cosmos is a servant. But knowledge is an essential attribute of God."[67] We cannot know the Reality by ourselves but only in, through, and by God himself. Thus perplexity clears the way for knowledge of, in, and through God, for it clears the way for knowing God in and through the Qur'an. Despite all his allusions to a religious universalism of a sort, Ibn 'Arabi maintains that human reason cannot come to the truth about God unaided by revelation, and this revelation in its most perfect and complete form is the Qur'an and the *Sunna*. Indeed, his universalism, far from implying a "religion within the bounds of reason alone," implies the opposite, precisely because religion has no bounds, least of all those of human reason.

But what is the salient characteristic of this knowledge such that it breaks the limits of reason? For Ibn 'Arabi, the gnostic is the one who is able to intuit *together* the incomparability or transcendence of God (*tanzīh*) and the comparability or immanence of God (*tashbīh*). "In knowing God, we must be able to put opposites together."[68] This is why Ibn 'Arabi, in the *Futūḥāt*, describes the realized knower as "having two eyes"—one that looks upon the incomparability of God and the other that looks upon his comparability:

The perfect man has two visions (*naẓar*) of the Real, which is why He appointed for him two eyes. With one eye he looks upon Him in respect to the fact that He is independent of the worlds. So he sees Him neither in any thing nor in himself. Through the other eye he looks upon Him in respect of His name All-Merciful, which seeks the cosmos and is sought by the cosmos. He sees His Being perme-

66. IV 278.33 in SPK, 351.                    67. III 411.27 in SDG, 134.
68. SPK, 70.

ating all things. Through the vision of this eye he is poor toward everything in respect to the fact that the things are the names of God, not in respect of their own entities. Hence, none is poorer toward the cosmos than the perfect man, since he witnesses it subjected to himself.[69]

So in the passing away of the "self," the Truth (al-ḥaqq) of the Real is unconcealed, for then the finite self no longer obscures or obstructs its disclosure. The realized knower becomes the locus where the Truth as such manifests itself, which is not to go so far as to say that the realized knower no longer sees his own form and sees the Essence of God as such—that is impossible. Nor does the realized knower become God; rather he knows himself as a theophany.[70] As Ibn ʿArabi puts it in his early work, Contem-

69. III 151.10 in SPK, 368. In bringing these opposites together, the true knower of God allows himself to be perplexed. As Michael Sells points out: "Bewilderment results from the union of subject and object implicit in the 'union hadith' ('I become the hearing with which he hears . . .'). Seeing, hearing, and other perceptions become the sole domain of the Qurʾanic all-seeing (al-baṣīr) and all-hearing (al-samīʿ), the divine perception of the secret of destiny within each human heart. These intensive gerunds are commonly translated with the locution 'all-,' but at this point a term like 'all-seeing' would mean not only 'seeing everything' but 'everything that really sees.'" Michael Sells, "Semantics of Mystical Union in Islam," in Mystical Union and Monotheistic Faith, ed. Moshe Idel and Bernard McGinn (New York: Macmillan, 1989), 108. For Ibn ʿArabi's use of a linguistic ḥayra in his works whereby he seeks to reproduce in his very language the very perplexity experienced by the gnostic, see another article by Sells, "Ibn ʿArabi's Polished Mirror: Perspective Shift and Meaning Event," Studia Islamica 67 (1988): 136–37, and his book-length comparative study on the subject, Mystical Languages of Unsaying (Chicago: University of Chicago Press, 1994).

70. "The passing away of the 'self' is a state of intuitive knowledge in which the essential unity of the Whole is revealed. This is the aspect of the mystical experience which Ibnul ʿArabi emphasizes. It is knowledge of an infallible nature that Ibnul ʿArabi is after. To say that I have become God or died to self in any real sense is ignorance, and to see your 'self' alone in a mystical experience is polytheism. The perfect mystic therefore is one who sees both God and 'self' in the mystical experience, both by mystical knowledge and feeling (ʿilman wa ḥālan) and sees his 'self' by mystical knowledge alone (ʿilman lā ḥālan), i.e., the perfect mystic is the one who recognizes both Essence and 'form' but realizes their essential unity and the absolute non-existence of the form. This is the most perfect fanāʾ a mystic can attain in this life according to Ibnul ʿArabi: the real fanāʾ is attained after death when the form completely disappears." Affifi, The Mystical Philosophy of Ibn ʿArabi, 142. The gnostic no longer knows himself as having any existence as such and thus becomes counted among what Sufis call "The People of Blame," i.e., those who shun any sort of company or activity that might make them consider themselves as "something"—even to the point of incurring opprobrium and scorn (hence, the name). As Ibn ʿArabi says of them, however: "They look at things with the same eye with which God looks at things. They never confuse realities" (II 16.15 in SPK, 373). This is because such people are no longer attached to creatures or created ideas and categories; for them, that which always was, not in any real sense, their own created form, has passed away and that which always truly was, the divine Essence, abides. Claude Addas puts this very well when she says, "«Celui qui Me voit et sait qu'il Me voit ne Me voit pas»:

*plation of the Holy Mysteries:* "Then He said, 'If you find Me you will not see Me but you will see Me if you lose Me.' 'Finding is losing Me and losing is finding Me. Were you able to discover taking, then you would know real existence.'"[71] And here we return to the essential point of this chapter: how does the realized knower "bring opposites together" and sustain this seeing "with two eyes"? For Ibn 'Arabi, it is always in and through his or her reading of the Qur'an. As we saw in our discussion of the chapter on Noah, it is the Qur'an that brings together *tanzīh* and *tashbīh;* in the chapter on Hūd, Ibn 'Arabi shows that God's essential self-limitation becomes known only in and through the imaginal world of the Qur'an. Nor, again, should we be misled by Ibn 'Arabi's statements in that same chapter on Hūd that the gnostic "transcends all religious traditions": for the Shaykh, the gnostic transcends all religious traditions not despite the Qur'an but *only in and through the Qur'an.* That is to say, only to the degree that the gnostic enters into the imaginal world of the Qur'an, only to that degree can he see the oneness of all revelations and the oneness of Truth. Thus, Ibn 'Arabi is very far from preaching some bloodless and abstract—and ultimately vapid—religious (or "spiritual") universalism. Only in a concrete and full-blooded engagement with the symbols and images of the Qur'an does a true, lived transcendent unity of all religions emerge.

---

telle est l'imprescriptible règle divine. La connaissance suprême de Dieu implique, paradoxalement, l'ignorance la plus absolue, et la vision de Son Essence n'advient, selon une célèbre sentence souvent citée par Ibn Arabi, que «lorsque disparaît ce qui n'a jamais été et que subsiste ce qui n'a jamais cessé d'être». Elle est donc réservée à celui qui, plongé dans la nuit de son néant originel, ne sait plus qu'il est." Claude Addas, *Ibn 'Arabi et le voyage sans rétour,* 62.

71. Ibn 'Arabi, *Contemplation of the Holy Mysteries,* trans. Cecilia Twinch and Pablo Beneito (Oxford: Anqa Publishing, 2001), 25. The translators add this explanatory note: the word "taking" refers to "the Quranic verse: 'And when your Lord *took* from the children of Adam—from their loins (literally, "backs": *zuhūr*)—their descendants and made them bear witness to themselves *(ashhada-hum 'alayhim)* [saying] 'Am I not your Lord?,' they said 'Yes, indeed *(bala)!* We do bear witness' (7:172)."

4

# "Unum est indistinctum"

*Meister Eckhart's Dialectical Theology*

Eckhart combined seamlessly in himself two roles which we have come to think of as entirely antithetical: on the one hand, he was a spiritual master or "mystic"; on the other, he was an academic theologian, teaching at the best universities of his day. It is often the case, therefore, that his existential insights rest on a very elaborate and subtle scholastic scaffolding. The current theme of our chapter is no exception: the realization of the primal identity of subject and object, of the coincidence of the divine transcendence of the universe and the divine immanence in the soul, is a realization gained through a lived union of the soul with God. Eckhart argues, however, that such a realization must transform the way we think about the basic principles of philosophy, just as these transformed principles must, in turn, transform the way we read, understand, interpret, and, ultimately, *live* Scripture.

This is one way of understanding why Eckhart undertook to write what was planned to be a vast work of scholastic theology and philosophy, called the *Opus tripartitum* or "The Tripartite Work."[1] This work was to be composed, as its title states, of three parts: (1) an *opus propositionum*, or "work of propositions" in which

1. The dating of the writing of the prologues to *Opus tripartitum* is a matter of some debate. Until recently, it was argued that the prologues date from relatively late in Eckhart's career (i.e., sometime after 1314) and that, therefore, they might possibly repre-

Eckhart would lay out, in an axiomatic form similar to Proclus's *Elements of Theology*, the basic principles of theology; (2) an *opus quaestionum*, or "work of questions" in which he would give, in the manner of Saint Thomas Aquinas's *Summa Theologiae*, responses to some one thousand disputed questions in theology; and finally, there was to be (3) an *opus expositionum*, or "work of commentaries" in which he would, using the framework of the previous two works, draw out the inner meaning of Scripture by commenting on all the books of the Bible as well as collect sermons on specific scriptural passages. Thus, following the proposition that Eckhart puts forward first, *Esse est Deus* or "to be is God," he then puts forward the question in his second part, *Ut Deus sit?* or "Does God exist?" This proposition and question then form the basis for his third discussion, interpreting the beginning of Genesis, "In the beginning, God created the heavens and the earth." The exegete is now prepared to uncover the inner, hidden meaning of this passage as containing the first proposition, *Esse est Deus*, Being is God. According to Eckhart, the *Lebemeister*, the principle *Esse est Deus* becomes a truth *for us*, that is to say, a *lived truth* to be appropriated by the soul in its union with God, only when that principle is in turn applied to the interpretation of a specific scriptural passage.

Eckhart says that it was his students who urged him to undertake the *Opus tripartitum*, and, we can see, Eckhart conceived it on a massive scale

---

sent a new and even fundamentally different approach than that found in the *Parisian Questions* and some of the scriptural commentaries. This is the view of Maurer (1974); Kurt Ruh, *Meister Eckhart: Theologe, Prediger, Mystiker* (Munich: C. H. Beck, 1993), 29; and Alain de Libera and Edouard Wéber, *Maitre Eckhart à Paris: Une critique médiévale de l'ontothéologie—Les Questions parisiennes no. 1 et no. 2* (Paris: Presses universitaires de France, 1984). Loris Sturlese, however, in his important article "Meister Eckhart in der Biblioteca Amploniana: Neues zur Datierung des 'Opus tripartitum,'" in *Die Biblioteca Amploniana*, ed. Andreas Speer, 434–96 (Berlin: de Gruyter, 1995), has convincingly shown that the prologues must date from relatively early in Eckhart's career (i.e., the first decade of the fourteenth century) and are more or less contemporaneous with the *Parisian Questions*. It is thus questionable, at best, to make much of any contrast between "the doctrine of the *Opus*" and "the doctrine of the *Parisian Questions*." That said, it is evident that Eckhart's thought underwent many modifications and revisions over the years and in places (i.e., *Sermo XXIX* and in his *Expositio Libri Sapientiae*, 7.27) he seems to base his arguments more on those of the *Parisian Questions* than on those of the prologues to the *Opus tripartitum*. But, again, it is questionable whether there is any fundamental conflict between these two works. In *Sermo XXIX*, Eckhart's argument is that "nowhere and never do we find God as God as in intellect" (n.304). If the argument of this chapter is convincing, this statement fully harmonizes with the metaphysics of the prologues of the *Opus tripartitum*. The reader should simply be aware that, although the prologues to the *Opus tripartitum* are of enormous importance in coming to any understanding of Eckhart's thought, they do not represent its definitive, let alone final, statement.

but ultimately did not finish it. All that we have are two prologues to the *Opus*—one a general prologue to the whole work, the other a prologue to part 1, The *Opus propositionum*—along with his commentaries on Genesis, Exodus, the Book of Wisdom, the Gospel of John, sermons on Ecclesiastes, and multiple Latin and vernacular sermons. Except for the vernacular sermons, all were presumably planned as part of the Tripartite Work.

We find in his prologues to the Tripartite Work, both the general prologue and the prologue to the Work of Propositions, a schematic but profound outline of his thought. In particular, central to Eckhart's preoccupations is the dialectical logic of Being expressed in the thesis *Esse est Deus*, or "Being (or Existence) is God." We are confronted here with a paradox that, we have seen, also forms the core of Ibn 'Arabi's thought about existence: Being, as being, is everything, for otherwise nothing else would exist; but at the same time, Being is not anything in particular, because no thing is Being as such. We are thus confronted with a paradox: Being is at once everything and nothing. Being, as the existence of all things, is indistinct from all existents, but Being, as existence in itself, is distinct from all existents. This paradox is implied in the very logic of the idea of Being itself.

## Esse est Deus

In his general prologue, Eckhart gives a list of the propositions that he will be treating in the first work. He lists fourteen, but prominent among these fourteen, because they appear first, are what the medievals called the *transcendentals*. Thus, Eckhart says, "The first treatise is about existence and being and its opposite, which is nothing. The second, about unity and the one and its opposite, which is many. The third, about truth and the true and its opposite, which is false. The fourth, about goodness and the good and its opposite, evil," etc. The transcendentals are what Eckhart calls *termini generales*, or "general terms," since we apply them to all beings without exception insofar as they are existent.[2] But precisely because the

2. Among recent scholars of medieval thought, Jan Aertsen has convincingly argued that the doctrine of the transcendentals is central to the medieval philosophical project and is, indeed, what makes that project distinctive. This, he asserts, is very much the case with Meister Eckhart, for whom the development of the doctrine of transcendentals is a central preoccupation and who, in his usual original fashion, contributes much to the medieval project as a whole. In the following passage, Aertsen also give a good summary of the structure and function of Eckhart's

transcendentals are what are most common to things, they refer, Eckhart argues, to what is not only cognitively but also ontologically prior to all things, i.e., God. This is because the transcendentals are not "in" things in the same manner as accidents. As Eckhart argues:

First we should by no means imagine or think of universal terms like existence, unity, truth and wisdom, goodness, and so on, after the manner and nature of accidents. Accidents receive existence in and through their subject and through its change. Moreover, they are posterior to the subject and take on existence by inhering in it. . . . The case is completely different with the general terms mentioned above. Existence itself, and the terms convertible with it, are not added to things as though posterior to them; on the contrary they are prior to every aspect of things.[3]

Because these general terms are presupposed by all other predicates which we may apply to beings, they are not said of beings *(entia)* in the same way that we predicate other terms of things. These *termini generales* are

<hr>

own account of his planned *Opus tripartitum* in the context of the medieval philosophical project based as it was on the doctrine of the transcendentals as the most fundamental concepts of the human intellect corresponding, of course, to the most fundamental properties of reality: "Meister Eckhart remains the most controversial thinker of the Middle Ages. But in the 'General Prologue' to his *Opus tripartitum*, he makes a number of observations, which he apparently considers as foundational for this grand project. According to one of them, the second book, the Work of *Quaestiones*, and the third, the Work of *Expositiones*, are so dependent on the first, namely, the Work of *Propositiones*, that without it they are of little use. Eckhart's first observation in the Prologue is instructive for his understanding of an axiomatic metaphysics. General terms *(termini generales)*—'being,' 'one,' 'true,' and 'good'—must not be imagined in the manner of accidents, since they precede everything and are the first in things. The first four treatises of the Work of *Propositiones* deal therefore with these general terms, which provide the philosophical foundation of the *Opus tripartitum*." See Jan Aertsen, *Medieval Philosophy and the Transcendentals: The Case of Thomas Aquinas* (Leiden: E. J. Brill, 1996), 19. It should be noted, however, that Aertsen's assertion of the centrality of the transcendentals to the medieval philosophical project is a contested one. Alain de Libera, for one, has given a quite different picture of the medieval philosophical project in his book *Penser au moyen âge* (Paris: Editions de Seuil, 1991). There he argues that the development of medieval philosophy was toward a closer and more systematic synthesis of the spiritual ideal of Christian ascesis and the Aristotelian/Averroistic ideal of the sage—a synthesis in which Meister Eckhart's thought played a decisive role by translating both literally and conceptually the technical language of theology and philosophy into the language of the "vulgar." By doing so, Eckhart made the practical dimension of these disciplines primary, i.e., they were now primarily understood as "ways of life." (De Libera here is obviously indebted to Pierre Hadot and his classic study of ancient philosophy, *Philosophy as Way of Life*.) For a critical discussion of de Libera's thesis, see Carlos Steel, "Medieval Philosophy: An Impossible Project? Thomas Aquinas and the 'Averroistic' Ideal of Happiness," in *Was ist Philosophie im Mittelalter?* ed. Jan Aertsen and Andreas Speer, 152–74 (Berlin: de Gruyter, 1998).

    3. *Prol. op. trip.*, n.8; LW I, 152–53/Mauer, 82–83.

the predicates presupposed by all other predicates which we may say of all beings and thus refer to what is prior to them as particular existent things. Or to put it in other words, these transcendental terms denote *perfections* of creatures and not mere accidental qualities. To say that a book is red is not to attribute any perfection to the book: for a book to be red, yellow, or green does not add any greater or lesser perfection or being to the book. But to say that the book is true insofar as it is known by an intellect or good insofar as it is desired by a will does add perfection to the book, because then it comes to have a higher immaterial existence in the intellect that knows it, or a higher end, purpose, or final cause in the will that desires it. As such, unity, truth, and goodness are not accidents of creatures but perfections prior to any particular creature that are simply realized temporally and spatially in the creature.

Eckhart explains how the logic of transcendental predication reflects the nature of existence in the following way: "It is not the nature of existence itself to be something or from something or through something; neither is it added or joined to anything. On the contrary, it precedes and comes before everything. So the existence of everything is immediately from the first and universal cause of things. All things exist from existence itself, and through it and in it; for what is different from existence is not or is nothing."[4] Since the general terms or transcendentals refer to the perfections presupposed by any other predicate we may attach to a thing, such as "white" or "human," they are "general" and universal. But, precisely because these terms are general and universal, they do not refer to anything based or found in the creature itself because every creature, as creature, is a particular being, a "this or that."[5] Existence *(esse)* is prior to all beings *(entia)* as substances; existence, therefore, does not "inhere" in creatures in the manner of an accident nor does it receive being in any way from creatures.[6] What is most common or universal thus refers nec-

4. *Prol. op. trip.*, n.8; LW I, 153/Mauer, 83.

5. This phrase, *"ens hoc vel hoc,"* is, as Ruh points out, Eckhart's "key" formulation (or *Schlüsselformel*) of created being. See Ruh, *Meister Eckhart*, 63.

6. In this way, Eckhart follows Thomas's critique of Avicenna, for whom (at least according to Thomas's reading of the great Persian philosopher) existence and the transcendentals are the most general *accidents* of things. Wouter Goris shows well how Aquinas's as well as Eckhart's doctrines of the transcendentals are a move *away* from the Avicennian concept of metaphysics. Goris, *Einheit als Prinzip und Ziel: Versuch über die Einheitsmetaphysik des 'Opus tripartitum'* (Leiden: E. J. Brill, 1997), 56.

essarily to what is most separate and particular, i.e., the "existence" and its synonymous terms refer not to mere abstractions but to existence itself, which gives existence to all that is and is thus in itself more "particular," "separate," and "real" than any concretely existing, finite creature. In asserting this, Eckhart follows not only in the Augustinian tradition but the broader Platonic tradition as well.[7] For the latter, concepts denoting "perfections" such as "being," "truth," "oneness," and "good" cannot have their basis in limited conditioned beings, which includes the created human intellect, but can have their basis only in the Absolute Being, and if we apply these terms to creatures at all, it is then only by analogy with the Absolute Being.

It follows, then, that creatures add nothing to and subtract nothing from our knowledge of God. Creatures of themselves give only diverse significations of the transcendental perfections, but these significations have their truth only in the divine existence itself because only there do they signify a *unity*. Thus Eckhart invokes several times the principle, drawn from Neoplatonism, that the inferior derives all of its perfection and intelligibility from what is superior but that the superior itself is unaffected by the inferior.[8] The inferior has existence, oneness, truth, and goodness in a divided fashion as "this or that existence," "this or that oneness," "this or that truth," and "this or that goodness."[9] Thus, we can know the inferior through the superior but not the superior through the inferior, at least not without significant qualification. There is nothing in the creature itself, be it in its essence or its real existence, that can form the basis of any knowledge of God's existence as such. All that the creature can do is point to God's existence. Eckhart will say, therefore, that the term "being" or "existence," when attributed to a creature, points only to the purity of existence, just as a wreath hung outside a tavern points to the wine that is served inside.

Just as a circular wreath which has nothing of wine in it [signifies] wine . . . [so] being or existence and every perfection, especially general ones such as exis-

7. For an illuminating discussion of the "Platonic" nature of Eckhart's understanding of the transcendentals, see Jan Aertsen, "Ontology and Henology in Medieval Philosophy (Thomas Aquinas, Master Eckhart, and Berthold of Moosburg)," in *On Proclus and His Influence in Medieval Philosophy*, ed. E. P. Bos and P.A.. Meyer, 120–40 (Leiden: E. J. Brill, 1992).

8. *Prol. op. trip.*, n.10; LW I, 154.          9. *Prol. op. trip.*, n.10; LW I, 155.

tence, oneness, truth, goodness, light, justice, and so forth, are used to describe God and creatures in an analogical way.[10]

I shall return to this significant image of the wreath and the wine later, because the doctrine of analogy indicated here is quite important and very different from that developed by his fellow Dominican Thomas Aquinas.

Thus creatures signify existence, even though they in and of themselves have nothing of existence either essentially or really. They can be said to have existence only insofar as their existence is understood as merely a referring to existence itself. But outside of existence itself they are nothing. Creatures are *signs* of existence itself and thus can be said to exist in some way, but only as signs. They have no existence in themselves and are thus utterly distinct from God; but insofar as they do exist, they are utterly *in*distinct from God.

This is the heart of Eckhart's dialectical theology. The very unity and unique oneness of God necessarily implies God's immanence in all things. It is not dissimilar to what Ibn 'Arabi says about how the absoluteness of God would not be absolute if it did not also include its own limitation in the existence of creatures. Creation is a free expression of God's unique oneness. It is free, because it flows lovingly from his nature as pure existence. *"Est igitur sciendum quod li unum idem est quod indistinctum"*— "It must therefore be known that the one is the same as that which is indistinct."[11] Eckhart, in his commentary on Wisdom, devotes a great deal of exposition to this thesis.[12] His commentary follows the verse from Wis-

---

10. *In Eccli.*, n.52; LW II, 280–81: "sicut [significat] circulus vinum, quo nihil vini in se habet. Ens autem sive esse et omnis perfectio, maxime generalis, puta esse, unum, verum, bonum, lux, iustitia et huiusmodi, dicuntur de deo et creaturis analogice." "The *esse formaliter inhærens* is not really *esse* and has no real basis within itself for being similar to *esse absolutum*. It is at best a sign of *esse*, as the wreath hung outside the tavern is a sign of the wine within." Frank Tobin, *Meister Eckhart: Thought and Language* (Philadelphia: University of Pennsylvania Press, 1986), 59.

11. *In Sap.*, n.144; LW II, 482, where he discusses the verse, "Cum sit una, omnia potest." Also, *In Ioh.*, n.562; LW III, 489: "Ipsum vero unum ex sui proprietate indistinctionem indicat. Est enim unum in se indistinctum" where he discusses the verse, "Domine, ostende nobis patrem, et sufficit nobis."

12. Eckhart's characterization of the One as indistinct may have been inspired by his reading of the Pseudo-Dionysius—in particular of the ninth chapter of the *Divine Names* (IX, 6–7, 913–16). It should also be mentioned that Aquinas himself is not averse to using the language of distinction-indistinction in describing the relation of creatures to God. Thus, in the *Summa Contra Gentiles* (C.G. I. 29.), he remarks: "Deus ... cum omnibus similitudinem habet et dissimilitudinem simul. Et inde quod Sacra Scriptura aliquando inter eum et creaturam commemorat, ut

dom *"Et cum sit una, omnia potest"* (Ws 7:27). In explaining this passage, Eckhart refers to a verse from Genesis and Deuteronomy, *"Deus unus est."* This verse is commonly understood to be the foundation statement of all the monotheistic religions, stating that there is not a plurality of gods but only one God. But for Eckhart, as for Aquinas, this statement by Moses means "something deeper" *(altius aliquid)*[13] than the mere fact that there is numerically only one God. If we understand the verse in this way, we are taking only the most literal and thus most superficial meaning of the text. The true import of the verse *"Deus unus est"* can be understood only by the application of dialectic and *rationes naturales* to holy Scripture. As Eckhart says, it is "of the nature of God" to be indistinct because he is infinite and not determined to the limits of any genus or "entity." There can, therefore, be no such thing as two infinite beings.[14] This means, of course, that a plurality of gods is impossible, because God, by his very nature as *esse* and as indistinct unity, is distinct from nothing else.[15] Eckhart's primary intention is not so much to prove the singularity of God; rather it is to explore, by means of *rationes naturales,* the *"aliquid altius"* that the verse "God is One" "insinuates" and its implications for understanding the nature of God and of the relation of God to creatures.

Since existence itself is God, all the perfections which are common to all creatures insofar as they exist can be properly attributed only to God and thus no distinction can be introduced into God. But God is distinct from creatures by this very indistinction.[16] Here, Eckhart follows the lead of Thomas, who argues: "The very being of God is distinguished and individuated from every other being through itself, because it is being subsistent in itself and does not enter into composition with any other nature,

---

cum dicitur Gen. 1:26: 'Faciamus hominem ad imaginem et similitudinem nostram'; aliquando similitudo negatur, secundum illud Isaiae 40:18: 'Cui ergo similem fecestis Deum, aut quam imaginem ponetis ei?' et in Psalmo: 'Deus, quis similis erit tibi?' Huic autem rationi Dionysius concordat, qui in IX cap. de Div. Nom. dicit: 'Eadem similia sunt Deo et dissimilia: similia quidem, secundum imitationem eius qui non est perfecte imitabilis qualem in eis contingit esse; dissimilia autem, secundum quod causata habent minus suis causis.'" See also Alois Dempf, *Meister Eckhart* (Freiburg: Herder, 1960), 209.

 13. *In Sap.,* n.144; LW II, 481.      14. *In Sap.,* n.144; LW II, 482.

 15. *In Sap.,* n.146; LW II, 484.

 16. *In Sap.,* n.144; LW II, 482. "The key to the analysis is to understand *unum* as the 'not-to-be-distinguished.' That is its *distinguishing* mark." Bernard McGinn, "The God beyond God: Theology and Mysticism in the Thought of Meister Eckhart," *Journal of Religion* 61 (1981): 7.

which may be other than its own being."[17] But Eckhart reverses Thomas's starting point, beginning with the transcendent One, who is God and who is not only common but also prior to every *"unum hoc vel hoc."* Oneness, then, is said of creatures only insofar as they are understood to receive what oneness they have directly from God. And they receive oneness from God by the very indistinction of the transcendent One. God's indistinction—which for Eckhart is to say his oneness—is not the absence of being nor an imperfection,[18] but rather the purity and what Eckhart calls the "exuberant goodness" of God's being: "Therefore, saying that God is one is to say that God is indistinct from all things, which is the property of the highest and first existence and its overflowing goodness *(bonitas exuberans)*."[19] God's indistinction is due to the purity of his being, not the absence or lack of being in him.[20] To think of any distinction in God is incompatible with our conception of God as pure existence. Eckhart's

17. *Quaestiones Disputate de Potentia Dei* 7. 2. ad 5: "ipsum esse dei distinguitur et individuatur a quolibet alio esse per hoc ipsum, quod est esse per se subsistens et non adveniens alicui naturae, quae sit aliud ab ipso esse."

18. The Greeks, by contrast, saw all indetermination as imperfection: even the Good of Plato and the God of Aristotle are finite, determinate forms.

19. *In Sap.*, n.144; LW II, 482–83: "Dicens ergo deum esse unum vult dicere deum esse indistinctum ab omnibus, quod est proprietas summi esse et primi et eius bonitas exuberans." See also: *In Ioh.*, n.263; LW III, 218.

20. Aquinas expresses very much the same point, though not in the dialectical fashion of Eckhart, in the eighth article of question four of the *De veritate*. In this article he asks whether all that is made is life in the Word (*Utrum omne quod factum est sit vita in Verbo*). His response is that, in a sense, all things are life in the Word and therefore indistinct from God in that, since God's thinking is identical with his being and his life, that which he thinks in making is identical with his being as well. In the human maker, by contrast, the thing made has a being other than that of the maker even in his or her intellect because the human intellect is not identical with human being or human life: "In nobis autem nulla operatio ad quam nos movemus est esse nostrum, unde intelligere nostrum non est vita nostra proprie loquendo nisi secundum quod vivere accipitur pro opere quod est signum vitae, et similiter nec similitudo intellecta in nobis est vita nostra; sed intelligere Verbi est suum esse, et similiter similitudo ipsius, unde similitudo creaturae est quodam modo ipsa creatura per modum illum quo dicitur quod 'anima quodam modo est omnia'; unde ex hoc quod similitudo creaturae in Verbo est productiva et motiva creaturae in propria natura existentis, quodam modo contingit ut creatura se ipsam moveat et ad esse producat, in quantum scilicet producitur in esse et movetur a sua similitudine in Verbo existente, et ita similitudo creaturae in Verbo est quodam modo creaturae vita." Thus, the similitude of the creature which is in the Word and which is identical with the being of the Word is, *in some way (quodam modo),* the life of the creature insofar as it is that through which it comes into its own created nature and it is that to which it strives. The creature is thus also utterly distinct from the Word insofar as its being is other than the essence it has in the Word. But it also, in some way, has its life and true being in the Word.

dialectic of the One, then, amounts to this: because the *esse commune* that is predicated of creatures insofar as they exist belongs properly to God alone, God is indistinct from all creatures. But precisely because God's being is common to all creatures, it is utterly distinct from the being of creatures because the being of creatures is a particular being, an *"ens hoc vel hoc"* and not *esse* in any absolute sense. In this way, the *esse commune* of all things, or God, is also absolutely One, because indistinct from all things.

In his commentary on the verse from Wisdom cited above, Eckhart makes a basic logical point: if anything were distinct from *esse*, it would not exist. Therefore nothing is distinct from God or can be distinct from God. Existence is God; therefore God is indistinct (i.e., not "this or that existence"), which is to say One. Everything exists through God, who is existence or *esse*; what does not exist through God, the *esse* that is common to all things insofar as they exist, does not exist at all:

> God is one which is indistinct. This signifies the highest divine perfection by which nothing exists or is able to exist without him or distinct from him. This is most clear if in place of the word "God" we use the word "existence." God is existence. It is clear that existence is indistinct from everything which exists and that nothing exists or can exist that is distinct and separated from existence.[21]

On this point, Eckhart appeals to the words of Augustine who says, "'You were with me and I was not with you.' 'You were with me,' because God is indistinct from all things; 'I was not with you,' because I am distinct and something created," that is, an *"ens hoc vel hoc"* who is distinct from other existent things and, in that degree, distinct even from God himself.[22] God, however, is not a *"hoc"*—a this—because he is infinite and not determined by a genus or species and, therefore, cannot be distinct from creatures in the same fashion as creatures are distinct from God and from each other.[23]

Eckhart attempts to understand the thesis that nothing is so indistinct and yet as distinct as God and creatures by asking the reader to consider several *rationes naturales*. These "natural reasons" basically reduce either to analogies from the natural world where two principles, such as form and matter or act and potency, are in a relation simultaneously of identity and difference, or to the notion, common in Neoplatonic thinkers, that between the cause or principle and its effect there arises a relation simul-

21. *In Sap.*, n.145; LW II, 483/TP, 166.   22. *In Sap.*, n.145; LW II, 483/TP, 166.
23. *In Sap.*, n.144; LW II, 482.

taneously of identity and difference or, to use Eckhart's words, of distinction and indistinction. The first *ratio naturalis* which Eckhart employs is one in which he compares God's distinction in indistinction to that of the eye to color. He remarks that that which does not have any color at all is more distinct from that which has color than two objects of a different color are distinct from each other.[24] Thus, that which does not have any color is more distinct from colored objects than a white object is from a black one. The eye, however, which according to medieval thought has no color at all since otherwise it would not be able to receive all colors, is most distinct from all colored objects. And yet, by virtue of the eye's very absence of color, it is able to receive all colors. It is, therefore, indistinct from all color. In a similar manner, since God, as pure existence, is indistinct from all creatures, God is also most distinct from creatures. The second *ratio naturalis* that Eckhart gives is also brief: "Nothing is further from something than its opposite. But God and the creature are opposed as the One and Unnumbered is opposed to number, the numerated, and the numerable. Therefore, nothing is as distinct from any created being."[25] That is, nothing so differs from the principle as that of which it is the principle and yet nothing is so identical as the principle and that of which it is the principle. Just so, the point is completely distinct from the line, yet nothing is so indistinct as the point from the line, because it is the line's beginning and "principle."

God, then, as the principle of all that is, is both identical to that of which he is the principle—all being in general—and yet utterly distinct from that of which he is the principle—every *"ens hoc vel hoc."* He is "distinct by his very indistinction":

Everything which is distinguished by indistinction is the more distinct the more indistinct it is, because it is distinguished by its own indistinction. Conversely, it is the more indistinct the more distinct it is, because it is distinguished by its own distinction from what is indistinct. Therefore, it will be the more indistinct insofar as it is distinct and vice versa, as was said. But God is something indistinct which is distinguished by his indistinction, as Thomas says in Ia, q. 7, a.1, at the end. For God is a sea of infinite substance, and consequently indistinct, as Damascene says.[26]

24. *In Sap.*, n.154; LW II, 489.
25. *In Sap.*, n.154; LW II, 490/TP, 169.
26. *In Sap.*, n.154; LW II, 490/TP, 169.

God is that which is most indistinct because God is an ocean of infinite substance which, being self-subsistent, is not distinguished from limited substance by any mark of distinction; and yet, as an ocean of infinite substance, God is completely distinct from all creatures. As an infinite ocean of substance, God is a reality that is sui generis and yet if God, as self-subsistent existence itself, were not indistinct from creatures, nothing would exist. As God in his indistinction is free from every creature, he is also free from all difference and thus utterly "detached" from all creatures.[27] It can also be inferred from Eckhart's text that God's distinction in indistinction means also that God is eminently an individual.[28] That is, God, in his indistinction, is he who is most distinct from all creatures and is therefore he who does not fall under a genus or species, but is pre-eminently individual.

The allusion to Aquinas in the passage cited above is significant here.[29] Eckhart refers specifically to the question in the *Summa* where Thomas asks whether God is without end. There he answers the objection that God is not infinite with respect to his substance, since otherwise he would not be distinguishable from determinate substances. Aquinas argues that God is self-subsistent substance and, precisely because he is infinite, he is by his infinite nature distinct from all other substances. Eckhart takes up this argument in his own words: "Deus autem indistinctum quoddam est quod sua indistinctione distinguitur, ut ait Thomas p. I, q. 7, a. 1 in fine." Most important in this citation is, as Goris remarks, the "identification of being with indistinction."[30] We predicate unity or the One of indistinction primarily because of the transcendental, cross-categorical nature of indistinction. We name God "existence" insofar as he is indistinct from all things as their *esse commune*; but we name God "One" insofar as he is distinct from all things by his very indistinction as the *esse commune* of all things.

This dialectic of distinction in indistinction is carried by Eckhart over into his commentary on Exodus. Here, however, Eckhart prefers to use

27. See Werner Beierwaltes, *Platonismus und Idealismus* (Frankfurt a.m.: V. Klosterman, 1972), 41.

28. See W. Bange, *Meister Eckharts Lehre von göttlichen und geschöflichen Sein* (Limburg: 1937), 90.

29. The passage in Thomas referred to by Eckhart here runs as follows: "ex hoc ipso quod esse dei est per se subsistens non receptum in aliquo, prout dicitur infinitum, distinguitur ab omnibus aliis, et alia removentur ab eo etc" (ad 3). See also Goris, *Einheit*, 222.

30. See Goris, *Einheit*, 222.

the terms *simile* and *dissimile* rather than *distinctum* and *indistinctum*. That is, Eckhart argues that we must say, at the same time, that nothing is so similar as God and creature and yet nothing is so dissimilar as God and creature:

You should know that nothing is as dissimilar as the Creator and any creature. In the second place, nothing is as similar as the Creator and any creature. And in the third place, nothing is as equally dissimilar and similar to anything else as God and the creature are dissimilar and similar in the same degree.[31]

God and creatures are identical insofar as God is existence and that he is the existence of all things without mediation (*immediate*). He is, therefore, not "foreign" (*alienus*) to any being. Eckhart gives six *rationes* for this, of which the first three, strikingly similar to some of the arguments used by Ibn 'Arabi in his *Bezels*, will be cited here: "The second issue to study is why it says 'strange gods.' You must recognize that God is foreign to no being, and this for six reasons: The first because he is existence and every act of existence comes immediately from him. Existence, however, is foreign to no being. One to whom existence is foreign is nothing."[32] If God were not the *esse* of all things, then nothing would exist. The consequent is false. Therefore, God is the *esse* of all things. The second reason states that God and creature are similar because God is infinite: "The second reason is that 'God is infinite.' The infinite is foreign to no being, but only to nothing, since outside it there is nothing, or, more properly speaking, outside it is only nothing."[33] In the third *ratio*, Eckhart returns to the language of his commentary on Wisdom, arguing that indistinction applies properly to God, distinction properly to creatures and that, therefore, nothing can be distinct from God who is indistinction itself: "The third reason is this. Indistinction belongs properly to God, distinction to creatures. Nothing that is indistinct from something is foreign to it."[34] By contrast, every creature is distinct and something other than existence or *esse*. Every created being, in that it is distinct and different from existence, is foreign (*E converso omne creatum, utpote distinctum et aliud ab esse, alienum est*). As we have seen, for Eckhart to be "foreign" (*alienum*) with respect to existence is to "exist from another" (*ab alio*): "*Alienum enim ab alio dictum est.*" It follows that, among creatures, every essence is distinct from every other essence

31. *In Exod.*, n.112; LW II, 110/TP, 81.   32. *In Exod.*, n.104; LW II, 105/TP, 79.
33. *In Exod.*, n.104; LW II, 105/TP, 79.   34. *In Exod.*, n.104; LW II, 106/TP, 79.

while existence, *esse*, is indistinct from every essence and every being *(ens)*: "Therefore, it is clear that every essence is foreign to or other than every other essence, as something distinct in relation to what it is distinguished from. But existence is indistinct from being and essence."[35] That is, God as *esse* is indistinct from every being and every essence—God and creature are identical insofar as the *esse* of every creature is the divine *esse*. But insofar as the essence and being of every creature is distinct from each other— insofar as every creature has a finite essence and a being that is proper to it—it is utterly dissimilar to God and different from him.

With these principles laid down, we can now get to the heart of Eckhart's mystical philosophy: that existence in itself can be nothing other than God. "Existence," and those terms convertible with "existence," can refer properly to nothing created but to God alone:

*Existence is God.* This proposition is evident: first, because if existence is something different from God himself, God neither exists nor is he a god. How can that be, or be something from which existence is different and distinct, or to which it is foreign? Or if he is a god, in that case he exists by another, since existence is different from him. Therefore God and existence are identical, or God has existence from another, and then he is not God himself, as was said above, but something else is before him and is the cause of his existence.[36]

---

35. *In Exod.*, n.106; LW II, 107/TP, 80.

36. *Prol. op. trip.*, n.12; LW I, 156–57/Maurer, 85: "*Esse est Deus*. Patet haec propositio primo, quia si esse est aliud ab ipso deo, deus nec est nec deus est. Quomodo enim est aut aliquid est, a quo esse aliud, alienum et distinctum est? Aut si est deus, alio utique est, cum esse sit aliud ab ipso. Deus igitur et esse idem, aut deus ab alio habet esse. Et sic non ipse deus, ut praemissum est, sed aliud ab ipso, prius ipso, est et est sibi causa, ut sit." Wackerzapp draws attention to Eckhart's frequent use of the "Quomodo?" question structure of his arguments not only here but in other places as well: *Prol. op. trip.*, n.17; *Prol. op. prop.*, n.9, n.13; *In Exod.*, n.29; *In Ioh.*, n.14, n.53, n.215, n.219; *Sermo IV*, n.23; *Proc. Col._II*, n.142. He remarks: "Diese rhetorischen Fragen haben alle dieselbe Struktur: ein Abstraktum, vor allem das Sein, wird dadurch als notwendige Bedingung eines konkreten Seienden erwiesen, daß gefragt wird, wie man das konkrete Seiende verstehen soll, wenn man jenen Bedingungszusammenhang leugnet." H. Wackerzapp, *Der Einfluß Meister Eckharts auf die ersten philosophischen Schriften des Nikolaus von Kues (1440–1450)* (Munster. Aschendorff, 1962), 62. This "abstraction," since it refers to God himself, is actually that which, for Eckhart, is most concrete and singular because the abstractions of perfections like existence, oneness, wisdom, and justice refer not to a universal of predication but to the universal of "separation"—i.e., of "separate," particular self-subsistent existence. That is, the "common" or *commune* in Eckhart is always not simply prior by predication but also ontologically prior as a sort of *separate* "Platonic" reality. Thus Dempf notes: "Die Wahrheit und Gutheit und Gerechtigkeit selbst sind nichts anderes als Gott, Gott selber. Also wahrlich nicht ein Abstraktum, sondern das Allerkonkreteste." See: Dempf, *Meister Eckhart*, 60.

If God were other than existence itself, then either God is outside of existence and thus nonexistent, or God receives his existence from another in the manner of a creature, both of which are impossible. Existence, then, must be God, because all things have existence in and through existence only and not through themselves or another finite existent or creature. What we mean by God is precisely that which must have existence through itself (*per se esse*), while all things other than God can have existence only in and through another (*ab alio esse*). Thus a creature can only *modify* the being of another creature (that is, effect on the existential level what Aristotle calls an *alteratio*, but not a substantial change, as fire, for example, modifies or alters wood). But no creature can give existence *absolutely speaking* to another creature (fire cannot give existence itself to the wood, since it presupposes wood as something that is pre-existent). Only God can give existence absolutely.[37] Therefore existence itself must come from God.

But not only that: existence itself must *be* God. It is absurd to think that existence itself could have "its" existence from another. It follows that existence itself must be God. From this fundamental thesis, Eckhart argues, the existence of God is evident.[38] Again, the logic of transcendental predication points to the a priori nature of existence and thus to the necessary conclusion that existence itself must be God. In short, it points to the analogical nature of all beings other than God, who is being properly speaking, just as diet, as a cause of health, or urine, as a sign of health, are both ordered to health in the animal. Thus, Eckhart notes:

37. *Prol. op. trip.*, nn.14–22/LW V, 159–65; and *Prol. op. prop.*, n.20/LW V, 178: "Igitur nihil hoc aut hoc dat esse." Given the nature of existence as God, Eckhart discusses almost immediately the *creative* nature of existence itself as distinguished from the non-creative existence characteristic of creatures. No creature, i.e., this or that being, can give existence in any absolute sense; only God can give existence absolutely. That is why he gives after his explanation of the thesis "Existence is God" an extended discussion of the opening verse of the Bible, "In principio creavit deus caelum et terram," in the general prologue. In particular, Eckhart makes the point that the analogy of God as "artisan" or "maker" can carry us only so far in understanding God's creative act: the analogy presupposes a pre-existent material out of which the artisan shapes the final product. But God does not merely "modify" the creature but gives it its very existence out of nothing.

38. Eckhart gives an argument in the form of a *modus tollens*, i.e.: If existence did not exist, then nothing would exist; but finite beings exist and existence is God, therefore, God exists. *Prol. op. trip.*, n.13; LW I, 158: "Quaestio prima est: *Utrum deus sit*. Dicendum quod sit. Ex propositione iam declarata primo sic: si deus non est, nihil est. Consequens est falsum. Ergo et antecedens, scilicet deum non esse. Consequentia probatur sic: si esse non est, nullum ens sive nihil est, sicut si albedo non est, nullum album est. Sed esse est deus, ut ait propositio. Igitur si deus non est, nihil est."

Being or existence and every perfection, especially general ones such as existence, oneness, truth, goodness, light, justice and so forth, are used to describe God and creatures in an analogical way. It follows from this that goodness and justice and the like (in creatures) have their goodness totally from something outside to which they are analogically ordered, namely, God. That is what Augustine says about existence near the middle of the first book of the *Confessions*, that there is no "vein by which existence comes from a source other" than God who is the supreme and "the Highest Existence," as was said above.[39]

This point, namely, that creatures have the *fundamentum* of their existence and thus of their oneness, truth, and goodness in God, is important. As he continues:

Analogates have nothing of the form (according to which they are analogically ordered) rooted in positive fashion in themselves. But every created being is analogically ordered to God in existence, truth, and goodness. Therefore every created being radically and positively possesses existence, life, and wisdom from and in God, not in itself as a created being. And thus it always "eats" as something produced and created, but it always hungers because it is always from another and not in itself.[40]

I shall have an opportunity to explain more fully Eckhart's image of the creature "eating" and "drinking" from the divine existence at the end of the next section. But suffice it to say here that, for Eckhart, the metaphysical structure of created being points beyond itself necessarily. Creatures are nothing but analogical inflections of God's absolute Being. But, at the same time, the possibility of union with God is always there, because the creature, in itself, adds nothing to God's mode of being. Remove the creaturely mode of existence or, better, realize the inherent nothingness of the creature, and one is left with God in the naked purity of his existence.

## The *Negatio negationis*

The crux of the problem in coming to an understanding of God and of God's existence is, of course, the structure of propositions in ordinary human discourse.[41] When human beings talk of things, they generally

---

39. *In Eccli*, n.52; LW II, 281/TP, 178.　　　40. *In Eccli*, n.53; LW II, 282/TP, 178.

41. For the intellectual-historical roots of Eckhart's teaching on the *negatio negationis*, see Goris, *Einheit*, 197–206.

predicate various attributes of a subject. The attributes are thought of, in general, as "properties" that "inhere" in the subject. Thus we tend to think of the subject as what is primary, in the sense of being a "substance," while we tend to think of the attributes predicated of the subject as somehow "inhering" in the substance either accidentally or substantially. When we say that "Socrates is a human being," we predicate "humanity" of Socrates as indicating what Socrates is substantially, but we still think of the individual substance pointed out by the name "Socrates" as what is primary.[42] In almost all cases, the subject is rightly understood to "precede" the predicate, since it refers to the substance in which the property designated by the predicate inheres. We implicitly understand, for example, in the proposition "The rose is red" that the subject "rose" is at least logically prior to the predicate "red." And we usually understand it to be ontologically prior as well, since what we call "redness" cannot exist apart from particular roses of which we may predicate it.

This normal predication of subject and object cannot, however, be the case with existence. When we say, for example, "The rose exists," we do not mean to say that "existence" presupposes the existence of some substance, such as rose, of which we may predicate it. To the contrary, in this case it is the predicate that precedes the subject: it is the substance "rose" that must, so to speak, "inhere" in the predicate "existence" and not the other way around, because, as we have seen, "existence" precedes both ontologically and cognitively every "this or that"—i.e., every particular substance.

Eckhart therefore says, right at the beginning of his prologues, "We must speak and judge differently of being and this being, similarly of the one and this one, of the true and this truth, of the good and this good":

When something is called being, one, true, good, each of these is a predicate of a proposition, and it lies second to the subject. But when something is called this being, this one, this true, or this good (for example, a man or a stone or the like), then the "this" and "this" are the predicate of the proposition, and the general terms just mentioned (for example "being") are not predicates, nor do they lie second to the subject, but they connect the predicate with the subject.

---

42. Thus Aristotle's metaphysics of substance, despite its great sophistication, is, in many ways, a "common sense" philosophy in that it follows more or less closely ordinary human discourse. It assumes that the structure of predication as found in (Greek) human discourse directly mirrors the ontological structure of things.

For instance, when I say, "This is a man or stone," I do not predicate existence but I predicate man or stone or something of the kind. . . . When I say, "A rose is red," I do not assert or affirm that a rose exists, nor that redness exists, but only the natural connection of terms. So "existence" or "is" is not a subject or predicate but a third term besides them: it is the copula of the predicate with the subject.[43]

Whenever we talk about a "this" or "that"—i.e., a creature—we use the term "existence" not absolutely, as a predicate, but as a copula or, to coin a phrase, as a "binding agent" in which the copula "binds" one term, the predicate, to another term, the subject. We therefore talk about "this or that being" using what medieval logical terminology called propositions *tertium adiacens:* i.e., propositions in which the copula "is" "lies third" after the subject and predicate. Propositions *secundum adiacens,* such as "Socrates is," are propositions in which the copula "lies second" after the subject. But we never predicate existence of creatures as such: we always say *"This is a man"* or *"This is a stone"* and not "Man *is*" or "Stone *is*."[44] What is crucial about propositions *tertium adiacens* such as "Martin is a man" or "A rose is red" is that they are true even if Martin or the rose never existed. As Eckhart says above, in such propositions we are not asserting the existence of Martin or the rose, or of humanity or redness, but simply the connection between the terms or between a "this" and a predicate. When we talk about "this or that being," then, we are never talking about existence in any absolute sense but only about the thing's essence. That is why Eckhart says that we must "speak and judge differently of being and this being, similarly of the one and this one, of the true and this truth, of the good and this good." When we talk of "this or that being," i.e., creatures, we are not referring to being or existence in its proper sense. We cannot really speak of creatures in propositions *secundum adiacens.*

What Eckhart wants to say is that the existential import of the cop-

43. *Prol. op. trip.,* n.3; LW I, 131–32/Maurer, 78–79. Eckhart refers to the peculiar status of existence in predication again at the conclusion of his prologue to the "Book of Propositions" (n.25). He also refers to it explicitly in his defense at his trial for heresy at Cologne: "cum dicitur 'homo est animal,' non praedico esse; le enim 'est' non est praedicatum, sed est tertium adiacens, copula praedicati non dicens existentiam, sed solam inhaerentiam praedicati, quod est animal, cum subiecto, quod est homo." See: *Proc. Col. I,* n.123 in: G. Théry, "Edition critique des pièces relatives au procès d'Eckhart contenues dans le manuscrit 33b de la Bibliothèque de Soest," in *Archives d'histoire doctrinale et littéraire du moyen age* 1 (1926), 129-268.

44. See Thomas Aquinas's *Expositio in Peri Hermeneias II,* lect. 2, n.2.

ula "is" mostly gets lost in our ordinary discourse about finite beings. The meaning of "is" becomes abstracted into that of a "binding agent" and loses its existential reference. But if we understand the true existential import of the copula "is," we must assert that "is" refers properly to God, for "is" refers to what is beyond and prior to every "this or that"—i.e., every finite being or creature. Eckhart, of course, recognizes that here we uncover a layer of reality that human propositional language is incapable of handling. Thus, Eckhart casts his fundamental thesis, "Existence is God," in the form of a proposition *tertium adiacens* where the "is" functions as a copula: it "connects" or "binds" the notions "existence" and "God." But the subject of the proposition "Existence is God" is, notably, existence itself. In other words, the *copula*, "is," becomes the *subject*, signified by the verb "to be," *esse*, of the proposition. Eckhart therefore asserts that the "to be" of every proposition *tertium adiacens* can signify nothing other than what we mean by God and that the only predicate that can be said formally and substantively of *esse* is God.[45] This is because God cannot be a "this or that": nothing can exist apart from God.

From Eckhart's standpoint, then, what ordinary human discourse regards as positive is, quite to the contrary, fundamentally *negative* in character. Every creature, insofar as it is a particular existence, is a "negation" because, implied in its status as a "this," it negates all other existent things

45. We encounter an almost identical conception of the relation of existence itself to existent things in Ibn 'Arabi and his teaching of *wādhat al-wujūd* (or the "unity of existence"). Toshihiko Izutsu explains this analysis of the structure of transcendental predication as he finds it in Islamic mystical writers: "Thus the structure of external reality which is indicated by the proposition: 'The flower is existent' proves to be completely different from what is suggested by the grammatical form of the sentence. What is existent in the fullest sense of the word is existence as the absolute Indeterminate, not the flower. Being-a-flower is but a special self-determination of this absolute Indeterminate. It is but a particular phenomenal form in which existence reveals itself in the dimension of the so-called external, sensible world. In other words, the 'flower' here is an accident qualifying 'existence,' and determining it into a certain phenomenal form. Existence in itself, that is, in its purity, is without attributes. It is absolutely simple unity or an absolute indiscrimination." See *Creation and the Timeless Order of Things: Essays in Islamic Mystical Philosophy* (Ashland, Ore.: White Cloud Press, 1994), 73–74. Also: "The Iranian existentialists take the position that in the pre-conceptual order of things, what is really real is existence, and existence only. Existence is the sole absolute, all comprehensive Reality that runs through the whole universe. Or rather, the whole universe is nothing other than the reality of existence. All the so-called quiddities are like shadows cast by the absolute Reality as it goes on evolving itself. They are no other than internal modifications or phenomenal forms under which the absolute Reality reveals itself in the empirical dimension of human experience characterized by time-space limitations." Izutsu, 181. This unfolds reasonably well the implications of Eckhart's thesis *Esse est Deus*.

as other than itself. As soon as we "speak and judge" about this or that being, we are already abstracting from existence by dividing off the thing spoken about from every other thing. Every creature is a *hoc vel hoc* or, in Thomistic language, an *aliquid:* a creature, insofar as it is conceived as a "this," can be said to "deny" that it is another creature. It is "this" existence and not "that" existence. But nothing can be denied to existence itself; it resists all combination or division into subjects or predicates. And since existence is God, then nothing can be denied of God except the "negation of the negation of all existence":

Absolutely nothing of entity, then, can be denied to being or existence itself. It follows that nothing can be denied to the being itself which is God except the negation of negation of all existence. This is why unity, which is the negation of negation, is most closely related to being.[46]

The same, Eckhart adds, can be said for the transcendentals: nothing can be denied to the one, the true, and the good, except the negation of the negation of these perfections. Thus, the true or the good is not any particular truth or good but rather it is the negation of creaturely limitations that make all truths and good only partial truths and goods. Presupposed by these partial truths and goods is the Truth in itself and the Good in itself, which are nothing other than God. That is why these transcendental perfections are convertible with "being" or "existence," which is God:

Moreover, nothing, or no existence, can be denied to being or of being; rather, the negation of negation is aptly ascribed to it. So nothing one, or no unity, can be denied to one except the negation of negation of unity or one; and the case is the same with the true and good.[47]

What is of prime interest for Eckhart, therefore, is that the formula "negation of negation" *adds nothing* to what we call "God" either really or conceptually. To add any sort of property to God in thought, even such properties as goodness or wisdom, would be tantamount to treating God as some sort of delimited object, subject to the sorts of predications we make of such objects: that "it," the subject, "has" these sorts of predicates.[48] But

46. *Prol. op. prop.,* n.15; LW I, 175–76/Maurer, 100. On this passage, see also H. Fischer, *Meister Eckhart: Einführung in sein philosophisches Denken* (Munich: Alber, 1974), 140.

47. *Prol, op. prop.,* n.12; LW I, 170/Maurer, 97.

48. Lossky sees the *negatio negationis* as a dialectical play between the assertion of an "*identité exclusive*" that affirms the *purity* of the divine being and an "*identité inclusive*" that affirms the

as Eckhart says in one of his vernacular sermons, nothing can be added to pure existence nor can anything be denied of pure existence because pure existence includes everything: "But God has a negation of negation; he is one and negates everything else, for outside of God is nothing."[49]

By talking of God in a doubly negative form—negation of negation—Eckhart wants to emphasize not only God's transconceptual nature but also and most importantly God's *preconceptual nature* as the basis of all human thought and willing. For, as Eckhart argues as did Thomas before him, the first concept that "falls" under the intellect is being and those predicates that are convertible with being, namely, the one, the true, and the good, for to know or conceive anything, we must first presuppose its existence, either really or ideally. These—the inherent indivisibility, intelligibility, and desirability of being—are presupposed in all our thinking and, hence, so is God presupposed in all our thinking.

Genuine knowledge of God, therefore, comes only after a process not of adding predicates to our notion of God but rather of stripping them away. Only when the soul adds *absolutely nothing* to its concept of God but abides in existence itself does it truly *know* God. Thus Eckhart says that we must pray that we be free even from conventional notions of "God," for insofar as these notions are formed by the created intellect they are a hindrance to any genuine encounter with God. As Eckhart says in Sermon 21, "*Unus Deus et pater omnium, quiest super omnes, et per omnia, et in omnibus nobis*" (Eph 4:6), the "soul receives the Godhead as it is purified in itself, where nothing has been added":

A master says: "One is a negation of negation." If I say God is good, this adds something [to him]. *One* is a negation of negation and a denial of denial. What does *one* mean? One means something to which nothing has been added. The

---

*plenitudo* of the divine being. This dialectic, of course, already puts God outside the possibility of being grasped within any "objective" knowledge. God is the plenitude of being that makes all existence possible, and yet, precisely due to the priority of that existence, God cannot be known with reference to anything other than himself. God is thus *omninominabile* because God is the ground of every existent thing; thus "nothing can be denied to existence itself," which is God. But God is also *innominabile* because God is nothing in particular but what is prior to every particular existence; God is the negation of negation of whom we cannot predicate anything as of a subject. See: Vladimir Lossky, *Théologie négative et connaissance de Dieu chez Maître Eckhart* (Paris: Vrin, 1998), 68.

49. Pr. 21; DW I, 363/TP, 281: "Aber got hât ein versagen des versagennes; er ist ein und versaget alle ander, wan niht ûzer gote enist."

soul receives the Godhead as it is purified in itself, where nothing has been added, not even in thought. *One* is a negation of negation. All creatures have negation in themselves; one creature denies that it is the other creature. One angel denies that it is some other angel.[50]

Eckhart therefore calls the negation of the negation the *medulla* or *apex* of pure affirmation that affirms the purity of existence: "It should be recognized now that the term 'one' is a negative word, but in reality it is affirmative. Moreover, it is the negation of negation, which is the purest form of affirmation, and the fullness of the term affirmed. Fullness, superabundance, and 'what is said by way of superabundance belong to the One alone,' as the Philosopher says."[51]

And also, in his *Commentary on Exodus*, Eckhart remarks:

> But to existence itself no existence is denied, just as to animal itself is not denied this animal, for example, "lion." Therefore, no negation, nothing negative, belongs to God, except for the negation of negation which is what the One signifies when expressed negatively.... The negation of negation is the purest and fullest affirmation—"I am who am".... Existence cannot deny that it is Existence Itself.[52]

God, then, is the primal affirmation of existence that every partial affirmation of existence in this or that creature presupposes. But as primal affirmation that is the *prius* of all thought, God cannot enter into human discourse or thought as a positive entity or concept. God can enter into human thought and discourse only negatively as the negation of negation, which as the principle of all conceptual thought is prior to all concepts— even that of "existence." The upshot of this is that God reveals himself positively to us only in sacred Scripture.

The full sense of the meaningfulness of being, therefore, comes to fruition only in revelation; indeed, the meaningfulness of being can only be recognized in and through the interpretation of Scripture. That is why, in the structure of his *Opus tripartitum*, the capstone and fulfillment of his project was to be in his *opus expositionum*, or "work of commentaries," where he would reveal the inner sense of both the work of propositions and the various disputed questions in the living metaphors and parables of Scripture. In these metaphors and parables the meaningfulness of created

---

50. *Pr.* 21; DW I, 361–63/TP, 281.
52. *In Exod.*, n.74; LW I, 77/TP, 68.

51. *In Sap.*, n.147; LW II, 485/TP, 167.

being, i.e., being insofar as it is inherently one, knowable, and desirable, is *lived* and *experienced*, as Scripture reinserts the abstraction of the transcendentals back into the lived experience of the soul of its inner union with God. Revelation begins with the soul's lived experience of God in its inner ground and ends with that lived experience. For it is in the intellect, which abstracts from the *hic et nunc*, that the eternal enters into the flow of time. By itself and in itself, the intellect remains in the eternal abstractions of metaphysics, but when turned toward the interpretation of Scripture, it sees how these eternal abstractions or transcendental qualities of being are born in the temporal life of the soul. But this statement itself remains abstract unless we look at a specific example of how Eckhart uses biblical exegesis to recover the inner, existential truth of metaphysical categories like the transcendentals.

Eckhart interprets the verse from John *In propria venit*, or "He came into His own" (Jn 1:11), in terms of his doctrine of the transcendentals: "Remember that nothing is so much its own as a being's act of existence or a creature's creator. But God is existence itself and is also the creator. This is the meaning of 'He came to his own.'"[53] Thus, the inner meaning of the second person of the Trinity, "coming to his own," i.e., becoming human, is that only God properly possesses true existence and only he is truly one, true, and good, while creatures only have these transcendental properties in and through God:

The passage can be taken in a second way as follows. The things that are his own into which God came are Existence or Being, the One, the True and the Good. These four things are God's own, for he is "the First which is rich through itself." He possesses these because he is "rich"; he possesses them as his own because he exists "through himself." In the case of everything that is below the First these four things are "guests and strangers" (Eph 2:19); with God they are "members of the household." Therefore, we teach first that God exists and works in all things and comes to all men and all things insofar as they exist, insofar as they are one, and insofar as they are true and good. Second, we teach that through his coming and presence God immediately and with no other agent causes being, unity, truth and goodness in all things in an analogical fashion.[54]

53. *In Ioh.*, n.96; LW III, 83/EE, 158–59.
54. *In Ioh.*, n.97; LW III, 83–84/EE, 159. Goris rightly criticizes Karl Albert, *Meister Eckharts These vom Sein: Untersuchungen zur Metaphysik des Opus tripartitum* (Saarbrücken: Kastelaun-Henn, 1976), for his assertion that Eckhart's doctrine of the transcendentals must be understood

To say that creatures have being, oneness, truth, and goodness in a way *analogous* to that of the being, oneness, truth, and goodness of God is to say that creatures and God share in these qualities, but creatures do so in only a limited or finite way, while God has them in an infinite mode. The problem for the human intellect, however, is that it cannot know being, oneness, truth, and goodness in God simply by abstracting their features from creatures and conceiving them without limit. To do so would be to come up with purely general, and thus purely empty, abstractions. But the divine Being, in its perfection, is not an idea or an abstraction but the most "concrete" existence there is, *esse ipsum subsistens*. The metaphysical speculations of the human intellect are, therefore, without content if pursued out of the resources of the human intellect alone. The result of this is that, for Eckhart, the transcendental predicates of creatures can become knowable as such only through a reflection on Christ. In Christ, God comes to dwell among us, which is to say that being, the one, the true, and the good come to dwell among us. They do so not as metaphysical abstractions but in the person of Christ, who, by being born in the ground of the soul, allows the soul to live *in* and *out* of pure existence, unity, truth, and goodness.

Eckhart tries to clarify this by an exegesis of the following verse in John, "And His own received Him not." Now, the literal meaning of this verse, as Eckhart mentions, is that Jesus was rejected by his own people and put to death on the cross. But for Eckhart, the deeper meaning is that "neither things that exist nor things that are one, true or good possess their being, unity, truth and goodness from themselves . . . but they possess them from the Word himself, the Son of God." Creatures have no existence, unity, truth, or goodness that is their own; these come directly from God insofar as he became Word and entered into creation himself as a human being. And insofar as creatures hold on to their created distinction, they do not receive the Word of God, which is to say his existence, unity, truth, and goodness. These transcendental predicates cannot take root in creatures, for, as Eckhart says, "indistinct existence is proper to God and he is distinguished by his indistinction alone, while distinct existence is proper to

_____

as a purely philosophical undertaking. Goris adduces the passages cited above to show that, in Eckhart's mind at least, the transcendentals and their relation to God, to creatures, and to each other cannot be understood apart from the processions of the divine Trinity and the Incarnation as revealed to us in the sacred text. See Goris, *Einheit*, 96.

a creature. It does not belong to what is distinct to receive what is indistinct. So Augustine, addressing God, says: 'You were with me, and I was not with you.'"[55] As Eckhart's citation of Augustine emphasizes, there is no one so intimate to ourselves as God. God is closer to us than we are to ourselves. The great paradox is that, the more we possess something of our own, the farther away we are from what is most intimate to us, God. Thus the soul falls away from the living Truth, Christ, and into metaphysical and philosophical abstractions. The soul substitutes its own "ideas" of God for a living relationship with God, Christ, himself.

Eckhart makes this point clear in the following passage:

Again, "He came to his own." Note that everything created, because it is a particular being, something distinct, belongs to some genus, species or individual thing. God is not anything distinct or proper to some nature, but is common to all. He is outside and above every genus. The proof of this is that being, God's effect, is not a genus and does not belong to any genus, but is common to every genus. When God came into this world, assumed a created nature and was made man, it was as if he came to what is proper from the height of what is common. This is what the text clearly means, "He was the true light that enlightens every man," for this light is common and superior to all. There follows, "He was in the world, and the world," that which contains every genus, "was made through him." Finally, John concludes, "He came to his own."[56]

In Christ, what is utterly common, existence, becomes united to what is most intimate and particular, the inner ground of the human soul. Eternal being intersects with temporal man. Thus, it is not simply the case, for Eckhart, that the doctrine of the transcendentals gives us the true meaning of Christ, but rather it is Christ that gives us the true meaning of the transcendentals and, from them, of all rational thought, for the doctrine of the transcendentals is the most fundamental of metaphysical truths. The truths of metaphysics can help us to understand Scripture, but ultimately it is Scripture that reveals to us the truths of metaphysics, because in Scripture, the truths of metaphysics are not abstract but concrete: they are understood as expressions or articulations of the soul's innermost, personal encounter with the person of Christ.

Thus, it follows that all creatures and all *rationes naturales* are simply

55. *In Ioh.*, n.99; LW III, 85 /EE, 159–60.
56. *In Ioh.*, n.103; LW III, 88–89/EE, 161.

analogues of this unity of humanity with God in Christ. But, as we have seen above, creatures in and of themselves cannot reveal to human reason existence, oneness, intelligibility, or goodness properly speaking, since creatures, including human reason, limit these transcendentals to finite beings. Creaturely existence, truth, or goodness is only analogous to God's pure existence, truth, and goodness. As Eckhart puts it in this passage from his commentary on Ecclesiasticus:

> Again, note . . . that these three are to be distinguished: "the univocal, the equivocal and the analogous. Equivocals are divided according to different things that are signified, univocals according to various differences of the [same] thing." Analogous things are not distinguished according to things, nor through the differences of things, but "according to the modes [of being]" of one and the same simple thing. For example, the one and the same health that is in an animal is that (and no other) which is in the diet and the urine [of the animal] in such a way that there is no more health as health in the diet and urine than there is in a stone. Urine is said to be "healthy" only because it signifies the health, the same in number, which is in the animal, just as a circular wreath which has nothing of wine in it [signifies] wine.[57]

Since there can be nothing outside of God's existence, there cannot be an equivocal relationship between God and creatures, for this would imply that God, who is existence itself, and existing creatures exist independently of each other, which is absurd because existing things can exist only by virtue of being caused by existence itself. Nor can there be between the creature, as creature, and God a univocal relationship, since that would imply a mere conceptual difference between God and creatures: they would both belong to the same genus (just as a deer and a moose both belong to the genus "mammal"), but would only differ by certain specific differences. But this is not the case at all between God and creatures. Creatures subsist in and through God's existence, but in an entirely different mode than that in which God exists. God exists infinitely, creatures finitely.

Creatures, therefore, do not, according to Eckhart, exist as such, because to exist is to exist without restriction. As he asserts above, creatures exist only insofar as they are *signs* of God's absolute existence. Their entire being consists in signifying the divine Being and nothing more. Hence,

---

57. *In Eccli.*, n.52; LW II, 280–81/TP, 178. Here Eckhart is referring to Thomas Aquinas's Sentences commentary, *Sent. I*, d. 22, q. 1, a. 3, ad 2.

Eckhart compares creatures to the hoops or wreaths that would hang outside of medieval taverns to signify the wine served within. Just as there is no wine in the wreath, but only the signification of wine, so there is nothing of existence in the creature, except the *signification of existence*—as well as of oneness, truth, and goodness. One can even extend the analogy further and say that, just as the wreath is an *invitation* to the traveler to drink the wine within, so is the creature an invitation to drink the divine existence, oneness, truth, and goodness within all creatures.

This image is, in fact, an invitation for the soul to turn within him or herself and drink the wine of divine being and truth in the soul's very ground. Indeed, this discussion of analogy occurs in the midst of Eckhart's exegesis of Ecclesiasticus 24:29, "They that eat me, shall yet hunger: and they that drink me, shall yet thirst." Since the creature is, in him or herself, nothing, the more he or she "eats" or "drinks" of the divine existence, the more he or she "hungers and thirsts." Just as the divine existence is inexhaustible in its infinity, so is the creature's need for God to fill its own existential nothingness. The whole point of Eckhart's exegesis, therefore, is to lead the soul actually to "drink" directly from God's pure existence. It is to lead the soul from the creaturely sign, i.e., "wreath," outside to the ground of the soul, i.e., "tavern," within, where God's being, truth, and goodness may be "drunk."

### Isticheit

While it appears relatively rarely in Eckhart's vernacular works, the Middle High German term *isticheit* or "is-ness" nevertheless provides a crucial insight into the hermeneutics of existence we have seen at work in Eckhart. Surely, in coining the term, Eckhart was thinking of existence as the copula "is" that binds predicate to subject. But he transforms this copula into an abstract noun to draw our attention to the primordial existence that every existent thing and every predication about existent things presupposes. What Eckhart, however, emphasizes in his vernacular works to a much greater extent than he does in his scholastic Latin works is that this primordial existence is something that can be known not through discursive rational thought but only *experientially* in and through the inner ground of the soul that gives birth in itself to the inner sense or *logos* of revelation, Jesus Christ.

Eckhart employs the term *isticheit* or "is-ness" in a particularly important passage in his sermon *Renovamini spiritu*. Here Eckhart takes up Paul's statement in his letter to the Ephesians about how the Christian may be "renewed in spirit," which in the Vulgate is translated as *mens* or "mind." Eckhart starts by remarking that the mind is, according to the best authorities, such as Augustine, a "store or a coffer of spiritual forms or formal images." This characteristic is what makes the soul akin to God. Just as God pours forth his image in the Son and the Holy Spirit, in the same way the soul "pours forth" spiritual forms and images. What is important for Eckhart, though, is that the soul resembles God not by having or possessing images of God, but precisely in this "pouring forth" of the image of God within itself. The soul is united to God only to the degree that it possesses nothing of itself but rather becomes a vehicle in and through which the divine Trinity may emanate into creation. For this reason, Eckhart remarks:

So when the soul with these powers contemplates what consists of images, whether that be an angel's image or its own, there is for the soul something lacking. Even if the soul contemplates God, either as God or an image or as three, the soul lacks something. But if all images are detached from the soul, and it contemplates only the Simple One, then the soul's naked being finds the naked, formless being of the divine unity, which is there a being above being, accepting and reposing in itself. Ah, marvel of marvels, how noble is that acceptance, when the soul's being can accept nothing else than the naked unity of God![58]

For Eckhart, to be "renewed in spirit" is to prevent any image or likeness coming between the soul and God. Indeed, all creation can be renewed, but God, technically speaking, cannot be renewed, because God is in eternity and renewal cannot come to what is eternal. So it is with the soul: insofar as I am a creature, I am renewed by God; but insofar as I am an image of God, I am in eternity: "To a soul, too, renewal happens, so far as 'spirit' is its name. It is called spirit because it is detached from here and now and from the whole natural order. But when it is an image of God and as nameless as God, then no renewal happens to it, but only eternity, as in God."[59] Thus, not to *have* but to *be* an image of God allows the divine eternity to break into the flow of our human temporality. It is this that is

58. *Pr.* 83; DW III, 437–38/EE, 206.
59. *Pr.* 83; DW III, 440/EE, 206.

the inner truth of the Trinity and the Incarnation and it is the breaking through of the eternal into the temporal of the mind or spirit that is its recovery, enactment, and fulfillment.

It would therefore be a mistake to read the passage cited above where Eckhart cautions us to go beyond the image of God "as three" as a denial of the dogma of the Trinity. Quite to the contrary, Trinitarian theology is essential to understanding how the soul appropriates in the ground of its existence the truth of revelation. For it is by *becoming an image of God* and giving birth to that image in our renewed mind or spirit that we participate in the life of the Trinity, and the Trinity comes to live in us. Indeed, for Eckhart, the doctrine of the Trinity shows us in what precise way being is meaningful by showing us how, in Christ, the divine eternal being intersects with, sustains, and gives meaning to the temporal being of our daily lives; how the being, oneness, truth, and goodness of things are eternal perfections that yet make possible the temporal existence of all creatures.

To help us understand this, Eckhart engages in a rather radical bit of negative theology, emphasizing that, to the degree that we think of God in abstraction, as an *ens perfectissimum* cut off from the world and aloof from the flow of temporality, then God literally "is not." In fact, such a "God" is neither good nor true. Eckhart states, "If I say: 'God is a being' (*Got is ein wesen*), it is not true; he is a being transcending being and a [being] transcending nothingness (*swebende wesen und ein uber wesende nitheit*)." To be renewed in spirit, therefore, we must "be silent" and "not chatter about God; for when you do chatter about him, you are telling lies and sinning." For "if you can understand anything about him, it in no way belongs to him."[60] We are sinning when we think that we understand God by predicating attributes of God in the same manner that we predicate attributes of creatures.

Knowledge of God is not purely a matter of thought for Eckhart but a matter of experiencing, in our innermost ground, the primal "is-ness" that is both manifest in all things and, at the same time, hidden in them. The obstacle to knowing God is the conviction of my own separate existence, my "mine-ness" or "this-ness" as absolute when, in reality, existence in itself is God and God alone. Here the practical and lived significance of all

---

60. Pr. 83; DW III, 442/EE, 207.

the logical distinctions that we observed Eckhart make earlier becomes clearer: by the term "is-ness" it seems that Eckhart wants to draw our attention to the concrete reality of the little copula "is" that joins predicate to subject when I make statements about any creature. What is prior to any subject or predicate is the "is-ness" that makes all subjects and predicates possible. Indeed, that "is-ness" is God, which is also the ground of my soul and which I appropriate in and through the Incarnation of Christ. My sense of existing in any absolute sense is an illusion; I am a negation of absolute or pure being that itself must be negated in a sort of "lived" *negatio negationis*. To break this illusion, I must let go of any sense of my existence being absolutely separate from existence itself, which is God:

Then what ought I to do? You ought to sink down out of all your your-ness (*dinesheit*), and flow into his his-ness (*sinesheit*), and your "yours" and his "his" ought to become one "mine," so completely that you with him perceive forever his uncreated is-ness (*isticheit*), and his nothingness, for which there is no name.[61]

This primal "is-ness" is as much "nothingness" as it is existence insofar as this is-ness is beyond every "this or that." It is literally "no-thing" precisely because it is existence itself. That is why Eckhart remarks, as mentioned above, that God transcends both being and nothingness, which means that even God must cease being a "god," i.e., a "this," and must divest himself of all his properties (*eigenschaften*) as a "this" and unite himself *to me* and *my is-ness* if God is truly and really to be God. Indeed, in this union of practical freedom between God and the soul there is fundamentally only one "working" apart from which "God" and "creature" are nothing but reified abstractions. Thus to the question of how we are to "perceive" God, Eckhart answers:

You should perceive him without images, without a medium, and without comparisons (*ane bilde, ane mittel, und ane glichnis*). But if I am to perceive God so, without a medium, then I must just become him, and he must become me. I say more: God must become me, and I must just become God, so completely one that this "he" and this "I" become and are one "is," and, in this is-ness, eternally perform one work (*in der isticheit ewiklich ein werk wirkent*), for this "he," who is God, and this "I," which is the soul, are greatly fruitful. But let there be a single

---

61. Pr. 83; DW III, 443/EE, 207.

"here" or a single "now," and the "I" and the "he" will never perform anything or become one.[62]

We cannot know God, then, through discursive thought. The soul can come to understand God only through a direct *participation* in the primordial "is-ness" that every existent thing and all discourse about things presupposes. This participation can come about, however, only when the soul has negated every negation in its own mode of being not only in every thought but also in every action. The detached soul must be free from all distinction in its thought, will, actions—which is to say in its very existence.

The soul that is free and detached no longer thinks of itself as "this person" as opposed to "that person." Rather, such a soul becomes detached from all that is creaturely, including its very self, and thinks, lives, and acts out of its pure, undivided humanity.[63] Such a soul therefore loves all things equally, without clinging or possessiveness, for it is dead to itself. And, as Eckhart remarks in Sermon 46, "*Haec est vita aeterna* (Jn 17:3)," it is in this pure, undivided humanity that existence itself in all its purity shines forth:

Man is an accident of nature. Therefore, abandon everything that is accident in you and preserve yourself as free, undivided human nature. Since this same nature which you possess has become the Son of the eternal Father through its being assumed by the eternal Word, you become the Son of the eternal Father with Christ because you have the same nature which has become God. Therefore, be careful not in the least to hold onto yourself as you are *this* person or *that*, but preserve yourself as a free, undivided human nature. And so, if you want to be one Son, separate yourself from all nothing because nothing causes distinction. How is that? Note the following. That you are *not* a certain person,

---

62. Pr. 83; DW III, 447/EE, 208.

63. Eckhart therefore argues that God never negates existence as such nor the creature insofar as it exists. God is the negation of negation, not the negation of anything positive or affirmative. In this way, God both preserves all creatures in existence and at the same time affirms his utter distinction from all creatures as the purity of existence (see Lossky, *Théologie négative*, 68). This makes possible, then, the most intimate unity in the most radical distinction. Eckhart uses the example of the unity of form and matter and parts and whole. He also points to the doctrine of the Incarnation and its teaching of the union of God and humanity in the person of Jesus Christ: just as the Incarnation of God in Christ did not destroy Christ's humanity but rather perfected and fulfilled it, so God's existence does not destroy the existence of creatures but perfects and fulfills it. See *Prol. op. trip.*, n.20; LW I, 178/Maurer, 101.

it is the *not* which differentiates you from this person. If you want to be without distinction, rid yourself of *not (nihte)*. There is a power in the soul which is separated from nothing since it has nothing in common with any things. Nothing is in this power but God alone. He shines naked into this power.[64]

God is no stranger to us because ultimately our very is-ness is God's is-ness—human nature in its purity is nothing other than the divine nature itself. For existence or "is-ness" is God; and to the degree that we live out of our very own "is-ness," we live out of God's "is-ness." By existing in our undivided humanity we accept God into us just as God becomes fully God only to the extent that God becomes fully human in Jesus Christ—and by extension, *in us*. So how do we negate our creaturely distinction—i.e., perform a *negatio negationis* not conceptually but *existentially* in all our willing and acting? For Eckhart, it is only by receiving Christ in the ground of our souls and allowing him to dwell and work there. It is Christ, not just by his historical example but more importantly by his eternally indwelling presence, who frees the soul from its particularity and allows it to dwell in its "undivided" human nature which, in Christ, is none other than the divine nature.

### Mystical Hermeneutics and the Dialectic of Existence

We have seen how both Ibn 'Arabi and Meister Eckhart see the relationship between God and creatures as a dialectical one in which God is both he who is utterly transcendent to all creatures and also, by the very virtue of that transcendence, also utterly immanent in all creatures. As Eckhart puts it, God's very distinction from creatures is his indistinction from creatures; while for Ibn 'Arabi, all creatures are both he and not he, where the incomparability of God necessarily implies God's comparability with all things.

It would be a mistake, however, to abstract from the thought of these two thinkers some universal or natural religion, for, apart from revelation, these metaphysical dialectics are simply just that: the juggling of abstract ideas, dialectical fireworks. For both Ibn 'Arabi and Meister Eckhart, any

---

64. *Pr.* 46; DW II, 380–82/TP, 304–5. For an almost identical passage see also *Pr.* 24; DW I, 420.

understanding of the dialectical nature of the creature's relationship with God springs from the revealed text and takes on significance and meaning for the individual only insofar as it is applied to the understanding of the revealed text. For Ibn 'Arabi, it is the Qur'an that brings together the transcendent and the immanent into a focused and coherent vision. Without the Qur'an and its assimilation into the heart of the believer, human reason is stuck in division and thus estranged from Reality. It is the same for Eckhart: God's transcendence and immanence come together in Christ. Not only is this *coincidentia oppositorum* revealed in Christ, but the grace of Christ also *effects* this coincidence of opposites by appropriating to himself in a complete, fully distinct, but inseparable way the divine and human natures. By allowing Christ to be born in the ground of the soul, the individual believer recovers and appropriates Christ's unification of the divine and human and lives it, for by living their unity he or she lives in God himself. It is therefore in the reading and interpretation of the revealed text, in the taking into oneself the message of the Qur'an or by accepting into oneself the inner *Logos* of Scripture, who is Christ, that the fundamental categories of metaphysics become meaningful. The soul experiences in his or her being the truth of existence as such. Out of this experience of pure being or existence comes a full understanding of being qua being, that is, a true metaphysical knowledge. This knowledge is not theoretical but practical and existential, that is to say, a lived basis of all action and thought. But for revelation, this knowledge would have been unattainable by human reason alone, according to our two mystics. For Ibn 'Arabi, only the imaginal world revealed by the Qur'an brings together properly the transcendent and immanent nature of existence; for Eckhart, Christ alone does this. The Qur'an and Christ make true metaphysics possible because they both make the true understanding of being something *lived in the ground of the believer's own existence.*

This is not to say that the specific characteristics of the Qur'an and the Bible do not have an effect on the way Ibn 'Arabi and Eckhart understand this dialectic. For Ibn 'Arabi, it is the Qur'an's fundamental message of *tawḥīd*, the assertion that God is one without a partner, that unites the opposites of comparability and incomparability. It is the divine *book* that serves as the locus of the individual soul's union with God and his divine Unity. The individual, realized knower of God, then, sees him or herself as a *theophany*: i.e., as an outward manifestation of the hidden divine reality, in the same way as the language of the Qur'an is an outward manifestation of the divine meaning within. It is thus by assimilation of the language of the Qur'an into the inner, hidden or *baṭinī* dimension of the realized knower that he or she turns inward. To the person who has fully assimilated the Qur'an, it is not he or she who "carries" or absorbs the book but rather it is the other way around: it is the book that "carries" or absorbs the knower. And in doing so, the realized knower recognizes him or herself for who he or she really is: a theophany or a manifestation of the divine without any inner core other than the hidden Real itself.

To designate creation as theophany is also to designate it as *imaginal*. As we saw in chapter 1, for Ibn 'Arabi, creation is an imaginal world insofar as it is analogous to a dream, without any existence or reality in itself. Compared, of course, to the dreams that human beings have, this imaginal world, i.e., creation, has far more reality than even our sensible experience, precisely because it is a *divine*, and hence, truly *creative* dream, bringing something out of nothing. In this realm, the spiritual and the material or sensible meet: spiritual realities take on material forms while material forms take on spiritual meanings. As truly expressive of the ambiguous nature of creation, as hovering between God's absolute Being and nothing, the world as imagination is also most fully expressive of the dialectical nature of creation and of God's relation to it. It brings together most clearly and powerfully the comparability and incomparability of God's absolute Existence. Insofar as the Qur'an both expresses and gives access to the imaginal world, the creation as viewed "imaginally" if you will, it is the only means by which human reason can know this fundamental truth about God and reality.

For Eckhart, by contrast, the core and marrow of revelation is a *Person*, Jesus Christ. It is in Jesus Christ that the unity of God as the coincidence of the opposites of transcendence and immanence not only comes to light but is also effected. Christ is the key to the inner meaning of both Scripture and human reason. In Christ, one confronts the inadequacy of any reflection or action that remains on the level of pure materiality or pure conceptuality. Whereas for Ibn 'Arabi, the transcendent eternity intersects with immanent temporality in the Qur'an, for Eckhart they intersect in Christ. That this intersection occurs in a Person, the Incarnate

Word, and not a book, has implications for how this unity of transcendence and immanence is appropriated by the individual believer. The Incarnation, therefore, plays a central role in Eckhart's thinking and writing. The Incarnation both reveals and effects the unity of the transcendence and immanence of God in every person who accepts Christ. Eckhart, therefore, uses not so much the language of theophany as the language of *ground* and *birth*. It is through Christ being born in the ground of the soul that the soul is united to God and knows God. The divine *Logos*, then, is not the revealed Book itself, the Bible, but he who is revealed in and through the Bible. As such, the Incarnation is, again, analogous to the world of imagination in the writings of Ibn 'Arabi.

Since, for Eckhart, creatures derive all their perfections, such as existence, intelligibility, goodness, and unity, directly from God, they have no perfections in themselves. Eckhart develops this notion at length, as we have seen, putting forth his thesis *Esse est Deus*. Creatures are only analogically differentiated limitations of the infinite divine existence, truth, goodness, and unity and, as such, are nothing in themselves. What is unique to the human soul is that, by giving birth to Christ in its inner ground, it can come to *realize* its own nothingness and thus become fully conformed to God's pure existence. This is the practical fruit of understanding abstract metaphysics through Scripture.

Thus, the revealed text is ultimately to be transcended precisely insofar as Christ, the divine Word, becomes the very *substance* of the soul of the believer. For Eckhart, the Word has become flesh and, as such, has redeemed human nature in its entirety, making it a vehicle, especially in its suffering and death, for a return to union with the Godhead. As Eckhart is never tired of repeating, the essence of the Christian dialectic is the patristic formula: God became man so that man might become God. Or transcendence became immanence, so that immanence might become transcendent or, yet again, eternity became temporal so that temporality might become eternal. In this way, then, we can characterize the "mystical" path, whether Christian or Muslim, as the way of pure interiority, of penetration to the innermost ground of human being, which, at the same time, is effected by understanding oneself and creation in and through the sacred text.

PART III

## ✤ Intellect

The Sufi saint, according to Ibn ʿArabi, is someone who understands how his own limited created nature shapes and, in fact, distorts his reception of God's gift of existence and his gift of intellectual illumination. But because he has this realization, the Sufi saint
is also able to rise above this limitation. Through the exercise of the
analogical imagination, he is able to see God in all things and in all
thoughts. The saint becomes a pure mirror in and through which
God is reflected. As a pure, polished mirror, the Sufi saint sees the
Real with the "heart," in the special sense that we shall see below.
When he knows the Real with his heart, the Sufi's entire being—
body, soul, and, particularly, intellect—"beats" to the rhythm of
divine manifestations in creation. In this sense, the Sufi saint rises
above mere rationality and becomes pure intellect, that is to say, a
pure and undistorted mirror of the divine Essence fully conformed
to the divine Reality. What allows the saint, however, to conform
to the divine manifestations in creation is the Holy Qur'an. By assimilating the words of the Qur'an into his or her heart, the Sufi
saint becomes conformed to the activity of the divine as a key to
its proper lock. Hence, the Sufi saint becomes annihilated in his
or her self only to become more receptive to the words of the Holy
Qur'an.

For Eckhart as well, the goal of the spiritual life is not to "know"
an image of God or to "have" an image of God, but *to be* the image of God. Eckhart explains that it is the nature of an image qua

image not to have any being of its own but to reflect entirely and wholly that of which it is the image. Its essence is through and through relational. Thus, to be an image of God for the soul is to be wholly related to God without any attachment to any possession or even being of one's own. The being of such a soul *is* to reflect God's Being. For Eckhart, the essence of intellectuality is fulfilled when there is perfect conformity between knower and known. Insofar as the human being is a finite creature, the essence of intellectuality remains unfulfilled, because there cannot be a perfect conformity to the divine image. He or she can only know God by analogy. But when he or she is an image of God, there is perfect conformity and thus true intellectuality. This, for Eckhart, is the true sense of *imagination:* actually *to become an image qua image.* What this means in practical terms, for Eckhart, is that the human being must reflect God's Word in his or her every thought and action, to allow the divine Word and his or her relation to it to become the ultimate basis of his or her life and action.

Hence, there is an absolute necessity for scriptural exegesis in the writings of both Eckhart and Ibn 'Arabi for the fulfillment of true intellectuality. For both Ibn 'Arabi and Meister Eckhart, scriptural hermeneutics is an eminently *philosophical* or *metaphysical* activity, essential to any science of being that is true, because it conforms the soul to the inner and transcendent *Logos* of all things. Reason becomes intellect in the interpretation of the revealed text in that revelation pulls the soul out of itself, forces it to let go of its finite attachments and calls it to subsist in the *Logos* of all things, which is intellect in all of its purity. Left to its own devices, reason becomes egocentric, relating reality only to itself and its finite concepts. As such, reason without revelation is cut off from true intellectuality. It is only when reason is called out of itself by revelation that it rises to the level of intellect, where is becomes a pure and detached reflection of truth in itself.

5

# Ibn 'Arabi and the Mirror of the Intellect

While I shall be pointing out the philosophical implications of
Ibn 'Arabi's thought, it bears repeating that Ibn 'Arabi never saw
himself as a philosopher or what he was doing as philosophy, *falsafa*, as understood by the Arabs. His aim was not a rational understanding of the world or even of God. Rather, he sought the
unveiling of the divine Reality *(al-ḥaqq)* in and through a unitative
intellection that he sometimes calls *gnosis (ma'rifa)*. In other words,
Ibn 'Arabi saw himself as doing what he called *wisdom (ḥikma)* or
what we might call "meta-philosophy": thinking that leads back
into the primal ground or presupposition of thinking which is the
self-disclosure of the Real, or Truth *(al-ḥaqq)* that illuminates all
thinking. As Claude Addas puts it:

In Ibn 'Arabi's eyes the only true philosopher, the only philosopher who
deserves the name of "sage" *(ḥākim* here becomes a synonym for *'ārif,*
gnostic), is he who endeavors to perfect his knowledge by means of contemplation and spiritual experience. The model for this type of philosopher is the man named by Ibn 'Arabi in the passage just cited: the "divine
Plato" *(Aflaṭūn al-ilāhi)*. The rest—those who rely only on their intellect
*('aql)*—will never grasp any more than a minuscule part of the truth.[1]

Reason or *'aql*—what Addas translates as "intellect"—is discursive
and analytic. As such, reason knows by dividing its proper objects
into classes and categories, as Aristotle taught. In this way also,

---

1. Claude Addas, *Quest for the Red Sulphur*, 105.

reason separates the knower from the known: the subject of knowledge, the knower, is radically separate from its object, the known, because, as Aristotle showed, the rational faculty of the human soul abstracts the immaterial form of a sensible thing from the material conditions of its existence. What human reason knows in a thing properly speaking is not "this (material) thing here" but the immaterial form that makes the thing what it is. Hence, the knower, as an immaterial thing, is radically separate from the material thing known.

But this is not the whole story. Even for Aristotle, reason presupposes a higher faculty, one that unites the knower in knowledge to the thing known. As Aristotle also argued, something is known only insofar as it becomes, in some way and to a certain extent, the knower, and the knower knows, only to the extent that he "becomes"—qua immaterial form—the known. This union is possible, according to Aristotle, because the knower and known are united not materially—they each remain in their separate material substrates—but *formally*: when I know the stone, I *am* the stone insofar as I have in my intellect the *form* of the stone, and the stone is me insofar as its form, in its immaterial purity, is in me as knower. This union of knower and known is the foundational insight not only of Aristotle, but also of Islamic epistemology and, by extension, the thought of Ibn 'Arabi as well. As Izutsu explains:

The problem of the unique form of subject-object relationship is discussed in Islam as the problem of *ittiḥād al-'ālim wa-al-ma'lūm*, i.e. the "unification of the knower and the known." Whatever may happen to be the object of knowledge, the highest degree of knowledge is always achieved when the knower, the human subject, becomes completely unified and identified with the object so much so that there remains no differentiation between the two. For differentiation or distinction means distance, and distance in cognitive relationship means ignorance. As long as there remains between the subject and the object the slightest degree of distinction, that is to say, as long as there are subject and object as two entities distinguishable from one another, perfect cognition is not realized.[2]

The drive behind all knowing, therefore, is toward *unity*, i.e., unity between knower and known, and though this unity is implicit in Aristotle's account of knowledge, it is more explicit in Plato (which is perhaps why for Ibn 'Arabi only Plato, among the *falāsifa*, rose above mere reasoning to

2. Toshihiko Izutsu, *Creation and the Timeless Order of Things*, 7.

the level of *ḥikma* or wisdom, i.e., an intuitive and unitative vision of the Good). To put all this into the language of a medieval Christian scholastic like Eckhart, inherent in reason is a drive toward *intellectus*, the knowledge of and therefore perfect union with the Real as such. Because the knower and known remain distinct materially on the level of abstraction, human reason is only an imperfect mode of cognition. Nevertheless, insofar as it *is* the immaterial form of the thing it knows, human reason "participates" in the act of unitative intellection that is the essence of divine knowledge. Such, I would argue, is also the view held by Ibn 'Arabi: *'aql* or reason has as its essential and inherent dynamic a drive toward unitative knowledge, which Ibn 'Arabi calls knowledge of the *heart* (*qalb*).[3] Through the heart, understood as the organ of unitative knowledge, the individual soul is united with God and knows God, not as an object of reason or even of faith, but as the ground of the soul's very existence and every act of knowing.

In and through this spiritual organ of the heart, God becomes both the knower and known in and through the gnostic. There is no separation of subject and object. To know God, then, one must first know oneself: the gnostic must know in what ways his own finite essence conditions, limits, reflects, and distorts the divine Essence.[4] Such self-knowledge is not attained, needless to say, by rational thought, because reason cannot grasp its own ground but only what is given to it as object. Self-knowledge, on the other hand, is the product of ascetic self-control and detachment

3. For the sake of clarity and consistency, I shall translate the term *'aql* by the English word "reason" or "discursive reason." The word "intellect" causes confusion in Western languages insofar as it does not correspond at all to what the Christian scholastics meant by "intellect" or *intellectus*. "Intellect" for them corresponded much more closely (though not exactly, as we shall see) to what the Sufis called the "heart." The problem is that it has been the custom to translate the term *'aql* in the works by the medieval Muslim scholastics by the term "intellect," as Affifi reminds us: "It [the heart] is not identical with the 'intellect' (as understood by the philosophers) which Ibnul 'Arabi definitely regards as phenomenal and dependent on the body, but rather an inseparable 'part' of the Principle of Universal Reason, which, though it functions through a body, is neither the body itself nor dependent for its existence on a body nor bound in any way by material limitations." A. E. Affifi, *The Mystical Philosophy of Ibnul 'Arabi*, 115.

4. "For Ibn 'Arabi the foundation of all knowledge, no matter how objective or impersonal some forms of knowledge may appear to be, has its grounds in self-knowledge: the kind of knowledge which cannot be ultimately divorced from the knower nor from the thing known. To put the matter in contemporary existentialist terms Ibn 'Arabi's is a participatory view of knowledge which recognizes that in every act of knowing stands the knower." Peter Coates, *Ibn 'Arabi and Modern Thought: The History of Taking Metaphysics Seriously* (Oxford: Anqa Publishing, 2002), 4.

from all created things, in thought, will, and action.[5] In other words, true intellectuality, for Ibn 'Arabi, is attained only by the saints and comes to fulfillment only in sainthood. Thus, before looking at the role and nature of the heart in Ibn 'Arabi's thought as expounded in the chapter on Shu'aib in the *Bezels*, we must first understand what he says about the nature of sainthood and self-knowledge in his chapter on Seth.

### The Wisdom of Expiration in the Word of Seth

As Affifi notes in his remarks on the text of the *Bezels*, Seth, as the son of Adam, is also the first manifestation of the Adamic principle. The Adamic principle, which we shall look at in more detail in part 4, is, in short, the principle of all manifestation, outward and inward, matter and spirit. It is the Universal Man of which the individual human being is but a small-scale reflection or microcosm. As the word of "expiration," Seth is the first emanation of the Adamic Universal Man into the inner man that is, relative to material reality, hidden or nonmanifest. In Neoplatonic terminology, the word of Seth as expiration is the emanation of the inner, intellectual principle of all things, the transcendent Intellect or νοῦς.[6] In the first chapter of the *Bezels*, the chapter on Adam, Ibn 'Arabi has in view the universal manifestation of God in creation and the vision that God has of himself in the "mirror" of creation and, in particular, the "mirror" of the word of Adam. In the chapter on Seth, on the other hand, Ibn 'Arabi has in view the "interior revelation" of God in humanity and the knowledge or "vision" that the human being has of himself in the divine "mirror."[7] This chapter, therefore, explores how God is known—in fact, best known—through knowledge of one's own self as a reflection of the di-

5. "Pour Ibn 'Arabi, en effet, il y a un constant parallélisme entre le phénomène ascetique et le phénomène mystique, entre les vertus et les charismes ou faveurs divines; à l'acte extérieur de vertu correspond toujours, comme fruit, une expérience (intuitive ou émotionelle) intérieure et spirituelle · mais cette expérience, à son tour, engendre, si elle est authentique, un autre acte extérieur de vertu plus haute, un autre phénomène ascetique." Asin Palacios, *L'Islam christianisé: Etude sur le Soufisme d'Ibn 'Arabi de Murcie*, trans. Bernard Dubant (Paris: Guy Trédaniel, 1982), 99.

6. Affifi, *Remarks*, 20.

7. "Alors que le chapitre sur Adam décrit la manifestation universelle de Dieu, ou la «vision» qu'a Dieu de Lui-même dans l'Homme universel, le chapitre sur Seth a pour sujet la révélation intérieure de Dieu ou la connaissance qu'a l'homme de lui-même dans le «mirroir» divin." Burckhardt, *La Sagesse des Prophetes*, 41 n.1.

vine Essence. And for Ibn ʿArabi, the *saints*, or "friends" *(āwlyāʾ)* of God, are those who know, because they realize in themselves this inner intellectual principle. They are able to do this because of two complementary movements: they detach themselves from all creatures through *fanāʾ* or self-annihilation and, simultaneously, they "remain" *(baqāʾ)* in and uncover the inner meaning of the Law, revealed through the Prophet. In other words, true intellectuality cannot for Ibn ʿArabi be separated from sainthood, and sainthood cannot be separated from prophecy, the Law, and revelation.

Ibn ʿArabi begins the chapter on the word of Seth with a discussion of the divine "gifts" and the types of people who ask for these gifts and receive them.[8] There are basically two types of people who ask and receive the divine gifts: those who ask and receive according to what they know is determined by their own fixed entity or essence (in Sufi terminology, their *qadar*), and those who ask for what they desire without regard to what has been determined by God in their fixed essence or *qadar*. This immutable essence or *qadar* is akin to a Platonic idea, but with the essential difference that it designates not a universal, in which many particulars share (like the universal "beauty," which is the transcendent form by which many particular things are beautiful), but rather a particular, the unique immaterial essence of a thing or person, which, however, may or may not have existence. It signifies the "destiny" that is "measured out" to a creature by God; not, however, by an arbitrary decree, but rather in accordance with the essential nature of the creature that pre-exists it and which God, by his creative power, simply makes manifest in existence.[9] As

8. As al-Qaysari remarks, the name "Allah" or "Lord" or "The Merciful *(ar-raḥmān)*" itself denotes the source of the giving of being. *Sharḥ,* I 223.

9. See William Chittick, trans. and ed., *Faith and Practice of Islam: Three Thirteenth Century Sufi Texts* (Albany: State University of New York Press, 1992), 213–14. Here Chittick quotes the commentator Jandi on this section of the *Fusus*, explaining why the *qadar* of a creature does not contradict free will and responsibility on the part of the creature for good or evil actions: "No one can say—as the ignorant wrongdoers say in judging about God—that He measures out truth-concealing, disobedience, and ignorance for the truth-concealers, the disobedient, and the ignorant, and then takes them to task for that and demands from them what is not in their capacity and scope. On the contrary, God writes, decrees, and measures out only that which is required by the thing that receives His ruling through its beginningless, specific preparedness, which is not made by God. This preparedness demands that God rule that the thing become manifest according to what it is in itself and that He make manifest what is latent within it through giving it existence." Muhyaddin al-Jandi, *Sharḥ fuṣūṣ al-ḥikam,* ed. S. J. Ashtiyani (Mashhad: Danishgah-i-Mashhad, 1361/1982), 483–84.

to the distinction between those who receive divine gifts or graces, only the first, those who know what is determined by their immutable identity, have any knowledge, because only they know themselves, i.e., only they know a priori their own preparedness to receive the divine gifts. The second kind of worshipper knows his or her *qadar* only "after the fact," or a posteriori,[10] by reflection on the course of events in one's life.

Thus, for Ibn 'Arabi, those who are perfect ask only that their will conform to the divine command, as he puts it a little later:

Similarly, the praising of God usually means its [the request's] articulation, whereas in the inner sense the praise is necessitated by the [spiritual, *fi'-l* or *bi'l-ma'nā*] state, for that which impels you to praise God is that essential element in you that binds you to a Divine Name, whether expressing His activity or transcendence.[11]

The life of a prophet or saint is an outward expression or form (*ṣurā*) of the inner meaning (*ma'nā*) that is in the divine Essence. Here we have an important distinction that Ibn 'Arabi makes between "form" (*ṣurā*) and "meaning" (*ma'nā*). The form of something is what makes that thing manifest in space and time; its meaning, however, is the reality that is intended by that form but which is nonmanifest in space or time. Thus, mercy is a quality that does not manifest itself in space or time except through, say, the forms of a mother and her child. Mercy is not a spatio-temporal quality, but is the meaning or intention of the forms of the mother and her child. "Mercy is a *meaning* expressed through these formal entities."[12] In the same way, colors have a form but also mean something: green has a certain form that distinguishes it on the spectrum of color; but it also has a supersensible meaning inherent in it (of life, say, or of the Prophet, etc.).

For Ibn 'Arabi, all the prophets themselves constitute the forms of specific meanings of the divine Essence. Each prophet hides a meaning that approaches with a greater or lesser degree the universality of the divine Essence, with Muhammad, of course, representing the one whose formal reality is the most perfect vehicle for what the divine Reality means or intends. It is the saint, however, who realizes (or *recovers*) in him or herself the inner meaning of the outer form of the prophets, and it is the "seal of

10. *Bezels*, 62–63/58–59.    11. *Bezels*, 63/60.
12. Dagli, *Ringstones of Wisdom*, 22 n.19.

the saints" who realizes the inner meaning of the outer form of the "seal of the prophets," Muhammad.

Therefore, in the Laws of the prophets and, particularly, in the Law of the "seal" of the prophets, the saint finds his own *qadar* or "secret of destiny" or, to be more precise, the *meaning (ma'na)* of his existence. The true saint is one who knows that his true self, his essential unfolding, pre-exists in the mind of God and that the events of his life are but the unfolding in time of this unique *qadar* or destiny that he has in God, but whose knowledge comes about by a meditation on the particular excellences or graces of the various prophets.[13] While all creatures are created according to a divine archetype in the mind of God, only humanity can know its own archetype through his or her own self-consciousness.[14] Among human beings, it is the saint who realizes this possibility to the fullest: "Such a one," Ibn 'Arabi asserts, "in respect of his knowledge of himself, knows himself as God knows him, since the object [of knowledge] is the same in both cases. However, in respect of his creatureliness, his knowledge is nothing but a favor from God, one of a multitude of predetermined [spiritual] states [inherent] in his essence."[15] If this is the case, even the act of knowing God through oneself does not come from any created will but is part of the unfolding of one's eternal archetype or identity. The saint sees all events as the unfolding of his proper destiny, not attributing any secondary causality to creatures. Thus, to receive such a gift, the soul must also be gifted with utter "poverty" (*iftiqār*) if it is to know the "secret" of its "destiny" or that meaning *(ma'nā)* of the form of his particular existence; for only by being utterly devoid of attachment to creatures and their supposedly causal effects, which is what the Sufi means by being "poor" of all

---

13. *Bezels*, 64/60.

14. "Everything in the world is eternally and permanently determined by its own archetype. The inner structure or content of that archetype, however, is an impenetrable mystery because it is part of the Divine Consciousness. But there is only one small aperture, so to speak, through which man can have a peep into this unfathomable mystery. That aperture is the self-consciousness of man. Very exceptionally, when the spiritual force of a man is unusually elevated in the experience of 'unveiling,' he may be given a chance of witnessing directly the content of his own archetype. And in such a case, his knowledge about his own archetype is the same as God's knowledge about him, in the sense that both derive from one and the same source. And by knowing his own archetype, not externally but internally, he takes a peep at the great mystery of the *qadr*." Toshihiko Izutsu, *Sufism and Taoism*, 180.

15. *Bezels*, 64/60–61.

creatures, can the saint observe with clarity the unfolding of his destiny and thus know and abide in God.[16]

As an analogy for this sort of self-knowledge achieved by the saints, Ibn ʿArabi uses his famous metaphor of the mirror. God reveals himself only through the perfected self-knowledge of the saint. God is the "mirror" in which the saint is able to see himself, that is, his immutable identity, as well as the immutable identities of all creatures. Just as the mirror is the condition for the reflection of one's image, so God is the condition for self-reflection upon one's immutable essence. But just as the mirror cannot itself be seen, indeed, becomes more invisible the more perfect its surface is, so God cannot be seen directly by the saint, but only insofar as the divine mirror is polished and made smooth by the law of a prophet:

Returning to the subject of the divine gifts, we have already maintained that these stem either from the Essence or from the Divine Names. As for favors or gifts of the first kind, they can result only from a divine Self-revelation, which occurs only in a form conforming to the essential predisposition of the recipient of such a revelation. Thus, the recipient sees nothing other than his own form in the mirror of the Reality. He does not see the Reality Itself, which is not possible, although he knows that he may see only his [true] form in It. As in the case of a mirror and the beholder, he sees the form in it, but does not see the mirror itself, despite his knowledge that he sees only his own and other images by means of it. God makes this comparison so that the recipient of a divine Self-revelation should know that it is not Him Whom he sees. The analogy of a mirror is the closest and most faithful one for a vision of a divine Self-revelation.[17]

The reflection that the perfectly realized saint sees of himself in himself is the same reflection that God sees of the saint in God himself. Of course, the saint does not and cannot *see* God just as, in looking at ourselves in the mirror, we are able to see our image in the mirror but cannot see the backing of the mirror that makes that image possible. Indeed, the mirror works as a mirror only to the degree that it is absent or invisible in the production of its images. So, too, does God, as a fully self-conscious being, make possible self-conscious awareness in his creatures, to the

---

16. As al-Qaysari explains, the one who receives must be utterly poor in everything except Allah. In order to realize his "secret of destiny" of his own immutable essence in God, the servant must annihilate himself (*fanāʾ*) and abide in God (*baqāʾ*). Thus the servant receives consciously only what is given to him by Allah, including his own being. *Sharḥ,* I 232.

17. *Bezels,* 65/61–62.

degree that God is not seen directly but only in and through that self-consciousness. "We know that our existence subsists through God, just as we know that the image we see 'subsists' through the mirror."[18] God is the dark, nonmanifest ground that makes possible all self-manifestation and all self-disclosure. God resists all attempts to make him or his Essense an object of reason, as the mirror resists all attempts to be seen. Yet, it is as the mirror of the self or soul (*nafs*) that God makes self-reflection possible and, in that sense, is more intimate to the soul that it is to itself. In the mirror of the divine intellect, the soul comes to know itself as a reflected Name of God:

Try, when you look at yourself in a mirror, to see the mirror itself, and you will find that you cannot do so. So much is this the case that some have concluded that the image perceived is situated between the mirror and the eye of the beholder. This represents the greatest knowledge they are capable of [on the subject]. The matter is [in fact] as we have concluded, and we have dealt with it also in *The Meccan Revelations*. If you have experienced this [in the spirit] you have experienced as much as is possible for a created being, so do not seek nor weary yourself in any attempts to proceed higher than this, for there is nothing higher, nor is there beyond the point you have reached aught except the pure, undetermined, unmanifested [Absolute]. In your seeing your true self, He is your mirror and you are His mirror in which He sees His Names and their determination, which are nothing other than Himself. The whole matter is prone to intricacy and ambiguity.[19]

The reflection is mutual. The servant sees his own essence reflected in the divine Mirror while God sees his Names reflected in the mirror of the servant's essence, which, of course, is nothing apart from the divine Essence itself.[20] Neither God nor the human being can see each other as separate objects but only as what, in the case of God, manifests his Names, namely, the human being, and as what is, in the case of the human being, the inscrutable ground of his self-knowledge.

In the divine mirror, the saint "both sees his form and does not see his form." That is, the saint sees his own essence in self-reflection, but cannot see the *ground* or backing of his self-reflection, for the ground or backing to his self-reflection is the divine Reality. Thus, Ibn 'Arabi is fond of quot-

18. Dagli, *Ringstones of Wisdom*, 25 n.36.    19. *Bezels*, 65/62.
20. *Sharḥ*, I 241.

ing the saying of Abu Bakr: "To realize that one cannot know [God] is to know."[21] No human being can ever know or experience God outside of what is determined by his or her immutable identity or *qadar*, which is to say, his or her inherent possibilities as a created being, for the divine Reality is refracted only through the limits of one's *qadar*. What makes this whole affair prone to "intricacy and ambiguity" is that, ultimately, the saint is the one who realizes that his own self, his entire immutable identity or *qadar*, is itself but an image of the surface of the divine Reality and, even more, that the true knower or observer of his own image is not the saint but God. The saint knows himself as merely an image or a "name" in and through which God sees and knows himself. The saint knows himself as having no substantiality either as a substrate for an image or as the knower of that image.

For Ibn 'Arabi, the saint, then, thinks not in and through himself but in and through the divinely revealed Law, which has its roots in the Qur'an. So in and through the Qur'an and the Law, the saint reads the true inner meaning of his or her existence by interpreting it within the context of the Muhammadan Law and the various other previous laws of the ordained prophets. The prophets are keys through which one's immutable identity can be read, compared, and interpreted, in other words, the prophets are *bezels* in which are set the various stones of the *saints*. The saint is the gnostic who, being "set" in the "bezel" of a particular prophet, realizes the inner meaning or *ma'nā* of the law of a prophet; and the seal of the saints is the saint who realizes the inner meaning of the seal of the prophets, Muhammad, which is the law that is most comprehensive and universal because expressing most clearly and comprehensively the divine Will. Hence, the seal of the saints is the one who realizes an immutable identity or *qadar* that is coterminous with the Universal Man, the divine Intellect in its unfolding manifestation. The saint in general, then, is the one who finds, realizes, and fulfills the inner meaning of the outer law. So, while prophethood, which is the giving of a law, is limited to definite historical events, the realm of sainthood transcends time: "This is because the office of apostle and prophet [by prophet I mean the bringer of Sacred Law] comes to an end, while Sainthood never ceases."[22] Sainthood, there-

---

21. *Sharḥ*, I 239.                     22. *Bezels*, 66/62.

fore, is the precondition for all prophethood and apostleship because it is also their fulfillment. As Chodkiewicz puts it, "Sufism and sainthood are inseparable."[23]

Based on a dream in which he completed the "wall" of prophethood and sainthood in the sanctuary of Mecca with two bricks, one of silver representing prophethood and one of gold representing sainthood, Ibn 'Arabi claimed to be the "Seal of the Saints" in the same manner that Muhammad was the "Seal" of the prophets. For in his interior journey, the Seal of the Saints reveals the inner meaning not only of the Qur'an and *hadith*, but also of the insights of all previous saints (*āwliyā'*) in one comprehensive vision. Needless to say, this is a remarkable and bold claim! While Muhammad was temporally the last of the prophets, he was also their fulfillment and thus, in principle, he is the first of the prophets. Similarly, with the seal of the saints:

Every prophet, from Adam until the last of the prophets, derives what he has from the Seal of the Prophets, even though he comes last in his temporal, physical manifestation, for in his [essential] reality he has always existed. The Prophet said, "I was a prophet when Adam was between the water and the clay," while other prophets became such only when they were sent forth [on their missions]. In the same way the Seal of Saints was a saint "when Adam was between the water and the clay," while other saints became saints only when they had acquired all the necessary divine qualities, since God has called Himself *the Friend [al-Wali], the Praised One*.[24]

The function of the seal of the saints (which, it must be added, is a controversial topic in the history of Islamic thought)[25] is one that stems unceasingly from an eternal essence and precedes in principle if not in history all other manifestations of sainthood. The seal of the saints is the Platonic form or essence that makes possible all other manifestations of that essence, just as the reality of Muhammad is principially prior to all other instances of prophethood even though temporally Muhammad was the last of the prophets.

23. Chodkiewicz, *Seal of the Saints*, 13.       24. *Bezels*, 67/63–64.

25. The notion of the "seal of the saints" can be traced backed to the writings of the relatively early Sufi al-Tirmidhi, whose questions on sainthood form the basis for a long chapter in Ibn 'Arabi's *Futūhāt al-makkiyya*. Nevertheless, this notion of the "seal of the saints" was—and is—rejected by many prominent mainstream Muslim *'ulama'*. See Knysh, *Ibn 'Arabi in the Later Islamic Tradition*, 72ff.

Prophecy is thus the outer, efficient cause, so to speak, of inner realization, while sainthood is its inner, final cause. This fact, Ibn ʿArabi is always careful to add, does not impinge upon the primacy of Muhammad as prophet, because he combined within himself the nature of both prophet and saint; the ability to give the Law itself arises from an at least implicit understanding of its hidden, inner sense. Thus, the prophet and the saint represent together the inner and outer knowledge of the Real, remaining distinct ways of knowing though stemming from the same source, just as the divine Names are distinct among themselves insofar as they reveal different aspects of the Real, but are, fundamentally, identical with that Real.[26]

It is the realized knower, however, *insofar as he is a saint,* who embraces the inner and outer knowledge of revelation, taking on himself the opposing attributes of the divine Reality:

He [the gnostic] at once knows and does not know, taking on himself the attribution of opposites, as does the Source Itself, as being at once the Majestic and the Beautiful, the Manifest and the Unmanifest, the First and the Last, this *[coincidentia oppositorum]* being his own essence. He knows and does not know, he is aware and he is not aware, he perceives and yet does not perceive.[27]

We have here again a reference to the "learned ignorance" of the gnostic: he knows insofar as he intuits the Unity at the basis of all manifestations and at the basis of his own thought and self-reflection and self-knowledge; he does not know insofar as he can never know this Unity as something over and against himself, as an object to be grasped in rational, systematic discourse.

In this way, then, the saint brings together opposites. He or she brings together the created and the uncreated, knowledge and ignorance, the manifest and the hidden. As Chodkiewicz points out, the saint is both "close" (*qarīb*) and "far" (*baʿīd*) from God. "Closeness" or "proximity" comes about only when there is a "total de-creation of what has been created, when all that survives is the Divine Oneness (*ul-wāḥdu*),"[28] and this proximity, which is the literal meaning of *walāya* or sainthood, is twofold:

26. *Bezels,* 68/65.  27. *Bezels,* 69/66.

28. Chodkiewicz, *Seal of the Saints,* 168.

The *walī*, close to God, is not wholly a *walī* unless he is also close to created being. Ibn 'Arabi identifies the Perfect Man with the tree "whose root is firm and whose branches are in the heavens" (Qur'an 14:24). Earthly as well as heavenly, the saint is he who brings together the high and the low, the *ḥaqq* and the *khalq*. Like the Mohammedan Reality whose heir he is, he forms the "isthmus" (*barzakh*) of the "two seas."[29]

The saint is the locus, both to himself and to others, where the unmanifest becomes manifest, where the inner meaning of the divine Names and Scripture become not only known but seen and perceived. Thus, the saint is to other men and women like a mirror of the divine Essence precisely because he himself sees himself as but a reflection or theophany of the divinity—a theophany that is refracted through his own essential form or *qadar*: In this way, the saint is also *far* from God, in the sense that he or she is fully aware of the hiddenness of God in all manifestations:

Whenever a gnostic receives a spiritual intuition in which he looks on a form that brings him new spiritual knowledge and new spiritual graces, [he should know] that the form he contemplates is none other than his own essential self, for it is only from the tree of his own self that he will garner the fruits of his knowledge. In the same way his image in a polished surface is naught but he, although the place or plane in which he sees his image effects certain changes in the image in accordance with the intrinsic reality of that plane. In this way something big appears small in a small mirror, long in a long mirror, and moving in a moving mirror. It may produce the inversion of this image from a particular plane, or it may produce an exactly corresponding image, right reflecting right [and left reflecting left]. However, it is more usual with mirrors for the right to reflect the left. In contradistinction to this, however, the right sometimes reflects the right and reversion takes place. All this applies [equally] to the modes and properties of the plane in which the divine Self-revelation occurs, which we have compared to a mirror.[30]

Hidden from direct perception in this act of self-perception are two things: the knower and the mirror in which the form of the knower is reflected.[31] The true observer of all things, the true knower as we have

29. Ibid., 173.
30. *Bezels*, 69–70/66–67.
31. "As for mirrors and polished bodies, neither the site of the forms within them nor anything behind them is perceived. Rather, forms that are absent from the eye for their perceiver and are not within the object are perceived. Thus the seen forms are a veil between eyesight and the polished object. It is not said that these forms are subtle or dense, but eyesight witnesses them as

mentioned above, is not the human being or even the saint or gnostic, but God.[32] In other words, the saint is simply a transparent image or vehicle in and through which the divine Essence sees and knows itself. Thus the gnostic can never know God as object, precisely because God is both the subject and object of all the knowing of the gnostic. The gnostic can know God only insofar as God is reflected in the essential mode of the gnostic himself.[33] But as Titus Burckhardt comments on this passage, while the "self" that the gnostic sees in the mirror of the divine hides the divine, it also, in another sense, manifests it, just as the image in a mirror manifests the presence of a mirror.[34]

There is therefore a knowledge of the divine insofar as the saint knows his own immutable identity as a reflection in the divine Essence. He knows himself and all creatures as imaginal objectifications of that divine Essence, which is itself utterly one and beyond the polarity of subject/object or of image and observer. The gnostic, by contrast, cannot grasp

---

dense. Their shapes change with the change in the shape of the polished object. When it is wavy, they are wavy. When the thing whose form they are moves in the outside world, they move, and when it remains still, they remain still, unless the shiny object is moved." III 214.9 in SDG, 110.

32. Thus Burckhardt notes: "Selon la terminologie advaïtique, Dieu est le Sujet—ou le Témoin (sâkshin)—absolu qui ne deviendra jamais «objet» de connaissance. C'est en Lui ou par Lui que toute chose est perçue, alors qu'il en reste toujours l'arrière-plan insaisissable.—«Les regards ne L'atteignent pas, mais c'est Lui qui atteint les regards», dit le Coran (VI, 103)." Burckhardt, *La Sagesse des Prophetes*, 47 n.1.

33. "There is nothing in *wujūd* but He, and *wujūd* is acquired only from Him. No entity of any existent thing becomes manifest except through His self-disclosure. So the mirror is the Presence of Possibility, the Real is the one who looks within it, and the form is you in keeping with the mode of your possibility. You may be an angel, a celestial sphere, a human being, a horse. Like the form in a mirror, you follow the guise of the mirror's own essence in terms of height, breadth, circularity, and diverse shapes, even though it is a mirror in every case." III 80.14 in SDG, 15. Also: "In the same way, the possible things are like shapes in possibility. The divine self-disclosure imparts *wujūd* to the possible things. The mirror imparts shapes to them. Then angel, substance, body, and accident become manifest, but possibility remains itself. It does not leave its own reality." III 80.14 in SDG, 15–16.

34. "In reality it is as we have said above—that is, that the reflected 'form' does not essentially hide the mirror, since the mirror manifests the form and we know implicitly that we see it only by virtue of the mirror. The spiritual point of view inherent in this symbolism is analogous to that of the Vedanta. This impossibility of grasping the mirror 'objectively' at the same time as we contemplate our image in it expresses the ungraspable character of *Atman*, the Absolute 'Subject,' of which all things, including the individual subject, are only illusory 'objectivations.' Like the expression 'Divine Subject,' the symbol of the mirror evokes a polarity whereas the Essence is beyond all dualism such as that of 'subject' and 'object': this, however, is something no symbol could express." Titus Burckhardt, *An Introduction to Sufism*, trans. D. M. Matheson (San Francisco: Harper Collins, 1995), 113.

the divine Essence as object in contemplating his own destiny anymore than he can grasp the mirror at the same time as he sees himself in it. Any grasping of the divine in this "seeing" will be by necessity indirect and oblique; God's Essence is refracted through creatures just as, as Ibn 'Arabi notes above, an image is reflected differently depending on whether the mirror is concave or convex. And in an even more fundamental sense, just as a mirror inverts an image so that right is left and left is right, so the creature inverts the divine Essence insofar as its perfection lies in its utter "poverty" of being and its fulfillment lies in its absolute dependence on God. Of all earthly creatures, the human intellect alone can rise to an awareness of how his or her limitations refract the divine "light" and, from that knowledge, gain some insight into what that Reality is in itself. This is where knowledge of the particular qualities or hidden "meanings" (ma'ānī) of the prophets come in: they enable the gnostic to know and realize the many different spiritual states (āḥwāl) in and through which the divine is manifested so that the realized saint may come to a knowledge of the way in which he or she refracts the divine Essence in him or herself. In this way, as Ibn 'Arabi mentions above, the gnostic or saint can then see the "right as right" and the "left as left," which is what Ibn 'Arabi means when he says that "it is only from the tree of his own self that he will garner the fruits of his knowledge."

For Ibn 'Arabi and many other Sufis, therefore, true intellectuality is essentially linked with self-annihilation or fanāʾ. The Sufi dies to self by annihilating attachment to all creatures, most importantly his or her created self. Through fanāʾ, the Sufi eliminates all that may soil and mar the mirror of the heart.[35] Through fanāʾ, the gnostic attains to the essential attribute of sainthood:

35. As Ibn 'Arabi explains in the chapter on Adam (to be treated in the next section), the entire universe, as the manifestation of the divine Names and Attributes, is also a mirror of God; but it is the human being who polishes (potentially) this mirror and brings together all the "discrete things and properties that have been diffused and scattered all over the immense universe" into sharp focus in the mirror of his intellect so that God may view His Names and Attributes in it. For, although God needs no mirror other than Himself in order to "view" and know Himself, nevertheless, as Izutsu explains, "the Absolute has also an aspect in which it is an Essence qualified by Attributes. And since the Attributes become real only when they are externalized, it becomes necessary for the Absolute to see itself in the 'other.' Thus the 'other' is created in order that God might see Himself therein in externalized form" (Izutsu, *Sufism and Taoism*, 220). This divine image, therefore, comes into sharpest focus in the heart of the gnostic, which, being well-polished by detachment from created things, reflects without distortion the divine Names and Attributes.

This consciousness of the "oneness of Being" he obtains only by being "annihilated" and completely immersed in the Absolute. Through the experience of "self-annihilation" he transforms himself, so to speak, into the "inside" of the Absolute, and from there sees the reality of all things by "immediate tasting." The concept of "self-annihilation" (*fanā'*) in this sense plays an exceedingly important role in the theory of *walāyah*. The "self-annihilation" is, in fact, the first item in the essential attributes of the Saint.[36]

As Izutsu so aptly describes it, the saint is "inside" the Absolute and sees the reality of all things by "tasting," because the saint has passed away from his created self that is "outside" the Absolute. He "sees" God through "immediate tasting" precisely because, being no longer "outside" God, he does not see God as an object or thing over and against himself but as the ground of his being, "drinking and eating God" into himself, so to speak, or, perhaps more accurately, God "eating, drinking, and tasting" the saint into himself.

Thus, in Sufism annihilation or *fanā'* is not a nihilistic extinction: *fanā'* is always followed, with an almost rigorous logical necessity, by *baqā'* or "abiding" in God. As Chittick and Corbin point out, both *fanā'* and *baqā'* are relative terms: *fanā'* is always *'an* (from) while *baqā'* is always *bi* (through).[37] One is always "annihilated" *from* creatures *for* "abiding" *through* God. This is, for Ibn 'Arabi, the only route to genuine knowledge of Truth. As he says in the *Futūḥāt*:

Since this is the situation, the intelligent man who wants to know God should follow His authority in the reports He has given about Himself in His scripture and upon the tongues of His messengers. When a person wants to know the things, but he cannot know them through what his faculties give him, he should strive in acts of obedience (*ṭā'āt*) until the Real is his hearing, his seeing, and all his faculties. Then he will know all affairs through God and he will know God

36. Izutsu, *Sufism and Taoism*, 265.

37. "In a chapter of the *Futūḥāt* devoted to annihilation, the Shaykh points out that the term *fanā'* is used in its technical sense along with the [preposition] *'an* (from). Thus the Sufis speak of annihilation *from* something. Likewise the term *baqā'* is employed with the [preposition] *bi* (through). Hence one speaks of subsistence *through* something. In all cases, annihilation is lower and subsistence is higher." William Chittick, *Imaginal Worlds*, 59–60. "But again we must be careful to bear in mind that for Ibn 'Arabi *fanā'* is never absolute annihilation (the failure to do so has been a source of countless misunderstandings in regard both to Sufism and to Buddhism). *Fanā'* and *baqā'* are always relative terms. According to Ibn 'Arabi, one must always state *toward what* there is annihilation, and wherein there is survival, persistence." Corbin, *Alone with the Alone*, 228.

through God. In any case, there is no escape from following authority. But once you know God through God and all things through God, then you will not be visited in that by ignorance, obfuscation, doubts, or uncertainties.[38]

We cannot know God until we abide entirely in and through God, not with our mind and reason only, but with all our faculties, all our senses, our entire being. As Ibn 'Arabi points out very significantly here, this knowledge of God has, as its presupposition, revelation and the authority of the Holy Qur'an and the realization of the inner meaning of the Qur'an by the saints of Islam. Without the authority of Scripture and of the saints, human reason could never break out of the categories of thought that delimit it to created things, because laws given by the prophets call us beyond reason and the saints call us to the realization of the inner meaning of these laws. Such realization is made possible by a faculty of knowing, the *heart*, that is higher than and sits in judgment over reason, just as reason is higher than and sits in judgment over the senses.

### The Wisdom of the Heart in the Word of Shu'aib

There are, in Ibn 'Arabi, two faculties of the soul by which knowledge, as opposed to mere sensation, is acquired, reason (*'aql*) and the heart (*qalb*). In Chittick's words:

Knowledge can be acquired through reflection, unveiling, or scripture. The human subtle reality (*al-laṭīfat al-insāniyya*), also called the "soul" (*nafs*), knows in a variety of modes. When it knows through reflection, the mode of its knowing is called "reason" (*'aql*). When it knows directly from God, the mode of knowing is called the "heart" (*qalb*), which is contrasted with reason. Whatever the means whereby the soul acquires knowledge, the knowing subject is one. There are not two different entities known as "reason" and "heart," though there is a real difference between the modalities of knowing. As we have already seen, reason knows through delimitation and binding, while the heart knows through letting go of all restrictions. *'Aql*, as shown by its root meaning, is that which limits the free and ties down the unconstricted. *Qalb* means fluctuation, for the heart undergoes constant change and transmutation in keeping with the never-repeating self-disclosures of God.[39]

38. II 298. 2 in SPK, 167.
39. SPK, 159.

As emphasized here, "reason" and the "heart" are not two opposed or separate organs. Though distinct, they nevertheless overlap. Just as reason presupposes sense perception for its operation but is distinct from it in its act of judgment, so the heart presupposes the activity of reason although it is distinct from it by virtue of its act of unitative intuition. It follows, of course, that the "heart," understood in this specific sense, refers, for the Sufis, not to the physical organ that pumps blood, nor even so much to the "organ" of love or desire, as to an "organ" of gnosis or self-realization, a notion with roots in the Qur'an where the "heart" is primarily understood as an organ of discernment. And, as Chittick notes, one of the key attributes of the heart is that it fluctuates in constant harmony with the divine disclosures or theophanies of creation. Reason, by contrast, binds and constricts these disclosures to the measure of its limited concepts and categories derived from created things.

Reason produces knowledge by reflection. As Aristotle showed, logical reasoning is about how classes of things are necessarily related and how true propositions can be made about them and valid inferences made from them. As such, reflection proceeds by division of beings into categories and classes and then tries to see how they combine necessarily. The heart, by contrast, is the "organ" of "unveiling": it has a pure openness to being as such and thus does not delimit or divide. It is the organ by which we know being as such, precisely because being as such cannot be divided or demarcated in any way. The heart, therefore, is the place in which being as such is known or disclosed to itself, because nothing, including the heart, can stand outside of being in order to observe it as an object. It is an axiom of Ibn 'Arabi as well as many other Sufis that "none knows God but God,"[40] which is to say that none knows Being except Being itself, i.e., God. The saint, therefore, is one who knows God or Being "from the inside," as it were; he or she knows God in and through God.

As we saw in the previous section, for Ibn 'Arabi, God necessarily manifests himself in finite creatures, for he is not limited by even absoluteness itself: for to say that the Absolute is free from finitude is to limit it, because it negates finitude in God. In other words, finite manifestation or self-disclosure is a logically necessary consequence of the infinite richness of the divine Reality. As such, this self-disclosure cannot remain

40. SPK, 153.

static: it must be a continuous, dynamic manifestation splaying itself out into finite being with every moment being a new creation and no form or moment being repeated twice in creation. Indeed, as Nettler perceptively points out, the fact that the infinite Absolute must, if it is to be truly infinite, delimit itself in finite creatures and do so continuously in an infinite variety of forms has an epistemological consequence:

As we know, "God" in Ibn ʿArabi's outlook, whether designated as *al-Haqq* or *Allah*, possesses "two faces," "the remote" and "the manifest." Though ultimately reducible to one "combined" visage only, God does, from the perspective of His creation, evince this "dual nature," at least for man's purpose, the better to understand Him. For the remote God is in Himself unknowable to man, His existence being a conceptual necessity and a mystically-intuited presence. The manifest God, however, is for man the remote God's "appearance" or "self-manifestation" *in* and *as* the multiplicity and flux of the phenomenal world. The *absolute* must, then, be reduced to the *conditional* in order for it to be knowable to the conditional world.[41]

It is of the essence of God to communicate himself, first to himself and then to creatures. Being is self-communicative, giving both existence and intelligibility to finite creatures. This, however, does not mean that we come to know God through inferences from creatures to a "first cause," which, as we have seen, is not how Ibn ʿArabi conceives of the relation between God and the world. Creatures in themselves, for Ibn ʿArabi, give no positive knowledge of God because, as such, they only limit God and his being; they add nothing to God either really or conceptually. But they *manifest* the divine just as forms manifest hidden, unmanifest meanings, as the color green may manifest "life" or a mother and child may manifest mercy, though the forms through which these realities are manifested do not add anything really or conceptually to the meanings they manifest.

It is this continuous kaleidoscope of manifestations and their inherent unity to which the heart of the saint is tuned. Indeed, the root of the word for "heart" in Arabic *(qalaba)* means "to fluctuate, to turn over." The heart of the saint, therefore, is the faculty by which the saint conforms to the fluctuation of divine manifestations and thus to their inner meanings:

Know that the Reality, as is confirmed by Tradition, in His Self-manifestation, transmutes Himself in the forms; know also that when the Heart embraces

<hr />

41. Nettler, *Sufi Metaphysics*, 117.

the Reality, it embraces none other than He, since it is as if the Reality fills the Heart. By this is meant that when the Heart contemplates the Reality in Its Self-manifestation to it, it is unable to contemplate anything else whatever. The heart of the gnostic is, in respect of its compass, as Abu Yazid al-Bistami had said, "Were the Throne and all it comprises to be placed one hundred million times in the corner of the gnostic's Heart, he would not be aware of it." In this question, Junayd said, "When the contingent is linked with the eternal there is nothing left of it." Thus, when the heart embraces the Eternal One, how can it possibly be aware of what is contingent and created?[42]

As al-Bistami and Junayd indicate, when the heart of the gnostic or saint is conformed to the divine manifestations or "unveilings," there is, paradoxically, nothing left of the contingency of the created self and a fortiori of reason. In his or her heart, the saint is not a creature but rather the locus in and through which the uncreated becomes manifest. This truth, for Ibn 'Arabi, is best illustrated by a metaphor that is the master-metaphor of the entire *Bezels*—that of the bezel to the gemstone:

Since the Self-manifestation of the Reality is variable according to the variety of the forms, the Heart is necessarily wide or restricted according to the form in which God manifests Himself. The heart can comprise no more than the form in which the Self-manifestation occurs; for the Heart of the gnostic or the Perfect Man is as the setting of the stone of the ring, conforming to it in every way, being circular, square, or any other shape according to the shape of the stone itself, for the setting conforms to the stone and not otherwise. This is opposed by those who maintain that the Reality manifests Himself in accordance with the predisposition of the servant. This is, however, not the case, since the servant is manifest to the Reality according to the form in which the Reality manifests Himself to him.[43]

Just as the gemstone determines the shape of the bezel for which it is prepared, so the "destiny" *(qadar)* of the gnostic as prepared by God determines the shape of the life that the gnostic—whether prophet or mere saint—must lead. God, then, not the realized knower, determines through the *qadar* of the saint how the realized knower may receive him. As Ibn 'Arabi explains:

The solution of this question rests on the fact that God manifests Himself in two ways: an unseen manifestation and a sensible manifestation. It is from the

---

42. *Bezels*, 148/119–20.        43. *Bezels*, 148–49/120.

former type that the predisposition of the Heart is bestowed, being the essential Self-manifestation, the very nature of which is to be unseen. This is the divine Identity in accordance with which He calls Himself [in the Qur'an] He. This Identity is His alone in all and from all eternity.[44]

This "unseen, essential manifestation" refers not to the outward creatures but to the various essential natures of the prophets and saints pre-established by God and manifested only through the outward lives of these prophets and saints.

The *Bezels* represents, then, a kind of phenomenology of the manifestations of God's Essence in the words and wisdoms of the prophets as seen and realized inwardly by the saints. The saint returns the outer manifestation to its inner manifestation, the outer form to the inner meaning. The saint reduces the outward beliefs of the prophets and their laws to their inner essential destiny. And since Muhammad was the seal of the prophets, the seal of the saints (i.e., Ibn 'Arabi) is the one who realizes the inner truth of all outward manifestations by realizing how the word of Muhammad fulfills and realizes the essential natures of all previous prophets and saints.

## Himma

Ibn 'Arabi expresses the paradoxes that arise from this utter self-identity of knower and known in the Absolute in a poetic interlude in the text in the chapter on Shu'aib:

Who is here and what there?
    Who is here is what is there.
He who is universal ['amma] is particular [khassa],
    And He Who is particular is universal.
There is but one Essence,
    The light of the Essence being also darkness.
He who heeds these words will not
    Fall into confusion.
In truth, only he knows what we say
    Who is possessed of spiritual power [himma].[45]

44. *Bezels*, 149/120.        45. *Bezels*, 150/122.

Here we see Ibn 'Arabi sum up many themes already seen: the universal, the Real, is particular because only it, as Being itself, is truly substantial, while the Real as particular is universal because the source of the being of all creatures. Likewise, the light of the divine Intellect is darkness as the light of the sun is blinding to anyone who looks directly into it.

But important here is Ibn 'Arabi's notion of *himma*. Only through *himma* (zeal, ardor—here translated as "spiritual power") can there be knowledge beyond reason. There is an essential connection in Ibn 'Arabi between love and knowledge.

In this sense the heart can indeed be called also a faculty of love or desire. Only the impassioned lover can give him or herself over entirely to the play of appearances of his or her beloved. And by doing so, his or her self is annihilated and abides in the beloved. In this way, the universal becomes particular (the play of appearances becomes the play of the particular beloved), while the particular becomes universal (the particular beloved becomes manifest in all things).

As Corbin points out,[46] this *himma* of the realized knower is, therefore, ultimately *creative*, for it is able to make appear in the sensible world the qualities and names of the Beloved, hidden in the higher manifestation of the essential natures of the prophets. In quoting, therefore, the Qur'anic verse "Surely in that is a reminder for him who has a heart," Ibn 'Arabi contrasts this knowledge united to and infused with love or ardor with purely discursive reason *('aql)*, translated here as "intellect":

*Surely in that is a reminder for him who has a heart* [50:37], by reason of His [constant] transformation through all the varieties of forms and attributes; nor does He say, "for him who has intellect." This is because the intellect restricts and seeks to define the truth within a particular qualification, while in fact the Reality does not admit of such limitation. It is not a reminder to the intellectuals and mongers of doctrinal formulations who contradict one another and denounce each other . . . *and they have no helpers* [3:91].[47]

Those who make "idols" of their beliefs—whether literally in wood or stone or metaphorically in their desires and received ideas and concepts— *have no helpers* because they have made their idols limited created things, separate from and other than their worshippers. Devoid of any imma-

---

46. Corbin, *Alone with the Alone*, 226.
47. *Bezels*, 150/122.

nence, these idols are also devoid of power, incapable of helping their worshippers in any way.[48] Being products of reason, they are empty of any life and thus of any love and spiritual power *(himma)*. *Himma* sees the spirit or meaning behind the form. It is by *himma* that we distinguish a living human being from a corpse or statue. By *himma*, the Sufi saint perceives the meaning of creation behind its many forms. Thus, *himma* is perfective of the heart *(qalb)*.

The one who has heart, by contrast, directly perceives God in all forms and thus rises above their limitation, realizing God's Identity is his identity and that God is a loving entity, quite literally a heart "pulsing" with living manifestations underneath the "chest" of creation and manifesting "spiritual power":

For the gnostic, the Reality is [always] known and not [ever] denied. Those who know in this world will know in the Hereafter. For this reason He says, *for one who is possessed of a heart* [50:37], namely, one who understands the formal transformations of the Reality by adapting himself formally, so that from [or by] himself he knows the Self. [In truth], his self is not other than the divine Identity Itself, as also no [determined] being, now or in the future, is other than His Identity; He is the Identity Itself.[49]

Thus, Ibn 'Arabi links the name of the prophet of this chapter, "Shu'aib," with the Arabic word *tasha"ub*, meaning "ramifications" or "branching out," with the implication that the realized knower is the one who sees the one root, the divine Essence, at the source of all the ramifications of manifested, created existence. So, al-Qaysari, commenting upon this chapter, compares the realized knower to one who sees the ocean in drops of water, the tree in its fruits, and the seed itself in the tree.[50] He or she is able to see the root "in" and "through" its "branches" or "fruit."

Reason, therefore, insofar as it takes these distinctions and ramifi-

48. "Here it [Ibn 'Arabi's formulation of the unity of existence] gives deeper meaning to Qur'an 3:91, saying, in essence, that these false gods cannot help their believers because their very separation and objectification (in their believers' construction of them) imply a negation of the truth of metaphysical divine immanence. From the Qur'anic perspective, this negation renders the belief and its godly aspect *false* as well as *intellectually misplaced.*" Nettler, *Sufi Metaphysics*, 132.

49. *Bezels*, 151/122. As al-Qaysari comments on this section of the chapter, the gnostic or *'arif* not only is a theophany of God but also manifests the divine Essence most properly because, when annihilated to creatures and abiding in God, the gnostic's identity is nothing other than the divine Identity. *Sharh*, II 92.

50. *Sharh*, II 91.

cations as absolute without the heart beating in loving unison with the fluctuation of God's self-disclosure in creation, cannot begin to grasp the divine. Only the "one who has heart" can do this. For Ibn 'Arabi, failure to recognize the powerlessness of reason to put true or real determinations upon God was the error of the Mu'tazilites, a school of theology that developed early in Islam and that argued that God not only does not but *cannot* violate rational principles of justice and divine unity. According to Ibn 'Arabi, they were bound by the "knots" (*al-ʿuqūd*) of belief in rational thought.[51]

The realized knower or saint, on the other hand, is freed of such "knots," seeing multiplicity in the One and the One in multiplicity. Thus the Primal Substance is assumed in the case of every form. Thus also he who knows himself in this way knows his Lord, "for He created him in His image, indeed, He is his very identity and reality. None of the scholars, therefore, have attained to knowledge of the self and its reality, except those theosophists among the messengers and the Sufis."[52] On this basis, Ibn 'Arabi offers a critique of various schools of *kalam* and their conceptions of the nature of the relation between God and cosmos. *Kalam* was a term that covered a variety of different schools of what we in the West would call "theology," although its most basic meaning is "speech" or "discourse," which, in turn, came to mean "rational discourse." *Kalam* tried, on the basis of the Qur'an and the *hadith* of the Prophet, to provide rational demonstrations or justifications of certain Islamic beliefs and practices. The Mu'tazilites were one such school. But, for Ibn 'Arabi, the Mu'tazilites made the mistake of emphasizing too much the transcendence of God, raising an abstract idea of "god" to the status of a belief; the Ash'arites, another school of *kalam* opposed to the Mu'tazilties that nevertheless taught the createdness of human acts, did not realize that, compared to the Real, the entire universe is composed of nothing but accidents of the one substance who is God.[53]

But perhaps the most fundamental objection that Ibn 'Arabi has with the *mutakallimun* and the philosophers is that their understanding of God

---

51. *Bezels*, 152/123–24.     52. *Bezels*, 153/125.

53. Indeed, we can see that Ibn 'Arabi's doctrine of the Unity of Being is, in many ways, simply a transposition of the Ash'arite teaching on substance and accident onto the relation between God and the world.

remains abstract. One cannot free oneself from creatures by means of rational thought, for it is rational thought that ties these knots of belief in the first place. What is needed to untie the Gordian knot of belief is the sword of gnosis, insight into the continuous annihilation and abiding of all things in and through God:

As for those to whom the higher worlds are disclosed, they see that God is manifest in every Breath and that no [particular] Self-manifestation is repeated. They also see that every Self-manifestation at once provides a [new] creation and annihilates another. Its annihilation is extinction at the [new] Self-manifestation, subsistence being what is given by the following [other] Self-manifestation; so understand.[54]

The terms translated here as "annihilation" and "subsistence" are, in fact, none other than the Sufi terms *fanā'* and *baqā'.* Every creature, whether human or not (let alone a Sufi or not!), by the very fact that they are constantly dependent on God's creative power, undergoes a process of *fanā'* or extinction from creatures and *baqā'* or abiding through God. The only difference between the Sufi and other creatures is that the Sufi undergoes this process with explicit awareness.

The only way, therefore, that the Sufi saint overcomes the abstractions of the *mutakallimun* and the philosophers is not through more abstract reasoning but through spiritual praxis. Only in the annihilation or *fanā'* from creatures can there be, on the part of the knower, a true abiding or *baqā'* in and through God, which is to say, a true knowledge of God, for none knows God except God, and the saint whose *fanā'* is complete does not, strictly speaking, know God but is the "place" in which knowledge of God occurs. Such a saint is the "perfect" or "universal" man, to be discussed in the next section, who restores to the human condition humanity's function as the primal *Logos* in and through which the world is created and in and through which it returns in consciousness to God's self-knowledge.[55]

---

54. *Bezels*, 155/126.

55. "Hence everyone in the cosmos is ignorant of the whole and knows the part, except only the perfect human being. For God *taught* him *the names, all of them* [2:31] and gave him the all-comprehensive words, so his form became perfect. The perfect human being brings together the form of the Real and the form of the cosmos. He is a *barzakh* between the Real and the cosmos, a raised-up mirror. The Real sees His form in the mirror of the human being, and creation also sees its form in him. He who gains this level has gained a level of perfection more perfect than which nothing is found in possibility." III 397.3 in SDG, 249.

Through spiritual praxis oriented upon the remembrance of God and the recitation of the holy text of the Qur'an, the mirror of the intellect is polished smooth and thus returns the gnostic to God:

As for "rust," that is tarnish and cloudiness. It is nothing but the forms that are disclosed in the mirror of the heart and that God does not call the servant to see. These forms can be polished from the mirror through remembrance of God and recitation of the Koran.[56]

56. IV 25.1 in SDG, 316.

6

# "Deus est intelligere"

*Detachment, Intellect, and the Emanation of the Word*
*in Meister Eckhart*

In one of his sermons, Meister Eckhart makes the remarkable claim that "the same knowledge in which God knows himself is the knowledge of every detached spirit and nothing else. The soul receives its being immediately from God. For this reason God is nearer to the soul than it is to itself, and God is in the ground of the soul with all of his divinity."[1] What does Eckhart here mean by a "detached spirit"? What is so special about it that "God is the ground" of such a soul "with all of his divinity"? The answer to these questions will take us into Eckhart's notion of how we come to know God in an intellectuality that is as much practical as it is speculative and as much rooted in the revealed text as it is in the powers of the soul. Indeed, I intend to explore here how the practical or ethical dimension of intellect is essential to its speculative function and how the revealed text is a necessary precondition for the full awakening and unfolding of the intellectual nature of the soul.

"Detachment" is, of course, the common translation for the German term *Abgeschiedenheit,* and it usually means a simple non-attachment to all things and equanimity in the face of life's vicis-

1. *Pr.* 10; DW I, 162/TP, 261.

situdes.[2] It, therefore, has primarily an ethical or practical meaning. But detachment has, in Eckhart's thought, a deeper speculative dimension that makes it integral to his concept of metaphysics and its ultimate end, which is knowledge of God.[3] It is significant that "detachment" translates the Latin words *abstractus* and *separatio* that Eckhart uses in his more

2. "Detachment" is the usual English translation of the German *Abgeschiedenheit* (or the Middle High German *abegescheidenheit*). Other alternatives, however, have been suggested: Raymond Blakney, *Meister Eckhart: A Modern Translation* (New York: Harper and Row, 1941), translates it "disinterest," while Schürmann translates it as "releasement." The former translation is an unfortunate choice insofar as it reinforces in the modern reader the notion that detachment is a sort of aloofness or disengagement from the world, which, as will be clear from our presentation, it is not. Schürmann's "releasement" is better, insofar as it implies that detachment "releases" things from their use in human projects and "lets them be" as they truly are in God. But this term is Schürmann's own coinage and seems too intertwined with his own insightful, but heavily Heideggerian, interpretation of Eckhart to be employed for use here. Closely related to *Abgeschiedenheit* is the word *Gelassenheit* (or the Middle High German *gelâzenheit*) that appears frequently in Eckhart's writings as often interchangeable with "detachment." As Reiner Schürmann notes, this word has, at first glance, primarily a moral sense: one of "resignation" or "serenity" in the face of difficulties. But it also has the meaning of "letting be" or simply "to let" (Schürmann, *Wandering Joy*, 16). It thus has an affirmative quality that is essentially related to the activity of the intellect when it knows things in their truth: it simply "lets things be." Finally, Eckhart often discusses "detachment" in connection with the word *lûterkeit* and its adjectival forms, *lûter, ledic,* and *blôz*. These terms are usually translated as "purity, emptiness" and as "pure, empty, bare, naked." As Bernard McGinn remarks: "This complex of terms is very frequent in Eckhart; it signifies both the primal purity of the divine nature and the purity and emptiness that the soul must achieve through detachment in order to be united with God" (TP, 402).

3. The intimate relationship between detachment and divine knowledge in Eckhart's thought has not gone unnoticed. Bernard Welte remarks that "this is because detachment lets all things be what they are in truth, and by doing so becomes one with the Truth itself." See: Welte, *Meister Eckhart: Gedanken zu seinen Gedanken*, 55. Alain de Libera sees Eckhart's thought in this respect as a synthesis between the Aristotelian notion (as mediated through the Arabs) of "abstraction" and Dionysian "aphairesis" or "stripping away" of predicates from the "super-essential" (God). Eckhart thus seems to identify the "detached soul" with the Aristotelian "separated" or "abstracted soul," in this way trying to show how a Christian spiritual praxis is also essentially noetic in character. In essence, Eckhart renders Aristotelian the Dionysian "stripping away" of all created forms and images from the soul. "En se dépassant dans le néant; l'homme—l'homme noble; c'est-à-dire l'homme de l'intellect—se libère des entraves de l'être, il se libère pour Dieu, Intellect supreme mais aussi Néant suressentiel. En ce sens, *l'abime appelle l'abime*." See the introduction to: Alain de Libera, trans., *Maître Eckhart. Traités et Sermons*, 3rd ed. (Paris: Flammarion, 1995), 31 n.1. Thus detachment is the precondition for knowledge of divine truth in that it lets all things be what they are in their primal origin, undistorted by the projects and desires of the finite human consciousness. As Reiner Schürmann remarks: "He who has learned 'to let be' restores all things to their primitive freedom; he leaves all things to themselves. He has learned not to subject them to his projects; he has rid himself of any self-affirmation in which mixed curiosity and ambition inhibit him." *Wandering Joy*, 16. Schürmann sums up Eckhart's thought on this matter in these words: "one must let truth be in order to understand truth as letting-be." *Wandering Joy*, 190.

technical scholastic works.[4] In other words, in Eckhart's vernacular "detachment" designates the technical Latin terms that, for Eckhart, describe the operations proper to the intellect and its proper perfection, which is knowledge of divine Truth, a divine Truth that is known primarily and most fully through revelation.

For Eckhart, as for Thomas Aquinas, whom he follows closely in his epistemology, all knowledge proceeds by abstraction of the immaterial intelligible form from material sensible particulars. But for Eckhart, this "first abstraction" of forms from sensible substances must be followed by what we may call a "second" or "metaphysical abstraction" whereby the soul separates itself as intellect from all that is created so that it may become conformed to being or existence as such, which is the proper subject matter of metaphysics. So, while the "first abstraction" of the intellect strips away the material conditions of sensible things to reveal their immaterial essence or form, a second abstraction is necessary in order to strip away what is finite and limited in creatures in order to reveal the Existence in itself that causes all creatures to exist.[5] This abstraction, Eckhart argues in his *Commentary on John,* fulfills and completes the proper nature of the intellect and is indistinguishable from the spiritual/ethical praxis that he describes as "detachment" in his vernacular works:

Intellect moreover abstracts from the here and now and, according to its own nature, has nothing in common with anything; it is not mixed with anything and is separate as is argued in the third book of the *De anima.* . . . Be, therefore,

4. There is also the additional evidence of the translations of Eckhart's vernacular works into Latin made by the censors at Avignon, where *abegescheidenheit* is often translated as *separatio* or *abstractio.* Thus "daz ist eine ieglichen abegescheidenen geistes bekanntisse" becomes "hoc est uniuscuiusque abstracti spiritus cognitio." Eckhart himself, in his defense, never quibbles with the translation. See Koch, DW V, 439. See also Forman, *Meister Eckhart: Mystic as Theologian,* 81.

5. Detachment, therefore, perfects the soul not merely morally but also intellectually: it makes the soul a pure and undistorted mirror of divine truth and capable of knowledge of God. Here Eckhart parts ways with Aquinas, his spiritual master. For Thomas there is no second or "metaphysical abstraction"; or, if there is, all that the human intellect would know is created *esse commune* or the existence common to created beings, which is a pure abstraction, existing only in particular creatures. We know God only as *esse ipsum subsistens,* self-subsistent existence, who is the *cause* of the *esse commune* in creatures, but who is not identical with that *esse.* Aquinas is, therefore, surprisingly more of a negative theologian in this matter than Eckhart. As we saw in chapter 4, Eckhart does not hold to the distinction between *esse commune* and *esse ipsum subsistens* because, for him, the creature is so dependent on the divine being that its own existence is as nothing compared to God's. The creature has no positive existence of its own but merely limits the existence it receives from God.

like [intellect]: humble, that is, subject to God, separated from time and space, not mixed with anything and having nothing in common with nothing: [by doing this] you come to God and God comes to you.[6]

The intellect *as intellect* (and not simply as the substantial form of the body) is essentially separate, abstracted, or *detached* from the conditions of finite, created being, making it in essence "conformable" to being or existence as such.[7] The intellect is essentially open to existence or being as such. By the same token, being is the cause of truth in the intellect and, as such, is essentially knowable. Or, as Eckhart would put it, being is essentially *Word*, whose essence is to communicate—to communicate existence, truth, and goodness.

For Eckhart, therefore, metaphysics is an extension of scriptural exegesis. The passage from Eckhart that we cited above is from his commentary on John, in which he spends most of his time giving an exegesis of the first chapter, explaining how the "Word became flesh," i.e., how the divine Word becomes present in the inner ground of the flesh-and-blood human being. In this context, Eckhart talks about the necessity of humility. In explicating the first verse of the third chapter of John, *Erat homo ex Pharisaeis Nicomdemus nomine*, he notes that the Latin word *homo* ("man") is related to the other Latin word *humilis*, meaning of the "ground" or "dirt,"

6. *In Ioh.*, 318; LW III, 265–66: "Intellectus autem abstrahit ab hic et nunc, et secundum genus suum nulli nihil habet commune: impermixtus est, separatus est, ex III De anima. . . . Esto talis: humilis, scilicet subiectus deo, separatus a tempore et continuo, impermixtus, nulli nihil habens commune: venis ad deum, et deus ad te." See also, *In Ioh.*, n.38; LW III, 32.

7. In asserting this, Eckhart returns to a purely Platonic metaphysics for which knowledge of the essential exemplars is attainable by the human soul in this life and it is attainable through a process of *purification* whereby the intellect purifies itself of all that is limited and contingent. And this purification is what Eckhart means by detachment or an *abstraction* from the contingent conditions of existence. This is, for Eckhart, the properly metaphysical abstraction because it is what allows the intellect to be conformed to existence as such. Again, by contrast, abstraction for Thomas belongs only to the "first operation" of the intellect whereby the intellect receives the intelligible forms of sensible substances by prescinding from the material conditions of their existence. This first operation is followed, according to Thomas, by a process of "separation" whereby the intellect, by composing and dividing, "separates out," as it were, the essential features of the thing as such. But on Thomas's account, "abstraction" cannot be carried beyond the first operation of the intellect. (See Thomas Aquinas, *In Boethii de Trinitate Expositio*, V, 1 and 3.) For Eckhart, on the other hand, there is an abstraction beyond the second operation of the intellect (of composing and dividing) that is proper to metaphysical science and indistinguishable from the praxis of detachment. Thus Eckhart will argue that the metaphysician considers the formal causes of things alone, apart from their efficient and final causes, as we saw in chapter 2: see *In Gen. I*, n. 4; LW I, 187–88/EE, 83–4.

and, hence, related to the word "humility." And yet, *homo ab intellectu et ratione homo est*—"man is man by virtue of his intellect and reason." But this apparent contradiction is not so strange: by virtue of a human being's humility, indeed, beyond that by virtue of his or her detachment in the empty *ground* of the soul, the human being is intellectual insofar as he or she is able to receive in its purity the divine Word or Intellect. Most importantly, this connection comes to light only in and through the interpretation of Scripture, through a true understanding of its import. In this way, the soul becomes truly detached, for detachment is *nothing other than receiving the revealed Word of God in the ground of one's soul.*

Two works that are of central importance to Eckhart's theory of the intellect, the spiritual life, and their relation to scriptural exegesis are the first two of the *Parisian Questions* (in Latin) and his little treatise *On Detachment* (in Middle High German). These two works represent "both ends," so to speak, of Eckhart's thought: the *Parisian Questions* give us Eckhart the *Lesemeister,* the scholastic theologian and metaphysician writing in scholarly Latin, while *On Detachment* gives us Eckhart the *Lebemeister,* the practical master of the spiritual life, writing in his vernacular Middle High German. By looking at both together, I hope to show the essential link between scholastic metaphysics and ethico-spiritual praxis in Eckhart's thought as well as the connection between speculative philosophy and scriptural exegesis.


## Detachment and the Proper Subject Matter of Metaphysics

At the beginning of his little treatise *On Detachment,* Eckhart claims that he has searched "in many writings by the pagan teachers and by the prophets of the Old and New Law" with the following purpose in mind:

I have inquired, carefully and most industriously, to find which is the greatest and best virtue with which man can most completely and closely conform himself to God, with which he can by grace become that which God is by nature, and with which man can come most of all to resemble that image which he was in God, and between which and God there was no distinction before ever God made created things. And as I scrutinize all these writings, so far as my reason can lead and instruct me, I find no other virtue better than a pure detachment from all things; because all other virtues have some regard for created things, but detachment is free from all created things.[8]

Eckhart here makes three points:

1) Detachment is the virtue that makes us resemble that "image" that we were in God before we were created, before that image was made to "stand out" (*ex-sistere*) in existence.

2) Eckhart calls detachment a "virtue," but he also makes it clear that it is not a virtue in the accepted sense of the term because it is, in a sense, the source and principle of all the other virtues. A virtue, as understood by Aristotle and the Aristotelian tradition, is a habit that perfects a being in its essential function. In other words, a virtue perfects a being with regard to its finite essence and with regard to other created or finite things. But detachment is different: it perfects the creature with regard to its *existential source*; it perfects the soul in relation *to existence itself.*[9]

3) Eckhart sees detachment as the fruit of his understanding the revealed texts and of all of "heathen" philosophy. Thus, detachment is a "virtue" that is itself not detached from the reading and interpretation of Scripture nor of the texts used to interpret Scripture, the works of the Church fathers and the pagan philosophers, a fact to be kept in mind as I discuss the rest of his treatise.

To start with, for Eckhart, detachment is the highest virtue insofar as it perfects the soul in its *essential nothingness*, i.e., in the inner emptiness from all created being that Eckhart sometime calls the "ground," "little castle," or "little spark" of the soul. Thus Eckhart says:

Whatever is to be received must be received by something; but detachment is so close to nothingness that there is nothing so subtle that it can be apprehended by detachment, except God alone. He is so simple and so subtle that he can indeed be apprehended in a detached heart. And so detachment can apprehend nothing except God.[10]

---

8. *Vom Abg.*, DW V, 400–01/EE, 285.

9. Or to put it another way, while the Aristotelian virtues are "ontic" in that they perfect the creature in its finite essence and with regard to other finite beings, detachment is an "ontological virtue" insofar as it perfects the creature with regard to existence itself, which is infinite and, therefore, no particular thing.

10. *Vom Abg.*, DW V, 404/EE, 286.

Here Eckhart makes use of the principle, often cited by Thomas, that "whatever is received must be received in the mode of the receiver." If the soul is to receive God as God, i.e., not as a limited, created thing in a certain "mode," it must receive God "without any mode." Thus, the detached heart wants to be nothing so that it might be receptive to God: "Whoever wants this or that wants to be something, but detachment wants to be nothing at all. So it is that detachment makes no claim upon anything."[11] For this reason, detachment is, as a virtue, above even love and humility: love and humility still have regard for "something," be it the object loved or the self that is abased, but detachment has regard for "no-thing" other than the Absolute itself, who is, of course, "no-thing" in particular. Indeed, detachment transforms the intellect to such an extent that it can "apprehend nothing but God": it apprehends existence as such, in comparison to which all else is as nothing. Without the inner emptiness that detachment actualizes and perfects in the soul, there would be some obstruction in the soul that would hinder it from receiving and knowing God as God.

It should be noted from the beginning that Eckhart does not commit himself to the patently absurd position that the detached soul that has emptied itself and become "nothing" ceases to exist or ceases to be a creature. Eckhart makes a very important distinction between the "outer man" and the "inner man": the outer man is the whole psycho-physical composite of which the soul is the substantial form and which makes use of the senses in knowing things, but the inner man is that inner ground that is untouched by the senses or anything created. "Now you must know that the outer man may be active whilst the inner man remains wholly free and immovable."[12] The inner man represents the intellectual core of the soul that transcends its function as the form of the body and is free from all conditioned being. It is that "part" that knows without the senses. Eckhart compares the inner man to the hinge of a door and the outer man to the door itself: while the outer man swings and moves, senses and knows sensible things, the inner man may remain free and unmoved, unaffected by the door that it supports. The detached soul is simply one that lives out of this immovable inner ground of its being, which is both the principle of its knowledge of God and of its loving action. In other words, the inner

11. *Vom Abg.*, DW V, 406/EE, 287.
12. *Vom Abg.*, DW V, 422/EE, 291.

man refers to the inner "image" of God, which, Eckhart claims, detachment uncovers and activates. The detached soul retains all the features of created being outwardly, but inwardly, he or she has become empty and nothing.

What, however, makes this detachment possible? For Eckhart, the human soul's intellectual nature makes this possible; in turn, detachment perfects the soul in its intellectual nature. Thus Eckhart says, referring to the Muslim philosopher Avicenna (Ibn Sina):

An authority called Avicenna says: "The excellence of the spirit which has achieved detachment is so great that whatever it contemplates is true, and whatever it desires is granted, and whatever it commands one must obey" (*On the Soul*, 4.4). And you should know that this is really so; when the free spirit has attained true detachment, it compels God to its being; and if the spirit could attain formlessness, and be without all accidents, it would take on God's properties. But this God can give to no one but himself; therefore God cannot do more for the spirit that has attained detachment than to give himself to it.[13]

In this "formlessness" of detachment the soul becomes perfected intellectually precisely because it is of the nature of the intellect to be "formless" so that it may receive all forms. Eckhart continues:

And the man who has attained complete detachment is so carried into eternity that no transient thing can move him, so that he experiences nothing of whatever is bodily, and he calls the world dead, because nothing earthly has any savor for him. This is what Saint Paul meant when he said: "I live, and yet I do not; Christ lives in me" (Gal 2:20).[14]

Once the intellect has been purified through detachment, it has become empty of all created things and is able to be conformed completely to God. Eckhart puts this into a simple formula: "And you must know that to be empty of all created things is to be full of God, and to be full of created things is to be empty of God."[15] If we are to know existence as such, we must "become empty" in the "inner ground" of our own particular existence through the praxis of detachment. The detached soul, therefore, does not literally "become" God: quite the contrary, it empties itself of any inner attachment to its own existence so that it may "let God be God." And in doing so, the soul is perfected intellectually. To understand how

---

13. *Vom Abg.*, DW V, 410–11/EE, 288.      14. Ibid.

15. *Vom Abg.*, DW V, 413/EE, 288.

this is so, we must turn to Eckhart's doctrine of the nature and operation of the intellect as outlined in his first two *Parisian Questions*.

## The Nature of the Intellect in the *Parisian Questions*

It is best to start our analysis of Eckhart's doctrine of the intellect with the second of the Parisian questions, because it deals with the nature of the created intellect. The second question runs as follows: "Is an Angel's Understanding, as Denoting an Action, the same as its Existence?" In answering this question, Eckhart must make some distinctions crucial for the doctrine of the intellect that appears throughout his other writings, and these distinctions form the foundation for his teaching on detachment, setting forth his fundamentally hermeneutical understanding of the human intellect.

Eckhart begins his answer to the question with an approving exposition of the views of his predecessors. They convincingly demonstrate that the intellect is of a fundamentally different nature than existence as it is encountered and understood in finite created beings:

Some demonstrate this [that the angel's understanding is *not* the same as its existence] well, in the following manner: Every action is either transient or immanent. Now existence is not a transient action, for this sort of action goes outward, whereas existence remains within. Neither is existence an immanent action, like understanding or sensation, for this kind of action is unlimited, either absolutely, as in the case of understanding, or relatively, as in the case of sensation. Existence, on the contrary, is limited and determined to a genus and species.[16]

What distinguishes understanding from existence is its simultaneously transcendent and immanent nature. It is transcendent in that, as Thomas also notes, the operation of the intellect is directed to all being as such so that its actions are, at least potentially, infinite in their extent. But understanding is immanent insofar as it remains within the thinking subject, even as it is essentially directed outwards to all existence as such. Hence, Thomas says that the action of the intellect is said to have infinity absolutely and that of the senses to have infinity only relatively:

16. *Quaes. Par.* II, n.1; LW V, 49/Maurer, 51.

As an example of infinity absolutely, we have the act *to understand,* of which the object is *the true,* and the act *to will,* of which the object is *the good.* Both of these are convertible with being; and so, to understand and to will, of themselves, bear relation to all things, and each receives its specification from its object. On the other hand, the act of sensation is relatively infinite, for it bears relation to all sensible things; as sight does to all things visible. Now the being of every creature is restricted to one in genus and species, and God's being alone is absolutely infinite, comprehending all things in itself, as Dionysius says. Hence the divine being is its own act of understanding and its own act of will.[17]

The intellect essentially relates to all of being as such,[18] and therefore transcends in both its nature and operation all genera and species, whereas existence is always limited to some genus and species. For this reason, the existence of an angel, limited as it is to a genus, is not the same as its understanding.

But to this argument from his Dominican predecessor, Eckhart adds arguments of his own or, as he puts it: "I have other ways of proving this." He first appeals to Aristotle's notion of the intellect (as derived in part from Anaxagoras) that the intellect *as intellect* is "unmixed with anything."

The intellect, as an intellect, is none of the things it knows: it must be "unmixed with anything," "having nothing in common," so that it might know everything, as the *De Anima* III says. Similarly, sight must be colorless so that it can see all colors. If the intellect, therefore, insofar as it is intellect, is nothing, it follows that neither is understanding some existence.[19]

---

17. *S.Th.* I, 54, 2: "Secunda autem actio de sui ratione habet infinitatem, vel simpliciter, vel secundum quid. Simpliciter quidem, sicut intelligere, cuius obiectum est verum, et velle, cuius obiectum est bonum, quorum utrumque convertitur cum ente; et ita intelligere et velle, quantum est de se, habent se ad omnia; et utrumque recipit speciem ab obiecto. Secundum quid autem infinitum est sentire, quod se habet ad omnia sensibilia, sicut visus ad omnia visibilia. Esse autem cuiuslibet creaturae est determinatum ad unum secundum genus et speciem: esse autem solius Dei est simpliciter infinitum, in se omnia comprehendens, ut dicit Dionysius, 5 cap. *De div. nom.* Unde solum esse divinum est suum intelligere et suum velle."

18. For a good discussion of the centrality of this relation for the medieval metaphysical project see in particular the works of Jan Aertsen, *Medieval Philosophy and the Transcendentals: The Case of Thomas Aquinas,* "Is There a Medieval Philosophy?" and "Die Tranzendentalienlehre bei Thomas von Aquin in ihren historischen Hintergründen und philosophischen Motiven," in *Thomas von Aquin: Werk und Wirkung im Licht Neuerer Forschungen,* ed. Albert Zimmermann, Miscellanea Medievalia 19 (Berlin: de Gruyter, 1988), 82–102. See also: Wouter Goris, *Einheit als Prinzip und Ziel,* passim.

19. *Quaes. Par. II,* n.2; LW V, 50/ Maurer, 51.

This principle is, as we shall see, of capital importance not only for Eckhart's doctrine of the intellect but also for his understanding of the noetic dimension of detachment. It is a principle to which he appeals again and again, both in his scholastic writing and in his more practical or spiritual vernacular writings. For Eckhart, the intellect insofar as it is intellect must be something separate and detached from any finite existence, and in asserting this, he follows a much more Neoplatonic/Albertian notion of the intellect than that which Aquinas held.[20] Thus, the qualification "insofar as" (in Latin, *in tantum quam*) is of paramount importance: insofar as the intellect is a real power of the soul, it is indeed "some being."[21] This Eckhart makes clear. But the intellect, *considered only in itself or in its essence*, cannot be a delimited or conditioned existence and is thus not simply the substantial form of the human body.[22] In its essential nature, it is "separate," "abstracted," or "detached" from all existence in genera and species.

The process of cognition itself gives evidence of this assertion. Following Thomas,[23] Eckhart argues that the intelligible species or image has no being that can be qualified as either substantial or accidental, because otherwise it could not be that *by which* something is known:

Now the purpose of a [cognitive] likeness is to represent something to the intellect. Hence it should be such as to better represent that thing, and it represents it better if it is not a being than if it were a being. In fact, if it were a being it

20. Aquinas and Eckhart can be seen as developing in opposite directions their teacher Albert's doctrine of the soul. As Anton Pegis points out in his book *St. Thomas and the Problem of the Soul in the 13th Century* (Toronto: Pontifical Institute of Medieval Studies, 1934), Albert struggled to reconcile two very different traditions concerning the nature and proper function of the soul: the Aristotelian tradition which argues that the soul is the form of the organic body and a principle of composite being and the Neoplatonic tradition which emphasizes the separate and self-subsistent nature of the soul (at least in its highest activities). Aquinas opted to develop the Aristotelian side of Albert's thought. Since the intellect is immaterial in its operation, we must think of it as self-subsistent, but Aquinas always argues that the human intellect needs to be united to a body in order to be fully actualized as intellect. Eckhart, by contrast, chose to develop a more Neoplatonic notion of the human soul and intellect. For Eckhart, the human intellect is actualized as intellect only to the extent that it is separate and detached from created being, since the intellect is, at its root, "formless" and "mode-less" and thus prior to all form.

21. *Quaes. Par. II*, n.7 ; LW V, 53/Maurer, 53.

22. See *S.Th*. I, 76, 1. Thomas, of course, also says that the actuality of the intellectual form is not exhausted by its in-formation of the body and thus it has operations that transcend its purely "organic" functions. That is why Thomas calls the soul a "substantial form" that is capable of subsisting after death. Nevertheless, Thomas argues that intellection is impossible without the body and the sensible material that the body provides for thought.

23. *S.Th*. I, 85, 2.

would detract from its representative function. Consequently it is not a being—unless you call it a being in the mind.[24]

For Eckhart what holds true of the *operation* of the intellect holds true of the *nature* of the intellect itself: "The intellect, as such, is neither here, nor now, nor a definite thing. But every being or existence is in a definite genus and species. So the intellect, as such, is not a being, nor does it have an existence."[25] In other words, the intelligible likeness—and by extension, the intellect—is not a being belonging to any genus or species.[26] If the intellect is to know anything, the mode of its "existence" must be different than the mode in which creatures exist.

Of course, in the passage cited above, Eckhart does concede that we might call the cognitive form a "being in the mind." But then, as he indicates earlier in his *respondeo,* even this position is inadequate. The cognitive form (or "intelligible species") cannot be thought to "be in" or "subsist in" the mind in the same manner that an accident subsists in its substance:

If a [cognitive] likeness were a being it would be an accident, for it is not a substance. But a [cognitive] likeness is not an accident, because an accident has a subject that gives it existence. Now a [cognitive] likeness has an object but not a subject. Place and subject are not the same. A [cognitive] likeness is in the soul, not as in a subject but as in a place (cf. Aristotle, *De anima,* 529 a25–30); for the soul is the "place of [cognitive] likenesses," not the whole soul but the intellect. It is clear that the soul would be the subject of a [cognitive] likeness if it has a subject. Consequently, a [cognitive] likeness is not a being.[27]

The intellect, as intellect, transcends any finite or conditioned existence,[28] and this is further confirmed by Eckhart by the convertibility of "being" and "goodness" as held in the medieval doctrine of the transcendentals. "Being and good are convertible terms. But we do not find in the intellect the na-

24. *Quaes. Par. II,* n.6; LW V, 52/Maurer, 53.

25. *Quaes. Par. II,* n.7; LW V, 52–53/Maurer, 53.

26. See John Caputo, "The Nothingness of the Intellect in Meister Eckhart's 'Parisian Questions,'" *The Thomist* 39 (1975), 85. "Consciousness . . . is completely translucent and empty. It is a 'lack' and desire of the fullness of being. It is a freedom which cuts through the dead weight of matter. It is . . . not what 'is' (being) but the 'revelation' of what is (non-being)."

27. *Quaes. Par. II,* n.5; LW V, 51.

28. Or, as Caputo sums up Eckhart's argument, since the cognitive form "is neither substance nor accident but that by which both substance and accidents are made known," the intellective soul cannot be understood as substance but as the "place" "*where* knowledge occurs." See Caputo, "The Nothingness of the Intellect," 99.

ture of the good or of efficient or final causality."[29] On this point, Eckhart appeals to the third book of Aristotle's *Metaphysics*[30] where the Greek philosopher argues that mathematical entities, which are intellectual products in their essence, cannot be qualified as "good" or "bad." Eckhart, therefore, concludes that the intellect considered in itself and not as a power of the soul transcends the usual causal forces, such as efficient and final causality, that determine an essence to a particular existence. As Eckhart says in the prologue to his *Opus propositionum*, therefore, the intellect can "abstract from the here and now." "Existence is measured not by time but by eternity"[31]: because the intellect has as its proper object being or existence as such, it cannot in its essential nature be restricted by temporal and spatial conditions.[32] For these are accidents of a substance and, as we have seen, the intellect as intellect is, for Eckhart, neither a substance nor an accident. One must only remember that the human being is not an intellect pure and simple; otherwise, he or she would be uncreated and divine. But, *insofar* as the human being, through the humility of a detachment that is receptive to God's Word and separated from all that is finite and created, becomes more and more intellectual, to that degree he or she shares in the divine intellectuality and, hence, the divine life. If all of this is the case, then it follows that we must think of God primarily as pure understanding, rather than as pure existence or, to put it more precisely, we must see that God is pure existence *by virtue* of his being the pure act of understanding, and not vice versa.

In the first Parisian question Eckhart asks: "Are Existence and Understanding the Same in God?" At first, Eckhart simply responds to the question in the affirmative and appeals to the reasons given by Thomas in both the *Summa Contra Gentiles* and the *Summa Theologiae* to support his position.[33] These arguments follow from the basic insight that the essence of God is identical with his act of existence. It follows that if we

29. *Quaes. Par. II*, n.8; LW V, 53/Maurer, 53: "Sed in intellectu non invenitur ratio boni nec efficientis nec finis."

30. Aristotle, *Metaph.* III, 2, 996a 27.

31. *Prol. op. trip.*, n.9; LW I, 154: "Esse rerum omnium, inquantum esse, mensuratur aeternitate, nequequam tempore. Intellectus enim, cuius obiectum est ens et in quo secundum Avicennam ens cadit primo omnium, ab hic et nunc abstrahit et per consequens a tempore." *In Sap.*, n.10; LW II, 331: "Obiectum autem intellectus est ens."

32. According to Caputo, for Eckhart the intellect is "that which is 'detached' from being" and is "not bound by the conditions of being." Caputo, "The Nothingness of the Intellect," 94–95.

33. *Contra Gentiles*, I, 45, nn.2–6, and *S.Th.* I, 14, 4.

predicate understanding of God, it cannot be predicated of God as an accidental quality but as expressing the very substance of God. Therefore, we must say that God does not merely *have* understanding, but that God, in some way, *is* the act of understanding itself. In arguing this Eckhart simply repeats the position of Thomas. But Eckhart goes farther than this and indicates as much: "I declare that it is not my present opinion that God understands because he exists, but rather that he exists because he understands. God is an intellect and understanding, and his understanding itself is the ground of his existence."[34] Understanding or "intellection" is the *fundamentum esse* of God. For Eckhart, this statement is in perfect accord with revelation: God does not say at the beginning of the Gospel "In the beginning was 'being' *(ens),*" but "In the beginning was the *Word*," which Eckhart interprets to imply *intellect* or *understanding.*[35]

Indeed, for Eckhart, this distinction is more than in accord with revelation: for him, it means that intellect is prior to being and that, therefore, revelation is prior to reason and the ultimate rational science, the science of being as being, or metaphysics. The truth of the science of metaphysics therefore lies not in human reason but in the Gospels, for these treat most clearly and directly of being qua being: it is the Word, Christ, who is prior to all things and it is only in Christ, who is Word or pure understanding, and the Gospels that the Truth of being qua being is found.

As is clear, Eckhart knew very well he was parting company with Thomas. For Thomas, existence in itself *(ipsum esse)* contains virtually within itself every perfection of existence, so that it would also include pre-eminently within itself understanding.[36] But in the first Parisian

34. *Quaes. Par. I,* n.4; LW V, 43/Maurer, 45.

35. *Quaes. Par. I,* n.4; LW V, 40.

36. See: *S.Th.* I, 4, 2, ad 3; I-II, 2, 5, ad 2; *In Divinis Nominibus,* c.5, lect. 1, ed. C. Pera (Rome, 1950), 235–36, nn.632–35. It is interesting to note, as Maurer does (15–16, n.21), that many contemporary Thomists, usually labeled "transcendental," adopt a position closer to that of Eckhart. Lonergan says, for example: "Among Thomists, however, there is a dispute whether *ipsum intelligere* or *ipsum esse subsistens* is logically first among divine attributes. As has been seen in the section on the notion of God, all other divine attributes follow from the notion of an unrestricted act of understanding. Moreover, since we define being by its relation to intelligence, necessarily our ultimate is not being but intelligence." See *Insight: A Study of Human Understanding* (London, 1957), 677. We also have this remark from the Baroque commentator on Aquinas, John of St. Thomas: "ergo ipsum intelligere, ut est actus ultimus et formaliter constituit vitam intellectivam ut non determinabilem ab alio, formaliter constituit eam in ratione summi gradus et naturae divinae." See *Cursus Theologicus* (Paris, 1934) II, 339, n.11.

question, Eckhart is making use of a notion of existence that was put forth in the generation before Eckhart by Henry of Ghent and by Albert the Great, teacher of both Eckhart and Thomas. This earlier understanding of existence is quite different from Thomas's own conception. For Henry and Albert, existence is understood in its etymological sense as that which "stands out" (ex-sistere) from its ideal being in the mind of God. Thus, Henry put forward that the existence of a creature is its relation to God as its efficient cause.[37]

But perhaps the most important influence on Eckhart here is the anonymous *Book of Causes,* a short but dense epitome of ancient Neo-platonic philosophy composed in Arabic sometime in the ninth century, translated into Latin, and widely read and commented upon by scholastic theologians like Albert and Thomas. One of the propositions of this work that Eckhart explicitly invokes in his response to the question of whether understanding or existence is logically prior in the divine being is "the first of created beings is existence."[38] For Eckhart "existence" as something distinct from the essence of the thing is consequent only upon created being or existence. Thus, Eckhart says: "As soon as we come to existence we come to a creature. Existence, then, has primarily the nature of something creatable. This is why some writers [cf. Henry of Ghent, Albert, etc.] say that the existence of a creature is related to God only as to an efficient cause, whereas its essence is related to him as to an exemplar[y] cause."[39] In his response to the second question, Eckhart also says that the intellect, as such, is not determined by efficient or final causality: the intellect, as such, is distinct from existence and is logically prior to it, and on this

37. For the Albertian notion of the relation of existence to understanding see his *In I Sent.* Q. 5, a. 6: ed. Borgnet (Paris: 1893), vol. 25, 184. Thomas Aquinas, commenting upon Dionysius, also notes this Neoplatonic notion of the relation of existence to understanding: "[Dionysius] ostendit quod ens dictum de Deo, signat processum existentium a Deo." *In Divinis Nominibus,* n.632.

38. *Liber de causis,* prop. 4, ed. Otto Bardenhewer (Freiburg, Switzerland: 1882), 166. Thomas resolves this difficulty by interpreting the *"ens"* referred to in this proposition as the *ens commune* of creatures, which is distinct from the *esse ipsum subsistens* that characterizes the divine existence. See his *In Librum de Causis Expositio,* translated by V. Guagliardo, C. Hess, and R. Taylor as *Commentary on the Book of Causes* (Washington, D.C.: The Catholic University of America Press, 1996), 26–34.

39. *Quaes. Par. I,* n.4; LW V, 41/Maurer, 46: "Esse ergo habet primo rationem creabilis, et ideo dicunt aliqui quod in creatura esse solum respicit deum sub ratione causae efficientis, essentia, autem respicit ipsum sub ratione causae exemplaris. Sapientia autem, quae pertinet ad intellectum, non habet rationem creabilis."

point, one detects the influence of his fellow German Dominican Dietrich of Freiburg, who developed an elaborate scheme of emanations in which the emanation of the intellect is logically and ontologically prior to that of existence.[40]

Of course, in making this argument, Eckhart must address Thomas's assertion that existence in itself includes virtually within itself all perfections. Eckhart answers that if we consider the terms "existence" and "intellect" *in the abstract,* i.e., from the standpoint of the first concepts of the intellect, then "being" or *esse* is conceptually prior, because *conceptually* intellect presupposes existence, since all intellects must first be beings of some sort. But if we consider things with regard to their *mode of participation* in God, their first principle, then we must reverse the order. Or, as Eckhart puts it in a much fuller treatment of this ontological hierarchy in his *Commentary on John,* we must make a distinction between what these terms—existence, life, and understanding—mean in the *abstract (in abstracto)* and how they manifest themselves in *concrete* instances (*in concreto*).[41] A concrete being that lives and understands is more perfect than one that does not, in the sense that it "gathers" more of existence within itself and brings it to full and perfectly simple self-reflection. Understanding, therefore, is higher or more perfect than mere existence,[42]

40. In particular, see his *Tractatus de intellectu et intelligibili,* translated by M. L. Führer as *Treatise on the Intellect and the Intelligible* (Milwaukee, Wis.: Marquette University Press, 1992). For Dietrich's influence on Eckhart, see B. McGinn's *The Harvest of Mysticism,* 96ff.

41. *Quaes. Par.* I, n.6; LW V, 41: "'In principio' enim 'erat verbum,' quod ad intellectum omnino pertinet, ut sic ipsum intelligere teneat primum gradum in perfectionibus, deinde ens vel esse." Also *In Ioh.,* n.63; LW III, 52–53: "vivere, esse et intelligere evacuant sive implent totum ens. Secundum sciendum quod alius est ordo istorum in abstracto, puta cum dicimus esse, vivere et intelligere; alius in concreto, puta cum dicimus ens vivens, intelligens. In abstracto enim esse est perfectius inter tria. Ipsi enim esse nullus modus sive perfectio essendi deesse potest. Quomodo autem aliquid deesset per esse? Sed potius deest per non-esse vel abesse. Pari ratione vivere est nobilius intelligere. In concreto vero oppositi modo se habet: ens enim infimum tenet locum, vivum secundum, intelligens tertium sive supremum. Et est ratio: nam in concreto sunt participantia. Omne autem participans ut sic nudum et imperfectum est ex se ipso. Propter quod primo participat ex sui imperfectione in imperfectiori gradu participationis, et plus sapit naturam imperfecti. Hinc est quod res creata primo est ens, perfectius vivens, postremo et supremo est intelligens. Sic ergo intelligens perfectius est quam ens, eo quod includit ens."

42. See W. Beierwaltes, *Proklos: Grundzüge seiner Metaphysik* (Frankfurt: V. Klosterman, 1965), 117–18 ; and Lossky, *Théologie négative,* 350–58. One can also find a clear summary of Eckhart's position in Frank Tobin, *Meister Eckhart: Thought and Language,* 52ff. Hence, in the prologues to the *Opus tripartitum,* Eckhart will argue that "Existence is God" precisely because God, as pure intellectual unity, is the *ground and fulfillment* of existence.

for in and through the act of understanding, creatures participate most fully in the divine life. Existence, therefore, is prior if we regard creatures with respect to their *emanation* from God, but understanding is prior, insofar as we regard creatures with respect to their *return* to God. Through intellect as intellect, then, we are united to God and not through existence (or only secondarily through existence). Hence, all of creation is united to God through the human intellect: the human intellect, as microcosm, is the vehicle through which all things return to God. The human intellect is a microcosm, because it is the one that is in pure potentiality to all modes of existence, both spiritual and material. Thus insofar as the goal of human life is to return to God in loving union, the intellect, speaking *in concreto* or in the order of its return to its divine source, is prior to existence. The most adequate way to knowledge of God, therefore, is through the intellect and not through existence.

Drawing on a principle enunciated by Dionysius,[43] Eckhart argues that something cannot formally be both in the cause and the effect. So when we predicate a term of many things by analogy, such as "health," the thing referred to can exist formally in only one of the things referred to— so that, for example, "health" subsists formally only in an animal, but "in a diet or urine there is no more health than in a stone. Now all creatures are formally beings; hence God will not be formally a being."[44] It follows, then, for Eckhart, that God is "no-thing"—not in the sense of sheer nonexistence, but in the sense of that which transcends all finite and conditioned being.

Nothing in the creature is in God except as in its cause, and it is not there formally. Consequently, since existence belongs to creatures, it is not in God except as in its cause. Therefore existence is not in God but purity of existence.[45]

If one understands by "existence" as it is predicated of creatures, i.e., as existing in a finite mode, then "existence" in this sense does not apply to God. Since the creaturely mode of existence adds nothing to God's existence, it is more proper to say that God is the "purity of existence."

What Eckhart means by "purity of existence" is, of course, ambiguous:

43. See his *De Coelesti Hierarchia*, c.2, n.3: PG 3, 140.
44. *Quaes. Par. I*, n.11; LW V, 46/Maurer, 49.
45. *Quaes. Par. I*, n.9; LW V, 45/Maurer, 48.

it can be either possessive in meaning in the sense of "existence's purity" or it can be privative, in the sense of purity *from* existence. I think Eckhart means both senses here, because God contains pre-eminently within himself all existence, and so cannot be any existent. As the cause of existence, God cannot be limited to any determinate existence; but it entails no contradiction to think of God as pure understanding precisely because pure understanding is "separate," "abstracted," and "detached" from every existent and thus not limited in its essence to any form or nature:

Aristotle says that the power of sight must be colorless so that it can perceive all colors, and that the intellect is not a natural form so that it can know all forms. So also I deny existence itself and suchlike of God so that he may be the cause of all existence and pre-contain all things. Thus, as I do not deny to God anything that is his, so I do deny to him what is not his. These negations, as Damascene says in the first book [of *On Orthodox Faith*], signify in God an excess of affirmation. So I deny nothing to God that is his by nature, asserting as I do that God pre-contains everything in purity, fullness, and perfection, more abundantly and extensively, because he is the ground and cause of all things. And this is what he intended to say when he declared "I am who am."[46]

Through becoming intellect as such, and not simply through existing or even knowing existent things, humans become conformed to the divine nature.[47] In other words, the soul must become free, unmixed, and thus purely intellectual if it is to know God, for only insofar as it is intellect is the soul like God and thus knows God. Moreover, the soul becomes free, unmixed, and purely intellectual in and through the detached reception of his Word in the Gospel. While it is indeed true that the human intellect becomes actualized as intellect only in knowing created being, it can never be fully actualized as intellect insofar as it knows only finite things. Only when it is fully conformed to the Word of God, as revealed in the Gospel, does the human intellect become fully actualized as intellect, because only then as *intelligere* is it conformed to God, not analogically qua created being, but univocally, qua intellect.

---

46. *Quaes. Par.* I, n.12; LW V, 47–48/Maurer, 50.

47. Eckhart does not, of course, in asserting this say that God is not existence as such; he simply denies that God can be any determinate existent. We must understand that "understanding itself, and whatever has to do with intellect, belongs to a different order than existence." *Quaes. Par.* I, n.7; LW V, 43/Maurer, 47: "Secundo accipio quod ipsum intelligere et ea quae ad intellectum pertinet, sunt alterius condicionis quam ipsum esse."

As intellect, the soul subsists not in its created being (which always remains, in any case), but rather, it subsists in God's Word. As such, the human soul, qua intellect, no longer "stands outside" God's Being, but stands, so to speak, "inside" the life of the Godhead, sharing in its intellection. As intellect, the human soul returns to and stands inside its original cause. Eckhart explains in his *Book of the Parables of Genesis*, "And this is what the Philosopher means when he says that the principle of being and of knowing are the same. For Plato posited ideas of things, similitudes or notions, which are necessary as much for cognition as for generation."[48] He continues:

> It should be recognized therefore that the similitude of things exists in its own original causes, most especially in the first [cause], and is their notion and word—as is said in Jn 1:1, "In the beginning was the Word," the Greek calls "*logos*," which signifies notion or word. I say that this similitude, word or notion in its analogical cause has a double relation: as the principle of cognition or of knowledge and also as the principle of existence "outside" in the nature of things. For this name itself, "existence" (*existentia*) indicates a sort of "standing outside" (*extrastantia*).[49]

Thus, all creatures, insofar as they receive existence from God, receive it analogically: they "stand," so to speak, "outside" (*ex-sistere*) the divine existence. But God, as the principle of all existence, is also the principle of all cognition or knowledge. God stands also "within" all things as their intelligible principle or "word." Indeed, as we saw above, God's own principle of himself is as Word. Hence, to stand in relation to God, not so much as "existence," but as "word," is to stand, not "outside" God, but "inside" God in a relation that is not analogical but univocal.[50]

The thesis of Eckhart's *Parisian Questions*, "*Deus est intelligere*," is not, therefore, in conflict with the thesis of the general prologue of his *Opus tripartitum*, "*Esse est Deus*." The fact that "God" or "*Deus*" is the subject of the first thesis and the predicate of the second should indicate as much. According to the thesis *Esse est Deus*, God is the only predicate that is ad-

---

48. *In Gen. II*, n.52; LW I, 520.
49. *In Gen. II*, n.52; LW I, 520.
50. This dual relation of creatures to God, in the realm of existence and in the realm of intellect, owes much to Eckhart's older contemporary, Dietrich of Freiburg. See B. Mojsisch, *Meister Eckhart: Analogie, Univozität und Einheit*, passim.

equate to existence as such, to the pure act of "to be" *(esse)*. In other words, only the predicate "God" describes pure existence substantively. To say that existence in its purity is God, however, is to say something primarily about existence and not about God. The thesis *Deus est intelligere* says something about God: i.e., that God is the act of unrestricted understanding or pure intellect, for it is by virtue of his unrestricted understanding or intellection that God "purifies" his existence of all limitation and negation such that God is the purity of existence or *esse*. As such, the act of pure understanding or *intelligere* describes God's nature more adequately than the term *esse* does, even though it is indeed true that, as Eckhart argues in his *Opus, esse* or the pure act of being is nothing other than God. This is why Eckhart likes to use the Latin term *bullitio,* or a "boiling up," to describe this unrestricted act of understanding that dissolves all limits and negations, while he uses the term *ebullitio,* or "boiling over," to describe God's giving of existence to finite creatures. It is therefore to an analysis of these two terms that we shall turn.

### Bullitio et ebullitio

Eckhart's understanding of the nature and status of the intellect is inseparable from his understanding of the Trinity.[51] As the soul becomes more and more intellectual through detachment, the more does God emanate into the soul as Word or Intellect. In other words, the more the soul becomes detached and, therefore, intellectual, the more it comes to participate in the Trinity, which is constituted by the inner emanations of the Godhead.

Here it is relevant to look at the distinction that Eckhart makes between two "emanations" from God, the *bullitio* or "boiling up" and the *ebullitio* or "boiling over." Eckhart, like many other medieval thinkers, including Aquinas, has no qualms about talking of God's creation of the world as a sort of "emanation" from God, a term borrowed directly from the vocabulary of Neoplatonism. There were (and are) qualms about using the term "emanation" because, at least in its original Neoplatonic context, it seemed to deny God's creative freedom—"emanation" implies a necessary

51. McGinn, *The Harvest of Mysticism,* 133.

process devoid of free choice and hence of love, like light streaming from a lamp. Similarly, "emanation" seems to deny that God created the world *ex nihilo*, from nothing—because "emanation" implies that the "stuff" of creation comes from God. Eckhart, however, like Aquinas, understands "emanation" in a more narrow sense, as meaning that being "streams" from God as the *efficient and final cause* of creatures, not as their "stuff" or material cause. As such, God's creative activity is free because, at least for Eckhart, the inner emanation of the Persons of the Trinity within God makes God sufficient unto himself and therefore does not create the world out of necessity but out of love.

Eckhart uses the terms *bullitio* and *ebullitio* to describe this dual emanation. The *ebullitio* is that emanation or "boiling over" in which God gives existence to finite things. The image here is of a reality so full of dynamic being, so abundant with existence, that it "boils over" into giving existence to finite things. Eckhart connects this *ebullitio* of God into creatures with the phenomenon of grace, of which there are two sorts:

The first grace comes from God insofar as he is understood as a being, or rather as something good—as Augustine says, "Because he is good, we exist." The divine essence as such neither generates nor creates, only the divine subject does. The second grace comes from God as he is understood according to the property of "personal notion," for which reason only the intellective being which properly reflects the image of the Trinity can receive it. Further, God as good is the principle of "boiling over" on the outside; as personal notion he is the principle of "boiling within himself," which is the cause and exemplar of the "boiling over." Thus, the emanation of the Persons in the Godhead, the cause and exemplar of creation, is prior.[52]

The "first grace" that Eckhart here talks about is simply the free gift of existence to all creatures regardless of their merits, and this "first grace" is the product of the divine "boiling over" or *ebullitio*. The "second grace," however, is given only to intellectual creatures. By virtue of the first grace or *ebullitio* all creatures "flow out" of God; by virtue of the second grace all creatures return to God: "The first grace consists in a type of flowing out, a departure from God; the second consists in a type of flowing back, a return to God himself. Both first and second grace have in common that they are from

52. *Serm. XXV*, n.258; LW IV, 235–36/TP, 218. For an explanation of "personal notion" see Thomas Aquinas, *S.Th.* I, 32, 2 and 3.

God alone."[53] As Eckhart makes clear, the second grace, by which creatures are enabled to return to God, has its source in the divine *bullitio*. That is, it is by participation in the emanation of the divine Persons from and into each other, that the soul finds its true end and makes possible its blessedness.

Logically and ontologically prior, therefore, to the divine *ebullitio* is the divine *bullitio* within the Godhead. For human beings, the *bullitio* is, of course, temporally posterior because it is the end and fulfillment of our existence as intellectual beings; but absolutely speaking, it is prior. This is so because of two things. First, the divine *bullitio* is purely inward and purely intellective. In his exegesis of verse 3:14 from Exodus, "I am who am," Eckhart argues that the repetition in the verse

indicates the purity of affirmation excluding all negation from God. It also indicates the reflexive turning back of his existence into itself and upon itself and its dwelling and remaining fixed in itself. It further indicates a "boiling" or giving birth to itself—glowing into itself, and melting and boiling in and into itself, light that totally forces its whole being in light and into light and that is everywhere turned back and reflected upon itself.[54]

Here we can see why Eckhart likes the metaphor of *bullitio* or "boiling up" to describe the inner life of the Godhead. Just as with a boiling substance, there is no fixed, finite being in God's essence. All is transparent to itself, flowing into itself, *giving birth* to itself. It is purely *reflexive*, hence, an intellectual activity, and, as we saw above, for Eckhart, it is not that God understands because he exists, but rather that he exists because he understands. Hence, the *bullitio* is logically and ontologically prior to the existence of things in the divine *ebullitio*. As such, the divine *bullitio* is not only the inner life of the Godhead but also the principle of all existence and all intellectuality and so it is as intellect that the human soul returns to the Godhead and participates in its life. Second, the *bullitio* is prior to the *ebullitio* in that the life of God is utterly free, being constricted by no finite essence or existence and governed only by love. In God, emanation and return are part of the same movement, with the Godhead differentiating itself as Persons, and simultaneously reuniting itself in love. Hence, only those who have love in its purity, stripped of creaturely attachments and,

53. *Serm. XXV*, n.259; LW IV, 237/TP, 218.
54. *In Exod.*, n.16; LW II, 21–22/TP, 46.

therefore, purely intellectual, can participate in the divine *bullitio*. Pure intellectuality and pure love are not only compatible but also logically necessitate each other.

In Eckhart's thought, then, the divine *bullitio* is a formal emanation of the divine Word, *Logos,* or Intellect that remains completely within the Godhead. It is a purely formal emanation in that it receives no being or existence of its own; otherwise, it would have an efficient cause setting it "outside," so to speak, the divine essence. Yet, as a purely formal emanation, the divine Word remains totally within the Godhead, even as, at the same time, the Word is distinct from the Godhead. This is precisely why, for Eckhart, the divine Word, as the formal emanation of the divine *bullitio,* is the proper subject matter of metaphysics and why the Gospel, whose inner meaning is Christ, is the fulfillment of metaphysical science.

As we saw in chapter 2, Eckhart argues that metaphysics does not concern itself with efficient or final causes but with the formal causes only. The pre-eminent formal cause of all things is nothing other that the divine Word or *Logos,* which is manifest in Christ:

Note that an image properly speaking is a simple formal emanation that transmits the whole pure naked essence. The metaphysician considers it in abstraction from the efficient and final causes according to which natural scientists investigate things. The image then is an emanation from the depths in silence, excluding everything that comes from without. It is a form of life, as if you were to imagine something swelling up from itself and in itself and then inwardly boiling without any "boiling over" yet understood.[55]

In other words, the proper object of metaphysics is not created things but the *Logos* of creation, i.e., the Word of the Gospels, and insofar as the Christian hears the Gospel and appropriates its Word by detaching him or herself from all created things and becoming purely intellectual, he or she lives in and through this Word and participates in the inner *bullitio* of God. He or she becomes a metaphysician of the highest sort and in the fullest meaning of the word. This metaphysical knowledge, precisely because it has as its subject matter the Word of the Gospel, is no neutral, theoretical science, but one that necessarily implies the complete transformation, or *rebirth,* of the knower as the (adopted) son of God:

55. *Serm. XLIX,* n.511; LW IV, 425–26/TP, 236.

From what has been said it is clear first that the image properly speaking exists only in what is living, intellectual, and uncreated, inasmuch as we abstract from and do not consider efficient and final causality. Second, the image has the character of a birth, an offspring, and a son inasmuch as it comes forth in the same nature and is equal and similar in everything to what produced it. Hence the Son, the Image, is in the Father and the Father is in him; he is one in the Father (Jn 10:38, 30).[56]

For Eckhart, metaphysics, properly speaking, is the mystical science of the *image*, because only the image as image is that which emanates without efficient or final causality.

This science of the "image qua image," in fact, forms the basis of Eckhart's entire commentary on the Gospel of John, which he asserts, as we have seen, to contain also the innermost truth of metaphysics, the study of "being qua being" *(ens inquantum ens)*. If, as we saw in chapter 2, the metaphysian looks, properly speaking, to the *formal* cause of things and not to efficient or final causes, then the Gospel of John is a pre-eminently metaphysical work, treating as it does of the formal emanation of the Son as Image into the world. The opening to the Gospel of John, Eckhart explains, contains within itself the essence of all metaphysics: "In the beginning was the Word, and the Word was with God, and the Word was God." "Word" is also convertible with "Image." If one understands what the image is qua image, one understands also the import of the entire Gospel. As Eckhart explains: "An image insofar as it is an image receives nothing of its own from the subject in which it exists, but receives its whole existence from the object it images."[57] Or, as Eckhart puts it in one of Latin sermons, "An image, as image, is totally related to what it is an image of, and is ordered to it and to nothing else."[58] The entire being of the image is to reflect that of which it is the image. It has no other nature other than the nature it reflects, nor does it have an existence other than the reflecting of its exemplar. The image, as image, is utterly distinct from its exemplar, and, at the same time, it is utterly identical with it. Thus, the Word, Christ, is the perfect image of God, the Father, because Christ's entire being was to reflect or image the Father. Christ is, by nature, the *imagination* of the Father, in the sense that Christ images perfectly his source. But, as the per-

---

56. *Serm. XLIX*, n.512; LW IV, 427/TP, 237.     57. *In Ioh.*, n.23; LW III, 19/EE, 129.
58. *Serm. XXV*, n.266; LW IV, 242/TP, 220.

fect "imagination," Christ is no phantom or whimsy, but to the contrary, he shares most fully in the unlimited and living Being of the Godhead.

The nature of image that Christ has by nature, the human soul, insofar as it is intellect, can have by grace, insofar as it allows the Word of the Gospel to take root in the soul and that Word allows Christ to emanate into the soul from within. Thus, not only is the science of metaphysics the science of the imagination, as we have seen in Ibn 'Arabi, but metaphysics, properly speaking, does not come to fulfillment, to full awareness, without the presence of the full image of God, Christ, alive and working within the soul. This is how the soul becomes by adoption what Christ is by nature:

> We should not falsely suppose that it is by one son or image that Christ is the Son of God and by some other that the just and godlike man is a son of God, for he says, "We are being transformed into the same image." Furthermore, just as when many mirrors held up to a person's face and countenance are all informed by the same one face, so too each and every just person is completely and perfectly justified by the same justice. Otherwise they would not be just in a univocal sense, and no single just person would be truly just if justice were one thing in itself and another in the just person.[59]

The human soul is "imaged" into the image of God in and through the Image of God, who is Christ. That is, insofar as the soul shares in Christ's Image of the Father, the soul participates not analogically, but univocally in the life of the Trinity. Christ's perfect reflection of God the Father in both his human and divine natures makes possible the perfect reflection by the human soul of God's Trinitarian life.

But this is not all. In his birth through the intellectual self-reflection of God, the Son "breathes forth" love, or the Holy Spirit, who is also uncreated. Thus we have completed the Holy Trinity. As Eckhart here notes, though, two things must be kept in mind about the inner emanation of the Word in God. First, it is purely intellectual, and, indeed, it is the perfection and completion of all intellectual being. But second, it is also a *birth*: a Word or Intellect that *re-founds* one's very being and existence into a *new* life. Thus, the soul that has recovered its divine image within itself and is reborn in Christ repeats the pattern of the *bullitio* and *ebullitio*: insofar as the Word of Christ "boils up" within the Christian, he or she "boils over" in works of utterly detached and selfless love:

59. *In Ioh.*, n.119; LW III, 104/EE, 169.

For it is necessary for something first to "boil" itself totally and then finally to "boil over" so that it can be completely perfected in itself while overflowing [with fruitfulness] that is more than perfection. (See Avicenna, *Metaphysics* 8.6 at the beginning.) This is why nature first nourishes, then gives increase, perfects, and thus produces another being like itself.[60]

For Eckhart, the Word of revelation and the Word of the intellect are one and the same, which means the first principle of metaphysics is not only compatible with the Gospels but is, in a deep sense, revealed most fully and perfectly *in* the Gospels themselves. How then, do we become metaphysicians of the highest order? By listening with all of one's heart and mind to the Word of the Gospel, by listening to God's Word in an utter, interior silence, so that one *becomes* and not just has an image of God. In commenting upon the verse in the Book of Wisdom that contains the phrase "For when quiet silence kept all things . . . your Almighty Word leapt down from heaven," Eckhart notes:

For there is still a sixth principal reason why it is necessary that "quiet silence keep all things" so that God the Son may be born in us by coming into our mind. The Son is the Father's image, and the soul is [created] according to God's image. By its concept and property an image is a formal production in silence of the efficient cause and final cause which both properly look to the external creature and both signify "boiling over." But the image insofar as it is a formal emanation properly smacks of "boiling." This is what is says here, "When quiet silence kept all things"; and below, "Your Word," that is, you Son, the Word, O Lord, came.[61]

The Word of God emanates into the mind of the soul that has "kept silence," i.e., detached itself from the "noise" of created things, ideas, and their demands upon the intellect. The Word emanates into the soul qua intellect, and qua intellect the soul receives and understands God's revelation of himself in his Word. In detachment both metaphysics and revelation properly speaking find their fulfillment.

### The Metaphysics of Detachment

In light of this theory of the intellect, one can see how Eckhart's metaphysics of detachment is really an extension of the Thomistic principle

60. *Serm. XLIX*, n.512; LW IV, 428/TP, 237.

61. *In Sap.*, n.283; LW II, 615–16/TP, 172–73: "Adhuc autem sexto principaliter ad hoc, ut

that "whatever is known is known in the mode of the knower." When the soul knows material things, it knows them in an immaterial way through the cognitive form since the soul is immaterial in its operation. Normally there is not falsity or error, insofar as the intellect is instinctively aware of the distinction between what is known and the mode in which it is known.[62] This distinction, however, cannot be the case when it comes to knowledge of God, for any attempt by our intellect to grasp God is doomed to failure, precisely because we can know God only in the mode by which we know things, the finite and created human intellect. Thus our intellect automatically reduces God, who is uncreated, to created images and concepts, thus falsifying the very reality we, in our intellect, are trying to know.

Thomas concludes, therefore, that knowledge of God is impossible in this life, but Eckhart draws an entirely different conclusion. If the human intellect can normally receive God only in accordance with the mode in which it exists, then, through the praxis of detachment, it can come to subsist "without any mode" (ane wise) and thus receive God in accordance, not with the mode of the *receiver*, but with the mode of the *received*: "God does not work alike in every man's heart; he works as he finds willingness and receptivity." In other words, insofar as the soul is "without mode," it lets God conform the soul to himself in the mode that is proper to God (who is, of course, without any mode). Thus, Eckhart claims that the perfection of detachment lies precisely in its letting God conform the soul to himself rather than the other way around:

And yet I praise detachment above all love. First because the best thing about love is that it compels me to love God, yet detachment compels God to love me.

---

deus filius in nobis nascatur, in mentem veniens, oportet *quietum silentium continere omnia*. Filius enim imago est patris, et anima ad imaginem dei. Imago autem ex sui ratione et proprietate est formalis quaedam productio in silentio causae efficientis et finalis, quae proprie creaturam extra respiciunt et significant ebullitionem. Imago autem, utpote formalis emanatio, sapit proprie bullitionem. Hoc est ergo quod hic dicitur: *eum quietum silentium contineret omnia*, et infra: *sermo tuus, domine, id est verbum, filius, venit.*" This passage bears very close resemblance in its themes to Predigt 101, to appear in volume four of the *Deutsche Werke*, edited by Georg Steer. Pfeiffer published this key sermon as n. 1 in his edition.

62. See *S.Th.* I, 85, 1. According to Thomas, Plato was so bedazzled by his discovery of the formal cause of things, which was indeed an immense step forward in the history of human thought, that he forgot the crucial distinction mentioned above and which Thomas is at such great pains to correct and elaborate.

Now it is greater for me to compel God to come to me than to compel myself to come to God; and that is because God is able to conform himself far better and with more suppleness, and to unite himself with me than I could unite myself with God.[63]

Hence, the soul must be freed of any inner "mode" of created being through detachment—so that, as a clean wax tablet, it may be completely receptive to God's "writing":

And when the heart that has detachment attains to the highest place, that must be nothingness, for in this is the greatest receptivity. See an analogy of this in nature. If I want to write on a wax tablet, it does not matter how fine the words may be that are written on the tablet, they still hinder me from writing on it. If I really want to write something, I must erase and eliminate everything that is already there; and the tablet is never so good for me to write on as when there is nothing on it at all. In the same way, if God is to write on my heart up in the highest place, everything that can be called this or that must come out of my heart, and in that way my heart will have won detachment. And so God can work upon it in the highest place and according to his highest will. And this is why the heart in its detachment has no this or that as its object.[64]

The detached intellect is one that is pure receptivity; it is pure intellect *as such*, making the phrase "detached intellect" something of a pleonasm. In such pure receptivity, the soul is able to know God "without any mode" and share in God's pure act of understanding since understanding, in and of itself, is "without any mode" (i.e., unlimited by any act of finite existence). Most interestingly, however, Eckhart compares the soul to a wax tablet that can receive God's "writing" only to the degree that it is blank and free of all "words." The soul is the place where God "writes" his revealed Word, and it is the proper end of the soul to allow God to write himself as the divine Word or *Logos* in itself. For this reason, as mentioned at the beginning of the treatise, the detached soul is what makes possible the fulfillment of revelation as revelation. Indeed, the two go together: insofar as the soul is intellectual, to that degree it actually *becomes* the very writing of God's Word; and to the degree that God's Word "writes itself" in and on the soul, to that degree the soul rises to the level of pure intellect. Thus, Eckhart sees detachment as that "virtue" that unlocks the true

63. *Vom Abg.*, DW V, 402–03/EE, 286.
64. *Vom Abg.*, DW V, 425–26/EE, 292.

meaning of Scripture as well as of philosophy, because it is what allows God to write his revealed Word in the soul and raise it to the level of intellect that contemplates being in its purity.

Because the human intellect is pure potency to form, it also has a potency to be conformed to God. In his *De ente et essentia*, Thomas remarks that just as prime matter holds the lowest grade on the scale of material beings due to the fact that it is pure potency for substantial forms, so the human intellect holds the lowest grade among intellectual substances due to its greatest degree of potency toward all cognitive forms.[65] Since the intellect therefore is in need of material images in order to know, it does not have, as the angels do, the forms of things infused or "inborn" in it.

Far from being an irredeemable defect of the human intellect, however, the intellect's pure potency is for Eckhart precisely the essential condition for its knowledge of God. Being pure potency, and thus empty and free, it is, unlike other intellectual substances, able to be conformed completely to the divine understanding as its actuality and thus be the vehicle for the revelation of God's Word. Because of its pure potency, it is as unlimited and free *in potentiality* as the divine understanding is *in actuality*. Detachment, therefore, perfects the human being in his *intellectual potency* to receive God and become actualized in his knowledge of God, while God's Word perfects the human being as the *actuality* of his or her intellect.

Again, using the metaphor already encountered several times in Eckhart's works, in a famous passage from one of his sermons he says the detached man

is free and has left himself, and he must be free of everything that he is to receive. If my eye is to see color, it must be free of all color. If I see blue or white, the sight of my eye which sees the color, this very thing that does the seeing, is the same as what is seen by the eye. The eye in which I see God is the same eye in which God sees me. My eye and God's eye are one eye and one seeing, one knowing and one loving.[66]

The detached soul is so receptive to God—so much in potency to God's pure actuality—that all that subsists between God and the detached soul is one actuality in which God is the mover and the soul is the moved. That

65. *De ente et essentia*, ch. 4.
66. *Pr.* 12; DW I, 200–01/TP, 269–70.

is, as Aristotle puts it in his physics when describing his theory of motion, there is between God and the soul, just as between the mover and the moved, μία ἡ ἀμφοῖν ἐνέργεια, or "one activity for both."[67] Indeed, such is the unity between God and the soul that, as the passage above indicates, *what* is known and that *by which* it is known become identical. Thus, while God and the soul remain distinct, they subsist in one actuality, the soul by participation, God by his essence.

Eckhart remarks, therefore, that detachment "has no object." It does not relate to things via cognitive forms but rather it makes the soul into a cognitive form itself, in which "what is known" is also that "by which it knows." The soul emptied of all attachment to created being derives all of its being not from its subject or substratum but from that of which it is the image—God—and all of its knowledge from the very Word of God, which is revealed to it in Christ and the Gospels. Eckhart emphasizes this principle in his sermon *In hoc apparuit charitas dei in nobis*:

Where the creature stops, there God begins to be. Now God wants no more from you than that you should in creaturely fashion go out of yourself, and let God be God in you. The smallest creaturely image that ever forms in you is as great as God is great. Why? Because it comes between you and the whole of God. As soon as the image comes in, God and all his divinity have to give way. But as the image goes out, God goes in.[68]

And again in his sermon *Videte qualem caritatem* he says:

Everything must be driven out that is [merely] likeness, so that I can be placed above into God and become one with him, one substance, one being, one nature, and the Son of God. And after this has happened, nothing in God is hidden that does not become revealed or that does not become mine.[69]

## Intellect as Mirror and Image in Ibn ʿArabi and Meister Eckhart

For both Ibn ʿArabi and Meister Eckhart, the relationship between revelation and intellectuality is an essential one. Intellectuality or knowl-

---

67. See *Physica* Γ 202a 18, and Bernard Welte's article "Meister Eckhart als Aristoteliker," 64–74.

68. *Pr.* 5b; DW I, 92–93/EE, 184.

69. *Pr.* 76; DW III, 322/TP, 329.

edge of the heart is, in fact, an interior revelation, a recovery by reason of the inner meaning of revelation, a recovery, however, that raises reason to the level of intellect, which is to say, a unitative knowledge of God. Revelation as the revealed text for both men, in turn, is the objectified deposit of inner intellectuality, ready to be interiorized and actualized by the soul made receptive by spiritual practice. This inner actualization of revelation leads to a higher intellection, one that reveals the true meaning, not just of revelation, but of all creatures as the manifestation of the divine knowledge, power, and love.

Of course, the vehicle each man uses, the revealed text, affects the way in which that inner truth is actualized and interiorized. For Ibn 'Arabi, the Qur'an proclaims the utter unity of God and itself as the direct speech of God. The entire universe is a theophany or manifestation of the divine Essence, and the Qur'an is the hermeneutic key to that theophany. So how does the believer respond to the Qur'an in both its content and its form? He or she does so by submitting him or herself entirely, in both reason and will, to its message. Hence, the religion of the Qur'an is called *Islam*, "submission." For Ibn 'Arabi, though, this word has a deeper sense: the will and reason of the perfected believer is so submissive to the divine will and message through *fana'* or self-annihilation, that what he or she wills and thinks "fluctuates," "beats," or "abides" (*yabqa*) in and with the divine manifestations.

Hence, as I have indicated, the highest point of intellectuality for Ibn 'Arabi is that of the "heart" (*al-qalb*), which "fluctuates" (*yaqlub*) with the divine manifestations. The divine manifestations to which the heart of the realized knower conforms himself constitute, of course, all creation. But for Ibn 'Arabi, the Qur'an has a special, indeed crucial, role to play in this conformity, because it is by internalizing the sense of the Qur'an that the heart of the realized knower can "beat" to the rhythm of divine theophanies and understand them as divine theophanies. Through his internalization of the very music of the Qur'an, the realized knower becomes like a vibrating string in harmony with the divine symphony of creation. Any amount of rational reflection or calculation will not produce this harmony; only the interior realization of the inner meaning of the Qur'an and seeing that meaning at work in all of creation can produce it.

Hence, Ibn 'Arabi emphasizes the inability of human reason to grasp and realize in itself the inner unity of being. The Muslim can find the truth only in prophethood and sainthood, where prophethood makes possible sainthood, but where sainthood is the fruition and fulfillment of prophethood. Without the laws of the prophets, human reason remains locked into a mere assertion of God's transcendent Unity or *tanzīh* and does not "see" the manifestations of God's life and being in creation. With the prophetic laws, however, reason finds the lived inner meaning of its own categories and concepts. This "finding" or "existentiation" of the inner meaning of the categories of reason is the same as the finding of the inner meaning of the prophetic law and thus the inner meaning of all creatures. In other words, intellectuality is the same as sainthood in Ibn ʿArabi's point of view.

Sainthood is the annihilation of the self in order to abide in the pure revealed Law of God, which is God's pure self-manifestation: "the negation of the negation means pure affirmation: the removal of illusion results in the self-revelation of the Real."[70] The removal or negation of finite being— itself a negation of the infinite Being of the Real—means the fullness of divine revelation and the fullness of pure intellection. In short, the Sufi saint is a man or woman who is able to see, by means of the Qur'an, the spiritual meaning within creatures that, nevertheless, transcends them. The "heart" of the Sufi is one that is attuned to this imaginal world, takes it in and lives in it, but, by doing so, transcends all images to arrive at the "station of no station," where his knowledge is no longer limited by any fixed essence but where he is an empty vessel in which the Real or Truth (*al-ḥaqq*) becomes manifest.

In contrast to Ibn ʿArabi, Eckhart's Christocentric reading of the Bible informs his entire mystical epistemology. Logically speaking, prior to birth, there must be the emptiness of the "womb" or intellective soul. Hence, as has been pointed out by McGinn, the mystical theology of Eckhart is a mystical theology of the *ground* of the soul, that inner depth that is beyond any genus or species, category or entity in and through which the soul is united to God. Following the Christian revelation, Eckhart conceives this relationship as a dialectic of emptiness and birth, of silence and the speaking forth of the Word: by entering into the Word of the Gospel, the soul

70. Reza Shah-Kazemi, *Paths to Transcendence according to Shankara, Ibn ʿArabi, and Meister Eckhart* (Bloomington, Ind.: World Wisdom Books, 2006), 99.

that is detached from all created things enters into and participates in the formal emanation of the Son in the Holy Trinity, in the divine *bullitio* in which there is no distinction other than the going out and the returning in of love. The detached soul no longer stands "outside" the divine life as part of the divine *ebullitio* or creation. That is, the detached soul no longer stands within the realm of analogically differentiated being, but rather stands in univocal unity with the Godhead.

The detached soul that has as its existential foundation the living Word of God does not look upon God as a "first cause" of existence, as the prime mover of medieval physics. Rather it receives God formally into its ground as Word, a formal emanation that is an intelligible speaking out, and this formal emanation, for Eckhart, is the highest subject matter of metaphysics. Thus, Eckhart says that it is the Gospels that treat being qua being, because only in the Gospels do human beings encounter God *formally*, only in listening to and giving ourselves over wholly, body and soul, will and intellect, to the divine Word do human beings become *conformed* to God. Then and only then, the soul surpasses reason by moving from discursive thought to a conformity that is the essence of intellectuality. The analogical understanding of reason moves to a univocal relationship of the human intellect to God, for the intellect, as intellect, becomes the object known and subsists in the cause of its knowledge. As creatures, human beings are related analogically to the pure being of God; but as intellectual, human beings come to share univocally in the life of the divine unity. This relationship comes to fulfillment by means of the metaphysics of the image: *to be* and not just to have an image of God is to derive all of one's being from God, the exemplar, apart from any efficient or final causality. Such a relation can only happen in the innermost ground of the soul, where Christ "boils up" in a formal emanation that allows the soul, by grace, to share in the divine life, a life that Christ already shares in by his very nature. Such a sharing in the divine life is the completion and perfection of metaphysics, because it knows and lives out of God as the formal cause and the formal cause only of the soul's life, knowledge, and blessedness. But such a sharing in the divine life is the completion and perfection of revelation too, because in this formal emanation, Christ, who is the inner essence and marrow of Scripture, comes to be the World in and through whom the soul lives, understands, and has its being.

Despite the different traditions and revealed texts, however, the two approaches represented by Ibn ʿArabi and Meister Eckhart amount practically to the emptying of the soul of all created images and attachments so that it might rise to the level of intellect, where it is united to God as image to its exemplar. The realized saint or gnostic of Ibn ʿArabi must be empty of all created form in order for his or her heart to "fluctuate" with the ever-changing and ever-flowing divine theophanies in creation. The intellect of the Christian that has given birth to the Son in his or her soul is one that is conformed to the divine Image in and through whom all things were created, and is conformed to God's manifestations in all of creation, united to God and to creation. Thus, both Ibn ʿArabi and Eckhart see the process of intellection as inseparable from the internalizing hermeneutics of their respective revealed texts, describing the same process of mystical realization, realized in unique, irreducible, but nevertheless analogous ways.

PART IV

# ✤ The Noble or Universal Man

The ideals of the Universal or Perfect Man in Ibn ʿArabi and of the Nobleman in Eckhart represent the culmination of the "mystical" thought of both men. In each, these terms signify a believer who has realized the divinity in such a way that God is no longer the object of his or her knowledge, but rather the ground of his or her knowing, loving, and working. For such men, the divine *Logos* becomes the inner logos of their being, hearing and living the divine Word not as commands from without but as organizing principle *(logos)* of their inner life and being. As Eckhart puts it, the Nobleman is an "ad-verb" to the divine Word *(Verbum)*, in the sense of completely, in his or her entire being, oriented to *(ad)* the divine Word and only modifying and inflecting it in his or her creaturely mode.

Why do Ibn ʿArabi and Eckhart call this realized knower of God a "universal" or "noble" man? Of course, each theologian can only use the language available to him from his respective tradition, and these terms are no exception, with a long history in Muslim and Christian mystical literature.[1] The basic concept behind

1. For Eckhart's notion of the nobleman, see: Marie Anne Vannier, "Der edle Mensch, eine Figur in Eckharts Straßburger Werk," *Freiburger Zeitschrift für Philosophie und Theologie* 44 (1997): 318. For the notion of the perfect or universal man in Ibn ʿArabi, see: Annemarie Schimmel, *Mystical Dimensions of Islam* (Chapel Hill: University of North Carolina Press, 1975), especially chap. 4. The Arabic term for Universal Man *(al-insān al-kāmil)* is sometimes also translated "Perfect Man." I have, however, chosen to translate the term as "Universal Man" for reasons which will become clear

both is that the realization of unity with the divine is a restoration of our primal humanity or, in Sufi terminology, our "Adamic nature." This nature is, as both mystical thinkers point out, unique in creation: human nature lies on the border between material and spiritual reality, and, as such, encompasses the full range of created possibilities. Indeed, as Ibn 'Arabi remarks, the distinction of human nature is that it has no distinction, that it has no fixed essence or nature but is "universal." Eckhart echoes this notion in his description of the human intellect as being essentially "empty" and "free," in the language of the Neoplatonists a *microcosm*, reflective of the entire created universe and thus an adequate vehicle in whom God may come to be realized in creation.

In this way, the Universal or Noble man corresponds to the divine *Logos, ratio,* or *kalima* in and through which God creates all things. Such a person is, in a sense, an "incarnation" of the primal Word in and through which God first revealed himself to his creation. Of course, for Eckhart, only Christ is the incarnate Word of God, but the nobleman gives birth to Christ within himself, sharing by grace in the Incarnation of Christ, who is fully human and fully divine, not by grace, but by nature. In Ibn 'Arabi, the perfect man is the living embodiment of the message of the Qur'an, a vessel for and of the "Mohammedan Word," the *kalima muhammadiyya*, seeing all creatures as theophanies of the uncreated Word of the Qur'an.

As Meister Eckhart puts it, the realized believer is a "nobleman" because he is no longer a "serf" but a "friend" of God. So it is for Ibn 'Arabi: such a person is no longer a slave or *'abd*, but a *wali* or "friend" of God. Thus, neither the Nobleman nor the Universal Man is a "slave" to God "over and above," but rather a friend who lives "in and with" God. They live not merely for the "God of belief," as Ibn 'Arabi puts it, i.e., the exclusively transcendent God of traditional religion, but also and primarily *in and from* the *deus absconditus*, the "hidden God," who is the ground of all being. As such the Universal Man or Nobleman, as a self-emptying reflection of the divine, recapitulates all aspects of the real, whether material or spiritual. It is therefore no wonder that both Ibn 'Arabi and Meister Eckhart also speak of the Universal Man or Nobleman using both male

---

in the text. Suffice it to say that "universality" captures more of what Ibn 'Arabi means by *al-insān al-kāmil* than does "perfection," although, to be sure, the Universal Man in Ibn 'Arabi is also humanity in its perfection. Perhaps the best translation for *kāmil* is "comprehensive."

and female imagery: the Universal Man or Nobleman integrates and reconciles within himself all opposites, most notably the active and the passive, represented by the male and the female respectively. This is precisely why the Universal Man is "universal," being in some respects both male and female. In this way, the Universal Man or Nobleman integrates and transcends all created difference in an inner union with God.

7

# The Universal Man in Ibn ʿArabi

As Ibn ʿArabi asserts in his *Futuhat,* all knowledge of God, the Reality *(al-ḥaqq),* is rooted in knowledge of the self:

The root of existence of knowledge of God is knowledge of self. So knowledge of God has the property of knowledge of self, which is the root. In the view of those who know the self, the self is an ocean without a shore, so knowledge of it has no end. Such is the property of knowledge of the self. Hence, knowledge of God, which is a branch of this root, joins with it in property, so there is no end to knowledge of God. That is why in every state the knower says, "My Lord, increase me in knowledge!" (20:114). Then God increases him in knowledge of himself that he may increase in knowledge of his Lord. This is given by divine unveiling.[1]

To enter into the essence of the human self is, for Ibn ʿArabi, tantamount to entering into the essence of the divine, because human existence is essentially linked to the divine existence. But for Ibn ʿArabi, and subsequently for Sufis like Abdel-Karim al-Jili, strongly influenced by Ibn ʿArabi, there must be a mediating link between the individual human being and the divine Essence in its utter transcendence. This mediating link is the Universal Man: the transcendent principle or *logos* of creation that is, importantly, also the immanent essence of human existence. As Titus Burckhardt puts it: "Universal Man is not really distinct from God; he is

---

1. III 121.25 in SPK, 345.

like the face of God in his creatures. By union with him, the spirit unites with God."[2] As such, the Universal Man serves as the locus in and through which the individual human being, who, at least in principle, participates in the Universal Man by virtue of the comprehensive nature of his essence, may come to know God. He corresponds in many ways to the Universal or First Intellect or νοῦς of the Neoplatonists, the hypostasis that mediates between the unknowable, impenetrable divine Unity and creatures in general. As S. H. Nasr puts it:

> The Universal Man, who is also the Logos, is the total theophany of the Divine Names; he is the whole of the Universe in its oneness as "seen" by the Divine Essence. He is the prototype of the Universe as well as of man by virtue of which man, the microcosm, contains within himself all the possibilities found in the Universe. The microcosm and the macrocosm face each other as two mirrors in each of which the other is reflected, while both "echo" in themselves their common prototype, who is the Universal Man. The Universal Man is also essentially the Spirit, or First Intellect, which "contains" all the Platonic "ideas" within itself, like the Logos in the doctrines of Philo who is "the first born of God" and in whom all the "ideas" are assembled.[3]

Thus, the Universal Man is the mediating link or *isthmus* (or *barzakh*) between the divine Reality and the human knower.[4] He serves as the divine archetype for creation as well as the vehicle in and through which human beings return to God by realizing the full potentialities of their own humanity.

As such, the "words" of the realities of the various prophets in the *Bezels* represent various facets of the Universal Man or *Logos*, manifesting the qualities and attributes of the divine Unity, while at the same time calling human beings back to that Unity. But the realities of two prophets stand

2. 'Abd al-Karim al-Jili, *The Universal Man*, ed. and trans. Titus Burckhardt (Roxborough: Beshara Publications, 1995), viii.

3. Nasr, *Three Muslim Sages*, 110. For this Neoplatonic aspect of Ibn 'Arabi's thought, in which the Universal Man corresponds to the First Intellect of philosophers like Plotinus and Proclus, see Izutsu, *Sufism and Taoism*, 237 ("Thus the Prophet Muhammad on the cosmic level corresponds almost exactly to the Plotinian First Intellect"). By contrast, Affifi argues that, while there are many Neoplatonic elements in Ibn 'Arabi's thought, it is, strictly speaking, not Neoplatonic because of Ibn 'Arabi's doctrine of the *wāḥdat al-wujūd*, in which the Divine Essence gives existence to all creatures *directly* and without the intermediate emanations of divine intelligences. See his *Remarks*, 9.

4. See Salman H. Bashier, *Ibn 'Arabi's Barzakh: The Concept of the Limit and the Relationship between God and the World* (Albany: State University of New York Press, 2004), 122.

out in an eminent way: those of Adam, the first prophet, and Muhammad, the last prophet; not surprisingly, the first and last chapters of the *Bezels* are meditations upon the "words" of Adam and of Muhammad. Both are prototypes of the Universal Man, but in different ways: Adam represents the *Logos* under the aspect of creation or "going out," while Muhammad represents the *Logos* under the aspect of "de-creation" or return. Adam represents the First Intellect as infinite possibility: the word of Adam is the archetype of creation insofar as his "word" contains within itself *virtually* or *principially* all the divine attributes and *a fortiori* all those attributes manifested in the infinite variety of creatures.[5] Adam represents how the human being, as the intellectual mirror of the divine Essence, contains within him or herself a "pre-understanding" or implicit knowledge of God and his creation simply by virtue of the nature of his very essence.

But it is only through the "word" or principle of the prophethood of Muhammad that this virtual or pre-understanding is brought to unitative consciousness or gnosis. As Izutsu explains:

The Reality of Muhammad is not exactly the permanent archetypes themselves. Rather, it is the unifying principle of all archetypes, the active principle on which depends the very existence of the archetypes. Considered from the side of the Absolute, the Reality of Muhammad is the creative activity itself of the Absolute, or God "conceived as the self-revealing Principle of the universe." It is the Absolute in the first stage of its eternal self-manifestation, i.e., the Absolute as the universal Consciousness.[6]

Thus the word or reality of Muhammad actualizes what is potential in Adam. In this way, as we shall see, the reality of Muhammad has an ontological—though not a chronological—priority to the reality of Adam. While true Adamic man is the man of faith or *imān* who reflects virtually in his essence the divine Reality *(al-ḥaqq)*, the man who manifests the word or reality of Muhammad is the man of realized knowledge who unites in himself in one-pointed awareness consciousness of God's utter unity in multiplicity and thus actualizes and realizes what in faith is only implicit.

5. "On the one hand man only exists in relation to the macrocosm which determines him, and on the other hand man knows the macrocosm, and this means that all the possibilities which are unfolded in the world are principially contained in man's intellectual essence." Burckhardt, *Introduction to Sufism*, 75.

6. Izutsu, *Sufism and Taoism*, 236.

## The "Word of Adam" and Primordial Humanity

According to Ibn 'Arabi, contained in the "word of Adam" is the "wisdom of divinity." Humanity as such, therefore, reflects in itself the essence of divinity because God created humanity according to his image. Thus, the human being is a sort of "qualitative 'abridgement' of the great cosmic 'book,' all universal qualities being in one way or another expressed in his form."[7] Human beings, as "sons of Adam," pre-contain essentially within themselves all the names and forms that may give expression to the divine Essence in creation.[8] As such, the word of Adam is also the Universal Logos in and through which not only human beings come to knowledge of God, but God comes to an understanding of himself. Indeed, Ibn 'Arabi claims, God *could not* know himself without his reflection in the word of Adam:

The Reality wanted to see the essences of His Most Beautiful Names or, to put it another way, to see His own Essence, in an all-inclusive object encompassing the whole [divine] Command, which, qualified by existence, would reveal to Him His own mystery. For the seeing of a thing, itself by itself, is not the same as its seeing itself in another, as it were in a mirror; for it appears to itself in a form that is invested by the location of the vision by that which would only appear to it given the existence of the location and its [the location's] self-disclosure to it.[9]

In other words, for God to come to know himself in a reflexive act of self-consciousness, he needs an "other" in and through whom the divine intellect could come to self-reflection. This "other" is Adam (and by extension all human beings), but at the same time, Adam is not an "other," insofar as he merely reflects the divine Essence and does not have any essential properties of his own. The "otherness" of Adam is thus annulled in his very reflection of the divine Essence.

---

7. "It may also be said that the universe and man are forms of the Universal Spirit (*ar-Ruh*) or of the Divine Spirit, or that the two are complementary aspects of one single 'pancosmic' being, a symbol of God. However, the 'outward' or 'objective' form of the macrocosm cannot be grasped in its totality because its limits extend indefinitely, whereas the form of man is known. This leads us to say that man is a qualitative 'abridgement' of the great cosmic 'book,' all universal qualities being in one way or another expressed in his form. Again, the Prophet said that 'God created Adam in His (own) form,' which means that the primordial nature of man is as it were the symbolical final term and in a sense the visible 'sum' of all the divine essences immanent in the world." Burckhardt, *Introduction to Sufism*, 76.

8. See Hirtenstein, *The Unlimited Mercifier*, 67.

9. *Bezels*, 50/48–49.

In the end, therefore, there are never two "things"—God and Adam: there is only the self-disclosure of God refracted back upon himself in various modes according to the preparedness of creatures to receive and refract it. Moreover, it is in the reality or word of Adam that the entire divine Essence is reflected, which is to say, Being as such.[10] The human being, insofar as he or she is the Universal Man, is only the "place" in which God comes to self-awareness.

God's conscious disclosure of himself *to* himself comes to fruition in creation through humanity. Ibn 'Arabi compares creation to an unpolished mirror unable to reflect the divine Essence until the creation of Adam, in whom this mirror was polished, allowing God to contemplate his own image:

> The Reality gave existence to the whole Cosmos [at first] as an undifferentiated thing without anything of the spirit in it, so that it was like an unpolished mirror. It is in the nature of the divine determination that He does not set out a location except to receive a divine spirit, which is also called [in the Qur'an] *the breathing into him.* The latter is nothing other than the coming into operation of the undifferentiated form's [innate] disposition to receive the inexhaustible overflowing of Self-revelation, which has always been and will ever be. There is only that which is receptive and the receptive has been only from the most Holy Superabundance [of the Reality], for all power to act [all initiative] is from Him, in the beginning and at the end. All command derives from Him, even as it begins with Him.[11]

Without Adam, creation is an "unpolished mirror," Ibn 'Arabi here using the image of a medieval metal mirror, which needed constant polishing to retain its reflective quality. As al-Qaysari notes, truth is reflected according to the quality of the mirror, thus there can be no absolute reflection of God in any creature qua creature.[12] Being, i.e., *wujūd* or "finding," attains its goal or *telos* of self-reflection only in a being that can reflect the divine Essence as such and in which the divine Essence can "find" itself; this creature is an intellectual creature, i.e., Adam, and, as the inner *telos* of creation, he is also, in a sense, the cause of creation.

---

10. "The divine self-disclosure is one, but those who 'receive' (*qabūl*) it, or act as its 'receptacles' (*qābil*), are many. Each receptacle perceives the self-disclosure according to its own preparedness. To say that a receptacle 'perceives' the self-disclosure means that it 'finds' it through its own existence. 'Perception' and 'existence' are one. Subjectivity and objectivity are two faces of the same reality." SPK, 338.

11. *Bezels*, 50/49.       12. *Sharḥ*, I 160.

Ibn 'Arabi states this principle quite directly when he says:

Thus the [divine] Command required [by its very nature] the reflective characteristic of the mirror of the Cosmos, and Adam was the very principle of reflection for that mirror and the spirit of that form, while the angels were only
certain faculties of that form which was the form of the Cosmos, called in the
terminology of the Folk, the Great Man (al-insān al-kabīr). In relation to it the
angels are as the psychic and physical faculties in the human formation. Each
of these [cosmic] faculties or powers is veiled [from knowing the whole] by its
own self [being limited by its relative individuality], so that it cannot know anything that excels it.[13]

Important to note here is that the perfection of Adam with respect to all
other creatures, including the angels, lies not just in his intellectual nature
(for the angels are self-subsistent intellects) but also in his lack of any de-
terminative being. As both spiritual and material beings, human beings
are open to every nature and able to reflect in their being and intellect the
full range of created being.

This insight touches upon a very important existential truth. According to Ibn 'Arabi, in Adam and all the "sons of Adam," existence precedes
essence: as the microcosm or epitome of creation, the essence of humanity
is precisely to be open to existence as such. In this way, the human being
stands not over and against being, thus making it an object for its own
transcendent subjectivity, but rather he or she stands *in* being. Izutsu puts
this point quite clearly:

This fact that the universe was an "unpolished mirror" required the creation of
Man who was meant to be the very polishing of the mirror.
    This is a very important statement for determining the cosmic significance
of Man. We might interpret it in terms of modern philosophic thinking and say
that what is symbolized by the "polishing"—or rather "the state of having been
polished" (*jala'*)—of the mirror is the "consciousness" of Man. All beings other
than Man only reflect, each one of them, singly, one aspect of the Absolute. It
is only when put together in the form of the universe that they constitute a big
whole corresponding to the Consciousness itself of the Absolute. In this sense,
the universe, certainly, is "one," but, since the universe lacks consciousness, it
does not constitute real unity. Man, on the contrary, not only synthesizes all
the forms of the Divine self-manifestation which are scattered over the world
of Being, but also is conscious of this whole. This is why a true comprehensive

13. *Bezels*, 51/49.

unity is established by Man, corresponding to the Unity of the Absolute. Man is in this sense the *Imago Dei*. And because of this peculiarity, Man can be, as we shall see presently, the "vicegerent" of God on the earth.[14]

Unlike the angels, human beings gather into themselves all levels of reality, the spiritual and material, the inner and the outer, the manifest and the nonmanifest.[15] "Man gathers together in himself all the things of the universe in the sense that he is a synthesis of the non-material realities of the individual things. The Universal Man is an epitome of the Macrocosm only in this particular sense."[16]

The universality of Adam is such that it cannot become an object of thought since this universality is precisely the basis and precondition for all thought. As Ibn 'Arabi explains:

This [knowledge] cannot be arrived at by the intellect by means of any rational thought process, for this kind of perception comes only by a divine disclosure from which is ascertained the origin of the forms of the Cosmos receiving the spirits. The [above-mentioned] formation is called Man and Viceregent [of God]. As for the first term, it stems from the universality of his formation and the fact that he embraces all the realities. For the Reality, he is as the pupil is for the eye through which the act of seeing takes place. Thus he is called *insān* [meaning both man and pupil], for it is by him that the Reality looks on His creation and bestows Mercy [of existence] on them. He is Man, the transient [in his form], the eternal [in his essence]; he is the perpetual, the everlasting, the [at once] discriminating and unifying Word. It is by his existence that the Cosmos subsists and he is, in relation to the Cosmos, as the seal is to the ring, the seal being that place whereon is engraved the token with which the King seals his treasure.[17]

The word of Adam, or the Universal Man as the *Logos* of creation, serves as the "pupil" of the eye through which God looks upon creation and upon himself.[18] But the Universal Man is also the reality in and through which God bestows Mercy, i.e., existence, upon creatures, because it is in and through Adam that creatures are "found," which is to say both "exist" and are "known" (*mawjūd* being the same term for both).

14. Izutsu, *Sufism and Taoism*, 222.

15. Thus the Universal Man is the *barzakh* or limit between the inner and the outer, the nonmanifest and the manifest. See *Sharḥ*, I 178–79.

16. Izutsu, *Sufism and Taoism*, 226.      17. *Bezels*, 51/49–50.

18. "We can fairly say that for Ibn 'Arabi the human self is to be properly viewed as essentially and unequivocally a point of vision (or a locus of awareness) which acts as a mirror in the unitive Divine act of Self-Expression." Coates, *Ibn 'Arabi and Modern Thought*, 124.

Again, the Universal Man is the *Logos* or *Ratio* of creation, "transient in form" but "eternal in essence," the "word" in and through whom creatures come to be "found," i.e., "to exist" by being known and named. As the Arabic language implies, to be is the same as to be found or known; to be "lost" or not found in consciousness is not to exist at all. So all existent things are already known—"found" in the divine intellect to be sure—but it is the Universal Man in the word of Adam that mediates that knowledge or "finding" into created existence. In developing the master metaphor of the *Bezels,* Ibn 'Arabi characterizes the word of Adam as the divine "seal" on the "ring" of creation, the "token by which the king seals his treasure." The human being "exists" only to the extent that he or she "finds" his or her own being or essence in the Universal Man, expressed and actualized most fully through the word of Muhammad in the Qur'an. Thus, the human being, paradoxically, does not fully exist as human insofar as he stands "outside" of God like other creatures, but only insofar as he stands "inside" God as his reflection and as only his reflection.

As was mentioned above, the angels do not enjoy this universality of the human essence, even though in certain respects, as spiritual beings, they are ontologically and intellectually higher than human beings. They cannot serve as "seals" of creation precisely because they lack the comprehensive nature of humanity. As Ibn 'Arabi notes:

The angels do not enjoy the comprehensiveness of Adam and comprehend only those Divine Names peculiar to them, by which they glorify and sanctify the Reality, nor are they aware that God has Names of which they know nothing and by which they cannot glorify Him, nor are they able to sanctify Him with the [complete] sanctification of Adam.[19]

And, Ibn 'Arabi continues, "Adam enshrines divine Names the angels have no part in" (52). Al-Qaysari remarks that Adam receives all degrees of being without himself being a degree, which is why Adam represents (or *is*) the Universal Spirit.[20] Only Adam worships God with all his Names.[21]

19. *Bezels,* 52/50–51.
20. *Sharḥ,* I 156. For al-Qaysari, what the angels do represent are the ruling spirits of the world in the same way that the faculties of the rational soul are ruling spirits of the body. Thus we have here a correspondence between macrocosm and microcosm. Nevertheless, the human being represents the unifying "soul" of the world and, as such, is higher than the angels. See *Sharḥ,* I 167.
21. *Sharḥ,* I 183.

For Ibn ʿArabi, therefore, the realized individual (*fard*) or gnostic (*ʿārif*) has "two eyes": with one eye he sees the divine Light that makes possible all manifestation just as the universal makes possible the existence and knowability of every particular. With the other eye, however, he sees the darkness of the particular, including the darkness of his own particularity and thus the extent (or lack) of his own preparedness to know the divine Light.[22] The human being is, qua Universal Man, neither light nor darkness, but the limit or *barzakh* between the two: he is light insofar as he is a mirror of the divine Light but is darkness insofar as he is not the light itself.[23] As Ibn ʿArabi says in the *Futūḥāt*: "The Real is sheer Light; while the impossible is sheer darkness. Darkness never turns into light nor does light turn into darkness. Creation is the *barzakh* (isthmus) between Light and darkness. . . . In himself, man is neither light nor darkness, since he is neither existent nor non-existent."[24] There can be no commensurability between God and non-being: creation, therefore, is like the "limit" between the divine Light and the darkness of nonexistence. What is peculiar about the human being, however, is that he or she can *choose* to face the light or face the darkness. He or she can choose to "exist"—be "found" in and by God and by him or herself—or just "be," as a creaturely thing among other things.

Despite the general Platonic tenor of Ibn ʿArabi's thought, however, the Shaykh differs from Plato in one important point: the universals do not exist in and through themselves but only insofar as they relate the divine Essence in its various imitable aspects to particular creatures.[25] This

22. "The Real is sheer Light, while the impossible (*al-muḥāl*) is sheer darkness (*ẓulma*). Darkness never turns into light, nor does light turn into darkness. Creation is the Barzakh between Light and darkness. In its essence it is qualified neither by darkness nor by light, since it is the Barzakh and the Middle (*al-wasaṭ*) which has a property from each of its two sides. That is why He appointed for man two eyes and guided him on the two highways, since he exists between the two paths. Through one eye and one path he accepts light and looks upon it in the measure of his preparedness. Through the other eye and the other path he looks upon darkness and turns toward it." III 274.28 in SPK, 362.

23. "In himself, man is neither light nor darkness, since he is neither existent nor nonexistent. He is the firm impediment which prevents sheer darkness from taking away sheer light. He receives the two sides through his own essence, and he acquires, through this reception, that light whereby he is described as 'existent' and that darkness whereby he is described as 'nonexistent.' So he shares in both sides and protects both sides." III 274.28 in SPK, 362.

24. SPK, 362.

25. *Bezels*, 53–54/52–53.

is also true, maybe even especially true, of the reality of Adam. To be sure, the reality of Adam reflects the divine Essence in its totality, but it cannot imitate or reflect the divine Essence with respect to one thing and one thing only: its self-subsistent Existence.[26] God has existence from himself while Adam has no existence in himself, but derives all existence and actuality that he has from God:

It is established that the originated is [completely] dependent on that which brings it about, for its possibility. Its existence is [entirely] derived from something other than itself, the connection in this case being one of dependence. It is therefore necessary that that which is the support [of originated existence] should be essentially and necessarily by itself, self-sufficient and independent of any other. This it is that bestows existence from its own essential Being on dependent existence, in this way becoming related to it.[27]

God exists by necessity; Adam does not exist by necessity but exists only contingently upon God's creative activity—his existentiating command, "Be!" Thus Adam exists only in and through God.[28] Ibn 'Arabi continues:

Furthermore, since the former, because of its essence, requires the latter [the dependent], the latter has [in a certain sense] necessary being. Also, since its dependence on that from which it was manifested is [implicit in] its own essence, it follows that the originated should conform to all the Names and attributes of the cause [origin], except that of Self-sufficient Being, which does not belong to originated existence, since what necessary being it has derives [entirely] from other than itself.[29]

God is he who is "rich in himself" (ghanī bi-nafsihi)[30] while the creature is utterly "poor" (faqīr) of existence: without the giving of existence by God, the creature would simply vanish—be nothing.[31] Here, the word of Adam

26. Thus, as al-Qaysari notes, God is not the same as the *esse commune* (*mawjūd jāmi'*) of the world: i.e., God is not merely pure, abstract existence but rather the fullness and self-subsistence of existence that unites within his essence all potential existences. It follows that Adam alone reflects God, not the *esse commune* of things because only Adam has this virtual, unifying essence that is itself not a determinate essence as well. *Sharḥ*, I 158–59.

27. *Bezels*, 54/53.                                 28. Izutsu, *Sufism and Taoism*, 239.

29. *Bezels*, 54/53.

30. God and Man are mirrors of one another. The only difference between them is that to God belongs absolute "wealth" and to Man (as well as to all other creatures) absolute "poverty" of Being. See *Sharḥ*, I 198.

31. The created world has no existence whatsoever in itself: it is absolutely "poor" (*iftiqar*) with regard to God. That is why we must make a distinction between "God" and the "Godhead" (*ilihut*), insofar as the former is "in need" of creation in order to exist while the latter is not.

is no exception; unlike every other creature, it reflects every aspect of the divinity; but like every other creature it receives all of its existence from the Reality.

In a sense, then, Adam is also the *least* of all creatures: he not only has no inherent existence but also has no "known station" within creation, no fixed essence on the scale or hierarchy of created beings or essences. Only he can, through forgetfulness of God, no longer reflect, according to his primordial essence, the divine Essence and utterly erase the trace of the divine within himself.[32] Like a mirror, the word of Adam is utterly "poor" (*faqīr*) or lacking in any nature of its own.[33] But this also is, paradoxically, the very source of his nobility. The Universal Man *is* also the Real in his poverty, insofar as he (potentially, at least) reflects and sees nothing but the Reality (*al-ḥaqq*) in all things and in himself; he is, therefore, also utterly independent of creatures insofar as he sees not created entities but only the names and attributes of God and is thus independent and free from all creatures.[34]

Being utterly poor in relation to God, the Universal Man pays no re-

32. "Usually, Man is considered the highest of all beings because of his Reason (*'aql*). But, in truth, this very Reason which is peculiar to Man weaves around him an opaque veil which develops into an 'ego.' And the 'ego' thus produced hinders Man from knowing the Absolute as it really is. Precisely because of his Reason, Man cannot but be a 'mirror which reflects the Absolute only with inversion.'" Izutsu, *Sufism and Taoism*, 241.

33. "Perfect man has two visions (*naẓar*) of the Real, which is why He appointed for him two eyes. With one eye he looks upon Him in respect to the fact that He is Independent of the worlds. So he sees Him neither in any thing nor in himself. Through the other eye he looks upon Him in respect of His name All-merciful, which seeks the cosmos and is sought by the cosmos. He sees His Being permeating all things. Through the vision of this he is poor toward everything in respect to the fact that the things are the names of God, not in respect of their own entities. Hence, none is poorer toward the cosmos than perfect man, since he witnesses it subjected to himself." III 151.10 in SPK, 368.

34. "Hence, perfect man is the Real in his poverty, like the names, and the Real in his independence, since he does not see that which is subjected to him, only that which possesses effects. In other words, he sees the divine names, not the entities of the cosmos. Hence he is poor only toward God, within the entities of the cosmos, while the cosmos knows nothing of that." III 151.10 in SPK, 369. As Chittick notes: "The Shaykh understands the hadith of God's creating Adam in His own form to mean that God brought human beings into existence possessing the inherent attributes of *wujūd*. Hence *wujūd* itself designates the original disposition of human beings. To be human is to manifest *wujūd* as *wujūd*, while to be anything else is to manifest certain qualities of *wujūd* rather than others. Notice, however, that 'manifestation' is the issue here, not identity with *wujūd* in every respect. Although identity is desirable, it is, in a real sense, impossible, because *wujūd* belongs to God alone. Hence difference always remains. God's two hands retain their rights even in the experience of *waḥdat al-wujūd*." *Imaginal Worlds*, 57.

gard to created things, customs, or institutions, going so far as to bring opprobrium upon himself, becoming one of the "People of Blame." As Ibn 'Arabi says of them in his *Futūḥāt*: "They look at things with the same eye with which God looks at things. They never confuse realities."[35] This is so because they are purified of any attachment to created things or ideas or mere "imitation" *(taqlīd)*, i.e., blind following of religious authority, and are thus able to see things for what they are—in God. "Thus He suggests that knowledge of Him is inferred in knowledge of ourselves. Whenever we ascribe any quality to Him, we are ourselves [representative of] that quality, except it be the quality of His Self-sufficient Being."[36] Again, genuine gnosis or realized knowledge of God is a matter of self-knowledge and self-knowledge is knowledge of one's utter poverty with respect to God.

The realized knower, however, knows that in that poverty he reflects the divine Essence, and the greatest of the realized knowers are the prophets in and through whom God reveals himself to us—and to himself: "It is for this reason that the divine revelations come to us through the mouths of the Interpreters [the prophets], for He describes Himself to us through us. If we witness Him we witness ourselves, and when He sees us He looks on Himself."[37] The knowing of the gnostic, then, is essentially *hermeneutical*: he interprets the world in the light of his utter existential poverty and the utter richness of the divine Existence or Truth *(al-ḥaqq)* that gives existence and illumination to creatures and to the created intellect. He does not know God, world, or self as objects to be discovered by his rational gaze; rather, he knows both creatures and himself as theophanies of God where the divine Existence illuminates all existent creatures and his own intellect, and it illumines his intellect through the *ayāt*, "signs" or "verses," of the Qur'an. Thus, in a deep sense he knows that all creatures, including his intellect, *are* the Reality *(al-ḥaqq)* by virtue of his very poverty.

With such an understanding of God, though, comes the notion of God's concealment. Creation both reveals God, insofar as it is his manifestation, and also conceals God, insofar as its manifestations are not-God. For Ibn 'Arabi, the cosmos cannot perceive the Reality as it perceives itself, for the cosmos is a play of disclosure and concealment, of light and dark. As a result, no cosmic being, qua created being, can know the Real-

---

35. II 16.15 in SPK, 373.  36. *Bezels*, 54/53.
37. *Bezels*, 55/53.

ity, since it does not have any share in self-sufficient Being.[38] This dialectical play of light and dark, disclosure and concealment, being both God and not-God is brought to its highest and sharpest contradiction in the ignorance and knowledge of the Reality which is the natural state of the human being.

As 'Abd al-Karim al-Jili, a prominent disciple of Ibn 'Arabi, puts it in his work *The Universal Man (Al-insān al-kāmil)*:

Know that with regard to thyself thou art in a state of obscurity—"to God is the supreme symbol"—in this sense that the totality will scarcely manifest itself to thee, whatever may be the horizon of thy knowledge of thyself; now, in this respect, thou art an essence hidden in obscurity; hast thou not learnt that God is thine essence in thine ipseity (*huwīyah*)? Now, thou art conscious of that which eminently is thy reality; thou art then, with regard to thyself in the darkness, although, in relation to the Divine Reality, thou art not veiled from thyself, for the principle of this reality requires that It be not unconscious of Itself; it follows that thou art Divinely revealed to thyself and at the same time, because of thy created nature, unconscious of thy Divine Reality; thou art, then, simultaneously manifested and hidden from thyself. This then is one of these symbols "that God formulated for mankind" and which is not understood except by those who know.[39]

Just as concealment conditions all disclosure, so does ignorance condition the highest knowledge. As our very existence, God is the very essence of our selfhood. But precisely because God is our very selfhood, God lies in darkness, because he cannot become an object of our rational gaze. And yet, God reveals himself as the existence by which we exist and the light by which we know. The world, including our very selves, acts as a veil upon God; hence the need for God to reveal himself to us in a special revelation. To respond properly to the revelation, then, means making a twofold movement: on the one hand becoming utterly receptive to all the divine

38. "The Cosmos is the sensory realm [subtle and gross] and the Vicegerent is unseen. For this reason the Ruler [God] is veiled, since the Reality has described Himself as being hidden in veils of darkness, which are the natural forms, and veils of light, which are the subtle spirits. The Cosmos consists of that which is gross and that which is subtle and is, therefore, in both aspects, the veil [covering] its [own] true self [reality]. For the Cosmos does not perceive the Reality as He perceives Himself, nor can it ever not be veiled, knowing itself to be distinct from its Creator and dependent upon Him. Indeed, it has no part in the [divine] Self-sufficiency [of being] of the Reality, nor will it ever attain to that. In this sense the Reality can never be known [by cosmic being] in any way, since originated being has no part in that [Self-sufficiency]." *Bezels*, 56/54–55.

39. Al-Jili, *The Universal Man*, 37.

Qualities, and on the other hand annihilating the finite ego that stands in the way of that receptivity.[40]

The human essence, then, is a meeting of contraries: of existence and nonexistence, of knowledge and ignorance, of manifestation and non-manifestation, of inner and outer, of universality and particularity. This "unity of polarities" is, for Ibn 'Arabi, actually what "confers distinction" on humanity:

> God unites the polarity of qualities only in Adam, to confer a distinction on him. Thus, He says to Lucifer, *What prevents you from prostrating to one whom I have created with my two hands?* What prevents Lucifer is the very fact that he [man] unites [in himself] the two modes, the [originated] Cosmos and the [originating and original] Reality, which are His two hands.[41]

Here, Lucifer represents the positivist or analytical impulse to break things down into their particulars and fail to see or even deny their ultimate unity,[42] extending even (or especially) to particular qualities that seem to be opposed or contradictory. Such is not the case for the Universal Man, who unites within himself light and dark, existence and nonexistence, knowledge and ignorance, since this unity is a reflection of their unity in God, whose ninety-nine names express the same "opposites in unity" (thus God is called the Forgiving and the Avenger, etc.).[43] This synthesis of qualities makes the Universal Man the pinnacle of creation and vice-regent of God on earth: "In short, the Regency is fitting only for the Universal Man."[44] Ibn 'Arabi continues:

> His outer form He composed of the cosmic realities and forms, while his inner form He composed to match His Own form. Thus He says in the Sacred Tradi-

---

40. "The two Divine 'dimensions' of transcendence and immanence correspond, in a certain manner, to Divine Unity and Divine Unicity, for Unity is exempt from all direct grasp; one can only comprehend it by successive negations, whereas Divine Unicity appears in the very qualities of things. . . . Only he who has already realized a qualitative aspect of his own soul can realize the Universal Qualities. As for the comprehension of Unity (*al-āhadīyah*), it implies the annihilation of the ego." Al-Jili, *The Universal Man*, xii–xiii.

41. *Bezels*, 56/55.

42. Thus al-Qaysari notes that the name "Iblis" signifies the "particular" or the power of illusion. *Sharḥ*, I 208.

43. Which is why al-Qaysari reminds us that some divine names imply negative attributes. *Sharḥ*, I 187.

44. *Bezels*, 56/55. As Nettler explains, the outer meaning of Adam is that he is the pinnacle of creation. But the inner significance of Adam is that he is the mirror in which the divine Reality is reflected and known. Nettler, *Sufi Metaphysics and Qur'anic Prophets*, 21–22.

tion, "I am his hearing and his sight," and not, "I am his eye and his ear," in order to show the distinction between the two forms [the imperceptible and the perceptible]. Likewise He is [implicit] in every cosmic being according as the essential reality [manifested] in that being requires it, providing it is understood that no other being enjoys the Synthesis [of divine realities] possessed by the Regent. It is only by virtue of this Synthesis that he is superior [to all other beings].[45]

While God is not the things themselves, he is nevertheless the sight and the hearing in and through which the Universal Man sees and hears, since the Universal Man clings to no one attribute of the divine Essence but unites them all.[46] God is the *wujūd* in which all creatures are *found* (*mawjūd*) and thus brought to consciousness and full existence.

Which brings up the question asked by Affifi some seventy years ago:

Is the Perfect Man [i.e., Universal Man], therefore, perfect in his *being* or in his *knowledge* or both? . . . That is to say, is the Perfect Man so called because he *is* a *perfect manifestation* of God, or is it on account of his *realizing*, in his mystical experience, the significance of his essential oneness with God? Ibnul 'Arabi certainly means both, but he does not make the distinction between these two questions clear.[47]

This is an important question but, with all respect due to Affifi, I think that Ibn 'Arabi was hardly confused or unclear on the matter: for the Shaykh, being (the "outer" or *Ẓāher*) and knowledge (the "inner" or *bāṭin*) are essentially intertwined; they are flip sides of the same coin. To *realize* one's essential oneness with God is truly *to be* what one is: an illuminated theophany of God. All creatures, of course, are illuminated theophanies

---

45. *Bezels*, 56/55.

46. With regard to the inner and the outer, al-Qaysari makes some further subtle distinctions: There is a distinction between the (1) absolute inner, which is the divine essence itself, and (2) the relative inner, which is the realm of the spirit and which, in relation to the absolute inner, is "outer" but in relation to the absolute manifest or outer is "inner." There is also a distinction between the (3) absolute outer or manifest, which is the world of corporeal bodies, and (4) the relative outer or manifest, which corresponds to the relative inner (no. 2). *Sharḥ*, I 210. It is thus partially in virtue of his very bodily, material nature that Adam and the "sons of Adam" reflect, unlike the angels, the divine Reality and it is by synthesizing within themselves both affirmative and negative attributes that the sons of Adam also reflect most perfectly, at least potentially, this same divine Reality. Thus, Adam, in his potential for both good and evil is much more a reflection of the divine Reality than any creature who is capable only of good, because, by having this bipolar potential, Adam reflects the infinite all-possibility of the divine Essence. Thus, the divine possibility necessitates even hell (see, for example, *Sharḥ*, I 176).

47. Affifi, *The Mystical Philosophy of Ibnul 'Arabi*, 81.

of God insofar as they have and are illuminated by Existence. But only the human being can reflect upon that illumination as illumination. As sons of Adam, we are potentially this unity in being, for in our very lack of a "fixed station" in the scale of Being, we reflect the divine Reality in our essence; and we are potentially this unity in our knowledge, for in reflecting the divine Essence in our own essence, we also know, if in a non-thematic way, the divine Qualities and Names.[48] To *become* a theophany is to *know* God as God knows himself, because God knows himself in and through his theophanies.

To bring, however, this unity of being and knowledge in realized knowledge or gnosis to actuality, the word of Adam needs to be completed by the word of Muhammad. For, as al-Qaysari explains, the Truth or inner word of Adam is the spirit of Muhammad or the First Intellect, made manifest and effective in the verses, "signs" [*ayāt*], of the Holy Qur'an.[49]

### The "Word of Muhammad" and the Universal Man

If the reality of Adam is the starting point of creation, then the reality of Muhammad is the endpoint or goal of creation. The Mohammedan Word is the principle in and through which creation returns to God.[50] As such, the word of Adam is the principle of universality, i.e., that through which all the divine names and fixed essences of things are reflected, while the word of Muhammad is the principle of singularity, i.e., the word through which all the divine names and fixed essences of things are united in God's self-subsistent Existence:

His [Muhammad's] is the wisdom of singularity because he is the most perfect creation of this humankind, for which reason the whole affair [of creation] begins and ends with him. He was a prophet when Adam was still between the water and the clay and he is, by his elemental makeup, the Seal of the Prophets, first of the three singular ones, since all other singulars derive from it.[51]

48. "Properly speaking, the term *insān kāmil* is applied to man insofar as he is *in actu* what he was intended and created to be, that is to say, insofar as he realizes in an effective manner his original theomorphism; for God created Adam 'according to His form.'" Chodkiewicz, *Seal of the Saints*, 70.

49. *Sharḥ,* I 213, 216.

50. Thus the word of Muhammad manifests the divine name Allah, because it manifests the divine essence in its unified singularity or "unity in multiplicity."

51. *Bezels,* 272/214.

Philosophically speaking, then, the word of Muhammad is akin to the First Intellect of the Neoplatonists through which both the created universe comes into being and the individual human intellect rises to and is united with God. In this return to the One, the human intellect no longer remains "scattered" among the multiplicity of lower things but becomes united or one in the origin or source of all being and intelligibility. It returns to the "singularity" of the One out of the "universality" of its "dispersal" in the many.

This facet of Ibn 'Arabi's thought has been pointed out by both his medieval and modern commentators,[52] and as such, it bears repeating that the word of Muhammad, like the words of all the other prophets in the Bezels, must be clearly distinguished from the historical personality of the Prophet himself. As we have seen, these "words" are aspects of the divine Logos or Universal Man that make possible particular historical prophets in the first place. But in this scheme, the words of Adam and Muhammad are particularly important, for they "frame" the prophetic words and, as such, define the Universal Man in his nature and in his perfection: Muhammad is the inward fulfillment of the promise or potential of Adam. The word of Adam is the *explication* or "unfolding" in creation of the divine Essence while the word of Muhammad is its "enfolding" in the reality of the realized gnostic, whose being coincides with that of the Universal Man. The reality of Muhammad actualizes in a singular, concrete unity or union the universal word of Adam. And in turn the saint or gnostic realizes or actualizes inwardly the singular unity manifested by Muhammad by participation in the *ḥaqīqa muḥammadīyya*, or the primal Word, *kalima*, of Muhammad.[53]

As the starting point for his discussion of the reality or "word" of Muhammad, Ibn 'Arabi refers to a *ḥadīth* in which Muhammad mentions three things of "this world" *(al-dunyā)* that "were made beloved" to him:

52. See *Sharḥ*, II 456.

53. "In any case, the terms *ḥaqīqa muḥammadīyya* and *insān kāmil* are not purely synonymous, but express differing views of man, the first seeing him in terms of his primordiality and the second in terms of his finality. The *kāmil* or perfections of the *insān kāmil* should not be understood in a 'moral' sense (so as to correspond with the 'heroic virtues'), but as meaning 'fulfillment' or 'completion.' Properly speaking, this perfection is possessed only by Muhammad, the ultimate and total manifestation of the *ḥaqīqa muḥammadīyya*. Yet, on the other hand, it is equally the goal of all spiritual life and the very definition of *walāya*. Hence, the *walāya* of the *walī* can only be participation in the *walāya* of the Prophet." Chodkiewicz, *Seal of the Saints*, 71.

"Three things have been made beloved to me in this world of yours: women, perfume and solace in prayer."[54] The rest of this last chapter in the *Bezels* is an extended exegesis on this *ḥadīth*. In the three things mentioned, Ibn ʿArabi sees expressed in symbolic form three essential unions that produce and manifest the fully realized knower who is an actualization, in union with God, of the Universal Man: the union of active and passive in his love for women, the disinterested love of all creatures as good in themselves in his love for perfumes, and his realization of union with God in his love of prayer.

Ibn ʿArabi begins by stating that Muhammad mentions in the *ḥadīth* women as the first of those things made beloved to him. Why? Because as fellow human beings, women were closest to the Prophet in nature and the human being's "knowledge of himself comes before knowledge of his Lord":

> Now man's knowledge of himself comes before his knowledge of his Lord, the latter being the result of the former, according to his saying, "Whoso knows himself, knows his Lord." From this one may understand either that one is not able to know and attain, which is one meaning, or that gnosis is possible. According to the first [interpretation] one cannot know oneself and cannot, therefore, know one's Lord, while, according to the second, one may know oneself and therefore one's Lord.[55]

Separated, male and female do not realize the full unity of the human essence and thus do not realize the full human reflection of the divine Essence in the human essence. Thus the male is drawn to the female in much the same way that the universal is drawn to its existential instantiation and fulfillment in the particular: "Women were made beloved to him and he had great affection for them because the whole always is drawn toward its part."[56] In his love for woman, man as universal is completed and made whole, for without this love for woman, man remains a truncated activity, in danger of not being open to God completely due to a lack of passivity. This passivity that is found eminently in woman is a figure for any union with God, for God yearns for union with the soul in much the way that the man yearns for union with woman.[57] This yearning of God for

---

54. *Bezels*, 272/214.  55. *Bezels*, 272/215.
56. *Bezels*, 273/215.
57. Thus we have these remarkable lines of erotic poetry right in the middle of this discus-

creation is analogous to the yearning of man for woman. Just as the man seeks his own image in woman and seeks to unite his activity with her passivity, so God seeks his image in man and seeks to unite his creative activity with the sublime passivity of his own inaccessible and hidden Essence. This parallels in many ways the Akhbarian principle that it is logically necessary for the divine perfection to manifest itself in created imperfection and for the divine infinity to manifest itself in created finitude, because otherwise, to exclude imperfection or finitude or passivity from the divine Being is to limit the plenitude of that Being and render it other than divine.

Thus, love and the desire to see his own image reflected in creation are the primary motivations of creation as well as of the necessary unfolding of the divine Essence. Ibn ʿArabi indicates this right at the beginning of the *Bezels* by citing the *ḥadīth* that God was a "hidden treasure that wished to be known." By perceiving this divine love for creation, the Prophet was able in his love for women to rise to an unitative love for God. For in being united with woman, man becomes passive for the divine unitative activity.

In the words of Ibn ʿArabi:

Then God drew forth from him a being in his own image, called woman, and because she appears in his own image, the man feels a deep longing for her, as something yearns for itself, while she feels longing for him as one longs for that place to which one belongs. Thus women were made beloved to him, for God loves that which He has created in His own image to which He made His angels prostrate, in spite of their great power, rank and lofty nature. From that stemmed the affinity [between God and man], and the [divine] image is the greatest, most glorious and perfect [example of] affinity. That is because it is a syzygy that polarizes the being of the Reality, just as woman, by her coming into being, polarizes humanity, making of it a syzygy. Thus we have a ternary, God, man, and woman, the man yearning for his Lord Who is his origin, as woman yearns for man.[58]

Here, as mentioned above, we have a clear analogy: just as woman "polarizes" humanity by creating a passive and active aspect to one human es-

<hr />

sion: "The Beloved longs to see me, / And I long even more to see Him, / The hearts beat fast, but destiny bars the way, / I groan in complaint and so does He.

Since He has explained that He breathed into man of His spirit, He is yearning [in reality] for Himself. Consider, then, how, because of His spirit, His creation is in His own image." *Bezels*, 273/216.

58. *Bezels*, 274/216.

sence, so humanity "polarizes" the divine Reality by creating a passive and active aspect to the one divine Essence. But this polarization is the necessary precondition for unity. This is evident in the erotic union between man and woman: "When a man loves a woman, he seeks union with her, that is to say the most complete union possible in love, and there is in the elemental sphere no greater union than that between the sexes."[59]

Such is also the case in the union of the Universal Man in God:

When man contemplates the Reality in woman he beholds [Him] in a passive aspect, while when he contemplates Him in himself, as being that from which woman is manifest, he beholds Him in an active aspect. When, however, he contemplates Him in himself, without any regard to what has come from him, he beholds Him as passive to Himself directly. However, his contemplation of the Reality in woman is the most complete and perfect, because in this way he contemplates the Reality in both active and passive mode, while by contemplating the Reality only in himself, he beholds Him in a passive mode particularly.[60]

By loving and beholding the beauty of woman, man comes to a fuller understanding of the union of opposites in God—most particularly, the union of one of the most basic polarities: that of activity and passivity (or actuality and potentiality to put it in Aristotelian terms). On the union of this polarity is based the union of the manifest and nonmanifest, of the transcendent and the immanent, of the inner and the outer, etc.

Man cannot win this understanding, however, without a formal or concrete support: "Contemplation of the Reality without formal support is not possible, since God, in His Essence, is far beyond all need of the Cosmos. Since, therefore, some form of support is necessary, the best and most perfect kind is the contemplation of God in women."[61] For any attempt at an abstract understanding of this unity of the active and passive in the Reality would simply be an assertion of male activity and thus of non-understanding, for male reason alone cannot understand how God can also be passive or "female" as much as active or "male." Only in an understanding of the close union—even, on a certain level, essential

59. *Bezels*, 274/217. The "split" between man and woman in the chapter on Muhammad only leads to a recognition of their unity—so it is also with the "split" between God and creation. See Nettler, *Sufi Metaphysics and Qur'anic Prophets*, 187. It goes without saying that Ibn 'Arabi sees a continuity everywhere between physical and spiritual love. See Asín-Palacios, *L'Islam christianisé*, 185.

60. *Bezels*, 275/217.

61. *Bezels*, 275/217.

identity—of the erotic union between man and woman and of that between God and human being can a true understanding of mystical gnosis
be achieved:

In relation to him they [women] are as the Universal Nature is to God in which
He revealed the forms of the Cosmos by directing toward it the divine Will and
Command, which, at the level of elemental forms, is symbolized by conjugal
union, [spiritual] concentration in the realm of luminous spirits, and the ordering of premises toward a conclusion [in the realm of thought], all of which
correspond to the consummation of the Primordial Singularity in all these aspects.[62]

In the *ḥadīth* quoted by Ibn ʿArabi as the basis for his discussion in this
chapter, woman comes first because she represents the primordial, passive
"universal nature" that is logically prior to the existence of all individual
creatures and, it follows, to all other types of polarity or opposition. She
represents the divine Eros that is both the root of division and duality in
creation and also the means for its overcoming in union with God. That is
why Ibn ʿArabi says that woman represents the passivity of "Universal Nature" or the material substrate or "cause" of creation; but this "Universal
Nature" is itself the product of the "breath" of the Merciful.[63]

As is usual for the Shaykh, he asserts that the ontological structure of
Reality is reflected in the very grammar of the Arabic language. Of the
next two things beloved of the Prophet—perfume and prayer—the former is grammatically masculine and the latter is feminine. For Ibn ʿArabi
this is significant, because, while in some passages he implies that, ontologically, man is superior to woman,[64] nevertheless here he notes that in
this *ḥadīth*, the feminine takes precedence over the masculine. For in mentioning these "three things" the gender of the word "three" is feminine, not
masculine, which is significant, since Arabic, like many other languages,
uses the masculine gender for a plurality of things even if only one of these
things is masculine. Here, however, the *ḥadīth* flagrantly breaks the rules

---

62. *Bezels*, 275–76/218.        63. *Bezels*, 277/219.

64. "Just as woman [ontologically] is of a lower rank than man, according to His saying, *Men
enjoy a rank above them*, so also is the creature inferior in rank to the One Who fashioned him
in his image, despite his being made in His image." *Bezels*, 276/219. For a more comprehensive
overview of Ibn ʿArabi's very nuanced views on gender, one can consult the index of the following work with profit: Sachiko Murata, *The Tao of Islam: A Sourcebook on Gender Relationships in
Islamic Thought* (Albany: State University of New York Press, 1992).

of Arabic grammar, using the feminine gender to refer to all three things, even though the word "perfume," being male in gender, should convert the "three" to the masculine gender. The implication is that man as Universal Man is, for the Shaykh, ontologically conditioned by two feminine realities: "Thus he [the Universal Man] is between two feminine entities, the one substantively feminine, the other feminine in reality, women being feminine in reality, while prayer is not."[65] The Universal Man stands between the passivity of the Universal Nature out of which he springs as a human being and prayer, which renders him passive to the divine activity. In love of woman man unites his activity with passivity, making him receptive to the divine activity and readying him for prayer and in prayer man becomes fully united to God.

Still, I do not wish to skip over the significance of perfume for Ibn 'Arabi's understanding of the Universal Man, for this "middle term" brings the realized knower from his virtual universal nature represented by woman to realized unity with God represented by prayer. The Arabic word for "perfume," *ṭib*, is, as was mentioned above, masculine in gender. As such, it refers to the nature of the Universal Man insofar as he lives and acts in "this world" (*al-dunyā*) where the masculine takes precedence. As woman relates man to his universal created matrix and as prayer relates him vertically to his Creator, perfume relates man horizontally to his fellow creatures. Here, Ibn 'Arabi interprets the *ḥadīth* as saying that the realized knower is one who treats all of creation with equanimity and detachment.[66] After all, perfumes or odors can be sweet-smelling or foul-smelling, but whether something smells sweet or not is not an indication of its inherent goodness or badness. As Ibn 'Arabi says:

However, being at source divine, it [creation] is all sweet smelling and good, but according as it is approved of [by separative attitudes] or disapproved of, it may be considered good or bad. Of garlic, Muhammad said, "It is a bush whose odor I detest"; he did not say "I detest it." Thus, it is not the thing itself that is to be detested, but only that which issues from it. Such an aversion may be a question of custom, natural antipathy, law, deficiency, or something else. If then the

65. *Bezels*, 277/220.

66. "God Himself has put perfume [*tib*, also goodness] in the context of conjugal union with reference to the innocence of 'A'ishah when He says, *Evil [malodorous] women are for evil men and evil men are for evil women, just as good [sweet-smelling] women are for good men and good men for good women, who are innocent of what they allege.*" *Bezels*, 278/221.

distinction between good and bad is to be made, then Muhammad was made to love the good and not the bad.[67]

In short, to the Universal Man, as embodied in the Prophet, *all creatures as such are good.* Evil is only a malodorous product of a selfish soul that clings to created things. Affifi puts the Shaykh's position well when he notes: "Nothing is evil: all that *is* is good. In other words what we call evil is *subjective,* not an objective reality. But even *'good' as contrasted with evil* is subjective and relative. The only good that is *absolute* is Pure Being (God, *the* Good)."[68] The gnostic, then, is a concrete manifestation of the Universal Man insofar as he treats all created things as good because they are reflective of some divine Name or aspect of the divine Essence. If we may speak of the prime virtue of the gnostic it is this: to love all creatures without distinction. For God shines the light of existence upon all creatures, good and bad alike, giving their essences actual existence, and likewise does the realized knower with his love. If an entity is "misguided" or "evil," it is misguided not by God, who simply gives it existence, but by the inherent possibilities of its own essence.[69] Yet, the existence of any creature, as existent, is good and, as such, loveable and desirable.

Indeed, what makes the realized knower of God himself good is not anything in his own essence, but precisely because the realized knower re-

---

67. *Bezels,* 278/221.

68. Affifi, *The Mystical Philosophy of Ibnul 'Arabi,* 158. As Ibn 'Arabi states in his *Bezels:* "The Apostle of God was made to love only the good in everything, which is [in reality] everything that is. [We might ask] whether there can be anything in the Cosmos that sees only the good in everything and knows no bad. We would say that there is not, since in the very source from which the Cosmos is manifested, which is the Real, we find aversion and love, the bad being that which is loathed, while the good is that which is loved. Now the Cosmos is [created] in God's image [macrocosm] and man has been made in both images [microcosm], so that there cannot be anything that sees only one aspect of things. There are certainly those who can distinguish the good from the bad, that a thing is bad by [sense] experience, but in whom perception of the good predominates over perception of the bad. As for the idea that one might remove the bad from the Cosmos of created being, such a thing is not possible, since the Mercy of God inheres in both the good and the bad. From its own standpoint the bad is good and good bad. Indeed, there is nothing but good, but seems, in some way, bad to some bad thing, and vice versa" (279/222).

69. "To the objection that this means that God makes people sin and then punishes them for sinning, the Shaykh replies that the entities are immutable and God does not 'make' (*ja'l*) them do anything. He simply gives them existence. If misguidance is the property of an entity, the entity will be misguided when it enters into existence. God shines the light of *wujūd* on the entities, and they come to exist as they are, doing what they do. God can no more change the entities than He can change His own Essence, *wujūd* itself." Chittick, *Imaginal Worlds,* 143.

alizes (in a real, effective, and unitative sense) that he *has no defined essence*. As such, he is at the *station of no station* in which he is no longer fixed at any degree of existence, but actualizes in himself his primordial Adamic nature and simply abides in existence as such. The realized knower does this to the extent that he recognizes all things as inherently good and, alternately, to the extent that he sees all things as good, the gnostic abides in the *Real (al-ḥaqq)*, pure existence. As Ibn ʿArabi explains in his *Futūḥāt:*

> The final end and ultimate return of the gnostics—though their entities remain immutably fixed—is that the Real is identical with them, while they do not exist. This station is possessed only by the gnostic. Hence they are contracted in the state of their expansion. . . . Hence the gnostic is known only through the fact that he brings opposites together, for all of him is the Real. Thus Abu Saʿid al-Kharraz was asked, "Through what have you known Allah?" He replied, "Through the fact that He brings opposites together," for he witnessed their coming together in himself, and he knew that he was upon His form. He had heard Him say, "He is the First and the Last, the Manifest and the Nonmanifest" (57:3); and it was this verse he brought in proof of his statement.[70]

The realized believer or gnostic brings together in himself all the divine Names and Attributes because he himself clings to nothing created, not even himself. As such, the realized believer manifests the Universal Man or the Word of Muhammad, which is manifested most clearly in the Qurʾan. Through the Qurʾan—and especially through prayer informed by the Qurʾan—this Universal Man comes to be realized in the believer. Thus, the Qurʾan is like an active principle or form that actualizes the Adamic nature of man and conforms him to the Word of Muhammad and, through this Word, to God. Naturally, therefore, a realization of the inherent goodness of all things passes over into prayer, because to realize the inherent goodness of all things is to refer that goodness always to the One who is good in himself and the source of the goodness of all things.

As Ibn ʿArabi explains, in the height of prayer, it is not the realized knower who prays but God who prays through the realized knower. This is the level of perfection or *iḥsān:* "pray to God as if you see Him, for if you do not see Him, He surely sees you." In the state of perfection or *iḥsān,* there is no longer any duality: the seeing of the servant becomes God's seeing, and the prayer of the servant becomes God's prayer. In fact, if one ef-

70. II 512.9 in SPK, 375.

fects a stop in the Arabic wording in the middle of the phrase *(lam takūn: tarāhu)*, then it reads, "if thou are not, thou seest Him."[71] When one is no longer attached to any created being, especially oneself, then one can see God, but under no other condition. Hence, gnosis or realized knowledge of God is fundamentally prayer rather than discursive thought, audible speech, or blind feeling: in gnosis the objective is known as subjective and the subjective is known as objective.

This notion represents the essence of *dhikr* or "remembrance of God." To know that the one who sees and the one who is seen, the one who prays and the one to whom one prays are the same. As Izutsu reminds us:

It must be kept in mind that "remembrance" *(dhikr)*, for Ibn 'Arabi, does not simply mean the act of remembering God with one's tongue and heart; the word is rather synonymous with mystical "self-annihilation" in God. The *dhikr* in this meaning is a spiritual state in which a mystic concentrates all his bodily and spiritual powers on God in such a way that his whole existence is united with God completely, without any residue.[72]

True *dhikr*, therefore, requires that the finite ego undergo a sort of "spiritual death" to itself in *fanā'* or "annihilation." The only way that the gnostic may know God is by "un-becoming," for only in un-becoming may there be room for the in-working of God in the heart and mind of the gnostic. Prayer or *dhikr*, if performed with selfless devotion, loosens the bonds of the ego and its attachments, including its conceptual categories. As Ibn 'Arabi puts it regarding the highest levels of prayer:

Consider, then, the sublimity of the rank of prayer and to what degree of dignity it brings the one who performs it. However, the one who does not attain to contemplative vision in his prayer has not reached its summit and cannot find [true] solace in it, since he cannot see Him with Whom he has discourse. If also he cannot hear the Reality's response, he cannot be listening carefully enough. Indeed, he who is not present with His Lord in prayer, neither hearing nor seeing Him, is not really praying at all, since he does not listen and watch [for God]. While it lasts, there is nothing like the prayer rite to prevent preoccupation with other things.[73]

Prayer or *dhikr* shifts the center of the Sufi's thought and being from him or herself to God, which is why it is only in prayer that the gnostic

71. Shah-Kazemi, *Paths to Transcendence*, 102.

72. Izutsu, *Sufism and Taoism*, 250.     73. *Bezels*, 281/223–24.

comes to know the Reality as it is, and not as he or she *thinks* or *feels* it to be. The blind follower of tradition knows only what he or she is told and the person of rational consideration knows only the apparent and the phenomenal.[74] But the realized knower "tastes" through prayer the Reality as it is in itself and recognizes the essential unity of the divine Essence and the manifest created forms of the world—including his or her own. "The perfect mystic therefore is one who sees *both* God and 'self' in the mystical experience."[75] Or, in other words, the realized knower sees both himself and all other creatures as theophanies of the one divine Essence, and prayer accomplishes this because, ultimately, prayer, if done with selfless devotion, is a *response* to God's word to us rather than a projection of one's preconceived ideas upon the unity of existence. Thus prayer is always prayer in and through the Qur'an. Prayer is always *revealed* prayer, for this is the only type of prayer that is efficacious.

It is therefore not at all strange, as it would first appear, that the teacher of the "Unity of Existence" would enjoin or even talk about prayer. Prayer, to be sure, presupposes a duality, but it posits this duality only to overcome it, as was the case in the Prophet's mention of women and perfume: love of both is an overcoming of duality. But in prayer we have the highest unity, because in prayer we know and experience the divine speaking in and through us:

That which is called prayer has also another aspect in that He has commanded us to pray to Him and has told us that He prays for us, the prayer being both from us and from Him. When it is God Who prays, He does so in His name the Last, as coming after the creation of the servant, being, indeed, the God the servant

74. "The only difference is, as Ibnul 'Arabi tells us, that the believer knows the real, being in immediate contact with it; the philosopher knows only the apparent and the phenomenal." Affifi, *The Mystical Philosophy of Ibnul 'Arabi*, 111.

75. "The passing away of 'self' is a state of intuitive knowledge in which the essential unity of the Whole is revealed. This is the aspect of the mystical experience which Ibnul 'Arabi emphasizes. It is *knowledge* of an infallible nature that Ibnul 'Arabi is after. To say that I have become God or died to self in any real sense is ignorance, and to see your 'self' *alone* in a mystical experience is polytheism. The perfect mystic therefore is one who sees *both* God and 'self' in the mystical experience, both by mystical knowledge and feeling (*'ilman wa halan*) and sees his 'self' by mystical knowledge alone (*'ilman la halan*), i.e. the perfect mystic is the one who recognizes both Essence and 'form' but realizes their essential unity and the absolute non-existence of the form. This is the most perfect *fana'* a mystic can attain in this life according to Ibnul 'Arabi: the *real fana'* is attained after death when the form completely disappears." Affifi, *The Mystical Philosophy of Ibnul 'Arabi*, 142.

creates in himself (in his Heart), whether by his reason or through traditional learning. This is the "God of belief," which is various according to the predisposition inherent in that particular person; as al-Junaid said, when asked about the gnosis of God and the gnostic, "The color of the water is the same as that of its container," which is a most precise answer, showing the matter as it is.[76]

As Ibn 'Arabi indicates with the phrase "the God the servant creates in himself (in his Heart), whether *by his reason* or through traditional learning," human beings have the tendency to project onto the notion of "God" images of their own making. Well before Feuerbach, the Shaykh realized that human beings tend to worship idols that are images of themselves and not of the true divinity, Allah. These idols are not God as such; rather they are "gods of belief." A "god of belief" is God understood under the name "the Last," for this is a "god" created by the thought or imagination of the believer (or the tradition to which the believer belongs). So that whatever praise the servant gives this "god of belief" is really praise of himself, not of God: "Similarly, the God of belief is made for the one who has regard for it, being his own production, so that his praise for that which he believes in is self-praise."[77] Thus, when Ibn 'Arabi cites, as he often does, the *ḥadīth* in which it is said, "to know one's self is to know one's Lord," what he is referring to is the constant temptation to create quasi-divine "idols" in our thought or imagination that we then worship. But anything that we create is only a creature and thus utterly unlike the true God who addresses us in the Holy Qur'an.

Thus, to know oneself is to know the sorts of "gods" finite egos such as we project upon the Reality and to know that the Reality is utterly unlike those "gods." Yet at the same time, it is also to know that the Reality is "much closer than your jugular vein" and the "seeing with which he [the realized knower] sees and the hearing with which he hears." In this understanding God is understood under the name "the First," i.e., the Reality as prior to all prayer, indeed as the necessary precondition for all prayer. As "the First," God is the *subject* of prayer; as "the Last" he is the *object* of prayer. In the chapter on the word of Muhammad, Ibn 'Arabi therefore goes through the verses of the opening prayer of the Qur'an, the *Fatiḥa*, and shows how it is *God* as well as the human being who prays this prayer

76. *Bezels*, 282/225.
77. *Bezels*, 283/226.

every time it is uttered. For the realized knower, then, God is both "first" and "last" and thus both the object and subject of all his prayer.

In other words, Ibn ʿArabi does not reject the "gods of belief" as invalid; in fact, he implies that they are necessary: we cannot, as we saw in a previous chapter, understand the divine Essence except in and through its theophanies. Every "god of belief" reveals a way to the divine Essence. What the realized knower understands, though, is the "relatively absolute" nature of the "gods of belief": they are relative insofar as they are a reality contingent upon the relationship of the creature to the divine Essence, which is beyond all finite relations, but absolute insofar as the creature must submit absolutely to a "god of belief" in order to overcome its limited nature.

Particularly important in this connection is Ibn ʿArabi's reference above to the notion of the great tenth-century Sufi al-Junayd, who said that the "color of the water is conditioned by the color of the container." Ibn ʿArabi continues his discussion of al-Junayd's image:

If he were to understand truly what Al-Junayd said regarding the color of the water being that of its container, he would allow to every believer his belief and would recognize God in every form and in every belief. His attitude, however, is merely a matter of opinion and not knowledge. Thus, He has said, "I am in my servant's opinion of Me," that is to say that He is manifest to him only in the form of his belief, whether it be universal or particular in nature. The God of beliefs is subject to certain limitations, and it is this God Who is contained in His servant's Heart, since the Absolute God cannot be contained by anything, being the very Essence of everything and of Itself. Indeed, one cannot say either that it encompasses Itself or that it does not do so; so understand! God speaks the truth and He is the [sole] Guide along the Way.[78]

The "color" of the container, i.e., the finite ego, colors the "water" which is the divine Essence. In itself, the water is colorless just as the divine Essence is in itself without limiting qualities or attributes. But, just as the container of water colors the water, so the finite ego colors the divine Essence in various ways, due to its finitude, according to its thoughts, categories, passions, and desires. Ibn ʿArabi explains this even more directly in his *Futūḥāt*:

---

78. *Bezels*, 283–84/226.

Junayd was asked about knowledge (*ma'rifa*) and the knower (*'ārif*). He replied, "The water takes on the color of its cup." In other words, the container displays its effects in what it contains. Junayd said this to let you know that you will never judge your object of knowledge except by yourself, since you will never know anything but yourself. Whatever may be the color of the cup, water becomes manifest in that color. The person without knowledge judges that the water is like that, since sight gives that to him. Water discloses itself in the forms of all the cups in respect to their colors, but it does not become delimited in its essence. You only see it that way. In the same manner, the shapes of the containers in which water appears display their effects in it, but in all of them it is still water. If the container is square, the water becomes manifest as square.[79]

For Ibn 'Arabi, the realized knower never knows God directly or without a medium: he or she always knows God through the limits of his or her created nature and, by extension, through the formal limits of his or her religious tradition. Nevertheless, the realized knower knows these limits *as limits* and therefore knows that God is not "the color of the container." As William Chittick puts it: "Perfect human beings are transparent before every self-disclosure of *wujūd*. In contrast, all other created things have delimited capacities that impose upon *wujūd* specific knottings and colorings that result in distinct beliefs."[80]

Thus, for the realized knower, to be conscious of oneself is to be conscious of the unity of existence that underlies and manifests itself in all phenomena, including the phenomena of his own consciousness and in all beliefs, including those of his own religious tradition, all the while knowing that its particular revelation is absolutely necessary for this realization.[81] The realized knower goes beyond thoughts and images and things and actually *drinks* from the source of existence and comes to *taste* it. Ultimately, the dualism implicit in the senses of seeing or even hearing is not the best approach to the sort of knowing characteristic of the Universal Man or realized knower, but rather the actions of tasting and eating and drinking. For in these images, there is an assimilation of consumption, not by the realized knower, of course, but by God. As the Shaykh puts it in the chapter of the *Bezels* on Abraham: "You are His nourishment as bestow-

79. III 161.24 in SPK, 341.
80. Chittick, *Imaginal Worlds*, 149.
81. "For Ibn 'Arabi consciousness of the Self, in its metaphysical depths, is nothing less than consciousness of the Unity of Being." Coates, *Ibn 'Arabi and Modern Thought*, 172.

ing the contents of His Self-Knowledge, while He is yours as bestowing existence, what is assigned to you being assigned also to Him." For "food penetrates to the essence of the one fed, permeating every part. So also with God, although in His case there are no parts but only Divine Stations or Names through which His Essence is manifest."[82] God and the realized knower of God "nourish" each other, one giving self-knowledge through the mirror of his essence the other giving existence through his own self-subsistent Being.

Thus, as Corbin says, it is not to "God in general" that the realized knower of God returns, to some "general idea" or "concept" of God, but rather he tastes and is consumed by the most particular and concrete Reality that there is.[83]

82. *Bezels*, 94–95/83–84.
83. See Corbin, *Alone with the Alone*, 132–33.

8

# The Nobleman in Meister Eckhart

There is no need to dwell on the centrality of the notion of the *Logos* to Christian thought. From the very beginning of the Gospel of John, Jesus is understood as the *Logos* or *Ratio* of all creation made flesh among humanity. This central assertion of the Christian tradition is also the linchpin of Meister Eckhart's mystical thought. For Eckhart, by becoming flesh, the *Logos*, Christ, who is also God, *ennobled* humanity, becoming what we are, as the Patristic formula claims, so that we might become what he is. We can no longer think of God as the Lord of the manor on which we work as serfs; rather, we are true sons and *noblemen* by adoption. We only need to claim our inheritance by listening to that *Logos* or Word, made known to us in the Gospel, and giving birth to that Word in the ground of our souls.

## The Nobleman

Eckhart asserts, as we noted above, that a true Nobleman is one who attains by grace a sovereign detachment from or "letting-go" (*gelâzenheit*) of all created things, such that he is a slave or vassal to no created man, angel, or thing. True nobility, then, for Eckhart, is not a social status only but first and primarily a metaphysical status. In the Nobleman, being as such is realized by humanity in and through the divine Word.[1] Indeed, as Marie Anne Vannier ex-

---

1. Vannier, "Der edle Mensch," 318.

plains it, "the nobleman is freely not the Man that has attained perfection, but rather, one who lives fully in God."[2] That is, the Nobleman is the man who lives not in or for his *own* perfection qua creature but who rather lives only for and in God. But in doing so, the Nobleman, paradoxically, fulfills and recapitulates all that is fully human in himself as well as all that is divine. In other words, the Nobleman is, by grace, what Christ was and is by his own nature: fully God and fully human.

Vannier points out that the theme of the Nobleman is one that is characteristic of the time of Eckhart's preaching in Strasbourg, near the end of his career. Indeed, one can see this theme as an attempt by Eckhart to extend his mystical teachings to the masses in a form more amenable to their understanding.[3] Eckhart is attempting in this period to situate his own mystical-exegetical teachings within the social context of his time, with the proviso that he is trying to describe something that transcends all periods and social contexts. In his long sermon from this period entitled *Of the Nobleman*, Eckhart makes liberal use of themes that he had already developed in one of his earliest writings (c. 1290s), called *Counsels on Discernment*. These consist of transcripts of talks given to young Dominicans while Eckhart was vicar of Thuringia.[4] In these, Eckhart talks about letting-go or *gelâzenheit* as the heart of the spiritual life, and what is at issue is the soul's proper comportment to God.

In the *Counsels*, letting-go is the opposite of self-will.[5] Once the spirit is "empty," Eckhart asserts, it "can do everything" because then it is an empty and hence serviceable vehicle for the divine in-working. And what is an "empty spirit"? Eckhart answers: "An empty spirit is one that is confused by nothing, attached to nothing, has not attached its best to any fixed way of acting, and has no concern whatever in anything for its own gain, for it is all sunk deep down into God's dearest will and has forsaken its own."[6] Thus in the third chapter, Eckhart says:

Therefore, make a start with yourself, and abandon yourself *(lâz dich)*. . . . Then what ought he to do? He ought to begin by forsaking himself *(sich selber lâzen)*, because then he has forsaken everything *(alliu dinc gelâzen)*. Truly, if a man renounced *(lieze)* a kingdom or the whole world but held on to himself, he would

---

2. Ibid., 323.     3. Ibid., 319.

4. For the place of the *Counsels* in Eckhart's career, see Kurt Ruh, *Meister Eckhart: Theologe, Prediger, Mystiker*, 30ff.

5. Ibid., 33.     6. *Counsels* 2; DW V, 190/EE, 248.

not have renounced anything *(nihtes gelâzen)*. What is more, if a man renounces himself, whatever else he retains, riches or honors or whatever it may be, he has forsaken everything. . . . For whoever has renounced his own will and himself has renounced everything *(alliu gelâzen)*.[7]

Letting-go is that process by which, as the Gospel itself teaches, the soul loses itself so that it may find itself again in God. For Eckhart, loss of self is the key: to lose everything except oneself amounts to losing nothing, but to lose oneself is to lose everything else. Only when the soul loses itself, however, is it prepared to be united with and know God.

Obviously, then, Eckhartian letting go is much more than a moral principle or virtue, effecting a transmutation in our very being and hence in our very mode of knowing and acting. Indeed, for Eckhart, this latter is so fundamental that Kurt Ruh himself talks of Eckhart teaching an *Ethik des Seins* or an "Ethics of Being," where "goodness" and "justice" are not simply ethical qualities but rather "participations" in the divine goodness and justice themselves.[8] They are, therefore, in traditional Aristotelian terminology, not accidental to the released *(gelâzen)* soul but "substantial" to it insofar as the released soul lives, acts, and thinks "in" God's goodness and justice and does not "have" or "possess" them. Thus, the soul must be "empty" or "free" of all created things, ideas, and qualities if it is truly to live in and out of God's substantial goodness and justice. In this, Eckhart is simply developing on the practical, lived plane what he asserts is true on the metaphysical or speculative plane as presented in chapter 4 of his thesis *Esse est Deus:* all being, oneness, truth, and goodness come from God and God alone, while the creature gives nothing of being, oneness, truth, or goodness. These transcendental qualities would disappear from the creature if God should not exist, just as all illumination in the air would cease if the sun were to stop shining.

Eckhart treats this process by which the released soul comes to subsist in God's essence or *wesen* as the result of what can almost be described as a law of "spiritual physics": "This is indeed a fair exchange and an honest deal: By as much as you go out in forsaking all things, by so much, neither less nor more, does God go in, with all that is his, as you entirely forsake everything that is yours."[9] For Eckhart, then, the observance of rites, pen-

7. *Counsels* 3; DW V, 193–94/EE, 249–50.
8. Ruh, *Meister Eckhart: Theologe, Prediger, Mystiker,* 35.
9. *Counsels* 4; DW V, 197/EE, 250.

ances, and even moral codes is a necessary but not sufficient condition for living in and out of God:

People ought never to think too much about what they could do, but they ought to think about what they could be *(waz sie waeren)*. If people and their way of life were only good, what they did might be a shining example. If you are just, then your works too are just. We ought not to think of building holiness upon action; we ought to build it upon a way of being, for it is not what we do that makes us holy, but we ought to make holy what we do.[10]

Here Eckhart simply applies the scholastic principle that *actio sequitur esse* to the spiritual life. Nothing our created self does is holy because everything that it does has a created origin; it is a mere expression of our limited, finite desire and plans for the gratification of our self-will. But letting-go "hallows" our works insofar as it releases us from self-will and into God's mode of existing, knowing, and acting, even if the action be identical to one done out of self-will.

As Kurt Ruh reminds us, Eckhart is not concerned with the repression of our "sinful nature": much more important in Eckhart's thinking is the status of the "I" *(das Ich)*—both knowledge of it and its overcoming.[11] At the end of the third chapter after referring to the beatitude "Blessed are the poor in spirit," Eckhart says: "Take a look at yourself *(Nim dîn selbes wâr)*, and whenever you find yourself, deny yourself. That is the best of all."[12] Eckhart, therefore, does not conceive this disclosure of truth in letting-go as something that gives us God as an object for a pure, thinking "I." For Eckhart, not only is such contemplation not possible, it is not even desirable:

This true possession of God depends on the disposition, and on an inward directing of the reason and intention toward God, not on a constant contemplation in an unchanging manner, for it would be impossible to nature to preserve such an intention, and very laborious and not the best thing either. A man ought not to have a God who is just a product of his thought, nor should he be satisfied with that, because if the thought vanished, God too would vanish. But one ought to have a God who is present, a God who is far above the notions of men and of all created things. That God does not vanish, if a man does not willfully turn away from him.[13]

10. *Counsels* 4; DW V, 197–98/EE, 250.
11. Ruh, *Meister Eckhart: Theologe, Prediger, Mystiker*, 34.
12. *Counsels* 3; DW V, 196/EE, 250.          13. *Counsels* 6; DW V, 208/EE, 253.

In this very interesting passage, Eckhart offers a critique of theological discourse that makes clear that the created "I" can never capture "God" in a thought or an image. If it thinks that it can do so, it falls into idolatry. Thoughts and images of God are nothing but human creations that vanish as soon as the subject who thinks them vanishes. Letting-go, however, does not "think" of God in this manner, because it results in the abandonment of the "I" that makes such thinking possible in the first place. Letting-go brings us into a true "possession" of God in which God is "present" and "above the notion of men and of all created things."

Clear from the above passage is that Eckhart does not think God becomes present in the manner that Heidegger critiques in *Being and Time* as "present-to-hand"—i.e., the de-temporalized, "look" of the thing that becomes an "object" or re-presentation in the human mind in a "metaphysics of presence." Rather, Eckhart makes clear that God is present in the released soul as the primal "enveloping" ground of all of its actions, thoughts, and volitions. Thus, Eckhart says:

So a man must be penetrated (*durchgangen*) with the divine presence (*gegenwerticheit*), and be shaped through and through (*durchformet*) with the shape of the God he loves, and be present in him, so that God's presence may shine out to him without any effort. What is more, in all things let him acquire nakedness, and let him always remain free of things. But at the beginning there must be attentiveness and a careful formation within himself, like a schoolboy setting himself to learn.[14]

Only the genuine freedom that the soul finds in letting-go and love for God allows God to be present to the soul. What makes God present is not an objectifying gaze but the liberating letting-go of self-abandoning love.

Thus the soul, in being released into freedom, is also released into love. For love releases self-will from itself and this releasement from self-will, in turn, releases love from the soul. And with this love comes a knowledge that, Eckhart claims, is incomparably better than any knowledge imparted by God through an angel or a special illumination. The higher type of knowledge occurs

when a man, through the love and intimacy that exist between his God and him, trusts in him so fully and is so certain of him that he cannot doubt. What

14. *Counsels* 6; DW V, 208–09/EE, 254.

makes him so certain is that he loves God in all his creatures without any distinction. And even if all God's creatures were to deny him and adjure him, yes, if God himself were to deny him, he would not mistrust; for love cannot mistrust, love has trust in everything that is good.[15]

Again, here Eckhart describes a type of knowledge without a speculative object but rather a knowledge that wells up from the ground of the released soul's utter freedom. Because the soul has abandoned itself in love, it also has abandoned all distinctions and limits of finite being. In other words, such a soul becomes fully intellectual because the nature of the intellect is to transcend all distinctions of genera and species. In its loving freedom, the released or *gelâzen* soul transcends itself and all created things insofar as no created thing can satisfy its infinite desire and yet, in a dialectic very reminiscent of Augustine and Bernard,[16] the soul also finds the ground of its very being in this love that abandons all things because, in this abandonment, one finds the ground of the self.

Thus, in the chapter of the *Counsels* on the theme of "zeal," Eckhart remarks: "People ought to learn to be free of their works as they perform them."[17] Activity in the world is unavoidable; indeed, it is necessary for full unity with God to be released from self-absorbed inaction.[18] The "practiced man" is so abandoned from his created self that he sees all things not as in a re-presentation of "outward things" but as they are in the divine

15. *Counsels* 15; DW V, 240–41/EE, 264.

16. Thus, for Bernard of Clairvaux, the precondition for the love of God in which the soul is transformed into God is the annihilation of the self. To illustrate this process of mystical union through love, Bernard employs some striking metaphors: "o pura et defaecata intentio voluntatis! eo certe defaecatior et purior, quo in ea de proprio nil jam admistum relinquitur: eo suavior et dulcior, quo totum divinum est quod sentitur. Sic affici, deificari est. Quomodo stilla aquae modica, multo infusa vino, deficere a se tota videtur, dum et saporem vini induit, et colorem; et quomodo ferrum ignitum et candens, igni simillimum fit, pristina propriaque forma exutum; et quomodo solis luce perfusus aer in eamdem transformatur luminis claritatem, adeo ut non tam illuminatus, quam ipsum lumen esse videatur: sic omnem tunc in sanctis humanam affectionem quodam ineffabili modo necesse erit a semetipsa liquescere, atque in Dei penitus trasfundi voluntatem. Alioquin quomodo omnia in omnibus erit Deus, si in homine de homine quidquam supererit? Manebit quidem substantia, sed in alia forma, alia gloria, aliaque potentia." *De Diligendo Deo*, IX, 28. Eckhart most probably took over, at least in part, this dialectic of emptiness/annihilation and fullness from Bernard, except that Eckhart stresses much more the role and nature of the *intellect* as making this dialectic possible. For a fuller treatment of the relation between detachment and theories of the intellect see my article, "Meister Eckhart's Metaphysics of Detachment," 35–54.

17. *Counsels* 21; DW V, 276/EE, 274.

18. *Counsels* 21; DW V, 276–77/EE, 274–75.

inwardness, which is to say, in their divine idea. And this way of seeing results in a practical imperative: "A man should accustom himself to seeking and wanting nothing for himself in anything, and to finding and accepting God in everything."[19]

This dialectic of letting-go Eckhart expresses in this way: "If we strip ourselves of everything external *(wir uns blôz halten der dinge, diu ûzer uns sint)* . . . God will wholly become my own, with all that he is and all that he can bestow, as much my own *(mîn eigen sîn)* as his own, neither less nor more."[20] The soul, therefore, is not completely free and abandoned until God has moved into the soul and completed the work of abandonment. The whole point of letting-go is to let God be God, by whatever means he may work.[21] Thus ethical actions or works of love are not just accidental features or results of letting-go but their ground and completion. Eckhart remarks that it is not enough to have a "good will," for, he says, "will" must be understood in two senses: one that is "accidental" *(ungewerenter)* and one that is "determining, creative, habitual *(zuoverhengender, machender, gewenter)*."[22] All created wills are accidental; only the divine will is essential, which is to say, "determining, creative, habitual." Thus, we must surrender our accidental will to the essential, creative will. By doing so, we transcend time, for in such letting-go, we are detached from all that is past and all that is yet to come.[23]

In this context Eckhart expands upon his concept of the nobleman in *The Book of "Benedictus": Of the Nobleman*, from his later time in Strasbourg. Here, as always, Eckhart takes as his hermeneutical lead a passage from the Gospel of Luke (19:12): "A noble man went out into a far country to obtain for himself a kingdom and returned." Eckhart comments upon this verse, "Our Lord teaches us in these words how noble man has been created in his nature, and how divine that is which he can attain by grace, and also how man should attain to it. And in these words much of Holy Scripture is touched upon."[24]

19. *Counsels*, 21; DW V, 278/EE, 275.      20. *Counsels* 23; DW V, 298/EE, 282.

21. *Counsels* 23; DW V, 307–08/EE, 284–85: "There was a man who would dearly have liked to make a stream flow through his garden, and he said: 'If the water could be mine, I should not care what sort of channel brought it to me, iron or timber, bone or rusty metal, if only I could have the water.' And so anyone is quite wrong who worries about the means through which God is working his works in you, whether it be nature or grace. Just let him work, and just be at peace."

22. *Counsels* 21; DW V, 280/EE, 276.      23. *Counsels* 21; DW V, 280–81/EE, 276.

24. *Nobleman*, DW V, 109/EE, 240.

Three things are to be noted in this statement. The first is the "noble-ness" of man's created nature. By virtue of his intellect, man is potential-ly conformed to all being as such and thus to God. In this way, human nature mirrors the divine nature, enfolding all things, both material and spiritual in itself. The second thing to note is that man can attain to the divine by grace. While noble in his nature, man cannot attain to the divine except by God's grace. Nevertheless, man is capable of receiving that grace by virtue of the nobility of his nature. Third and most important is what Eckhart says at the end, that "in these words much of Holy Scripture is touched upon." Both the nobility of human nature and its actualization by divine grace are the marrow of sacred Scripture. Indeed, as we shall see, the Nobleman is not just the *message* of sacred Scripture, but more impor-tantly sacred Scripture is the *vehicle* in and through which the Nobleman is actualized, while the Nobleman is the one in whom the inner meaning of the Scriptures becomes known and lived among us..

That the human being is a microcosm reflective of all of creation and therefore of God is something that Eckhart mentions right at the begin-ning of the sermon, taking it, in fact, as a basic presupposition of what follows:

In the first place we should know what is very evident, that man has in himself a twofold nature, body and spirit. Therefore it is said in a treatise that whoever knows himself knows all created things, because all created things are either body or spirit. That is why scripture says about what is human that there is in us one outward man and a second inner man (2 Cor 4:16).[25]

Eckhart then goes on to develop considerably this distinction between the "inner man" and the "outer man." The outer man is that "part" or aspect of the human being which is directed outward toward sensible, created things, that aspect of the human being that is "fallen" insofar as it "falls from itself" into the created order and away from God (although the body and the created world as such are good). The "outer man" has become en-trapped in the "snares and traps" of the body as in the "snares and weeds" of the field (an allusion to the parable of the sower in Matthew 13:25), and as such, the "outer man is the bad tree that can never produce good fruit."[26] In other words, the human person, insofar as he or she acts according to

25. *Nobleman*, DW V, 109/EE, 240.
26. *Nobleman*, DW V, 111/EE, 241.

the "outer man," cannot produce works of love or of intellection, only acts of vice and wickedness.

By contrast, the "inner man" is that aspect of the human being that is directed toward God alone. Eckhart compares this inner man to a "seed" that, properly tended and cared for, blossoms into a tree that produces works of love and righteousness. This seed of the inner man is always there, even in those people who have chosen to live in and out of the outer man. Eckhart quotes Origen regarding this truth: "Because God himself has sowed and planted and given life to this seed, even though it may be overgrown and hidden, it will never be destroyed or extinguished completely; it will glow and shine, gleam and burn, and it will never cease to turn toward God."[27]

Eckhart then delineates six stages by which the human being turns from living in and out of the outer man to living in and out of the inner man. The details of these stages need not be elaborated here, except to say that in the final stage, the soul must become "free of images" and "transformed into the image of God's everlastingness," becoming oblivious to created things and temporality. In this final stage, the soul no longer *has* any images but *is* an image by grace of God and becomes a child of God, "for the end of the inner man and of the new man is eternal life."[28]

The "new man," meaning the soul that lives in and out of the inner man, has let all that is finite and temporal, all that is created, "drop away." Indeed, Eckhart compares this process to that of a sculptor who does not so much "create" a statue from scratch as simply "liberate" the form from the marble or wood:

And there is still another simile. The sun never stops shining; but if there is a cloud or mist between us and the sun, we are not aware that it is shining. And if the eye is diseased in itself or is ailing or covered, it knows nothing of the sunshine. And sometimes I have made an evident comparison: If a master craftsman makes figures out of wood or stone, he does not introduce the figure into the wood, but he cuts away the fragments that had hidden and concealed the figure; he gives nothing to the wood, rather he takes away from it, cutting away its surface and removing its rough covering, and then what had lain hidden beneath shines out. This is the treasure that lay hidden in the field, as our Lord says in the gospel (Mt 13:44).[29]

27. *Nobleman,* DW V, 111/EE, 241. See Origen, *Homilies on Genesis,* 13.4.
28. *Nobleman,* DW V, 112/EE, 242.        29. *Nobleman,* DW V, 113/EE, 243.

Thus is the inner man like the figure that is liberated from the marble or wood by the sculptor, who is, of course, God.[30] Eckhart sums up his point by quoting St. Augustine: "'When all of man's soul mounts into eternity to God alone, the image of God appears and shines'; but if the soul is distracted toward external things, even to the outward exercise of virtues, then this image is wholly concealed."[31] Thus, every Christian must "go out of" him- or herself so that he or she may "return" to what is within, formless and without image, which is for Eckhart the whole point of the verse from Luke:

> And that is what our Lord means by these words when he says, that "a nobleman went out," because man must go out of every image and out of himself and out of everything, he must go far indeed, and become quite unlike all this, truly, if he wishes to and shall receive the Son, and become son in the bosom and heart of the Father.[32]

The "far land" in which the nobleman obtained a "kingdom" is no other than the inner man, united continually with God and united with God in such a way that no form or image comes between the soul and God. In that inner "place" then, the soul receives the Son and becomes "born" in turn as a son of God. In this way, the inner meaning of Scripture is fulfilled in a pure intellectuality where the soul is "disposed" of all images so that it itself may be conformed to the Son of God, Christ, as his Image, who is also the core or marrow of Scripture.

As Eckhart argues further, "Every kind of medium is alien to God. 'I am,' God says, 'The first and the last' (Rv 22:13)." Since God contains within himself all distinction, God cannot be distinguished from anything; he is entirely one and indivisible. As such, there can be no medium in and through which the soul can know God; God himself must be he in and through whom one knows God. For Eckhart, only through Scripture does one come to know God as God, quoting the book of Revelation to that effect. Only to the degree that the human being is stripped of his or her usual ways of knowing, does he or she come to know God as God. Eckhart refers again here to the (probably fanciful) etymology of the word for

---

30. Here we have an echo, probably relayed through Augustine, of Plotinus's treatise on beauty in *Enneads*, I, 6, in which he uses the metaphor of "carving our own statue," liberating the divine within by cutting off the "excess" of worldly attachments.

31. *Nobleman*, DW V, 113–14/EE, 243.       32. *Nobleman*, DW V, 114/EE, 243.

"man" in Latin, *homo*, being derived from the world *humilis*, of the "earth" or "ground," and from which is derived the word "humility." But this "poverty" and "humility" of man is, as we have pointed out before, an indication for Eckhart of humanity's great nobility as well, because the human being is so poor that he lacks any defined or limited essence and thus becomes capable of unity with God:

> Nor, indeed, has man in one sense anything in common with anything, that is, he is not formed or made like this thing or that thing, and he knows nothing about nothing, so that one finds nowhere anything of this nothing in him, and this nothing is thus wholly taken away from him so that in him there is found only life, being, truth and goodness. Thus he who is such a man is "a nobleman," indeed neither less nor more.[33]

The great paradox here is that the Nobleman is the man who is so "poor" in himself that he lives only in and out of the being, truth, and goodness of God, becoming "noble" by grace or participation, though he or she is utterly humble by nature. Indeed, such is the conformity of the Nobleman to God and the divine Truth that he abandons all human ways of knowing God and subsists entirely in God's Word.

In this connection, Eckhart discusses a crucial question: which is superior and makes us more blessed—*to be* united to God, or *to know* that one is united to God? On the face of it, Eckhart says, it would seem that the latter is superior and makes us more blessed. After all, if, as he puts it, "I possessed all joy, and I did not know it, how could that help me and what joy would that be to me?" But Eckhart immediately follows, "Yet I say certainly that this is not so." He continues:

> It is only true that without that the soul would not be blessed; but blessedness does not consist in this, for the first thing in which blessedness consists is when the soul contemplates God directly. From there, out of God's ground, it takes all its being and its life and makes everything that it is, and it knows nothing about knowing or love or about anything at all. It comes to rest completely and only in the being of God, and it knows nothing there except being and God.[34]

Blessedness and knowledge consist in the direct (*blôz*) union with God. As soon as one "knows" oneself to be united to God, that unity and oneness are broken and one, paradoxically, has fallen away from that high-

33. *Nobleman*, DW V, 116/EE, 244.
34. *Nobleman*, DW V, 116–17/EE, 245.

est knowledge of God. As Eckhart further explains, knowledge consists in unity of being with what one knows, not merely in *having* an image or intelligible species of what one knows in the mind:

But when the soul knows and perceives that it contemplates, perceives and loves God, this is in the natural order a going out and return to the starting point; for no one knows himself as being white except the man who is in fact white. Therefore whoever knows himself as being white is building and erecting his knowledge upon being white, and he does not receive his knowledge without a medium or without previous knowledge of the color; but he derives his perception of it and his knowledge about it from things that are white, and so he forms his perception not purely from the color as such, but his perceiving and knowledge are formed from what is colored, that is, what is white, and he then recognizes himself as white. But "white" is far inferior to, more external than "being white." The wall is something very different from the foundation on which the wall is built.[35]

As we have seen before, according to Aristotle, all knowledge is a union of the form of the thing known with the intellect of the knower such that the form in the mind of the knower and the form of the thing known is one and the same. In knowing created things, the form in the mind of the knower is of a higher order, has more reality because it is pure form, than the form as it exists in the created, material thing itself.

But with knowledge of divine things, the situation is reversed: the form as it exists in itself is of a higher nature, has more "being" or reality, than the form as it exists in the mind of the finite, created knower. Thus, to the example of "white," Eckhart says, my knowledge of "white" is ultimately based upon "being white": knowledge must be rooted in actual being. Only by *existing in* God can we have any knowledge *of* God. And we exist in God by receiving and subsisting in Christ.

Hence, once more, Eckhart emphasizes the ultimate role of Christ in all human knowing: in being united to Christ, we do not *have* an image of God, but *become* that image by grace. In knowing Christ, our knowledge of God is based not on any medium, on any intelligible species or image, but on the actual *being* of Christ. Thus for the Christian, to know in its highest sense is, quite literally, to know all things *in* Christ, i.e., in Christ as the *fundamentum cognitionis,* not as an object of cognition but as the ontologi-

---

35. *Nobleman,* DW V, 117/EE, 245.

cal foundation of our knowing. And if Christ is the core and marrow of holy Scripture, then the Christian comes to know Christ and hence any metaphysical knowledge worth having, only in and through the careful reading of and listening to Scripture. In turn, in a typical hermeneutical circle, it is in knowing Christ that the Christian is able then to interpret Scripture properly by actually *enacting,* by *living out,* its inner meaning.

Thus, toward the end of the sermon, Eckhart reminds us that the order of nature and the divine order are, in many respects, opposite, mirror images of each other:

> Nature begins its work in what is feeblest, but God begins his work in what is most perfect. Nature forms the man from the child and hen from the egg, but God makes the man before the child and the hen before the egg. Nature makes the wood first warm, then hot, and so it forms the being of the fire; but God first gives being to all created things, and thereafter gives in time, and yet gives outside of time and outside of everything that pertains to it. And God gives the Holy Spirit before the gifts of the Holy Spirit.[36]

Here Eckhart refers to the Aristotelian principle that actuality is ultimately prior to potentiality: although in time, the egg is prior to the hen, it is the hen that has ontological priority because it is the end or goal toward which the egg develops and is actualized. Likewise in human cognition, we first receive the sense data, from which are then abstracted the intelligible forms by which we know the objects *as* this or that thing. Our intellect is first in potentiality to the forms of things; only in the act of cognition does the intellect acquire actuality by acquiring the actual forms of things.

But in divine matters, Eckhart argues, it is the reverse: the pure actuality of God's Being is prior to any knowledge we may have of God. We do not come to a knowledge of God by abstracting the divine Word from our sensible experience, but rather the divine Word first speaks to us, and only then do we, can we, make sense of its meaning in our sensible and corporeal existence. Christ is the self-subsistent Word, *Ratio,* or *Logos* that makes possible any knowledge of God on the part of the creature. All our talk about God and thinking about God presuppose this highest unity of the Word in God beyond language or thought, just as the heat of the fire presupposes the being of the fire:

36. *Nobleman,* DW V, 118/EE, 246.

So I say that there is no blessedness unless man perceives and knows well that he contemplates and perceives God, and yet God forbid that my blessedness should consist in that. If someone is satisfied with something else, let him keep it for himself, but I pity him. The heat of the fire and the being of the fire are quite different, utterly separated in nature from one another, and their only proximity is in terms of time and place. God's contemplating and our contemplating are wholly separate and different from one another.[37]

Eckhart does concede here that the truly blessed man does indeed know that he knows and loves God, but merely emphasizes that this is not the foundation for his blessedness. Nothing human or created can be such a foundation. God can know God and the human soul can know God only in and through God, just as the soul can know the potential only through the actual, the less perfect through the more perfect. To contemplate God truly, one must contemplate God through God, and that means contemplating God in and through Christ, who is revealed to us in the Gospel. Again taking up the theme of the sermon drawn from the Gospel of Luke, Eckhart notes that the Nobleman "went into a far country," meaning he went out of himself and the finite categories of his human reason and "inherited a kingdom," blessed union with God himself. In other words, the Gospel here refers to itself: it is that "far country" into which the Christian must enter in order to obtain for himself a "kingdom." Then he must return to "this world," to bear forth acts of love and mercy.

### Beati pauperes spiritu: "Blessed Are the Poor in Spirit"

The dialectic of Eckhart's Nobleman is clear: the more the believer empties himself of what is creaturely and becomes "nothing," the more he or she is united to and lives out of God's superabundant Being. His is a dialectic of emptiness and fullness: the more empty the creature becomes of himself, the more full he becomes of God. A similar dialectic is at work in Ibn 'Arabi as well. Indeed, in Eckhart, as in Ibn 'Arabi, this dialectic comes to be expressed in feminine metaphors, in Eckhart's case in the metaphors of virginity and birth. For both, the ability of the woman to conceive and give birth is pregnant, so to speak, with metaphysical meaning that surpasses merely biological or social facts. The woman here is a symbol and,

37. *Nobleman,* DW V, 118/EE, 246.

like all authentic symbols rooted in revelation, has great power. To the modern mind, such symbolism may seem arbitrary, but then again, it is no more arbitrary than the modern tendency to assert that the biological or social meaning of the phenomena is the "real" or "primary" meaning. For Eckhart, as for Ibn 'Arabi, the truth of the symbolism here is found not in biological research or sociological analysis but in the transformation that this symbol works on the inner life of the one who understands it.

One of the places in which Eckhart uses feminine metaphors most extensively is in his vernacular sermon with the Latin title *Intravit Jesus in quoddam castellum et mulier quaedam, Marthe nomine, excepit illum in domum suam* (Lk 10:38). This is translated as "Jesus entered a certain village, where a woman named Martha welcomed him into her home." Eckhart, however, translated the Latin of the Vulgate very freely into German as "Our Lord Jesus Christ went up into a little town, and was received by a virgin who was a wife." In this rather free translation, Eckhart will lay emphasis on all the elements of the verse.

First, Eckhart says, Jesus was received by a "virgin," and of this "virgin" he says: "'Virgin' is as much as to say a person who is free of all alien images, as free as he was when he was not."[38] Eckhart then immediately anticipates the objection, how is this possible? How can anyone think "nothing"? Eckhart responds that we can be free of images simply by being devoid of any possessiveness with regard to them. He does not hold to the absurdity that we can render our minds totally "blank," without content. He does think, however, that we can have images, thoughts, and concepts without any possessiveness, any sense of "mine" or "thine." Nor does being a "virgin" in this deeper metaphysical sense mean that the "virgin" soul must be free of any work or action. To the contrary, this "virginity" removes all obstacles to free and perfect action: "But I say that because a man is a virgin, that does not deprive him at all of any of the works he has ever done; but all this permits him to remain, maidenly and free, without any obstacles between him and supreme truth, just as Jesus is empty and free and maidenly in himself."[39]

Spiritual virginity, however, is not the end or goal of the spiritual life. This virginity must be perfected by becoming a "wife":

38. *Pr.* 2; DW I, 24–25/EE, 177.
39. *Pr.* 2; DW I, 26/EE, 177.

Now mark what I say and pay careful attention! For if a man were to be a virgin forever, no fruit would come from him. If he is to become fruitful, he must of necessity be a wife. "Wife" is the noblest word one can apply to the soul, much nobler than "virgin." That a man conceives God in himself is good, and in his conceiving he is a maiden. But that God should become fruitful in him is better; for the only gratitude for a gift is to be fruitful with the gift, and then the spirit is a wife, in its gratitude giving birth in return, when he for God gives birth to Jesus into the heart of the Father.[40]

The soul should not be a virgin for its own sake, but rather for the sake of being a "wife," i.e., bearing fruit in the form of acts of love, rooted in a continual awareness of God's presence in the soul. The emptiness of virginity must issue in the fullness and fruitfulness of the "wifely" state, which is why Eckhart asserts that the title "wife" is the *noblest* title: for it indicates a full participation in the mighty work of God. Eckhart, of course, here goes against the tendency of his time to exalt the "virginal" over the "wifely." But for Eckhart what is at stake is not so much the worldly or even spiritual status of these "states" but rather a deeper understanding of what they mean. For what their spiritual meaning reveals is the inner dialectical unity of the "virginal" and the "wifely" and thus of the contemplative and active life, and of the clerical and lay state.

Indeed, Eckhart continues the theme of nobility in this sermon by saying how the wife bears fruit (i.e., Jesus)

becoming fruitful from the noblest ground of all – or, to put it better, from that same ground where the Father is bearing his eternal Word, from that ground is she fruitfully bearing his eternal Word, from that ground is she fruitfully bearing with him.[41]

This "noblest ground" is the innermost ground of the soul, where God bears forth his only Son, the eternal Word. Here in this innermost ground, the soul touches eternity:

And I have often said that there is a power in the soul that touches neither time nor flesh. It flows from the spirit and remains in the spirit and is wholly spiritual. In this power God is always verdant and blossoming in all the joy and honor that he is in himself.[42]

---

40. *Pr.* 2; DW I, 27/EE, 178.    41. *Pr.* 2; DW I, 31/EE, 179.
42. *Pr.* 2; DW I, 32/EE, 179.

Here God eternally bears forth his Son, and if a soul could only have a glimpse of that power in itself, it would share in that great divine joy, even if wracked by extreme poverty and suffering. Eckhart says of such a soul:

Yes, even if after this God never gave him the kingdom of heaven, he still would have received a reward great enough for all that he had ever suffered, for God is present in this power as he is in the eternal now. If the spirit were always united with God in this power, the man could never grow old; for that now in which God made the first man, and the now in which the last man will have his end, and the now in which I am talking, they are all the same in God, and there is not more than the one now. Now you can see that this man lives in one light with God, and therefore there is not in him either suffering or the passage of time, but an unchanging eternity.[43]

To have access to this "noblest ground" is to have access to eternity and to the eternal meanings of all of God's Word as found in Scripture. In this noblest ground the soul lives and knows out of the eternal "now" in which God made the "first man" and God made the "last man." In this ground, the soul finds the Alpha and the Omega of humanity and, therefore, of God's revelation of himself to humanity. In short, one finds here the *eschatological* dimension of Eckhart's thought: the "end times" do not lie in any temporal future, but lie in the innermost ground of the soul, where the "now" of the end coincides with the "now" of the beginning and the "now" of the present.

This tapping into the eternal "now" of God's life is, for Eckhart, the mark of true intellectuality, for from this vantage point, the soul is able to view all things *sub speciei aeternitatis.* Eckhart, however, in this sermon calls this intellectual power a "spark" of the soul, a supernatural light within the soul that allows it to know *sub speciei aeternitatis.* But it is only a "spark," because it is also something higher than or "above" the soul, coming down into it like a spark that sputters forth into the darkness from a far larger raging fire. In fact, there can be *no name* that is adequate to describe or identify this intellectual power:

I have sometimes said that there is a power in the spirit that alone is free. Sometimes I have said that it is a guard of the spirit; sometimes I have said that it is a light of the spirit; sometimes I have said that it is a spark. But now I say that it is neither this nor that, and yet it is a something that is higher above this and that

43. Pr. 2; DW I, 33–34/EE, 179.

than heaven is above the earth. And therefore I now give it finer names than I have ever given it before, and yet whatever finer names, whatever words we use, they are telling lies, and it is far above them. It is free of all names, it is bare of all forms, wholly empty and free, as God himself is empty and free. It is so utterly one and simple, as God is one and simple, that man cannot in any way look into it. The same power of which I have spoken, in which God is verdant and growing with all his divinity, and the spirit in God—with this same power is the Father bringing to birth his Only-Begotten Son as truly as in himself, for he truly lives in this power, and the spirit with the Father brings to birth the same Only-Begotten Son, and it begets itself the same Son, and is the same Son in this light, and it is the truth. If you could look upon this with my heart, you would well understand what I say, for it is true, and it is Truth's own self that says it.[44]

Eckhart emphasizes that this power, this "spark," is "neither this nor that." As such, it is both purely intellectual and utterly free: intellectual because, as we saw in a previous chapter, intellect must be free of any "this or that" in order to know every "this or that" as "this or that"; free because, neither this nor that, it is not conditioned by any creature or thing. It is so utterly "one" that "man cannot in any way look into it." That is, man cannot look into it precisely because this power constitutes the *ground* of his knowing and of his freedom. He cannot make this power an *object* of his reason or will for the simple reason that this ground or spark makes all thought and free action possible. As a result, human reason can never have access to this inner ground; the human soul can have access to this inner ground only by the grace of Christ, because it is Christ who is born in this inner ground, and by allowing Christ to be born in me I enter fully into this inner ground and into its unfathomable understanding and absolute freedom.

Thus, the final metaphor that Eckhart uses to describe this innermost ground or spark of the soul is one that takes us back to the Gospel verse that forms the exegetical basis of the sermon—that of a "little castle" or "little town" (*castellum*). Eckhart says that we can conceive this innermost ground of the soul as a "little castle" or "town" out of which the soul looks down on all things, but which it is unable to look into. Indeed, this little town is so utterly one and simple that not even God can look into it, for it is above both the soul and "God" conceived as the first cause of all things and a distinct being, even if the highest being. Eckhart says:

44. *Pr.* 2; DW I, 39–41/EE, 180–81.

This little town is so truly one and simple, and this simple one is so exalted above every manner and every power, that no power, no manner, not God himself may look at it. It is as true that this is true and that I speak truly as that God is alive! God himself never for an instant looks into it, never yet did he look on it, so far as he possesses himself in the manner and according to the properties of his Persons. It is well to observe this, because this simple one is without manner and without properties. And therefore, if God were ever to look upon it, that must cost him all his divine names and the properties of his Persons; that he must wholly forsake, if he is ever once to look into it. But as he is simply one, without any manner and properties, he is not Father or Son or Holy Spirit, and yet he is something that is neither this nor that.[45]

This passage is quite striking indeed, for it implies that God must also become "detached" from all his properties and become a "virgin" who is also a "wife." Even more, he seems to say that the Trinity, with its three Persons of the Father, the Son, and the Holy Spirit, is a property true of God only on a certain level, to be surpassed by penetrating to the innermost Godhead or "ground" of God. Still, if we look at it in the context of the entire sermon, Eckhart's intentions appear far less radical, if no less profound. First, God must not "give up" his properties because, speaking precisely, God always is already detached from his "properties," which themselves acquire any sense only in God's relations with creatures. As for seeming to "surpass" the Trinity in this teaching, we must see this as a dialectical move on Eckhart's part: for the wife to bear fruit, she must become a virgin, just as for the soul to realize the fullness of God's Being, it must become nothing. So, too, with God himself: God in the fruitfulness of interpersonal love that is the Trinity must also be in himself utterly free and one in order for the fruitfulness of the Trinity to arise. Neither moment in this dialectic is ontologically or logically prior: emptiness must issue in fullness, and fullness must issue out of emptiness. So the oneness of God must necessarily bear fruit in the Trinity while the Trinity must presuppose for its selfless love the inner emptiness and oneness of the Godhead.

Perhaps the most striking of Eckhart's sermons on the Nobleman is *Beati pauperes spiritu*.[46] As the title of this sermon indicates, Eckhart deals

---

45. *Pr.* 2; DW I, 43–44/EE, 181.

46. *Pr.* 52; DW II, 486–506. Eckhart does not use the words "detachment" or "detaching" in this sermon, but, as Bernard McGinn remarks regarding it: "its fifteen references to the adjective 'free' (*vri*) and three uses of 'empty' (*ledic*)—both of God and the soul—show that it must be

with the notion of "*spiritual poverty*," which he argues has, beyond our usual notion of material poverty, an existential and noetic dimension. Thus, he says that a truly poor person, one who is not only materially poor but also "spiritually" or "inwardly" poor, "wants nothing, and knows nothing, and has nothing." Indeed, such a person is so inwardly poor that he "is as free of his own created will as he was when he did not exist." And, "so long as you have a will to fulfill God's will, and a longing for God and for eternity, then you are not poor; for a poor man is one who has a will and longing for nothing."[47] Indeed, the spiritually poor person is poor even of her own will: she is free of all subjectivity and subjectivism. Therefore, spiritual poverty, in the context of Eckhart's thought, has more than a mere social or moral meaning but an *ontological meaning*: it signifies the proper comportment of the soul to *existence itself*.

Indeed, such a spiritually poor soul is so free of subjectivity that it no longer knows, loves, or experiences God as an object, first cause, or ground of beings, because, according to Eckhart, in spiritual poverty, the soul comes to know God as its ownmost inner ground, which is no-thing. "My" ground and "God's" ground are the same, for when I am spiritually poor, I live not out of my own resources as a created being nor out of any other created being, but out of the divine living, working, and knowing. In spiritual poverty, we discover that what we call "God" is not some being "out there" like any other being. To think this way would be to reduce God to the level of another creature—an exalted one, to be sure, but still a limited, created being. The soul that is released from all finite things is also released from such a "God"; rather, it comes to live, know, and exist out of the living, knowing, and truly existent God revealed to us through Christ. The "empty" soul is so empty of creatures that it resides in God as God was before there was any creation:

When I stood in my first cause (*êrsten sache*), I then had no "God," and then I was my own cause (*sache mîn selbes*). I wanted nothing, I longed for nothing, for I was an empty being (*ledic sîn*), and the only truth in which I rejoiced was in the knowledge of myself. Then it was myself I wanted and nothing else. What I wanted I was, and what I was I wanted; and so I stood, empty of God and of

---

ranked among the premier Eckhartian texts on the need for radical deconstruction of the created self." Bernard McGinn, *The Mystical Thought of Meister Eckhart*, 135.

47. Pr. 52; DW II, 491/EE, 200.

everything. But when I went out from my own free will and received my created being, then I had a "God," for before there were any creatures, God was not "God," but he was what he was. But when creatures came to be and received their created being, then God was not "God" in himself, but he was "God" in the creatures.[48]

The "God" who is the "highest being," "first cause," and "ruler" of creation is only a consequence of creation, because creation presupposes a duality of creator and created. From the standpoint of created being, then, "God" stands apart from all things and is, therefore, a being as well, only one with infinite power.

But such a "God," Eckhart asserts, is only one, incomplete aspect of the God revealed in sacred Scripture,[49] because the God who is first cause is only the God of the philosophers—an abstraction and principle that is not a living concern for the soul in search of the living God of Scripture. It is significant here to note that the Middle High German word that Eckhart uses for "cause"—*sache*—also means "thing," "issue," "matter of concern."[50] When Eckhart thinks of God in German, it is not merely as a metaphysical principle but as *the* issue or matter of concern for the soul. To drive home his point in as emphatic a manner as he can, Eckhart goes so far as to say, "Now I say that God, so far as he is 'God,' is not the perfect end of

48. Pr. 52; DW II, 492–93/EE, 200. Michael Sells, in his book *Mystical Languages of Unsaying*, criticizes the use of the inverted commas, arguing that it diverts us from Eckhart's project of deconstructing our language about God in order to allow the soul to enter into a deeper experience of what the word "God" refers to (and besides, the original Middle High German text never uses the inverted commas). Sells is no doubt correct in this. Nevertheless, I think that McGinn is justified in adding the inverted commas in order to stress the crucial distinction that Eckhart is trying to make in the sermon between the metaphysical (or ontotheological) "God" and the living, revealed/concealed God "beyond 'God.'" To the reader, all I can say is that in reading the above passage from Eckhart, it would be good to read it again, but this time subtracting mentally all inverted commas.

49. In asserting this, Eckhart is only following Thomas Aquinas. For Aquinas, metaphysics does not treat of God per se but only being qua being. If it treats of God at all, it treats of God in an indirect manner as the *cause* of being qua being or *esse commune*. Only sacred Scripture deals with God per se. Thus theology is twofold: there is the indirect natural theology of metaphysics, which has being qua being as its subject matter, and there is the direct theology of revelation, which has Holy Writ as its subject matter. See Jan Aertsen, "Ontology and Henology in Medieval Philosophy," 120–40; Aertsen, "Die tranzendentalienlehre bei Thomas von Aquin in ihren historischen Hintergründen und philosophischen Motiven"; and Albert Zimmermann, *Ontologie oder Metaphysik?*

50. See Heidegger's essay "The Thing," in *Poetry, Language, Thought*, trans. Albert Hofstadter (New York: Harper & Row, 1971), 174.

created beings. . . . So therefore let us pray to God that we may be free of 'God' (*wir gotes ledic werden*)."[51] For Eckhart, the truly released or spiritually poor soul has no "God" precisely because such a soul has no "God" as object or metaphysical first cause. Such a soul is "empty" (*ledic*) of the notion of "god." Rather, its God is the living God who reveals himself in the ground of the soul; who is both within and without, transcendent and immanent, perfectly one, beyond all metaphysical distinctions. For Eckhart, God is "nothing" in that God is "neither this nor that."[52] In Eckhart's thought, however, to realize that God is "no-thing" is to open oneself up to God's giving birth to his Son in the soul. For it is out of the inner emptiness and nothingness that the divine birth comes.[53] "It is characteristic of creatures that they make something out of something, while it is characteristic of God that he makes something out of nothing."[54] This passage is important because it shows us that Eckhart is not indulging in some sort of existential nihilism; for Eckhart, the "nothingness" of God with respect to us is the utter fullness and overabundant reality of God in himself.

The released soul is, for Eckhart, *causa sui* because, released from all caused creatures, what it is and what it wills are in perfect conformity. Such a soul is so "empty" of creatures that all it wants is "itself," which is what it is in God or the Word. Indeed, Eckhart asserts that a spiritually poor soul does not live for "himself or for the truth or for God." He or she is completely free and unconditioned by any created thing. He or she lives in such a way that he or she does not know that God is "in" him or her, being as "free of his own knowing as he was when he was not." In other words, such a soul does not and cannot adhere to any immanentist pantheism, for to say that God is only "within" is to make God into some absolute "subject," which is just as erroneous as making God an absolute "object." The attitude of such a soul is, therefore, "Let God perform what he will, and let man be free," for to be released into the true, living, revealed God and not the "God of the philosophers" is also to be released into freedom.[55]

51. *Pr.* 52; DW II, 493/EE, 200.

52. See: *Pr.* 37; DW II, 331, and *Pr.* 71; DW III, 223. See also: Holger Helting, "Heidegger and Meister Eckhart," in *Herkunft aber bleibt stets Zukunft* (Frankfurt a.m.: Vittorio Klostermann, 1998), 94ff.

53. *Pr.* 39; DW II, 264.                    54. *Pr.* 39; DW II, 256.

55. *Pr.* 52; DW II, 494–5/EE, 201.

Thus, for Eckhart, blessedness consists neither in knowing nor in loving: "The authorities say that God is a being, and a rational one, and that he knows all things. I say that God is neither being nor rational, and that he does not know this or that. Therefore God is free of all things, and therefore he is all things (*Her umbe ist got ledic aller dinge, und her umbe ist er alliu dinge*)."[56] Only in God's utter freedom, in the groundlessness of God's nature, can anything be, because God, in his utter self-emptying letting-go, is the only one who can release all beings into existence. For Eckhart, creation, to the extent that we can talk intelligibly about it at all, is not some act of "making" (*techne*). Rather, it is an act of letting-go in which all beings, hitherto existing only as ideas in the divine intellect, are released into an existence of their own. Thus, for Eckhart, letting-go is both a creative and de-creative act, depending on one's standpoint: from the standpoint of the divine, it releases beings into existence and is therefore creative, while from the human or created standpoint, it "reverses" creation by stripping the creature of all that is created and returning it to its undifferentiated being in the divine.

The soul, then, lives out of God only when it is itself groundless and without even a "place" in which God can work, for the truly poor spirit is one whose "place" is not his own but God's. All this is difficult to understand, for Eckhart himself says that what he is saying "transcends grace and being and understanding and will and longing." According to Eckhart, divine grace does not give us a "new being" but rather returns us to what we primordially *are* in God: "When grace had finished and had perfected its work, then Paul remained what he was" (referring to Paul's rapture).[57] To become what we primordially are requires a metaphorical "death" to our created being and our created self, requires an utter trust and confidence in the workings of divine grace to make the soul "anew" into what it always was in its primordial being in God. The truth of human existence lies in the infinite openness that is the divine intellect in which all things subsist as ideas. What the fallen, sinful soul does, however, is make itself or some other created thing a finite god. As Eckhart says, "that God is 'God,' of that I am a cause; if I did not exist, God too would not be 'God'":

56. *Pr.* 52; DW II, 497/EE, 201.
57. *Pr.* 52; DW II, 502/EE, 202.

When man clings to place he clings to distinction. Therefore I pray to God that he may make me free of "God," for my real being is above God if we take "God" to be the beginning of created things. . . . And therefore I am unborn, and in the manner in which I am unborn I can never die. In my unborn manner I have been eternally, and am now, and shall eternally remain. What I am in the order of having been born, that will die and perish, for it is mortal, and so it must in time suffer corruption. In my birth all things were born and I was the cause of myself and of all things; and if I would have wished it, I would not be nor would all other things be. And if I did not exist, "God" would also not exist. That God is "God," of that I am a cause; if I did not exist, God too would not be "God." There is no need to understand this.[58]

In this "unborn" ideal mode, in which the soul was when it was not a creature and it had no objective "God," the soul is in eternity. To be "born" outside of God and into the distinction between creator and creature is to fall into time and corruption. As we saw in our introduction in discussing the work of Gershom Scholem, there is a Gnostic temptation (in the heretical sense) here: namely, to oppose the "evil" creator God to the "good" God "beyond God." But, I must repeat, this is not Eckhart's (or Ibn 'Arabi's) intention. The transcendent creator God of revelation is the *same* God who is beyond all relation to creation. Indeed, this point is the entire thrust of Eckhart's preaching: that God as he is in himself unites us to himself precisely *in and through* his general revelation in creation and especially in his specific revelation in the Word of the Gospel. God reveals himself to us first as creator, then as Word, but there is no contradiction or inconsistency here. Eckhart enjoins his listeners not to abandon the God of revelation but, to the contrary, to enter more deeply into that revelation, to actualize it and enact it in their own lives, in the here and now, in their created, temporal world, so that they may be joined in loving union with their Creator. This actualization of God in the human condition in all its fullness, including all its imperfection, for Eckhart, is the entire point of the Incarnation.

Eckhart says that a de-creative process must take place in the interior of the soul, if the soul is to know and be united with God. This process Eckhart describes with verbs like *entbilden* and *entwerden* ("un-form" and "un-become") as in this passage from the *Book of Divine Consolation:* "You must

58. *Pr.* 52; DW II, 502–4/EE, 202–3.

un-form (*entbildet*) yourself in such a way that you may be transformed (*überbildet*) in God alone."[59] That is, this process is one in which the soul becomes more deeply united to the same God revealed in creation, but as he is in himself apart from all reference to creation. For Eckhart, then, blessedness consists in "breaking through" to this "unborn" where there is eternity and where God is God not as first cause but as God:

A great authority says that his breaking through is nobler than his flowing out; and that is true. When I flowed out from God, all things said: "God is" (*got der ist*). And this cannot make me blessed, for with this I acknowledge that I am a creature. But in the breaking-through, when I come to be free of will of myself and of God's will and of all his works and of God himself, then I am above all created things, and I am neither God nor creature, but I am what I was and what I shall remain, now and eternally.[60]

To say that "God is" is to simply say that God is another being among beings and "is" just as a rock "is." But, as Eckhart says, this cannot make me "blessed" because it does not unite me to God in being, thinking, and acting. God's existence is dynamic and, most of all, *communicative*: it gives itself to creatures so that creatures may give themselves to him.

For Eckhart, we can think of God in truth only when we leave all created things behind and become receptive to the divine inflowing and become ourselves born of God as God's only-begotten Son. Only by returning to the point of birth, out of which all things come, can the soul then know God as God. Rather, for Eckhart, the God out of whom the detached soul lives, loves, and thinks is a "God beyond 'God,'" a God who is beyond all created concepts of God.[61] Indeed, Eckhart begins the sermon not by saying "Jesus said," but instead, "Blessedness opened its mouth to wisdom and said: 'Blessed are the poor in spirit, for the kingdom of heaven is theirs' (Mt 5:3)." The nature of true wisdom is such that it lets wisdom or blessedness speak for itself. The mark of the detached soul, the released intellect, is not to speak in any way for itself but to allow Wisdom to speak in and through itself. Thus, Eckhart follows by stating: "All angels and all saints and all who were ever born must keep silent when the Wisdom of

59. *BgT* 1; DW 5, 11.
60. *Pr.* 52; DW II, 504/EE, 203.
61. B. McGinn, "The God beyond God: Theology and Mysticism in the Thought of Meister Eckhart," *Journal of Religion* 61 (1981): 18.

the Father speaks, for all the Wisdom of the angels and of all created being is mere folly before the unfathomable Wisdom of God. It has said that the poor are blessed."[62] The Wisdom of the Father or God is none other, of course, than Christ. To be poor in spirit is, ultimately, to let Christ speak in oneself and through oneself to and in all things.

For Eckhart, the fact of the Incarnation contains the inner truth of Christianity. The Incarnation tells us that God in the person of Christ did not think "divinity something to be held onto" but that he "emptied himself" by becoming a human being (Phil 2:6–8). By doing so the eternal breaks into historical time and abiding truth into the world of shifting phenomena. The self-emptying love of the Trinity makes possible not only the releasement of all creatures into existence but also their return in and through the birth of the Son into the empty ground of the human soul. But for Eckhart, what is most significant about this teaching is that God did not become a human being once, in some distant time and place but that God is *always* giving birth to his Son and that this giving birth is always contemporaneous with the life of each and every released soul.

For Eckhart, the Christian life is the constant re-enactment of this birth into time and the created world. In a sense very reminiscent of Kierkegaard and Heidegger's notion of "repetition," the task of the soul is to be open to the birth of the Son in the *here and now* of his or her life, to make revelation operative out of the nothingness of the innermost ground:

"God has sent his Only-Begotten Son into the world." You must not by this understand the external world in which the Son ate and drank with us, but understand it to apply to the inner world. As truly as the Father in his simple nature gives his Son birth naturally, so truly does he give him birth in the inward part of the spirit, and that is the inner world. Here God's ground is my ground, and my ground is God's ground. Here I live from what is my own, as God lives from what is his own. . . . It is out of this inner ground that you should perform all your works without asking, "Why?"[63]

62. Pr. 52, DW II, 486/EE, 199.

63. Pr. 5b; DW I, 85–96/EE, 183. In connection with this notion of "repetition" in Eckhart, we should also cite the following striking passage from his sermon *Praedica verbum* (*Predigt* 30), which we cited in chapter 2. Eckhart discusses this same idea also in the same sermon: "Everything that God created six thousand years ago when he made the world and everything he will yet create in a thousand years (if the world last that long), all this he creates in the innermost and in the highest of the soul. Everything that is past, everything that is present, and everything that is future God creates in the innermost of the soul." *Pr.* 30; DW II, 95–6/TP, 292–93.

Through the birth of the Son in the soul, the soul comes to understand that its "ground" and the divine "ground" are one and the same. This understanding, however, is not a theoretical understanding but a practical one: the soul begins to *live and act* not out of any ground peculiar to itself—for as creature it realizes its own groundlessness—but out of the divine ground. Thus the soul *makes its own* God's own working, being, and knowing precisely in giving up anything of its own. Eckhart thus says that the truly detached soul lives "from what is my own, as God lives from what is his own." I live an existence that is truly my own when I no longer seek my ground as creature who, in the end, is just one "thing" interchangeable with other things, but as an only-begotten son of God. The truly free soul acts for nothing outside of itself but out of its own inner ground. It acts "without a why."[64] In other words, affective union with God does not annihilate or absorb the personality or individuality of the soul but rather enhances it and grounds it.

The soul that lives "without a why" does not have God as an "objective" or "highest value" but as the living ground of its being and its freedom. Such a soul is thus truly free, because it is grounded in God's absolute freedom, and God is absolutely free because God is completely released from all subjectivity (at least as it is understood from creatures), indeed, from all that is created. And further, since God is so released, God is perfectly creative. Thus to the extent that the soul is released from all "whys," to that extent it gives birth to the divine Word or *Ratio* in its innermost ground, abolishing in this "birth" all distinction between "transcendent ideas" and the sensible particulars of creation.[65] Rather, for the released

64. McGinn argues that this peculiar phrase is an original contribution of the high Middle Ages to mystical thought, having its origins in the early thirteenth century. It seems to have first occurred in the writings of Beatrice of Nazareth (c. 1215–35), and the phrase *sans nul pourquoy/ sine propter quid* occurs quite often in the writings of Marguerite Porete (d. 1310), which Eckhart probably knew quite well. McGinn says this about this new concept: "Living 'without a why' was a necessary implication of the new mysticism of the later Middle Ages, especially in its dialectically apophatic forms. A mysticism based upon a 'wayless way' to an unknown God of absolute freedom can only bear fruit in a 'whylessness' that will probably seem either empty of meaning or potentially dangerous to those who know nothing of it." McGinn, *The Mystical Thought of Meister Eckhart*, 154. See also his book *Meister Eckhart and the Beguine Mystics: Hadewijch of Brabant, Mechthild of Magdeburg, and Marguerite Porete* (New York: Continuum, 1994), passim.

65. Schürmann notes also how this constitutes an important break with the Aristotelian-Thomistic tradition. Aquinas, for example, had argued that the word "idea" designates (to use Schürmann's summation) "the form not insofar as it exists in the thing and gives being to it, but

soul, creatures, including the soul itself, have no "goal" or "why" "beyond" or "outside" themselves, but all subsist "from," "in," and "through" God. All the distinctions of traditional philosophy or metaphysics are broken in a dynamic process of union and birth.

To sum up, then, Eckhart's logic of letting-go is, if one may use the rather paradoxical expression, a "logic of freedom": the more the soul abandons its self-will and its practical or speculative grasping after created things, it becomes utterly free with respect to all things and is thus able to know them as they are in their truth and love them as they are in their goodness. But for Eckhart, this logic cannot be possible if it is rooted in anything created: for nothing created, in and of itself, can open up this infinite receptivity toward creatures. This logic of letting-go can be rooted only in a divine freedom that has no limits but is purely "empty." But this divine emptiness is also infinitely rich in intelligibility and desirability. This is because, in being released into existence, creatures are also *revealed* in their truth and goodness. Hence, as we have seen, Eckhart notes that the Gospel says not "In the beginning was being," but "In the beginning was the Word," or revelation. Of course, in letting creatures be, God himself is concealed "behind" or "beyond" this act. But that is why, for Eckhart, special revelation is necessary: Christ, the Word, by being born into the hidden, inner ground of the soul, makes possible the union of the soul with God and, thus, also knowledge and love of God.

---

insofar as it exists outside it. This separate existence can be twofold: as a principle of knowledge, the form is found in the human intellect; as a model of the thing, it is in God. While in the first mode, intelligible, the form can exist in any being whatever endowed with reason, created or uncreated, in the second it is by right reserved to a creating cause alone; this latter possesses in itself the primal image of the thing that will be produced. For Thomas Aquinas the original meaning of the 'idea' lies here: it is the title for the preexistence of an effect in the creating cause" (Schürmann, *Wandering Joy*, 34). But Eckhart argues that this distinction is overturned when the soul is detached and has "released" all created things. Insofar as the soul "wants nothing, knows nothing, and has nothing" it no longer grasps created beings in a creaturely way but in a divine way. It lets creatures be; and insofar as it lets creatures be, it lets them be as they are in their original idea or model in God. Such a soul no longer has its own intellect but participates in intellect as such, which, Eckhart claims, is uncreated and divine. Thus, as Schürmann explains: "According to Eckhart the intellect, being potentially the sum total of all possible representations, contains, inasmuch as it is detached from what it actually knows, the 'ideas' or models of things themselves. A detached man is no longer the place of contingent 'representations,' but of subsistent 'ideas'" (Schürmann, *Wandering Joy*, 34).

# Conclusion

## *The Unity and Diversity of the Mystical Path*

Listening not to me, but to the *Logos*, it is wise to agree that all is one.

> Heraclitus

Though the *Logos* is common, most men live as if they had a private source of understanding.

> Heraclitus

God does not become more divine when we push him away from us in a sheer, impenetrable voluntarism; rather, the truly divine God is the God who has revealed himself as "logos" and, as "logos," has acted and continues to act lovingly on our behalf. Certainly, love, as Saint Paul says, "transcends" knowledge and is thereby capable of perceiving more than thought alone; nonetheless it continues to be love of the God who is Logos.

> Benedict XVI

Throughout all four parts of this book, I have tried to show that the mystical thought and practice of Ibn 'Arabi and Meister Eckhart cannot be understood without reference to a revelation and a hermeneutics of that revelation that seeks the inner meaning of all revealed texts: the inner union of the soul with God. This mystical hermeneutic is what allows the soul to see creatures as embodied signs of spiritual realities. Just as, for Eckhart, the circle outside the tavern is the sign of the wine within, so are creatures signs of the "wine" of divine existence and truth accessible from within the soul. So, for Ibn 'Arabi, do the verses of the Qur'an, or *ayat*, have also the meaning of "sign" (*āya*), pointing to the spiritual significance of all things in creation. Thus, for both, the true nature of things is inaccessible to the human intellect without special revelation. But this mystical hermeneutic is not fulfilled until it leads to union of the soul with God.

This union occurs in and through the divine *Logos*: the soul remains a creature always for both Meister Eckhart and Ibn 'Arabi, but insofar as the soul realizes its own nothingness and allows itself to be conformed totally to God, it is made over into God. That is, there is no union until the soul becomes conformed entirely to the divine Word. Only then does the soul become, quite literally, an *image* of God and, as we saw, the image as image derives *all* of its being from that of which it is the image. It has no being of its own. Hence, the ultimate goal of the mystical life is *to imagine* God, not, it must be emphasized, in the usual way we think of "imagine"—as some particular or material image. But rather, in the very active and literal sense in which someone like Eckhart means the term: actually *to be* an image of God in one's entire intellect and being in which one derives all one's existence from God's existence. This is the true sense of the imagination. The imagination is analogical when it recognizes the very finitude with which the soul images God, and therefore opens itself up completely to God's infinity.

Such a soul is made over into God in and through the divine *Logos*, because it is as intellect or heart that the soul is made over completely into God by the divine *Logos*, just as the wood is transformed into fire by fire, to use an image of Eckhart's. While as creature, the human being is related to God's being analogically, as an intellectual being, he or she is related to God univocally, for in intellect, the knower and the known are the same. In this relationship, the soul becomes the Universal Man or Nobleman. Meister Eckhart and Ibn 'Arabi do not present us, therefore, with utterly private irrational ecstasies or with rational systems that can stand independently of revelation or religious tradition. Instead, they present us with a sustained attempt to use the tools that reason offers in philosophy, logic, and science in order to enter into and be transformed by the inner meaning of God's special revelation to humanity. By entering into the inner meaning of revelation, reason is, in turn, illuminated by revelation and is able to grasp, even if only imperfectly, what is beyond and above it. So transformed, the mystic relates to the divine Logos as Universal Man or Nobleman, the created reflection of God's creative and communicative power.

But this divine Truth is not an object of human reason; rather, the entire human being *lives* the divine Truth as the ground, not object, of all its thinking and acting. Revelation corrects the deficiencies of reason not with more reason, but *by transforming the soul from within*. The kind of knowledge that Ibn 'Arabi and Meister Eckhart talk about and that we properly call "mystical" is complete conformity to the divine *Logos* in the heart or ground of one's being. Mystical knowledge is not a discursive knowledge of "divine things" or an encyclopedic understanding of the Bible or Qur'an. As long as the innermost part of the self is not conformed to the divine *Logos*, such knowledge, as all worldly knowledge, is not only useless but can be dangerous when used with pride and in rebellion against God.

## *Logos* and the "Mystical"

A divine *Logos* is essential to the mystical paths of both Ibn 'Arabi, a Muslim, and Meister Eckhart, a Christian, because the *Logos* is the Word by which God communicates his being to creatures, and the Word in and through which he draws creatures, in their epitome, the human being, back to himself. For both mystical exegetes, being is coterminous with its communication, which is why for Meister Eckhart, Ibn 'Arabi, and Muslim and Christian scholastics generally, being is convertible with truth and goodness. To be is both to communicate being to the intellect, as truth, and to communicate existence to things, which is why being is called the good that is "diffusive of itself"—*bonum est diffusivum sui*. Thus, it is essential to God's nature to be self-communicative; in other words, to be a *Word* or *Logos*. For Ibn 'Arabi, God or being is *al-ḥaqq*, the True, and a term that can also be translated as "the Right," or the source or measure of right or just action, of goodness. Hence, both Ibn 'Arabi and Meister Eckhart assert that for metaphysics to grasp being qua being, being as such, one has to also grasp being as communicated in *revelation*. To be is to be revealed and to be revealed is to be. The Universal Man or the Nobleman is simply the human being who realizes this truth in his very being and not just in thought, word, or deed. The whole point of revelation and its interpretation is to make the divine Word not the object but the ground of one's thinking, acting, and entire being. In this sense, the *Logos* of an Eckhart or Ibn 'Arabi represents a radical rupture with the *Logos* of Greek philosophy, conceived as the objective rational order in the cosmos, knowable by reason alone.

There is, however, a great difference in how Ibn 'Arabi and Meister Eckhart conceive this relationship of humanity to the divine *Logos*, stemming from the differences contained in the Qur'anic and biblical revelations and in the Muslim and Christian traditions in general about how to conceive God and our relationship to him. While revelation, to be sure, communicates not a notion of "being," but existence itself, this communication is still received in a limited form since it is limited and finite creatures who necessarily receive it. As a Muslim, Ibn 'Arabi conceives of this *Logos* as the *kalima muḥammadīyya* or the "Muhammadan Word" that is the uncreated principle of the Holy Qur'an. In other words, this *Logos* manifests itself as a divine *book*, which, however, in God is uncreated and eternal. God is under no obligation to create it or any other thing. This book offers guidance to all the *banu Adam* or "sons of Adam" as to how to return to their primal Adamic nature or *fiṭra,* as described above. The Qur'an describes this nature as not so much fallen as obscured by unnecessary custom and blind imitation or *taqlīd.* Ibn 'Arabi calls the various objects of traditional customs and opinions the "gods of belief," being finite representations of the un-representable Absolute. But it should also be added that, important as the "book" is for the mystical element in Islam, the Qur'an is only fully actualized as book in the Universal Man and, to lesser degrees, in the "words" of the various prophets and saints, who actualize in their very lives the various meanings or words of the divine book.

As a Christian, Eckhart understands the *Logos* as a *Person,* Jesus Christ, who is the principle, core, or "marrow" of sacred Scripture. All of Scripture exists, Eckhart argues, so that we may encounter Christ within its pages. Thus, for Eckhart, our encounter with the *Logos* is a *personal encounter,* one that is based in the personal encounter of the three Persons of the Trinity with each other in their self-emptying and therefore utterly unifying love. Since Christ is both fully God and fully man, he both heals the break between the human and the divine and also serves as both the ontological and effective basis for their unity. Unlike the Muslim Ibn 'Arabi, Eckhart the Christian sees that the union between God and humanity has been broken by original sin and that only a mediator who is fully God and fully human can heal that breach and form the basis for their unity. Hence, for

Eckhart, there is the necessity for a *rebirth* whereby the Son is born in the ground of the soul and the Christian becomes, by the grace of adoption, a true son of God.

These are great differences and are not to be taken lightly. To acknowledge them is to take seriously the notion that the mystical path is one that is mediated necessarily by revelation as constituted by a body of scripture as accepted by a religious community or church. Any self-communication of God will necessarily take the form of a particular revelation with its own understanding of the divine and relationship of humanity to the divine. Leaving aside the important question of which revelations of the divine are more or less adequate or full than others, we must nevertheless note that, even if revelation is limited by the vessel that receives it, there is in mystical writers like Ibn 'Arabi or Meister Eckhart an inherent tendency to transcend those limitations and to incorporate elements of other traditions in their formulation of the essence of God and of his relation to us. It must therefore be admitted that the "universality" of the Sufi saint or the Christian mystic is only a relative universality: no human being, no matter how "realized" or "empty," can *in actuality* realize the absolute universality of God's fullness of being and existence. But what one can assert is that every revelation contains within itself elements of other revelations, which mystical thinkers bring to the surface, such that we can speak of a "Christian element" in Ibn 'Arabi and a "Muslim element" in Meister Eckhart, without implying at all any syncretistic deviations in either of their writings from orthodoxy as defined by their traditions.

I have intended to present here, in all four parts of this book, examples of such "trans-traditional" affinities. In the case of Ibn 'Arabi, for instance, we have the centrality of the notion of the *Logos* or *kalima* or *al-ruh al-muḥammadīyya* in his mystical path, a parallel of the Christian teaching of the Word or *Logos* in and through whom God communicates his being to all creatures and through whom he draws creatures back to him. Like Christ, the *Logos* is like the primal Adam in whom our full humanity is restored and, by being so restored, our full union in and with God. Of course, for Ibn 'Arabi, the Word was not "made flesh" and is not and cannot be identified exclusively with the prophet Jesus. The Muslim *Logos* is not a Person.

Likewise with Meister Eckhart there is an "Islamic element" in his emphasis on the Godhead "beyond" the distinctions of the Trinity. The inner ground of both the soul and God is of such oneness that no one can "look into it," not even the Persons of the Trinity, which is as good a formulation of the Islamic doctrine of *tawḥīd* or of the absolute unity of God *(lā illāh illā allāh)* as one can find. But, for Eckhart, this unity is only a moment in a dialectical process that necessarily issues in the Persons of the Trinity. In other words, this unity of the inner ground is only the necessary condition for the unity of the Persons of the Trinity. The soul breaks into this inner unity of the Godhead, not to go "beyond" the Trinity, but to share in the root of Trinitarian life and participate, by grace, in the unity and love of that life. Hence, for Eckhart, this unity of the Godhead is an affirmation and not a negation of the Trinity.

Overall, we can look upon these convergences as the implicit recognition by both Ibn ʿArabi and Meister Eckhart of the necessity for incorporating elements of other traditions into their own without compromising the orthodoxy of their traditions in any way. These incorporations, however, without necessarily attributing them to merely "spontaneous manifestations of the human spirit," cannot simply be explained by historical borrowings. As far as we know, Eckhart had no direct knowledge of the life or work of Ibn ʿArabi, nor does Ibn ʿArabi evince any knowledge of Christian theology or mystical literature. (Indeed, as has been noted, Ibn ʿArabi's knowledge of even *Muslim* philosophy is quite thin.)[1] But it is still noteworthy that Ibn ʿArabi saw the necessity for the incorporation of "Christian elements" in his thought and that Meister Eckhart saw

1. Indeed, it is the thesis of the well-known book by the Spanish priest Asin-Palacios, *El Islam Cristianado* (cited above in its French translation), that the phenomenon of Sufism simply represents the importation of Christian mystical thought into Islam. He sees this as particularly true of Ibn ʿArabi, especially when we consider that Ibn ʿArabi was born and grew up in Spain, where he had frequent contacts with Christians. The strong form of Palacios's thesis, formulated in the 1930s, has since been rejected by almost all scholars of Sufism and Islam, whose research has brought to light the essentially Islamic roots of Sufism and of the thought of Ibn ʿArabi. But nevertheless, Palacios's thesis is still convincing in its weak form: that Christian thought had a strong influence on the development of Sufism, and on the thought of Ibn ʿArabi in particular, as the exploration of the inner meaning of Islamic law. From the side of Meister Eckhart, we need only refer to the book by Kurt Flasch, *Meister Eckhart: Die Geburt der "Deutschen Mystik" aus dem Geist der arabischen Philosophie,* where he shows how many of the key concepts of Eckhart stem, via Albert the Great and Dietrich of Freiburg, from Averroes, who was himself someone known personally by Ibn ʿArabi. The convergences between Ibn ʿArabi and Meister Eckhart are, therefore, not purely accidental, even if it is impossible to establish a direct link between them.

the necessity of the incorporation of "Islamic elements" in his thought. They were both, to be sure, unaware of these teachings as "Christian" or "Islamic" but saw them merely as facets of the Truth. For as necessary as the exclusive and orthodox adherence of the mystic to his or her religious tradition is, some incorporation of elements from other traditions is also necessary if the fullness of the mystical life is to be realized and adequately described. The mystical understanding and appropriation of revelation, in whatever form it is found and accepted, requires, even *demands*, parallel and even identical hermeneutical and metaphysical moves on the part of the mystical writer, of whatever religious tradition.[2]

Yet, this incorporation can come, as we have seen above, only at the height and end of the mystical path, of the realization of the divine Word in the soul. Only one who has followed the path of his or her religious tradition in its fullness and in complete obedience to its orthodox interpretation has the right to make this incorporation. To do so at the *beginning* of the mystical path is to fall into a muddled, superficial, and contrived syncretism. In short, the authentic mystical traditions of Christianity and Islam converge not *despite* their complete and absolute grounding in their revealed texts, but, as I hope to have shown in presenting parallels in such detail, *because of* their grounding in the respective texts and traditions. Due to a common inheritance of Neoplatonic and Peripatetic categories, the works of Ibn 'Arabi and Meister Eckhart share many similarities, but ultimately, such similarities are superficial, for there is absent in the pagan Greek conception of the *Logos* the whole notion of *communication* in which the human being is both differentiated from and united to his or her origin. What they truly share with one another is an attempt to use these categories to enter more deeply into their scriptures and bring out

2. These sorts of moves among scholastic thinkers in medieval Judaism, Christianity, and Islam concerning the knowability (and unknowability) of God David Burrell traces brilliantly in his book, *Knowing the Unknowable God: Ibn-Sina, Maimonides, Aquinas* (Notre Dame, Ind.: University of Notre Dame Press, 1986). Burrell shows how coming to a deeper and more precise understanding of the relation of God, the Creator, to his creation was a common achievement of philosopher-theologians working in the three great Semitic monotheistic religions, with Ibn-Sina and Maimonides providing crucial conceptual precisions that made the grand theological-philosophical synthesis of Aquinas possible. Of course, as we have noted, there is no direct influence of Ibn 'Arabi on the thought of Eckhart; nevertheless, Eckhart works in and presupposes in his writing the same common intellectual and spiritual achievement of the three religious civilizations as does his intellectual and spiritual master, as well as fellow Dominican, Thomas Aquinas.

their inner meaning and, by doing so, to become united to God through the power and wisdom of God's own self-communication to man. What they share is an acute sense of hermeneutical reason that sees the transcendent in the immanent, the spiritual in the material, and the one in the many. As such, they, or those who study their writings, are in a better position to understand the "embodiedness" of divine Truth or its "incarnational" aspect in religious texts and traditions, and that that Truth cannot be understood except through entering imaginatively into these texts and traditions, attempting to discern their transcendent referent and source.

## Mystical Hermeneutics and Comparative Religion

Quoting al-Junayd, as we saw in chapter 7, Ibn 'Arabi notes that, as the "water takes on the color of the cup" so God takes on the "color" of our preconceived notions and fundamental rational categories. Our knowledge of God always and inevitably, according to Ibn 'Arabi, will be colored by concepts which human reason and religious tradition "lay over" the divine Reality, because human reason, being finite, cannot conceive the infinite. This limitation on our knowledge of God is real, such that Ibn 'Arabi could say with Thomas Aquinas and Meister Eckhart that reason alone cannot know God as he is in himself. There is, then, a real sense in which the "gods of belief" are God as conceived by various religious traditions and, further, a sense in which these "gods of belief" are not the absolute truth about God, but only relative approximations of the Truth that is God himself. The realized knower is, however, the one who sees God in all the "gods of belief," seeing them as so many approximations of the Truth about God that has its fullest expression in the Qur'an.

Neither Ibn 'Arabi nor Meister Eckhart is a relativist: even if the form of their own religious tradition is not the same as the Absolute manifested in that form, the form is essential. To return to the metaphor of Junayd, the water is not the color of the cup, but it is necessary to have the cup in order to drink the water. As Ibn 'Arabi says in his *Futūḥāt*: "The road to felicity is set down by revealed religion, nothing else."[3] Human happiness and perfection presuppose the self-communication of God to creation

3. *Futūḥāt* II, 148.12.

through his *Logos*. There cannot be any *mystical* imagination, thought, or practice without the revealed text. Without the revealed text, reason is reduced to its own concepts and ideas, reducing "reality" to conform to those concepts and ideas. Only when reason is confronted with the revealed text does it strive to go beyond itself. What revelation specifically discloses is the analogical nature of things: that all things refer, in finite or limited ways, to what is ultimately real and one. Without the revealed text, therefore, reason never rises above itself to intellect and, as a result, tries to "cut" reality down to its own size. It is precisely the *Logos* that is the essence of the revealed text and the principle of creation that not only calls the soul beyond itself but actually constitutes that soul's very being and life, insofar as the soul is truly and fully *intellectual*.

So while the Universal Man or Nobleman realizes the fullness of the *Logos* revealed to, through, and in his or her religious tradition, he or she realizes also potentialities latent in other traditions without for a moment ceasing to be fully a Muslim or a Christian (or a Jew or a Buddhist, etc.), because, in making fully immanent the revealed Word of their tradition, the Universal Man or Nobleman also fully realizes the limitedness of that tradition. Such a notion is, as we have seen, explicit in the writings of Ibn 'Arabi, but it is also in the thought of Meister Eckhart, even if only implicitly. For does not Eckhart say that the perfected Nobleman should pray to God to be free of "God"? Like Ibn 'Arabi, Eckhart is acutely aware of the difference between the "gods of belief" and the true, living God who is beyond all names and is utterly one and absolute. The living God who is beyond our conceptual or imaginative powers shatters every form. Mystical life and consciousness is essentially human life and consciousness radically re-oriented: away from the finite self and to the infinite Other, who is God. As such, the mystical path, while fully committed to the fullness of the religious tradition to which it belongs, does not grasp and cling to that tradition, for it knows that that absence of grasping and clinging is the precondition for its genuine perfection and renewal.

For Ibn 'Arabi, the Qur'an both affirms and puts into question Muslim "tradition" in the very specific sense of *taqlīd* or mere imitation: it affirms it insofar as it proclaims the fullness of Muhammad's message to humanity; but it puts it into question insofar as it also takes us beyond the "gods of belief" and makes us see, if we are realized knowers of God, the truth in every form or "knotting" of creation, because they are all divine manifestations or theophanies. As al-Ghazali pointed out well before Ibn 'Arabi, the point of the mystical path is to "put new life" into the tradition, which is why he spoke of *iḥyā'* or "giving life" in his monumental *Iḥyā' 'ulūm ad-din (The Revival of the Religious Sciences)*. William Chittick paraphrases Ibn 'Arabi's position thusly: "The revealed religions are diverse, because they cannot possibly not be diverse. They all point to a single *wujūd*, but each is a providential specification of that *wujūd* with a view toward human felicity."[4] Just as pure being, *wujūd* or God never repeats itself in its disclosures in creation, so it does not repeat its divine revelations. As Chittick further explains Ibn 'Arabi's view: "Since human dispositions are diverse, divine dispensations must also be diverse to take into account the diversity of these dispositions."[5] Since, in creating the world, God cannot *not* disclose himself in some fashion, all things are a revelation of God, what many call in both the Christian and Muslim traditions *primal*, or *general, revelation*, in which being or existence is communicated to creatures.

But to every community is a *special revelation* suited to the times, the place, and the temperament of the people. And the point of this special revelation is to lead all rational creatures back to God and to make them blessed. Ibn 'Arabi explains in his *Futūḥāt*, commenting upon the Qur'anic verse *We never chastise, until We send forth a messenger* (17:15):

God says, *We never chastise, until We send forth a messenger.* Note that He did not say, "until We send forth a person." Hence the *message* of the one who is sent must be established for the one to whom it is directed. There must be clear and manifest proofs established for each person to whom the messenger is sent, for many a sign (*āya*) has within it obscurity or equivocality such that some people do not perceive what it proves. The clarity of the proof must be such that it establishes the person's messengerhood for each person to whom he is sent. Only then, if the person refuses it, will he be taken to account. Hence, this verse has within it a tremendous mercy, because of the diversity of human dispositions that lead to a diversity of views. He who knows the all-inclusiveness of the divine mercy, which, God reports, *embraces all things* [7:156], knows that God did this only because of mercy toward His servants.[6]

---

4. Chittick, *Imaginal Worlds*, 156.     5. Ibid.
6. III 469.25.

Here, Ibn 'Arabi emphasizes that the diversity of authentic revelations is not only a divine mercy but flows necessarily from the divine mercy. But, and this is crucial for understanding Ibn 'Arabi and his writing, the universality of all religion comes to fulfillment *only in the Qur'an*. Only in the Qur'an, conceived as the eternal message of God to humanity, starting from Adam and finding its final written form in Muhammad, does the proper meaning of previous revelations come to light, according to Ibn 'Arabi and, thus, only in the Qur'an do previous revelations find their true meaning and effective power.

Ibn 'Arabi, therefore, notes that God does not say "until We send forth a *person*," but rather "until We send forth a *messenger*." That is, the true locus of meaning for Ibn 'Arabi, as for any Muslim, is the *message* or *Logos* that is born by the messenger. It is not the individual that is at issue, but the divine message. The prophet is such by virtue of the *Logos* he embodies, whether in whole or in part. For Eckhart, the Christian, Christ himself, the *Person, is*, of course, the message of Christ, and in the encounter with the person of Christ, the soul is made over as a person to his or her very ground in the image of Christ. In Christ, individual person and *Logos* are identical. Thus, Christ adapts but also transforms every person and every temperament into himself. For Eckhart, the diversity of revelation leads inevitably back to Christ. The living God shatters every form *in and through Christ*: it is Christ who unites the transcendent with the immanent, the divine with the human. This means that the birth of Christ must be recovered anew in the ground of the soul of every Christian by re-birth. It is the death of the mystical imagination and of religion in general when the soul gives him or herself over not to the divine *Logos*, Christ, but to a mere *idea*, the idea of the universality of religion or religious experience. Authentic religion or mystical reflection, for Eckhart, lies not in any idea, no matter how cogent or sound, but in the living out of the Word of God, who is a living Person. There is no doubt for Eckhart that Christ is the fullness and perfection of God's revelation to humanity, and thus is the fullness and perfection of being. For in Christ both message or *Logos* and individual or concrete existence are united in a *Person*.

The mystical path, therefore, is the path of the *Logos* or "Word" of Reality in which that *Logos* or Word becomes the ground and substance of the individual soul. Thus the mystical path is not irrational, for the *Logos*, if not "reason" in the sense of calculative ratiocination, is the transcendent source and measure of all reason. The mystical path, therefore, is *suprarational* and, as such, the *Logos* cannot be known by the efforts of the human mind. The *Logos* becomes known only by revealing itself to the soul prepared to receive it. "Revelation" or "unveiling," both in its general and specific senses, is essential to the *Logos* as *Logos*. In the general sense, the *Logos* communicates its being and goodness to all creatures; in the specific sense, the *Logos* communicates its own proper intellectual nature to intellectual creatures. And while the mystical writer seeks to bring out the "inner" sense of revelation—that sense that revelation has for the life and self-transcendence of the soul—the mystical path is, properly speaking, neither "inner" nor "outer." As we have tried to show in the cases of Ibn 'Arabi and Meister Eckhart, the "mystical" is not based on "experiences" of a discrete and self-contained subject. Rather it is the opening of that subject out onto the full plentitude of existence. In that sense, insofar as all medieval philosophy and theology, Muslim and Christian, seeks to conform the soul to the ultimate Reality that is God, then all medieval Muslim and Christian philosophy and theology is, properly speaking, "mystical." In this sense, there is a real affinity between the two religions, even if, on the level of doctrinal teaching, it would betray that very mystical affinity to appeal to some common and universal "religion of reason."

If, then, we are to learn anything from the writings of Ibn 'Arabi and Meister Eckhart about the relationship between revelation, religious tradition, and knowledge of God, it is that we must hearken to the *Logos* in humble silence. For this *Logos* does not speak to human beings privately, but to all.

# Bibliography

IBN 'ARABI

Works by Ibn 'Arabi and His Commentators

Ibn 'Arabi. *Futūḥāt al-makkīyya.* Edited by O. Yahia. 4 vols. Cairo: al-
Hay'at al-Misriyya al-'Amma li'Kitab, 1972–.

———. *Fuṣūṣ al-ḥikam.* Edited by A. E. Affifi. Beirut: Dar al-Kitab al-
Arabi, 2002.

———. *Tarjumān al-Āshwāq.* Beirut: Dar Sadr, 2003.

Al-Jandi, Mu'yyaddin. *Sharḥ fuṣūṣ al-ḥikam.* Edited by S. J. Ashtiyani.
Mashhad: Danishgah-i-Mashhad, n.d.

Al-Qaysari, Dawoud. *Maṭla' khuṣūṣ al-ḥikam fī ma'ānī fuṣūṣ al-ḥikam.* Edited by Muhammad Hassan al-Sa'adi. 2 vols. Tehran: 1995.

Translations of Ibn 'Arabi's Work

Ibn 'Arabi. *Sufis of Andalusia: The Rūḥ al-Quds and al-Durrat al-Fākhirah.*
Translated by Ralph Austin. Roxborough: Beshara Publications,
1971.

———. *La Sagesse des prophètes (Fuçuç al-hikam).* Translated by Titus
Burckhardt. Paris: Albin Michel, 1974.

———. *The Bezels of Wisdom.* Translated by R. W. J. Austin. Mahwah,
N.J.: Paulist Press, 1980.

———. *La Production des Cercles.* Translated by Paul Fenton and Mau-
rice Gloton. Paris: Editions de l'Eclat, 1996.

———. *Le livre des théophanies d'Ibn Arabi.* Translated by Stéphane Rus-
poli. Paris: Editions du Cerf, 2000.

———. *Contemplation of the Holy Mysteries.* Translated by Cecilia
Twinch and Pablo Beneito. Oxford: Anqa Publishing, 2001.

———. *The Ringstones of Wisdom (Fuṣūṣ al-ḥikam).* Translated by Caner
K. Dagli. Chicago: Great Books of the Islamic World, 2004.

Chittick, William. *The Sufi Path of Knowledge: Ibn 'Arabi's Metaphysics of Imagina-tion*. Albany: State University of New York Press, 1989.

———. *The Self-Disclosure of God: Principles of Ibn al-'Arabi's Cosmology*. Albany: State University of New York Press, 1998.

MEISTER ECKHART

Works by Meister Eckhart

Eckhart, Meister. *Die deutschen Werke*. Edited by Josef Quint and Georg Steer. 5 vols. Stuttgart: Kohlhammer, 1936–.

———. *Die lateinischen Werke*. Edited by Josef Koch, Albert Zimmermann, and Loris Sturlese. 5 vols. Stuttgart: Kohlhammer, 1936–.

Théry, G. "Edition critique des pièces relatives au procès d'Eckhart contenues dans le manucrit 33b de la Bibliotèque de Soest." In *Archives d'histoire doctri-nale et littéraire du moyen âge 1* (1926): 129–268.

Translations of Meister Eckhart's Work

Eckhart, Meister. *Meister Eckhart: A Modern Translation*. Translated by Raymond B. Blakney. New York: Harper and Row, 1941.

———. *Master Eckhart: Parisian Questions and Prologues*. Translated by Armand Maurer. Toronto: Pontifical Institute for Medieval Studies, 1974.

———. *Meister Eckhart: The Essential Sermons, Commentaries, Treatises, and De-fense*. Translated and introduced by Edmund Colledge and Bernard McGinn. New York: Paulist Press, 1981.

———. *Meister Eckhart: Teacher and Preacher*. Edited and translated by Bernard McGinn. New York: Paulist Press, 1986.

———. *Maître Eckhart: Traités et sermons*. Translated by Alain de Libera. 3rd ed. Paris: Flammarion, 1995.

SECONDARY LITERATURE

Abu Madyan. *The Way of Abu Madyan: The Works of Abu Madyan Shu'ayb*. Com-piled and translated by Vincent J. Cornell. Cambridge: Islamic Texts Society, 1996.

Addas, Claude. *Quest for the Red Sulphur*. Translated by Peter Kingsley. Cam-bridge: Islamic Texts Society, 1993.

———. *Ibn 'Arabi et le voyage sans retour*. Paris: Edition de Seuil, 1996.

Aertsen, Jan. "Die Tranzendentalienlehre bei Thomas von Aquin in ihren histo-rischen Hintergründen und philosophischen Motiven." In *Thomas von Aquin: Werk und Wirkung im Licht Neuerer Forschungen*, edited by Albert Zimmer-mann, 82–102. Miscellanea Medievalia 19. Berlin: de Gruyter, 1988.

————. "Ontology and Henology in Medieval Philosophy (Thomas Aquinas, Master Eckhart, and Berthold of Moosburg)." In *On Proclus and His Influence in Medieval Philosophy*, edited by E. P. Bos and P. A.. Meyer, 120–40. Leiden: E. J. Brill, 1992.

————. *Medieval Philosophy and the Transcendentals: The Case of Thomas Aquinas.* Leiden: E. J. Brill, 1996.

————. "Is There a Medieval Philosophy?" *International Philosophical Quarterly* 39 (1999): 403–5.

Affifi, A. E. *The Mystical Philosophy of Ibnul 'Arabi.* Lahore: Muhammad Ashraf, 1979.

Albertus Magnus. *Scriptum super libros Sententiarum.* Edited by Borgnet. Paris: 1893.

Anon. *Liber de causis.* Edited by Otto Bardenhewer. Freiburg, Switzerland: 1882.

Aquinas, Thomas. *Summa Contra Gentiles.* Rome: Editio Leonina Manualis, 1934.

————. *Summa Theologiae.* 5 vols. Ottawa: Cura et studio institute Studiorum Mediaevorum Ottaviensis, 1941–45.

————. *Quaestiones Disputate.* Edited by R. Spiazzi et al. 8th ed. 2 vols. Turin: Marietti, 1949.

————. *In librum beati Dionysii In Divinis Nominibus expositio.* Edited by C. Pera. Rome: Marietti, 1950.

————. *Super librum de causis expositio.* Edited by H. D. Saffrey. Louvain: Editions E. Nauwelaerts, 1954.

————. *In Boethii de Trinitate Expositio.* Edited by B. Decker. Leiden: E. J. Brill: 1955.

————. *Commentary on the Book of Causes.* Translated by V. Guagliardo, C. Hess, and R. Taylor. Washington, D.C.: The Catholic University of America Press, 1996.

Arnaldez, Roger. *Averroes: A Rationalist in Islam.* Translated by David Streight. Notre Dame, Ind.: University of Notre Dame Press, 2000.

Asin-Palacio, Miguel. *L'Islam christianisé: Etude sur le Soufisme d'Ibn 'Arabi de Murcie.* Translated by Bernard Dubant. Paris: Guy Trédaniel, 1982.

Averroes (Ibn Rushd). *Decisive Treatise and Epistle Dedicatory.* Translated by Charles E. Butterworth. Provo, Utah: Brigham Young University Press, 2001.

Bange, W. *Meister Eckharts Lehre von göttlichen und geschöflichen Sein.* Limburg: 1937.

Bashier, Salman H. *Ibn 'Arabi's Barzakh: The Concept of the Limit and the Relationship between God and the World.* Albany: State University of New York Press, 2004.

Beierwaltes, Werner. *Proklos: Grundzüge seiner Metaphysik.* Frankfurt: V. Klosterman, 1965.

————. *Platonismus und Idealismus*. Frankfurt: V. Klosterman, 1972.

Bernard of Clairvaux. *Sancti Bernardi Opera Omnia*. Edited by J. Leclerq, C. H. Talbot, and H. M. Rochais. 8 vols. Rome: 1957–80.

————. *Bernard of Clairvaux: Selected Works*. Translated by Gillian Evans. Mahwah, N.J.: Paulist Press, 1987.

Beyer de Ryke, Benoît. *Maître Eckhart: une mystique du détachement*. Brussels: Editions Ousia, 2000.

Brunner, Fernand. *Maître Eckhart: Approche de l'oeuvre*. Geneva: Editions Ad Solem, 1999.

Büchner, Christine. *Die Transformation des Einheitsdenkens Meister Eckharts bei Heinrich Seuse und Johannes Tauler*. Meister-Eckhart-Jahrbuch Beihefte. Stuttgart: Kolhammer, 2007.

Al-Bukhari, Muhammad ibn Isma'il. *Sahih Abi 'Abd Allah al-Bukhari*. 25 vols. Cairo: Al-Matba'a al-Bahiya al-Misriya, 1933–62. See also the translation by Muhammad Muhsin Khan, *The Translation of the Meanings of Sahih al-Bukhari*. 6th rev. ed. 9 vols. Chicago: Kazi Publications, 1983.

Burckhardt, Titus. *Introduction to Sufism*. San Francisco: Harper Collins, 1995.

Burrell, David. *Knowing the Unknowable God: Ibn-Sina, Maimonides, Aquinas*. Notre Dame, Ind.: University of Notre Dame Press, 1986.

————. *Freedom and Creation in Three Traditions*. Notre Dame, Ind.: University of Notre Dame Press, 1993.

Caputo, John. "The Nothingness of the Intellect in Meister Eckhart's 'Parisian Questions.'" *The Thomist* 39 (1975): 85–115.

Certeau, Michel de. *La Fable mystique: XVI–XVII siècle*. Paris: Gallimard, 1982.

Chittick, William. "Ibn 'Arabi and His School." In *Islamic Spirituality: Manifestations*, edited by Seyyed Hossein Nasr, 49–79. New York: Crossroad Publishing, 1991.

————, trans. and ed. *Faith and Practice of Islam: Three Thirteenth Century Sufi Texts*. Albany: State University of New York Press, 1992.

————. *Imaginal Worlds: Ibn 'Arabi and the Problem of Religious Diversity*. Albany: State University of New York Press, 1994.

————. *Science of the Cosmos, Science of the Soul: The Pertinence of Islamic Cosmology in the Modern World*. Oxford: One World Publications, 2007.

Chodkiewicz, Michel. "Ibn 'Arabi et la lettre de la loi." In *Actes du colloque: Mystique, culture et société*, edited by M. Meslin. Paris: 1983.

————. *An Ocean Without Shore: Ibn 'Arabi, The Book, and the Law*. Translated by David Streight. Albany: State University of New York Press, 1993.

————. *The Seal of the Saints: Prophethood and Sainthood in the Doctrine of Ibn 'Arabi*. Translated by Liadain Sherrard. Cambridge: Islamic Texts Society, 1993.

Clarke, W. Norris, S.J. *The One and the Many: A Contemporary Thomistic Metaphysics*. Notre Dame, Ind.: University of Notre Dame Press, 2001.

Coates, Peter. *Ibn 'Arab and Modern Thought: The History of Taking Metaphysics Seriously*. Oxford: Anqa Publishing, 2002.

Corbin, Henri. *Alone with the Alone: Creative Imagination in the Sufism of Ibn 'Arabi*. Princeton, N.J.: Princeton University Press, 1969.

Dempf, Alois. *Meister Eckhart*. Freiburg: Herder, 1960.

Dietrich of Freiburg. *Opera Omnia*. Hamburg: Felix Meiner, 1977.

———. *Treatise on the Intellect and the Intelligible*. Translated by M. L. Führer. Milwaukee, Wis.: Marquette University Press, 1992.

Dobie, Robert J. "Meister Eckhart's Metaphysics of Detachment." *The Modern Schoolman* 80 (2002): 35–54.

———. "Meister Eckhart's 'Ontological Philosophy of Religion.'" *Journal of Religion* 82 (2002): 563–85.

———. "Reason and Revelation in Meister Eckhart." *The Thomist* 67 (2003): 409–38.

———. "The Phenomenology of *Wujud* in the Thought of Ibn 'Arabi." In *Timing and Temporality in Islamic Philosophy and Phenomenology of Life*. Vol. 3 of *Islamic Philosophy and Occidental Phenomenology in Dialogue*, edited by A-T. Tymieniecka, 313–22. Dordrecht: Springer, 2007.

———. "Gnosis, Metaphysics and Revelation in Medieval Christian and Islamic Philosophy." In *Philosophy, Islamic Views and Modern Attitudes*. Papers presented at the Second World Congress on Mulla Sadra, Tehran, May 2004. Vol. 4. Edited by Ali Naqi Baqershahi, 309–22. Tehran: Sadra Islamic Philosophy Research Institute Publication, 2008.

Duclow, Donald F. "Hermeneutics and Meister Eckhart." *Philosophy Today* 28 (1984): 36–43.

———. *Masters of Learned Ignorance: Eriugena, Eckhart, Cusanus*. Variorum. Aldershot, England: Ashgate Publishing, 2006.

Dupré, Louis. "*Unio Mystica*: The State and the Experience." In *Mystical Union and Monotheistic Faith: An Ecumenical Dialogue*. Edited by Moshe Idel and Bernard McGinn, 3–23. New York: Macmillan, 1989.

———. *Religious Mystery and Rational Reflection: Excursions in the Phenomenology and Philosophy of Religion*. Grand Rapids, Mich.: Eerdmans, 1998.

Fischer, Heribert. "Grundgedanken der deutschen Predigten." In *Meister Eckhart der Prediger: Festschrift zum Eckhart-Gedenkjahr*, edited by Udo Nix and Rapheal Öchslin, 55–59. Freiburg: Herder, 1960.

———. "Zur Frage nach der Mystik in den Werken Meister Eckharts." In *La mystique rhénane*, 109–32. Paris: Presses Universitaires de France, 1963.

———. "Die theologische Arbeitsweise Meister Eckharts in den lateinischen

Werke." In *Methoden der Wissenschaft und Kunst Mittelalters*, edited by Albert Zimmermann, 50–75. Berlin: de Gruyter, 1970.

———. *Meister Eckhart: Einführung in sein philosophisches Denken*. Munich: Alber, 1974.

Flasch, Kurt. "Die Intention Meister Eckharts." In *Sprache und Begriff: Festschrift für Bruno Lierbrucks*, edited by Heinz Röttges, 292–318. Meisenheim am Glan: Hain, 1974.

———. "Meister Eckhart: Versuch, ihn aus dem mystischen Strom zu retten." In *Gnosis und Mystik in der Geschichte der Philosophie*, edited by Peter Koslowski, 94–110. Darmstadt: Wissenschaftliche Buchgesellschaft, 1988.

———. *Meister Eckhart: Die Geburth der "Deutschen Mystik" aus dem Geist der arabischen Philosophie*. Munich: C. H. Beck, 2006.

Forman, R. K. C., ed. *The Problem of Pure Consciousness*. Oxford: Oxford University Press, 1990.

———. *Meister Eckhart: Mystic as Theologian*. Rockport, Mass.: Element Books, 1991.

Al-Ghazali, Abu Hamid. *Al-Maqṣād al-asnā fī sharḥ maʿānī asmāʾ Allāh al-ḥusnā*. Edited by Fadlou A. Shehadi. Beirut: Dar El-Machreq, 1971.

———. *Deliverance from Error: Five Key Texts Including His Spiritual Autobiography, al-Munqidh min al-Dalal*. Translated by R. J. McCarthy. Louisville, Ky.: Fons Vitae, 1980.

———. *The Ninety-nine Most Beautiful Names of God*. Translated by David Burrell. Cambridge: Islamic Texts Society, 1992.

———. *The Niche of Lights*. Translated by David Buchman. Provo, Utah: Brigham Young University Press, 1998.

———. *Ihyāʾ ʿulūm ad-dīn*. 5 vols. Cairo: Dar al-Afak al-Arabiyya, 2004.

Goris, Wouter. *Einheit als Prinzip und Ziel: Versuch über die Einheitsmetaphysik des "Opus tripartitum."* Leiden: E. J. Brill, 1997.

———. "Ontologie oder Henologie? Zur Einheitsmetaphysik Meister Eckharts." In *Was ist Philosophie in Mittelalter?* edited by Jan Aertsen and Andreas Speer, 694–703. Miscellanea Mediaevalia, 26. Berlin: de Gruyter, 1998.

Grant, Sara. *Toward an Alternative Theology: Confessions of a Non-Dualist Christian*. Notre Dame, Ind.: University of Notre Dame Press, 2002.

Haas, Alois. "Aktualität und Normativität Meister Eckharts." In *Eckardus Teutonicus, Homo doctus et sanctus. Nachweise und Berichte zum Prozeß gegen Meister Eckhart*, edited by Heinrich Stirnimann and Rüdi Imbach, 205–68. Freiburg, Switzerland: Universitätsverlag, 1992.

Heidegger, Martin. *Being and Time*. Translated by John Macquarrie and Edward Robinson. New York: Harper-Collins, 1962.

———. *Poetry, Language, Thought*. Translated by Albert Hofstadter. New York: Harper & Row, 1971.

Helting, Holger. "Heidegger and Meister Eckhart." In *Herkunft aber bleibt stets Zukunft*, 83–100. Franfurt: V. Klostermann, 1998.

Henry of Ghent. *Summa Quaestionum Ordinarium Theologi praeconio Solemnis Henrici a Gandavo.* Paris: In Aedibus J. Badii Ascensii, 1529.

Hirtenstein, Stephen. *The Unlimited Mercifier: The Spiritual Life and Thought of Ibn 'Arabi.* Oxford: Anqa Publishing, 1999.

Hodgson, Marshall G. S. *The Venture of Islam: Conscience and History in a World Civilization.* Vol. 2, *The Expansion of Islam in the Middle Periods.* Chicago: University of Chicago Press, 1974.

Honnenfelder, L. "Der zweite Anfang der Metaphysik. Voraussetzungen, Ansätze und Folgen der Wiederbegründung der Metaphysik im 13./14. Jahrhundert." In *Philosophie im Mittelalter: Entwicklungslinien und Paradigmen,* 165–84. Hamburg: Felix Meiner, 1987.

Izutsu, Toshihiko. *Sufism and Taoism: A Comparative Study of Key Philosophical Concepts.* Berkeley: University of California Press, 1983.

———. *Creation and the Timeless Order of Things: Essays in Islamic Mystical Philosophy.* Ashland, Ore.: White Cloud Press, 1994.

———. *Ethico-Religious Concepts in the Qur'an.* Montreal: McGill-Queen's University Press, 2002.

Jarczyk, Gwendoline, and Pierre-Jean Labarrière. *Maître Eckhart ou l'empreinte du désert.* Paris: Albin Michel, 1995.

Al-Jili, 'Abd al-Karim. *The Universal Man.* Edited, translated, and annotated by Titus Burckhardt and translated from the French by Angela Culme-Seymour. Roxborough: Beshara Publications, 1995.

John of St. Thomas. *Cursus Theologicus.* Paris, 1934.

Jonas, Hans. "Myth and Mysticism: A Study of Objectification and Interiorization in Religious Thought." *Journal of Religion* 49 (1969): 315–29.

Katz, S. T., ed. *Mysticism and Philosophical Analysis.* London: Sheldon Press, 1978.

———, ed. *Mysticism and Religious Traditions.* Oxford: Oxford University Press, 1983.

———, ed. *Mysticism and Language.* Oxford: Oxford University Press, 1992.

Kelly, C. F. *Meister Eckhart on Divine Knowledge.* New Haven, Conn.: Yale University Press, 1977.

Knysh, Alexander. *Ibn 'Arabi in the Later Islamic Tradition: The Making of a Polemical Image in Medieval Islam.* Albany: State University of New York Press, 1999.

Landau, Rom. *The Philosophy of Ibn 'Arabi.* New York: Macmillan, 1959.

Largier, Niklaus. "*Figuratio Locutio*: Hermeneutik und Philosophie bei Eckhart von Hochheim und Heinrich Seuse." In *Meister Eckhart: Lebensstationen—Redesituatationen,* edited by Klaus Jacobi, 303–32. Berlin: Akademie Verlag, 1997.

———. "Intellekttheorie, Hermeneutik und Allegorie: Subjekt und Subjektivität bei Meister Eckhart." In *Geschichte und Vorgeschichte der modernen Subjekti-*

*vität*, edited by Reto Fetz, Roland Hagenbüche, and Peter Schulz, 460–86. Berlin: de Gruyter, 1998.

Levering, Matthew. *Participatory Biblical Exegesis: A Theology of Biblical Interpretation*. Notre Dame, Ind.: University of Notre Dame Press, 2008.

Libera, Alain de. *Penser au moyen âge*. Paris: Editions de Seuil, 1991.

Libera, Alain de, and Edouard Wéber. *Maitre Eckhart à Paris: Une critique médiévale de l'ontothéologie—Les Questions parisiennes no. 1 et no. 2*. Paris: Presses universitaires de France, 1984.

Lobel, Diana. "'Silence Is Praise to You': Maimonides on Negative Theology, Looseness of Expression, and Religious Experience." *American Catholic Philosophical Quarterly* 79 (2002): 25–49.

Lonergan, Bernard. *Insight: A Study of Human Understanding*. London, 1957.

Lossky, Vladimir. *The Mystical Theology of the Eastern Church*. Crestwood, N.Y.: St. Vladimir's Seminary Press, 1957.

———. *Théologie négative et connaissance de Dieu chez Maître Eckhart*. Paris: Vrin, 1998.

Lubac, Henri de. *Exégèse médiévale: Les quatre sens de l'écriture*. 4 vols. Lyon: Auber, 1959.

Maimonides, Moses. *The Guide for the Perplexed*. Translated by M. Friedlaender. New York: Dover, 1956.

Maritain, Jacques. *Distinguish in Order to Unite or The Degrees of Knowledge*. Translated by Gerald Phelan. Notre Dame, Ind.: University of Notre Dame Press, 1995.

McGinn, Bernard. "The God beyond God: Theology and Mysticism in the Thought of Meister Eckhart." *Journal of Religion* 61 (1981): 1–19.

———. "Meister Eckhart on God as Absolute Unity." In *Neoplatonism and Christian Thought*, edited by D. O'Meara, 128–39. Albany: State University of New York Press, 1982.

———. *The Foundations of Mysticism: Origins to Fifth Century*. New York: Crossroad, 1991.

———. *Meister Eckhart and the Beguine Mystics: Hadewijch of Brabant, Mechthild of Magdeburg, and Marguerite Porete*. New York: Continuum, 1994.

———. *The Mystical Thought of Meister Eckhart: The Man from Whom God Hid Nothing*. New York: Crossroad, 2001.

———. *The Harvest of Mysticism in Medieval Germany*. New York: Crossroad, 2005.

Mieth, Dietmar. *Meister Eckhart: Mystik und Lebenskunst*. Duesseldorf: Patmos, 2004.

Mojsisch, Burkhardt. *Meister Eckhart: Analogie, Univozität und Einheit*. Hamburg: Felix Meiner, 1983.

Morris, James. *The Reflective Heart: Discovering Spiritual Intelligence in Ibn 'Arabi's Meccan Illuminations*. Louisville, Ky.: Fons Vitae, 2005.

Murata, Sachiko. *The Tao of Islam: A Sourcebook on Gender Relationships in Islamic Thought*. Albany: State University of New York Press, 1992.

Nasr, S. H. *Three Muslim Sages*. Delmar, N.Y.: Caravan Books, 1964.

———. *Sufi Essays*. 2nd ed. Albany: State University of New York Press, 1991.

Nettler, Ronald. *Sufi Metaphysics and Qur'anic Prophets: Ibn 'Arabi's Thought and Method in the Fusus al-Hikam*. Cambridge: Islamic Texts Society, 2003.

Nwyia, Paul. *Exegèse coranique et langage mystique: Nouvel essai sur le lexique technique des mystiques musulmans*. Beirut: Dar el-Machreq Sarl, 1991.

Pegis, Anton. *St. Thomas and the Problem of the Soul in the 13th Century*. Toronto: Pontifical Institute of Medieval Studies, 1934.

Plotinus. *Enneads*. Translation by A. H. Armstrong. Loeb Classical Library. Cambridge, Mass.: Harvard University Press, 1984–88.

Ruh, Kurt. *Geschichte der abendländische Mystik*. Vol. 2, *Frauenmystik und Franziskanische Mystik der Frühzeit*. Munich: C. H. Beck, 1993.

———. *Meister Eckhart: Theologe, Prediger, Mystiker*. Munich: C. H. Beck, 1993.

Schimmel, Annemarie. *Mystical Dimensions of Islam*. Chapel Hill: University of North Carolina Press, 1975.

Scholem, Gershom. *Major Trends in Jewish Mysticism*. New York: Schocken Books, 1974.

Schürmann, Reiner. *Meister Eckhart: Mystic and Philosopher*. Bloomington: Indiana University Press, 1978. Republished as *Wandering Joy: Meister Eckhart's Mystical Philosophy*. Great Barrington, Mass.: Lindisfarne Press, 2001.

Seeskin, Kenneth. "Sanctity and Silence: The Religious Significance of Maimonides' Negative Theology." *American Catholic Philosophical Quarterly* 79 (2002): 7–24.

Sells, Michael. "Ibn 'Arabi's Polished Mirror: Perspective Shift and Meaning Event." *Studia Islamica* 67 (1988): 123–49.

———. "Bewildered Tongue: The Semantics of Mystical Union in Islam." In *Mystical Union and Monotheistic Faith*, edited by Moshe Idel and Bernard McGinn, 87–124. New York: Macmillan, 1989.

———. *Mystical Languages of Unsaying*. Chicago: University of Chicago Press, 1994.

Shah-Kazemi, Reza. *Paths to Transcendence according to Shankara, Ibn 'Arabi, and Meister Eckhart*. Bloomington, Ind.: World Wisdom Books, 2006.

Smart, Ninian. *Reasons and Faith: An Investigation of Religious Discourse, Christian and Non-Christian*. London: Routledge and Kegan Paul, 1958.

Staal, F. *Exploring Mysticism*. Harmondsworth, England: Penguin, 1975.

Stace, W. T. *Mysticism and Philosophy*. London: Macmillan, 1961.

Steel, Carlos. "Medieval Philosophy: An Impossible Project? Thomas Aquinas and the 'Averroistic' Ideal of Happiness." In *Was ist Philosophie im Mittelalter?* edited by Jan Aertsen and Andreas Speer, 152–74. Berlin: de Gruyter, 1998.

Sturlese, Loris. "Meister Eckhart in der Biblioteca Amploniana: Neues zur Datierung des 'Opus tripartitum.'" In *Die Biblioteca Amploniana*, edited by Andreas Speer, 434–96. Berlin: de Gruyter, 1995.

Tobin, Frank. *Meister Eckhart: Thought and Language*. Philadelphia: University of Pennsylvania Press, 1986.

Turner, Denys. *The Darkness of God: Negativity in Christian Mysticism*. Cambridge: Cambridge University Press, 1995.

Urvoy, Dominique. *Ibn Rushd (Averroes)*. Translated by Olivia Stewart. London: Routledge, 1991.

Vannier, Marie Anne. "Der edle Mensch, eine Figur in Eckharts Straßburger Werk." *Freiburger Zeitschrift für Philosophie und Theologie* 44 (1997): 317–34.

Wackerzapp, H. *Der Einfluß Meister Eckharts auf die ersten philosophischen Schriften des Nikolaus von Kues (1440–1450)*. Munster: Aschendorff, 1962.

Welte, Bernard. "Meister Eckhart als Aristoteliker." In *Philosophisches Jahrbuch* 69 (1961): 64–74.

———. *Meister Eckhart: Gedanken zu seinen Gedanken*. Freiburg: Herder, 1992.

Weiß, Konrad. "Meister Eckharts biblische Hermeneutik." In *La mystique Rhénane*, 95–108. Strasbourg: Presses universitaires de France, 1963.

Wilken, Robert Lewis. *The Spirit of Early Christian Thought: Seeking the Face of God*. New Haven, Conn.: Yale University Press, 2003.

Winkler, E. "Wort Gottes und Hermeneutik bei Meister Eckhart." In *Freiheit und Gelassenheit: Meister Eckhart Heute*. Edited by Udo Kern. Grünwald: Kaiser, 1980.

Zaehner, Robert. *Mysticism: Sacred and Profane*. Oxford: Oxford University Press, 1961.

Zimmerman, Albert. *Ontologie oder Metaphysik? Die Diskussion über den Gegenstand der Metaphysik im 13. und 14. Jahrhundert*. Leiden: E. J. Brill, 1965.

Zum Brunn, Emilie, and Alain de Libera. *Maître Eckhart: Métaphysique du Verbe et théologie négative*. Paris: Beauchesne, 1984.

# Index

Aaron (prophet), 54n81

*Abgeschiedenheit* (detachment), 4, 187

Abraham (prophet), 43, 45, 48

Abstraction, metaphysical, 189–90

Accidents, 126

Adam (prophet), 88, 164, 227, 235, 239n46, 241, 293; Adamic nature, 88, 164, 222, 227, 229–32, 234, 248, 286; *Bezels* on, 175n35; the primal, 287; as vice-regent of God, 90; word of, 228, 234, 235

'Abd al-Ghani al-Nabulusi, 25

Abu Bakr, 170

Addas, C., 5n3, 16n20, 38, 54n81, 121n70, 161

Aertsen, J., 69n31, 125n2, 128n7, 196n18, 275n49

Affifi, A. L., 26n9, 43n52, 44n53, 52n76, 121n70, 163n3, 164, 226n3, 239, 247, 250nn74–75

'A'isha, 29, 43, 55, 246n66

Albert, K., 145n54

Albertus Magnus, 70, 197, 288n1; doctrine of the soul, 197n20, 201

Allegory, 47–48, 80

Analogy, 13–19, 27, 93–94, 129, 138, 145, 148–49, 203, 205, 219, 291

Anaxagoras, 196

Angels, 77, 230–31, 232, 243, 255, 259, 279; intellects of, 195–96

*Aphairesis* (stripping away), 188n3

'Aql (reason), 161-62, 163, 177–78, 182, 183-84, 235n32; vs. intellect, 163n3. *See also* Reason

Aquinas, Thomas, 13n17, 60, 62, 63, 70, 71, 74, 115n55, 129n12, 130, 131, 133, 134, 143, 189, 190n7, 193, 195–96, 197, 206, 207, 212–13, 275n49, 281n65, 289n2, 290; critique of Avicenna, 127n6; *De ente et essentia*, 215; on existence and understanding in God, 199–200, 201, 202; on God's oneness, 131n20; *Peri Hermineas*, 140n44; *Summa Theologiae*, 124. *See also* Aristotelian-Thomisic tradition

Arabic language, 116; root system, 47n62, 49; grammar, 245–46

Archetypes, divine, 167, 227

*'Ārif (bi-Llāh)*, 51, 54, 98, 253. *See also* Gnostic

Aristotle, 21, 22, 23, 59, 65, 74, 80, 81, 103, 104n19, 161–62, 178, 196, 204, 205, 244, 257; alteration vs. substantial change, 137; *De anima*, 198; ideal of the sage, 125n2; *Metaphysics*, 199; metaphysics of substance, 139n42; on natural place, 81; and philosophy, 82; physics of motion, 216; "separated soul," 188n3; and virtue, 192

Aristotelian-Thomistic tradition, 281n65

*Āsbāb al-nuzūl* (occasions of revelation), 47n62

Ash'arites, 184

Asin-Palacios, M., 164n5, 244n59, 288

Attributes, divine, 106

Augustine, 74, 132, 147, 150, 207, 260, 264; *abditum mentis*, 74; Augustinian tradition, 60, 128; *Confessions* Bk. 1, 138; *Confessions* Bk. 11, 93; Eckhart's sermon on his feast day, 82–83

Dagli, C., 29n12, 32n20, 53, 166n12, 169n18
Damascene, St. John, 133, 204
Dempf, A., 129n12, 136n36
Descartes, R., 10, 11
Detachment, 79, 81-83, 87, 187, 213–16; and metaphysics, 191-95; and virtue, 192. *See also Abgeschiedenheit*
*On Detachment* (Eckhart), 81–83, 191
Deuteronomy, 130
*Dhāwq* (taste), 119n64, 250, 253
*Dhikr* (remembrance of God), 249–50
Dhimmis ("protected peoples" under Islamic law), 16, 54
Dialectic: of immanence and transcendence, 69; of the notion of God, 94–95, 112; and theology, 129
Dietrich of Freiburg, 202, 205n50, 288n1
Dominic, St., 76; and the Dominicans, 76
Dreams, 27; interpretation of *(ta'bir)*, 28, 47–49, 52
Duclow, D., 5, 57n1
Dupre, L., 24, 45, 53, 60n5, 65, 67n23

Ecclesiastes, 149
Eckhart, Meister: "Defense," 140n43; knowledge of Islamic thought, 288; Latin works, 149; as *Lebemeister*, 124, 191; as *Lesemeister*, 191; preaching in Strasbourg, 256; and religious controversy, 13–14; vernacular works, 149; as vicar of Thuringia, 256. *See also* Sermons of Eckhart
Emanation: formal, 73, 78, 209, 219; inner, 86; intellectual, 164; and the Persons of the Trinity, 73, 206–7
*Energeia* (actuality; Aristotle), 83n64
*Esse* (to be, existence): in the abstract, 202; *actio sequitur esse*, 258; and the copula "est/is," 141–42; and *esse commune/mawjūd jāmiʿ*, 132, 134, 189n5, 201n31, 234n26, 275n49; *Esse est Deus*, 74n44, 124, 125, 136–38, 157, 257; *Esse est Deus* vs. *Deus est intelligere*, 205–6; *esse per se/per alio*, 137; and God, 85, 95; and the intellect, 200; *ipsum esse subsistens*, 74, 200
Essence, divine, 8, 31, 32n20, 37, 38, 41, 42n50, 52n76, 100n9, 102n14, 106–7, 108, 111n44, 114, 116, 121, 159, 163, 165–66, 168, 169, 173–74, 175, 181, 183, 217, 225–26, 227, 228, 229, 233, 234, 235, 236, 239n46, 242, 243, 247, 250, 252, 254

Ephesians, Paul's letter to the, 150
Epistemology: Aristotelian-Islamic, 162; Thomistic, 189
Eros, divine, 245
Ethics, 72; the *ethicus*, 83
Exegesis: apophatic, 73; biblical, 58–59, 62, 66; goal of, 87; historical-critical, 67; medieval, 67; participatory, 12–13; qur'anic, 47n62
Existence, 2, 34, 39, 51, 155; God's, 62n10; nature of, 93–96; as prior to beings, 126–38; and detachment, 192; as "standing outside" (*ex-sistere*), 201, 205; and intellect, 202–3; and human nature, 230–40; divine, 233–34; pure, 248; and spiritual poverty, 274. *See also Esse; Wujūd*
Exodus, 81, 208; Eckhart's commentary on, 62, 125, 134, 144
Experience (mystical), 4, 9, 60, 86, 94, 250

Faith (*imān*), 227
*Falsafa* (philosophy), 161
*Fanā'* (annihilation), 4, 119, 175–77, 185, 217, 249. *See also Baqā'*
*Fard* (realized individual), 233
Feuerbach, L., 251
Fischer, H., 58n4, 64n15, 68n27, 142n46
*Fiṭra* (primal, original nature), 88, 286
Flasch, K., 58n4, 288n1
*Fountain of Life (Fons Vitae)*, 63. *See also* Avicebron
Forman, R. K. C., 10n13, 189n4
*Futūḥ* (opening, revelation), 97
*Futūḥāt al-makkiyya*, 26, 35n28, 37, 50, 55, 97, 107, 110, 118, 119, 120, 171n25, 221, 233, 236, 252, 290, 292

Gadamer, H. G., 57n1
*Gelassenheit* (letting-go), 4, 188n2, 255, 256-61, 277; logic of, 282
Genesis, book of, 130; Eckhart's commentary, 64n15, 70, 125
Al-Ghazali, Abu Hamid, 30, 42n48, 119n64; *Deliverance from Error*, 119; *Most Beautiful Names*, 37n32, 42n47; *Niche of Lights*, 30n15; *Revival of the Religious Sciences*, 89, 292
Gnosis (*ma'rifa*), 28, 106, 161, 178, 185, 227, 236, 240, 245, 249, 251, 253

Gnostic, the, 52n74, 52n76, 54n81, 55, 97n2, 107–8, 108n31, 110–13, 116–17, 163, 170, 175, 180, 183n49, 186, 220, 241, 247, 248, 249, 251; "having two eyes," 120–22, 233; "learned ignorance," 172-74. *See also* '*Ārif* (*bi-Llāh*)

Gnosticism, 8, 278

God, 2, 4, 6, 20, 21, 23, 28, 29, 30, 31, 32, 33, 34, 36, 38, 40, 41, 42, 44, 49, 51, 191–92, 194; of Aristotle, 131n18; as author of sacred scripture, 65–66; as being qua being, 81, 114–15; as Creator, 7, 137n37, 277, 278; as *deus absconditus* or concealed, 222, 236–37; dialectical nature of, 104; dual nature as manifest/non-manifest, 179; as *esse ipsum subsistens*, 146; essence of, 111n44; and existence, 152, 203–6; existence of, 94-96, 98n3, 93, 137; existing in God, 64; as final and efficient cause, 74, 85, 207; as first principle, 72; as formal cause, 74; as God "beyond 'God,'" 277, 279; as "Godhead" (*deitas, gottheit*), 7, 85, 86, 206–9, 211, 219, 273, 288; vs. "god of belief," 251–52, 286, 290–91; God of the philosophers vs. as revealed, 275–78; God's unity, 65; goodness of, 131; as "ground" of the soul, 221, 222, 272–73, 274–82; "in himself," 37, 279; as infinite ocean of substance, 133–34; as infinite Other, 291; as inner principle of existence, 68, as first cause, 70, 114–15, 219, 274–76, 279; as intellect, 86; as justice, 83; knowledge by the saint, 176–77, 178; knowledge in, 65; knowledge of, 62–64, 75, 85, 128–38, 143–44, 151–54, 193, 213–16, 236–37, 264–68, 279, 294; knowledge of himself, 50; and "letting-go" (*Gelassenheit*), 256–68; and metaphysics, 70n33; as negation of negation, 142–43; as non-being, 151–52, 276; as one or indistinct, 130–36; as ontologically prior to all beings, 126–38; as outer and inner, 114; and prayer, 250–52; preconceptual nature of, 143; presence within the soul, 259; as pure understanding (*intelligere*), 199–206; remembrance of (*dhikr*), 186; as "rich in himself," 102; as self-communication, 86; and self-knowledge, 102–3, 225–31; 252–54; and self-knowledge of the saint, 167–77; as self-manifestation, 218;

as subject and object of all knowledge, 107, 111; as transcendent and immanent, 68, 77, 95, 98; as true knower, 174; as ultimate Identity, 183; as union of opposites, 244; union with, 84–86, 245, 260–61, 284, 287; and Universal Man, 232; as *wali* ("friend"), 171

Good (Plato), 131n18

Goris, W., 60n6, 127n6, 134, 138n41, 145n54, 196n18

Gospels, the, 17, 23, 74, 87, 91, 200, 216, 257, 268, 277, 282; inner meaning of, 209; and the intellect, 204; and metaphysics, 212, 219

Grace, 71, 79, 80, 86, 211, 256, 262, 277; first and second, 207–8

Grant, S., 115n55

Ground of the soul, 59, 67, 73, 75, 76, 79, 81, 87, 90, 91, 149, 155, 157, 163, 191, 192–95, 218–19, 259, 260, 270–82, 288, 293; as "spark" or "little castle," 271–73

Haas, A., 58n4

Ḥadīth (tradition, saying of the Prophet), 25, 28, 29, 33, 51, 55, 102, 112, 121n69, 171, 184, 235n34, 241, 242, 243, 245, 246, 251

Hadot, P., 125n2

Ḥāl (pl. *āḥwāl*; inner state, station), 48, 175

Al-ḥaqq (the Real, Truth), 3, 27, 35, 36, 95, 97, 101, 110, 121, 161, 173, 179, 218, 225, 227, 235, 236, 248, 285; *ḥaqīqa* (reality), 51. *See also* Truth

Ḥayra (perplexity), 98, 108–9

Heart (*al-qalb*), 118n62, 159, 163, 175, 177–81, 217, 218; as perfected by *himma*, 182–83; root meaning, 179–80

Hegel, 6

Heidegger, M., 75, 275n50, 280; *Being and Time*, 259

Henry of Ghent, 201

Heraclitus, 283

Heresy, 14

Hermeneutics, 5, 17, 22, 28, 40, 57, 58; biblical-scriptural, 70n32, 160, mystical, 283–90; principles and method of, 67, 80. *See also* Dreams; *Ta'wīl*

Ḥikma (wisdom), 28, 161, 163

Himma (spiritual power), 181–86

Hirtenstein, S., 118n62, 228n8

Hodgson, M., 88

Holy Spirit, 211, 267

Honnenfelder, L., 70n33
Hūd (prophet), 109, 111, 112, 122
*Huwīyya* (ipseity), 106

I *(das Ich)*, 258–59
Ibn 'Arabi: attitude to Christians and
    Jews, 16; dream in Cordoba, 112; knowl-
    edge of Christianity, 288; and religious
    controversy, 13-14, 25; as "seal of the
    saints," 171, 181
Ideas, divine. *See* Platonic ideas
Identity: operative vs. substantial, 83n64
*Iftiqār* (poverty), 167–68
*Ihsān* (perfection), 248
Image: *imago Dei*, 228, 231; qua image,
    159–60, 209–10, 212, 216, 219, 284; in
    the soul, 192, 194
Imagination, 22-23, 28–39, 160; analogical,
    23, 25, 87, 88–91, 159, 284; the *mundus
    imaginalis*, 43, 46–47, 48, 89, 122, 155–56,
    218
Incarnation, 62n10, 68, 85, 86, 89, 151,
    153n63, 157, 278; as inner truth of
    Christianity, 280; "physics" of, 85n67;
    as temporal and eternal event, 90. *See
    also* Christ
"Inner man"/"outer man," 193–94, 262–64
*Innominabile* (un-nameable) and *omni-
    nominabile* (all-nameable), 42, 142n48
Intellect, human, 146; "First Intellect,"
    240–41; intellectuality, 160–64, 165,
    175, 216–17, 219, 271; as "mirror," 88, 159,
    164, 168-69, 173–75, 185n55, 186, 211,
    227, 228, 229–30, 233, 235n32, 238n44;
    nature of, 194, 195–206; operation of,
    62; "pure," 159; as pure potency, 215–16;
    and reason, 291; and revelation, 85–86,
    214–15; "superior" or "higher" *(intellec-
    tus)*, 79–80, 111–12, 163; as "un-mixed,"
    189–90, 196. *See also Nous*; Reason
Interpretation, 59, 65, 73. *See also*
    Hermeneutics
*Interpreter of Desires (tarjumān al-āshwāq;*
    Ibn 'Arabi's poetic *diwan*), 16
Isaac (prophet), 43, 55
Islam, 98–99, 97n2, 101, 106; compared
    with Christianity, 88–91; meaning of
    name, 217; mystical element, 286
*Isticheit* (is-ness), 149–54
Izutsu, T., 30n14, 32, 28, 102n13, 105, 108,
    109n33, 119n64, 141n45, 162, 167n14,

175n35, 226n3, 227, 230, 231n16, 234n28,
    235n32, 249

James (apostle), 63
Al-Jandi, Mu'yaddin, 165n9
Jesus (of Nazareth), 89–90, 146, 270, 287;
    as *Logos*, 255
Al-Jili, Albdel-Karim, 225, 237, 238n40
John, gospel of, 2, 74, 145, 255; Eckhart's
    commentary, 69, 71, 73, 83, 125, 189, 190,
    202, 210
John of the Cross, 13
John of St. Thomas, 200n36
Jonas, H., 69n31
Joseph (prophet), 28-39
Al-Junayd, Abu l- Qasim, 118, 180, 251-53,
    290
Justice/the just man, 83–84, 211
Justin (Martyr), 23

Kabbalism, 8
*Kalām* (dialectical theology), 184;
    *mutakallimūn* (practitioners of), 184,
    185. *See also* Ash'arites; Mu'tazailites
*Kalima* (word), 99n4, 222, 241; *kalima
    muhammadīyya* (of Muhammad), 222,
    232, 286. *See also Logos*; Word
Kant, I., 11
*Kashf* (unveiling, opening), 97–98, 106
Katz, S. T., 10n13
Kayka'us, Sultan of Konya, 16
Kelly, C. F., 58n4
*Kenosis* (emptying), 84
Al-Kharraz, Abu Sa'id, 248
Kierkegaard, S., 280
Knowledge, 80; goal of, 120; hermeneuti-
    cal, 236; "higher," 259–60; limitations of,
    117; metaphysical-philosophical, 74, 155,
    267; mystical, 285; nature of, 82; self-
    knowledge, 111–13, 258–68; tacit, 93
Knysh, A., 14, 171n25

Landau, R., 114n54
Largier, N., 19n1, 95n1
Law, Islamic *(shar'ia)*, 9, 16, 36, 51, 54, 89,
    118; 165, 170, 218
Letting-go. *See Gelassenheit*
Levering, M., 12n16, 13
Libera, A. de, 85n67, 123n1, 125n2, 188n3
Life: active vs. contemplative, 270
Light, intelligible, 30–36

Science, 22, 284; diversity/plurality of, 64–65, 72, 76, 78, 80

Scripture, 57, 58, 59, 64; allegorical sense of, 68n27; inner sense of, 68–75, 78, 80, 82, 87, 91, 124, 215, 264, 267; interpretation of, 80; literal sense of, 66; and the nobleman, 262; parabolic sense of, 68n27, 69. *See also* Bible

Seeskin, K., 64n14

Self, 225; essential, 112; inner, 103; loss of, 257. *See also* Bāṭin; Nafs

Sells, M., 121n69, 275n48

Sermons of Eckhart: *Beati pauperes spiritu* (Pr. 52), 268, 273–80; on Ecclesiastes, 125, 148; *Haec est vita aeterna* (Pr. 46), 153–54; *In hoc apparuit charitas dei in nobis* (Pr. 5b), 216; *Intravit Jesus in quoddam castellum* (Pr. 2), 269–73 *Iusti vivent in aeternam* (Pr. 6), 84–85; *Praedica Verbum* (Pr. 30), 76–79, 280n63; *Renovamini spiritu* (Pr. 83), 150–53; *Unus Deus et pater omnium* (Pr. 21), 143–44; *Videte qualem caritatem* (Pr. 76), 216

Seth (prophet), 164; *Bezels* on, 164–65

Shah-Kazemi, 218n70

Shankaracarya, 115n55

Shu'aib (prophet), 164 177; *Bezels* on, 181; root meaning of name, 183

Smart, N., 9n12

Soul, 58; as detached, 79, 80, 191–95, 214–16, 219; essence of, 85; as image of God, 150, 169–60, 263–68; medieval doctrines of, 197n20; perfection of, 192–94; as "released" (*gelassen*), 257–60, 276–82; transformation from within, 285; union with God, 59, 76, 81–82, 123, 145, 152, 157, 163, 284; as virgin/wife, 269–73

Species, intelligible, 197+98. *See also* Cognitive form

Staal, F., 9n12

Stace, W. T., 9n12

Station, of no station, 218, 248. *See also* Ḥāl

Steel, C., 125n2

Sturlese, L., 123n1

Sufism, 22n2, 109, 118, 288n1

*Sunna* (tradition of the Prophet), 120

Suso, H., 13

Symbols, symbolism, 27, 43–53

*Tahqīq* (realization), 3

*Tanzīh* (incomparability), 99–109, 119, 122, 218. *See also Tashbīh*

*Taqlīd* (imitation), 3, 236, 286, 291

*Tashbīh* (comparability), 99–109, 119, 122. *See also Tanzīh*

Tauler, J., 13

*Tawḥīd* (divine unity), 155, 288

*Ta'wīl* (interpretation), 22, 47–49, 50n69

*Termini generales* ("general terms"), 125–38. *See also Transcendentalia*

Testaments, Old and New, 61n8, 74

Theologian, the, 69, 71n36, 123; the *theologus*, 83

Theology, 50, 57, 62n10; dialectical, 98, 125n2; medieval, 294; negative, 151. *See also Kalām*

Theophany, 42, 90, 106, 108, 121, 156, 173, 178, 217, 220, 222, 225, 236, 239, 240, 250, 252, 292

Theresa of Avila, 13

*Timothy*, Paul's letter to, 76

Al-Tirmidhi, 28, 171n25

Tobin, F., 129n10, 202n42

Torah, 49n67

Transcendence, 7; in Bible, 67; self-limitation of, 113; self-transcendence, 82

*Transcendentalia* (the "transcendentals"), 72–73, 95, 142–43, 145, 198–99; and Christ, 146–49; logic of, 127–29. *See also Termini generales*

Trinity, the, 62n10, 73, 150, 151, 211, 219, 273, 280, 286, 288; and intellect, 206

Truth, 2–3, 59–61, 70, 78, 79, 80, 81, 110, 119, 121, 160, 176, 188n3, 189, 217, 265, 272, 285, 289; as Christ, 147; disclosure of, 258; incarnational aspect, 290; lived, 62; of metaphysics and physics, 71; oneness of, 65, 66. *See also Al-ḥaqq*

Al-Tustari, 44n53

Turner, D., 61n5

'Umar b. al-Khattab, 16

Unity: divine, 109–22, 217, 226, 227; of knower and known, 162-65. *See also Tawḥīd*

Unity of Existence (*wāḥdat al-wujūd*), 119n64, 226n3, 235n34, 250, 253n81. *See also Wujūd*

Universal (Perfect) Man (*al-insān al-kāmil*), 87, 88, 164, 170, 180, 185, 221–23, 225–54, 284, 285, 286, 291; as *Logos* of creation, 232

Vannier, M. A., 221n1, 255, 256
Vedanta, 174n32, 174n34
Vice-regent: man as, 43–44, 90, 238
Virginity: symbolism of, 268–69
Vulgate, the, 150, 269

Wackerzapp, H., 136n36
*Walī*, 97, 172–73, 222; *walāyya*, 97n2, 241n53. *See also* Saint; Sainthood
Weber, E., 123n1
Weiss, K., 63n13, 68n27, 70n32
Welte, B., 60n6, 83n64, 188n3, 216n67
Wilken, R. L., 23, 24
Winkler, E., 61n9
Wisdom , 279–80. *See also* Ḥikma
Wisdom, book of, 129–30, 132, 135, 212; Eckhart's commentary, 68, 125

"Without a why" (*ana warumbe*), 281–82
Women, 242-46
Word, divine, 10, 21, 24, 49n67, 54, 59–60, 66, 75, 76, 86, 99, 153, 157, 160, 211, 212, 214, 218–19, 221, 232, 255, 265, 267, 270, 271, 277, 284; as actuality of the intellect, 215–16; formal emanation of, 209; as ground of the soul, 293–94; incarnate, 190, 191; and the intellect, 204–5; realization in the soul, 289. *See also Logos*
Wrath, divine, 110. *See also* Mercy
*Wujūd* (existence), 37–38, 45n58, 100n7, 111, 174n33, 229, 231, 235n34, 239, 253, 292; Ibn ʿArabi on, 40–43; root meaning of, 40, 232. *See also* Unity of Existence

Zaehner, R., 9n12
*Ẓāhir* ("outer," "apparent"), 100
Zimmermann, A., 70n33, 275n49
Zum Brunn, E., 85n67

*Logos & Revelation: Ibn 'Arabi, Meister Eckhart, and Mystical Hermeneutics* was designed and typeset in Brioso by Kachergis Book Design of Pittsboro, North Carolina. It was printed on 60-pound House Natural Smooth and bound by Sheridan Books of Ann Arbor, Michigan.